VIXEN

VIXEN

A MAGGIE DEACON ADVENTURE

JARROD THALHEIMER

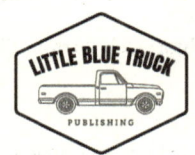

This is a work of fiction. Names, characters, places, and incidents either are the product of the author's imagination or are used fictitiously. Any resemblance to actual persons, living or dead, events or locales is entirely coincidental.

Copyright © 2024 Little Blue Truck Productions Inc.

Published in the United States and Canada by Little Blue Truck Publishing, a division of Little Blue Truck Productions Inc. A 100% Canadian company.

All rights reserved.

No part of this publication may be reproduced, stored, in a retrieval system or transmitted in any form or by any means – electronic, mechanical, photocopying or otherwise – without the prior written consent of the author.

ISBN: 978-0-9866095-1-0 (hardcover)
ISBN: 978-0-9866095-3-4 (paperback)
ISBN: 978-0-9866095-2-7 (ebook)

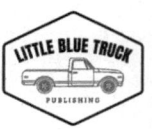

Little Blue Truck Publishing, BC, Canada

www.littlebluetruck.com

Designer: Alex Hennig

Editor: Jack Burton, ME

First Edition

Printed in Canada

For Dawn

...and Mom & Dad

PROLOGUE

THE VIEW it showcased was spectacular. An I.M. Pei original, to be sure, and Zevon Levi had the bank drafts to prove it. Stark white and encased in steel-supported limestone, the Malibu mansion looked more like a rock formation carved by alien lasers than some run-of-the-mill "dwelling." Interestingly, with his cheek lying flat against the floor, Zevon could make out four distinct geometric patterns within his immediate line of sight, each completely different, yet somehow still mutually complementary. Stunning. Pei really was a genius.

The tile felt cool on Zevon's face even as he blinked repeatedly, trying hard to focus on the activity surrounding him. He was lying in the fetal position, his back towards the open nano-door that framed the endless expanse of the Pacific Ocean. He could feel the breeze tickling at his lone, exposed love handle, and it bugged him. He tried to move his arm and pull his shirt down, but it wouldn't move. Not the shirt, his arm would not move.

Pei had agreed to do the house only because he was already working on the Reagan UCLA Medical Center at the time. Well, that and Zevon had offered double his rate, plus a significant contribution to MIT's design program. *Why do they always do that*, he thought? Why not just ask for more money and give it to them yourself, right? Zevon tried to catch his breath by shifting his weight slightly. It hurt to move, a lot.

As Zevon caught sight of the blood - his blood - pooling beside him, he felt pangs of despair instead of the anger he had initially displayed. Lesson learned. All that yelling had bought him was a solid pipe-shot to the back of the head, something he could happily have done without. *This was ridiculous* he wondered to himself. *Who in the* heck robs a house in broad daylight? In the middle of the day? With a friggen cube van?

When they knocked on the door, he thought it was just more stuff from the studio for his garage. Boy, was he wrong on that one. Zevon hated being caught stupid. He knew the Boolis were bad news from the start. He told them to wait, just a bit more time. That was all that was needed. More time.

Zevon didn't know how many there were. Everything went black at first, and when he finally came to, the steady stream of men going in and out of his house was almost hypnotic. Zevon tried to count them but somehow kept losing track. It was either a hundred men or four. He couldn't tell anymore. It was getting harder to focus. He tried to hear the two voices speaking, just off to one side of him.

"How hard did you hit him?"

"Not that damn hard."

"Look at his head, you asshole. You caved it in! Now what am I supposed to do?"

"He's breathing."

"Barely."

"Knocking someone out is not an exact science."

"Shut the fuck up, okay? Just help them. Let's get this done."

The movement of bodies and items being carried seemed to slow down and then speed up. At least Zevon thought it did. Time had turned fluid now, as he was having ever more trouble organizing his thoughts. Every time he felt like he finally had hold of one it slipped away, frustrating him. Things had been working out so well. The divorce was a week out from being final. The children were old enough not to have to take sides, and they were taken care of anyway. He had even managed to sell that godforsaken *Cliffhanger*-ripoff. How that dreadful script ever found financing in Germany made no cosmic sense. Those people were supposed to be intelligent. Zevon's thoughts turned dark. *Was it really going to end like this?* He had to do something.

As the men in black continued to haul armloads of boxes, electronics and art through the open concept living room to the waiting van parked outside, one of them started yelling.

"C'mon you guys! Fucking move it, will ya? We don't have all day."

Zevon tried to speak but found his mouth wouldn't respond to his attempt at sound. It came out more as an "uhhh" than anything understandable. He watched as they hauled out pieces of set dec and props from his latest picture. When *White Knight Light* had finally wrapped, he had been faced with a $2200 per month storage bill from Raleigh Studios. At the time, he figured why bother renting space? Just dump the crap in his garages until the next film goes up, create his own rental invoice, and let the next batch of investor-dentists foot the bill. Problem was there might not be a next one now. This really didn't feel like it was going to end well.

Zevon's breathing began to labour. He'd had a panic attack once and this sort of felt like that, except with a dull headache. He felt himself start to get angry. Not because he was probably dying, but because he realized that the divorce wasn't final-final yet, so that meant his wife was probably going to get the house after all. *That bitch,* thought Zevon. *I gave her the condo, the apartment, and the Aston Martin just so I could keep the house. Now she's going to get that too. Damn how things work out.*

"He doesn't look good."

"His eyes are open."

"Maybe, but he ain't in there I don't think."

"Ah, geez…."

Suddenly, one of the guys dropped a large-framed picture to the floor. Zevon saw it hit and spoke. "Not that one. No, you can't have that one. It's special." And with that, his head flopped oddly to the side as Zevon Levi breathed his last, still staring at the most precious thing he had ever owned.

"He said something."

"Check him." said the larger man.

The first guy bent down near Zevon, checking his head, careful to avoid the blood leaking around him.

"Shit, Tranko. He's fuckin' dead."

"Pack it up, now! ordered the larger man.

The men loaded the last of their haul into the cube van. Three of them jumped into the back while the remaining two got into the front driver seats.

Tranko Lutz put the van in gear, pressing the accelerator to take off from the hidden driveway only to be suddenly forced to stop short. A car had turned into the compound and was now facing Tranko and his van, blocking the way. Grinding his teeth hard, Tranko reached for the gun on the van's center console and shoved it down the back of his pants, aggressively stepping out to confront the offending driver. This job was getting messier by the minute.

1

"SO, do we put her in handcuffs?"

"What?"

Craig, the teenaged produce assistant, held up his hands, miming them as being locked together. "Ya know, handcuffs? Or a zip-tie maybe?"

His supervisor, a slightly older twenty-something with a nametag reading "Mr. Javins," shook his head and rolled his eyes before turning to face the slim, older woman the pair had just escorted into the back room. He gestured toward a folding chair in the corner of the small office.

"Ma'am? If you could?"

Calm but visibly annoyed, Maggie Deacon stepped to the chair and sat down. She faced the two directly.

Turning to his younger associate, the manager spoke. "You said you have her ID?"

The produce assistant immediately handed over a driver's license.

Sucking air across his teeth, the manager studied the ID, eventually reading out loud. "Margaret Deacon, 8161 Hunter Street, born in…ah…well, it looks like…58 years of age?"

"62. You did the math wrong." said the woman.

"Hmmmm…" The manager paused before looking back at Craig. "And you have the item in question?"

The produce assistant held out a small pack of triple AAA batteries. The manager took them and held them up.

"OK, ma'am. Why are you trying to steal batteries?"

Maggie Deacon said nothing.

"The loss prevention co-ordinator has it all on video, Dave." assured the produce assistant.

"So, security has you on video. Do you deny taking the batteries?"

Calmly, Maggie answered, "No, of course not."

Surprised by her quick agreement, Javins perked up. "So, you admit to stealing them then?"

Pausing to focus directly on the pair, Maggie sat up straight, took in a deep breath, then spoke.

"I came into your store to get a few things. I wanted a cart, but you charge for those now and I didn't have a coin, so I grabbed a basket. Then, I pick up a head of lettuce and four bananas. After that, a pack of Oreos, then a red pepper, some beef jerky, and a big bottle of pomegranate juice. The juice didn't fit inside the basket, at least not without crushing the cookies, so I had to carry that in my other hand, along with a flyer coupon I pulled from the shelf display. Then, remembering I needed batteries, I grabbed them off the rack with my other full hand, dropping them into a pocket so I don't drop anything. Then I go to check out."

The two staff nodded in understanding.

"Then, after putting all my items on the belt – and paying – I bagged them, because your store doesn't do that anymore either. All done, I go and walk out of the store, to no sound from any buzzer, I might add and suddenly I'm grabbed by junior snotnose over there and accused in public of being a thief."

"Well, I...." stammered the manager.

Maggie continued. "Now, in your vast experience as…whatever your job is here, do you think it's possible in all the confusion I just described that maybe, possibly, I simply forgot about putting the batteries in my pocket? Could that be an explanation for what happened? Or does it really make more sense that I'm some kind of super-criminal, out for kicks, stealing batteries while still paying for everything else that I pick up?"

The small room fell silent. No one spoke, as eyes darted from person to person. Maggie knew the next person to speak was the loser. She held her tongue, purposefully. Without fail, the junior associate piped up.

"I saw on *Seinfeld* where seniors steal batteries from stores all the time…"

"Craig, I don't think that's helpful right now."

"But it must be a thing, or why else......?"

"Enough!" interrupted the manager.

Maggie continued to stay silent, staring at the manager. She'd learned a long time ago to never interrupt an adversary when they were in the process of losing.

Unable to take the pressure of silence any longer, the manager clapped his hands on his knees. "Looking at all the evidence here, I'm thinking it's pretty clear to me that some sort of mistake has been made."

Momentum shift. Now it was time for Maggie to speak.

"But you called me a thief."

Immediately, the manager put his hands up. "Hey, now. Hold on. I never called you a thief. Craig? Did you call her a thief?"

Craig stammered. "I just, I don't remember...security saw you put the batteries in your pocket, so maybe..."

The two were floundering now. They wanted out of the situation. It was time for Maggie to throw them a line.

"I'm willing to forget this ever happened. Are you?"

The relief that crossed the manager's face was almost comical. In less than three minutes he had shifted from being a prosecutor out for blood to a drowning man praying for a life preserver. He almost lunged at the offer.

"Absolutely I think we can just acknowledge this was an unfortunate mix-up, dismiss it as such and all walk away with no harm done."

But Maggie wasn't finished just yet.

"What about my batteries?" she asked.

"You are perfectly free to go through the checkout and purchase them, of course." said Javins.

Slightly increasing the volume, and force, of her voice, Maggie shifted into interrogation-mode.

"Just to clarify, you humiliated me in front of the entire store, hauled me back here like some shoplifter, call me a thief, and now I'm supposed to go stand in line and buy them again? Are you kidding?"

"But you didn't buy them..." explained the junior assistant.

Seeing his calm, workable solution deteriorating in front of his eyes, the manager began to panic.

"Look, let's stop all this. How about you just take your groceries and your batteries and head on home, okay? Really, I'm very sorry for any inconvenience and I do hope you will continue to shop with us in the future. Really."

Satisfied, Maggie rose to her feet, reached over to the small desk, and grabbed her two grocery bags in one hand. Then, opening her other hand, she pushed it toward the manager, palm out.

"And the batteries?" she enquired.

"Of course, yes." Javins handed her the small package. "And I'm – we're, both – really sorry for ever calling you a thief."

Except that she was.

A thief.

In fact, Margaret Deacon was an extraordinary thief. And she had been so for a very long time. From precious stones to expensive jewelry to famous works of art. Once, she even walked out the front entrance of the *Louvre* with two – two! – paintings under her arm. Yet today she'd gotten tagged for lifting a package of batteries. And by two idiots, no less.

It was humiliating.

And Maggie knew her failure needed to be addressed sooner rather than later. Or else.

2

STILL ROLLING the events of the day around in her head, Maggie spat into the sink, rinsed her toothbrush, and dropped it into her *I Love NYC* coffee mug. Looking into the mirror she studied herself. Old age was here, there was certainly no denying that, but she still liked what she saw. She was older now, but still pretty. She had come to quite love her silver hair. Maggie's face had lines, but they weren't deep. And her eyes still had sparkle. Plus, the package it was wrapped in was pretty darn good. Maggie admired her trim figure.

The thing at the grocery store was stupid. She knew why she'd done it. And why she'd screwed it up. She was nervous. It had been almost two years since she last did a job for Ivan, and she was rusty. Not physically, but mentally. In her heart she knew this, which was probably why she'd pulled her little stunt yesterday. To test herself. And she'd gotten nabbed. So embarrassing.

Clicking off the bathroom light, Maggie stepped into her bedroom. As she approached the end of her bed, she quickened her pace and grabbed the maple foot board with both hands, tossing her body into a full handstand. She held herself aloft for a count of three before lithely collapsing into a ball and rolling smoothly onto her bed.

She still had the moves.

Most mornings began the same. Between 5 and 6am Maggie exercised, alternating between yoga, *Pilates*, and her own version of *Tai Chi*. She followed that with a shower and then prepared herself a breakfast of toast, fruit, and coffee to be enjoyed on her back patio rain or shine. Starting the day outside always reminded her of her years in Paris and the hours she would spend at the sidewalk cafes.

Her current neighbors to the east were renters. They had a little boy of about 2 and a half, who would often open his back door and stand on the top step calling out to Maggie when she was in her garden. She enjoyed his little round face with blond hair and liked his attention. His mother would smile and wave as she herded the little one back inside for breakfast. She was extra busy herself thanks to a new baby girl.

Maggie liked the woman. She was young, pretty, and seemed smart. Her husband was ok. A little dull but otherwise fine. She allowed Maggie to visualize what it might have been like to be married or have kids, neither of which she ever wanted.

The neighbors to the west were retired. Pleasant people who spent most of their time talking about some trip they just took or sharing plans about whatever impending voyage focused their attention.

Maggie enjoyed the neighborhood and the life that she now led. She had some money. Not a lot, but enough. She even had a best friend that she saw regularly. Things were good. The intrinsic beauty of life's daily mundanities was something she had come to revel in. She even had a part-time job on the customer service desk of a catalogue order center. It helped to fill the week, while providing a cover of sorts to ensure the "normal" life she always knew existed could continue.

Maggie liked normal life. At least, she thought she did. She was constantly telling herself she did, and she really wanted to believe it. But it was just so dull without any action. She needed a jolt every now and again. How did the nine-to-fivers handle it? She wondered. Is that what they used vacations for? She needed more. Two years was a very long time between jobs.

Maggie decided to reach out to Ivan.

Nothing provocative. Just a reminder that she was still available. That she hadn't "left the game." She hesitated before hitting send, hovering the mouse over the button. Did she want this? She had tried to leave it behind before. She was trying to do it again. But two years? Maggie pressed "send."

It was up to the universe now. She wondered what might happen.

Full of nervous energy, Maggie needed a distraction. She descended the stairs into her basement and walked toward her father's old piano. Tucked into a corner with only a plant separating it from the mirror reflecting its side, Maggie squeezed in beside it, reached low and pushed a small spot on the frame. Then she gave a solid, full-body push. The mirror panel instantly swung open, revealing a hidden steel door. Taking a silver key from the soil of the plant, Maggie unlocked the heavy door, walked in and then shut herself inside the hidden room.

Sliding onto a seat at her workbench, Maggie set to work spraying lubricant on the tiny metal wheels of her fast-descent harness to keep them quiet and slick. Technology had become tangentially important as her own physical abilities diminished. She was fitter and stronger than many men half her age, but it still meant she needed an assist when dropping 20ft in a single second. What once required only a cable and some nerve now required pulleys with small servo-assists. Even though she hadn't done a job in two years, the habits were ingrained, and the desire to be prepared never went away even though she worked less.

Increasingly, age was becoming the mental discussion Maggie didn't want to have with herself. Yes, she was older, but she didn't "feel" older, not in her mind anyway. Sure, the body had some tweaks here and there, but she was still in fighting shape. She leaned on her workbench.

Without necessarily wanting to, Maggie had been forced to become quite proficient in operating, cleaning, and maintaining the various pieces of equipment she was now relying on. Basic fears that she had never experienced before were increasingly becoming part of the job. Three years back, she did a job in Rome that led to a broken hip. You can't have a more "old lady injury" than to break a hip. The fact that she broke it diving out of a 3rd story window and landing in a 700-year old palazzo fountain was not lost on her, but the injury did precipitate a distinct change in attitude.

Maggie reached behind her and grabbed the butterfly knife stashed in the waist of her yoga pants. With a deft flip and spin of the wrist, she had an open blade and began trimming excess threads from her harnesses. The sharpness of the blade barely compared to its beauty. A jade handle with silver highlights worn smooth hinted that it was Maggie's favorite possession. The reality that it had saved her butt too many times to remember only confirmed it. She loved *Lola*, her butterfly knife.

The life Maggie had left was exciting, but not ultimately fulfilling. Years back she had decided she was done with it. She craved a home, friends, and a normal existence. Even her current job, as boring as it could be, provided a sort of honesty to her existence that she had always assumed regular people had. She didn't know for sure, though. When one becomes a cat burglar in their teens it's kind of hard to establish a moral compass of any kind.

Maggie had no ability nor desire to ask forgiveness for past sins. What was done was done. But she did control her future, even though trying to leave the business entirely was proving unsuccessful. Obviously, she needed the release it provided. The adrenaline.

But her new life wasn't without its own hooks. She found herself creating all-new mental rules for her old profession. Decisions like not wanting to steal from legitimate owners, or museums. It had to be theft from thieves. That was new. And over the last decade, much of the excess from her jobs either went to charities or people in need, anonymously, of course. That was new too. Still, Maggie did not fool herself into thinking she was any sort of true-blue innocent. She worked in the international world of art theft, and she was good at it.

Maggie finished. Her gear was checked and prepped, should Ivan come through with something. She would do the same every few days, needed or not. Bad gear could mean mistakes and mistakes could mean death. Maggie liked living.

Glancing at the clock, she realized the day had disappeared around her. It was almost 5pm and she was supposed to be somewhere in less than 30min. She stepped out of the hidden sanctum and headed upstairs, fretting about the consequences of being late for something this important again.

3

"UNDER THE O, 66……66, oh clickety-click." Maggie frowned.

She was a single number shy of winning the new car. The double blackout game had been going on for just under an hour and her cards were more ink than numbers. B-12 stared at her, mocking her waiting dabber. It stood almost alone, unmarked in a field of ink blotches. She flexed the muscles in her brain, trying to will the right ball from the spinning cage on stage.

The palatial hall was eerily quiet. Even the casino games next door seemed subdued. Everyone was focused on winning the car blackout game. The caller spun the cage again and pulled another number.

"And we have under the B, 14…14, oh, Luraleen."

Maggie looked to her left. Fatima was concentrating just as hard on her cards, though she was shy at least five numbers and maybe more. Often, she would get so flustered that she would miss a call, or three. Maggie knew she wouldn't win. Fatima never won at stuff like this. But she enjoyed trying.

"And again under the B, 2…..B2, oh whoop-de-doo."

"BINGO!!!" A shriek erupted from across the room and 200+ heads swiveled, let out a collective sigh, and then offered obligatory, and remarkably polite, applause as the winner's card was verified. Maggie pulled her failed collection together, stacked them and then tore them into sixes, dropping the pieces across the table like bits of paper snow. She turned to Fatima.

"Fati, do you know her?"

"No, I've never seen her before. I think she came with someone. Probably a newbie. They always win because they don't know they're more likely to lose."

"I only needed one number," complained Maggie.

"So did she. Now she has a Corolla. I didn't like the color anyway."

As the people began to empty out some headed for the slots area while others moved towards the restaurant. Maggie rose to her feet, casually felt for *Lola* (hiding lengthwise along the base of her spine) and adjusted her shirt. Satisfied that all was as it should be, Maggie and Fatima strolled out of the bingo palace and casino into the warm evening air.

Maggie squeezed Fatima's arm. "Did you have fun, honey?"

"Of course. I wanted to win, but I always have fun."

Maggie clapped her hands. "Well, good. What do you want to do now? We can go for a few more rounds if you like. Or we can grab a snack somewhere. Maybe hit a movie? It's still kind of early."

Fatima looked nervously to her left and right. Maggie caught her discomfort and quizzed her.

"What's going on? What aren't you telling me?"

"Oh, well…uh…I sort of…have some other plans."

"Now? Tonight?" asked Maggie. Fatima nodded her head.

"I have a date."

"But I thought we were spending your birthday evening together." Maggie was disappointed.

"I know, I know…and we did. But…it's just…"

"Him? The Brazilian? Again?"

Fatima smiled shyly.

Maggie didn't particularly like the Brazilian. She acknowledged his good looks. Sort of Omar Sharif-y. He was handsome and all, but he had a slightly condescending way about him that turned her off. She had known guys like him, years ago. Powerful, wealthy, and ever so full of themselves. And more than a few of them tried to bell her. Unsuccessfully. Maggie saw through them all. Well, most of them. Usually all they wanted were playthings. And she figured Aldo was just like them.

Fatima liked him quite a bit. And even though Maggie didn't know Fatima before her husband died, she had certainly seen a change in her recently, as a giggly teenaged girl seemed to emerge from her best friend. And that made Maggie smile. So, while she wasn't personally into the guy, she couldn't deny the effect he was having on her. Fatima was a big girl. She would have to deal with whatever happened herself. Still, Maggie was a little surprised at getting dumped for him tonight.

"You could have warned me, you know."

"I know, I know...and I should have. It's just...I was sort of embarrassed. I think maybe I thought he might, you know...change his mind?"

"Is it getting serious between you two?" asked Maggie.

"No, no, no. We're not exclusive or anything, I don't think."

"You're dating someone else too?" chided Maggie.

"No, of course not! I'm not that way. We're just having a little fun, is all."

"I bet it's fun. Fancy-pants Brazilian boy is loaded."

Fatima scowled at her. "It's not about the money for me, Mags. You know that."

"I do know that. But I also know it's pretty hard to say 'no' to a guy who can fly you to France for dinner and then dessert in Spain."

"He doesn't do that." Fatima pursed her lips.

"Where did he take you two weeks ago?"

"A *Lyle Lovett* concert."

"Where?"

Fatima looked left and right.

"Come on. Where was it, Fati?"

"Red Rocks...."

"Red Rocks...in Colorado?" finished Maggie.

Fatima blushed.

"Yeah, I think I rest my case on that one," smiled Maggie.

Fatima's face turned slightly stern. "OK, he's a little...fancy, but I'm not about that. Of course, it's nice and all but he seems like an interesting man. And so, what if he's rich? I mean, I'm kind of rich too. It's not that big of a deal."

Maggie smiled at her friend's protests. "You know I'm sort of teasing you, right?"

Fatima looked at her with big eyes.

"Like a big sister would, sort of?" Maggie made a face.

"You're younger than me." Fatima stuck out her tongue.

"Yeah, but I feel like I would be the older sister in this situation."

"Oh you!" Fatima slapped Maggie on the arm.

"Whatever. Go have fun. And don't get too attached, okay?"

"I'm just having fun, you know me." Fatima did a mini twirl on the sidewalk that made Maggie shake her head and laugh.

"Yes, I think I do know you. Anyway, don't worry about me. I'll go home and…check my furnace or write in my diary or something."

"Stop it!" said Fatima, laughing.

"Go! Be good, but not too good."

The two friends hugged, said their goodbyes, and went to their individual cars.

As Maggie drove off, Fatima checked the message she'd just received from Aldo. He had sent a cryptic text with no more than an address and instructions on where to park in downtown Vancouver. The instant mystery got Fatima excited. It was her birthday, after all, and here she was heading out on a date with a dashing suitor in the half-light of a beautiful summer evening. What could possibly go wrong?

4

"WHAT DO you mean he's dead? Don't tell me he's dead."

"Look things didn't go down the way they were supposed to."

Tranko Lutz, and his massive frame, sat squeezed into the passenger seat of a tiny Fiat 500, tucked near the back of the parking lot at Mel's Drive-In on Sunset Blvd. A small woman sat at the wheel of the car, fuming.

"You were supposed to scare him, knock him out maybe and then take a bunch of stuff. That was it. How the hell did you kill him? What am I supposed to do now?"

"Sorry Bunny, these kinds of things aren't an exact science ya know."

"This does not work for me. I'm not paying you." Suddenly, Elfrieda "Bunny" Levi began to scream and bang her hands and head against the steering wheel of the car. Tranko's brain searched for answers. *What the heck is this about?* He tried to calm her down.

"Bunny, hey Bunny. Look calm down. C'mon. People are looking, okay? Stop it? Stop it, okay?"

Bunny's screams eventually became guttural curses as she exited the tiny car and began pacing around the parking lot. Extremely fit and taut, yet sporting massive fake boobs, Bunny Levi presented about as "real" as a plastic palm tree. Her lips were bee-stung huge, and her eyes so blackened with shadow that a prostitute would point and laugh. She tipped around on sky-high heels, waving her arms in the air.

"So, what now you moron? What now?"

Tranko had exited the car as well. He lowered his voice as he spoke, "Look, it was clean. No one saw anything."

"Oh, that's good. So, you didn't kill anyone else then?" Bunny fixed him with a look.

"No." Tranko replied, remembering how close he had come to killing Howie. First the idiot had showed up late. Then, he thought clocking the guy with a blackjack was a good idea, which turned out great. As a finale, he had asked his idiot cousin to pick him up *from the job* instead of down the street. When the guy blocked in the van as they were trying to leave, Tranko almost shot the slack-jaw in the face. And Howie right after him.

"This will not go well. I can't get tied to this. I won't get tied to this. You killed him, I didn't. This is your fault. I'm turning you in."

Tranko took a deep breath. He hated doing freelance work. It never went the way it was supposed to. He was a professional mercenary, trained in eight different martial arts. He could handle any weapon known to man and had led entire armies. He had run freedom fighters in Central America and had even overthrown an interim government in Uruguay. Tranko had managed security teams in some of the hottest spots on earth and recruited the most skilled assassins around. Now he was left defending a crew of bona fide morons to a greedy, huge-titted bitch who thought that threatening to turn him in might score some sort of discount on the fee owed. This had to stop.

"You're not turning me in."

"Why not?"

"You know why not. The second they get me I hand them you."

"I'm not paying the full rate."

"Yes, you sure as hell are."

Bunny looked confused for a second, but the wheels kept turning.

"I don't have the money. And what if this ties everything up? I don't even know if that bastard had his will updated or changed. What if he did? I'm screwed then. Totally screwed."

"You have the money, Bunny," Tranko said calmly, even as his inner voice raged. *Never, never, never take a job from a woman. You can't argue with 'em, and it always goes bad. Always.* Tranko knew he could kill her if he had to, but he wanted to get paid more.

"Bunny, I have all the stuff in the truck. If you don't give me my money, I drive the shit over to the cops with a map to your house taped on the hood. Or you pay me like you agreed, and I make everything go away."

Bunny just stared at him with her crooked, mean-girl sneer, like he was stupid. It took most of Tranko's will not to put his fist through Bunny Levi's shiny face. He searched for the strength to continue.

"Look, the plan was to send the stuff back after a few days anyway. All we do now is let the van get found, make sure it's clean, and the cops tie the whole thing up as a home invasion gone wrong. It'll be fine."

Bunny was disbelieving. "Will it all be fine? Will it? 'Cause the kids will be fine, right? And I'll be fine, right? Your fuckup just ruined everything I had going on here. Everything!" Bunny hopped angrily in her heels. "You'd better make this thing go completely away or else."

Tranko stared at the tiny woman, more curious than worried about what kind of threat she could conceivably make.

"You think you're the only bad man I know? Don't make the mistake of thinking I'm helpless. Don't ever make that mistake."

Tranko sighed. No more. No more jobs like this ever. He had to find enough cash to get level and then get out of the country.

"I'm not giving you the money jerkoff. You killed him. I should go to the police."

"And tell them what? That you only hired me to beat and rob him? Like they'll believe that. They'll turn me to get you."

"Why is this my fault? You're the one who screwed things up."

She had him there. He had screwed things up. The first thing he'd done wrong was answer the damn ad in the first place. Being on *Craigslist* was bad to start with. He hated finding jobs this way. The old way, through trusted contacts and solid relationships, that's how a pro worked. Not this *Facebook/TikTok* bullshit way of dealing. It was the difference between playing in the big leagues versus scrabbling around with a bunch of amateurs.

Even his crew, a group of half-time bouncers and loan collectors, collectively dumber than a sack of hammers, were humiliating. If he hadn't had the navigation app on his phone, they would've gotten lost on the way to the beach house. It had been a comedy of errors from start to finish. And this was the icing on the cake. Now he had to apologize to a picky bitch he never should've been working for in the first place.

"I'm sorry this went down the way it did."

"Well, I'm glad you finally said that. It's not like I'm gonna miss him or something, but the kids are going to get all weepy now and then what am I supposed to do? I wanted to be free of that bastard but now I have to do the whole "grieving widow" routine. It's just not fair."

"Look, I paid real money out already but maybe we can work something out."

"I'm not paying."

"Bunny c'mon."

"Nothing."

"Geez Bunny, that means this job is actually costing me money. That's not fair. At least let me break even on it. I'll cut it by $2500. How's that?"

"Tranko, I've got a shit load of trouble now and it was caused by you and your stupid crew."

"Trouble for you? What are your costs on this? I hired guys, rented the truck. Who's paying for that?"

"Fine, here."

Bunny reached inside her gaudy D&G bag and pulled out two small pads of cash, handing them to Tranko. "That's $1200. You and I are done. I don't want to ever see or hear from you again, got it?"

"And the stuff in the truck?"

"Like you said. Let the cops find it. I just want this all away from me."

And with that she turned on her *Jimmy Choo* heels and tick-tocked back to her ridiculous little car, slipping sideways only once when her right stiletto pierced the warm asphalt near a storm drain.

As the small car left the parking lot, Tranko watched a black SUV turn in and head straight for him, stopping at the last possible instant. Then, the large man in the passenger seat got out and walked right up to him.

"Mr. Dachshund wants to see you. Now."

5

FATIMA WAS BLUSHING. No one was looking at her and she was not embarrassed, but she was blushing all the same. Reaching forward to press 'PH' in the elegant elevator, Fatima could not believe how wonderful she felt.

The last 24 hours had been magical. After Maggie, she had met Aldo for what turned out to be an exclusive candlelit concert at the Christ Church Cathedral downtown. Afterwards, he'd taken her to a lovely little bar where they spent hours laughing and telling stories late into the night. Then, he took her home, promising to send a car for a late breakfast at the Marine Club the next day.

Somehow, that led to a dare which resulted in him piloting a massive speedboat to see the underside of Lion's Gate bridge. Fatima could see him in her mind's eye, dressed so casually in white linen pants and shirt with two gold chains draped around his neck. He had handled the boat with a confidence that made her legs weak. They spent the rest of the early afternoon at the Quay, shopping, talking and handholding.

Aldo Neto was a dream.

The elevator continued to ding as it neared his penthouse.

Fatima checked her reflection in the elevator. Dressed in the most revealing piece she would ever dare to wear in front of her own mirror, she had finally declared herself ready and headed out to meet Aldo for a fancy dinner in his Vancouver nest.

His apartment encompassed the top three floors of a spectacular building overlooking Stanley Park and the bay. She hadn't seen it yet, and as the elevator reached the top Fatima wondered what Aldo had in store for her tonight.

Watching the door slide open, Fatima was surprised to find herself entering what appeared to be a decidedly non-private dinner party. There were people all over. And closer inspection revealed the people to all be women. Some were her age, some younger but all looked fantastic. Confused, Fatima stepped forward and looked around. Aldo was nowhere to be seen. A waiter appeared and offered a drink, which she accepted out of habit, only to stand awkwardly in a corner near the entrance alcove for what seemed like an eternity.

Eventually, a second waiter entered the room to announce that dinner was being served and showed the ladies into a dining room laid out for a feast. Still unsure of what was going on, Fatima approached the table. There were place cards at each setting. Finding her name, she sat down, still confused as to what was happening. Was she in the right place? Had she misunderstood his invitation? Was something else taking place?

After everyone was seated, Aldo entered the room. Unlike Fatima, he seemed perfectly at ease as he greeted each woman with a quick kiss on the cheek. When he reached Fatima, she tried to squeak out a question, but he was too fast, already moving on to the next. Fatima was too nervous to make a scene in front of so many people, though she wished she had the courage to do so. Aldo stepped to the front of the room and began ringing a wine glass with a spoon, indicating his desire to speak.

"Ladies, I wish to welcome you all here tonight. This is my home, and my fondest desire is for all of you to feel the utmost of comfort here. You are all very special to me, each in your own way. Please, get to know each other as we dine."

Fatima couldn't speak. She darted her eyes left and right, trying to read the other women at the table. She caught at least three other faces holding similarly shocked looks. Thank goodness she wasn't the only dupe. This arrogant fool thought he was running a harem. She seethed as the salad was placed before her. Fatima wanted to scream.

* * *

As dinner eventually gave way to drinks, Fatima finally found herself in conversation with Aldo. It was "her turn" she supposed. He still seemed oblivious to her discomfort.

"You seem bothered Fatima, why?"

Fatima was left open mouthed. Almost sputtering her words, she said. "I thought dinner tonight was for us. And I thought us meant 'you and me.'"

"We are adults Fatima, and I am a man of great appetite. I have no desire to settle down. I am enjoying my life and at certain times I choose to enjoy it with you. And I enjoy it very much. Is that not fair? I never claimed you were my one and only."

He had her there. He never had claimed that. But darn it, he'd implied it. Fatima's face burned with humiliation. She stepped away from him.

"I have to go, Aldo."

"No, no, you can't. Please come see my art collection. Come see *Peaches*. You mustn't act in haste, my Fatima."

The drink in her hand twitched. She wanted to throw it in his face so badly, but her timid nature would allow no such thing.

"Don't call me. Ever."

As Fatima turned and stormed toward the door, she noticed what could only be an expensive area rug. Venting her rage, she dumped the entire contents of her glass all over it. And with every fiber of her being wished she had been drinking red wine instead of the white.

Collecting her wrap, Fatima stepped into the waiting elevator and pressed at buttons until the door closed behind her. She cried all the way down, pausing just long enough to get from the lobby to the inside of a taxi.

Pulling out her cell phone, Fatima dialed the only number she could.

"Please pick up. Please pick up."

"Hello?" answered a sleepy voice.

"It's me. Can I come over? You won't believe what just happened to me."

6

GETTING TO the roof of Aldo's building had been reasonably easy. Surrounded by office towers on two sides that had all-night cleaning crews made access a breeze. All it had taken was a quick lock-pick followed by an even quicker elevator ride up. A few hallways, a couple doors, one eight-foot ladder and Maggie stood firm on the roof of Insurance Mutual, looking down on the highrise, rooftop home of Mr. Aldo Neto.

Fatima had come to Maggie's and relayed the humiliation of her evening, sparing no details about the "party" she had been lured to. Maggie was appalled, and she told her so.

"He's a jerk Fati, you're better off without him, you know that."

Fatima had continued to pour out her pain, saying how unimportant and cheap he had made her feel. Maggie had listened and patiently calmed her down, even offering Fatima a bed to stay over. She declined, wanting to be in her own space. "I just need some time, I guess. I'll be OK." They hugged, and a demoralized Fatima had gone home, sad but resigned.

Maggie was outraged. And she meant to do something about Aldo's abuse. Right now. Tonight.

Unfolding her collapsible kite, she attached the harness and stood motionless on the edge of her tower. It was 3:53 am. Sunrise was in about an hour and a half. Lots of time. She was 10 floors higher than the building she needed to land on. Plenty of distance for an easy glide across. She attached her only safety, a CO_2 propelled glove anchor. Maggie could feel her heart racing. It had been a long while since she'd tried anything this risky. Could she still do it? Did she still have the guts? Then, instinct took over as Maggie crouched slightly and jumped.

The night sky swirled around her. She felt invisible as she fell into the darkness. It was only a few seconds before her kite caught the wind, but the experience of free-fall never ceased to slow time. She glided in a large circle, then a smaller one and finally came to a soft, if somewhat awkward, landing on Aldo's roof. Stowing her gear behind some air conditioning units, Maggie identified a lower parkade less than two blocks away as her primary escape route via kite. She proceeded to head for the west corner of the building.

As Fatima had relayed the events of the night, Maggie's ears had perked up at one point. She'd mentioned Aldo's vain attempt to show off "his *Peaches*". That stuck out to Maggie. The original *Peaches* by Édouard Manet had been stolen back in 1977. It was recovered in 2000 and subsequently resold, back to its original owners by the insurance company. In turn, they donated it to a private museum where it still hangs today. Maggie knew it. She had seen it. That meant Aldo was not just a jerk but a phony too. And tonight she would prove it to the world, at his expense.

Her plan was simple. Get in, steal the fake *Peaches*, get out and then return it anonymously to a newspaper with a note explaining that after stealing it, and finding out it was a fake, there was no point in keeping it. The press would run with the story of "Annoyed Art Thief Returns Fake Art," causing no end of embarrassment to Aldo. Then let Mr. Big Shot explain his cheap copy to the home audience. Maggie accepted that her revenge was not particularly elegant. As such plots go it was admittedly petty, but it just needed to humiliate the creep. Which it would.

Finding the ventilation system, Maggie encountered her first snag. The building plans had indicated a Webber system, but it was, in fact, a Trane Commercial. It must have been replaced since then. Not a big deal. Maggie could find her way through both, but she detested surprises. And Trane sometimes used slightly different ducting, meaning even the best athlete's body was bound to get some bruises on the journey through.

As Maggie squeezed her way in, she had to admit there was another, even stronger reason for doing what she was doing. She wanted a serious workout. She needed to feel the pressure of a heist.

She knew she was going a little stir crazy without having pulled one for so long.

Maggie's on-the-fly calculations indicated approximately 75 feet of distance to cover before she could drop safely into a side room. Fati had said the painting was in the main floor living area, so barring any sophisticated alarm systems, Maggie needed only to run down some stairs and pinch the painting.

After much careful, but productive struggling later, Maggie emerged from the vent into the laundry room. It was 25ft farther than she expected, but it had the necessary opening she needed to get out again quickly.

Carefully, she scanned the door for wiring, poked her head into the hallway and began to move like a cat along the floor. She knew that most residential motion alarms were set to allow cats or dogs a certain amount of free movement at night. If she stayed in their zone, she would be fine. So far, she had not seen any indication of alarms at all. She guessed fake art didn't really need protection. She also realized her mind was wandering a bit more than usual, but to a seasoned thief a gig like this was akin to visiting the fridge at night. Aldo was making it easy.

Finding a staircase, Maggie made her way down, finding the bedroom level. No lights were on, and it seemed like no one was home. A surprise considering the dinner party earlier but fine with her. She continued down again, finally coming to the bottom of the stairs. She crouched with her back to a corner on the main floor and surveyed the area.

She was about to move when a tiny blue light caught her eye. She looked hard and recognized a laser port.

"What the hell does he need a laser system for?" She mumbled to herself.

Maggie reached in her pocket, grabbed a small handful of climber's powder, and tossed it into the air. As it fell it illuminated a basic checkerboard pattern of blue lasers across the floor of the main apartment room. She smiled.

Rich boys and their toys, she thought, hearing the discussion now: "I want lasers, and I want blue ones." She smirked to herself.

He had spent the cash for lasers but then ordered the simplest, easiest system in the world to bypass. Easier even than motion sensors. The pattern was static. It never moved. So, beating it was like walking on flagstones through a pond. She tossed some more dust, memorized the distances, and simply measured her steps as she lily-padded her way toward the living room.

From 10ft away she could see the picture. It looked like *Peaches* alright. But as she got closer, she began to admire the skill of the forger. It was an exceptional copy. There were really no visible flaws.

Reaching behind her for *Lola*, Maggie spun the knife open and prepared to cut the painting out of the frame. Suddenly, a voice came from behind her.

"Please, not with a knife, I'll have to reframe it even smaller again."

Maggie froze. She didn't turn around. She didn't move. What the hell was going on?

"It is a beauty, isn't it? I love having a painting that every amateur does in art class. A bowl of fruit, except this one is worth a million dollars or so."

Maggie turned and faced Aldo Neto. He was dressed in a robe, with slippers and pajamas on. He did not seem to have a weapon.

"I won't be able to convince you to remove your mask, will I?"

Maggie said nothing, frowning under her mask. *What was going on?*

"The one in the private collection is a forgery, though I'm sure you knew that. Why else would you bother coming here to steal this one, eh?"

The man did not seem scared or agitated one bit. He was as cool as if he was having lunch on the veranda.

This worried Maggie, a lot.

Aldo sighed audibly. "I've no intention of standing here having a one-way conversation all night. Either explain yourself, or leave the way you came in. I will not call the police, for obvious reasons. And for the record, you are quite shabby as cat burglars go. You made enough noise to wake the dead coming in. Good night."

And with that he turned and left the room.

Maggie did not hesitate. The painting was now officially an afterthought. She sprinted up the stairs, back into the ducting and out onto the roof as fast as she could.

Less than 3 mins later she was landing on the lower parkade roof and hurriedly disassembling her kite. *"Wake the dead?" Who the hell does he think he is?* Thoughts swirled in Maggie's head. And for a moment, just a single moment, she too found herself quite impressed with Mr. Aldo Neto.

Reversing her clothing, Maggie removed her mask and exited the parkade to the street. She jumped a bus and headed in the opposite direction. Only when convinced that she was not being followed or tracked did she change direction and go home.

It would seem she had approached the "get revenge on Aldo Neto" job a little too casually.

Maggie's bruises seemed to hurt just a little bit more than usual.

7

DAVID MUST HAVE been the only insurance agent in history who loved his job. It didn't matter how it came up, without exception whenever his career was mentioned, eyes would roll back inside people's heads. And that was fine. They truly had no idea how awesome his life was and that worked perfectly well for him.

Sure, it seemed boring and all, but insurance work was great work for an ex-art thief. David checked his watch. She was late. She was always late.

In truth, David Teck had never been particularly good at being a thief. He liked attention far too much. As a result, he found himself saddled with a burning desire to be a "famous" art thief as opposed to a good one. That led to more than a few run-ins with the authorities and other assorted bad dudes, which finally led to a resolve to stop getting caught.

Unfortunately, it also meant he had to wave goodbye to the *James Bond*-like life he'd always dreamt such great art thieves lived. Fancy parties and whispered discussions with permanently horny arm candy that moved in and out of the rooms of power. David imagined he'd be able to write his own ticket easily, especially considering the average intelligence of your garden variety crook.

Most of them were smash and grab specialists at best. All they did was figure out it was easier to grab a painting from some dozy museum than robbing cash from an armed liquor store. And it was. It didn't take many smarts to realize which was easier. The harder part was making sure you stole something that was valuable. It was almost comical the number of newbie art thieves that thought grabbing something like *Dogs Playing Poker* would net them a half-decent haul. Didn't these morons bother to watch one or two episodes of *Antique Road Show*? Hell, even *Pawn Stars*. Chumlee was quicker on the draw than most of these dolts.

David learned early, by accident. His father was a bank manager. David was expected to follow in his footsteps but found that college life was far too much fun. He was working on his eighth year at Harvard, having adjusted his major twice, and quite enjoyed the ride. The contacts, the parties, the 'Master of the Universe' feeling you got from being at the high end of life. It was great fun.

Things changed for David when he joined a party planning committee. They had been organizing a poetry slam at the main library. The group was in the atrium discussing plans and making notes on who was going where when campus security burst in and started yelling at people not to move. A work of art had gone missing, and they were locking down the university in hopes of corralling it. Back then at Harvard there were something like 300 works on permanent display, with thousands more stored in archives.

A huge case was made of the whole thing, but it wasn't until a full week later that it was all revealed as nothing more than a simple screwup. Apparently, some janitor had noticed one of the paintings hanging crooked. The old guy had taken it upon himself to fix the hook it was hung on. He lifted the painting off the wall, storing it in a broom closet while he went to find a new hook. Evidently, something distracted the janitor and he forgot to put the picture back before his shift ended. Then, plot twist: that night he got sick with the stomach flu and was off work for almost a week. When he finally came back, he realized all the hell that broke loose was over the painting he'd moved. Even that was only because some tweedy professor had noticed that it was missing during his weekly commute down that specific hallway. They went to the closet he left it in and there it was. Mystery solved.

The amazing part had been realizing how easy it was to rip art from them in the first place. No alarms, no security. There wasn't even a written record of what was hanging where. It had taken them three days to even know what picture was missing. No one had known, not even the twit that reported it in the first place. The whole thing was ridiculous. Anyway, the event served to educate David better than any class he had ever taken, which was why David Teck decided "art thief" was a far more promising career than banking.

Thus, it began. David lifted multiple works from Harvard's archives. One small piece here, a tiny sculpture there. He never made much in the way of money, but the thrill was worth the point. And he never got caught because no one even knew the stuff was missing. And in the end, that was the problem. David needed the credit. He wanted folks to know that he was the thief. It wasn't any fun if you had to keep it a secret.

So, David started to talk. Usually, it was close buddies, or girls he wanted to sleep with. And in the end, it gave him an edge that he loved to flash every now and again. Never specific, always just below the surface. And it was working great until he told the wrong person: an art major he wanted to bang, who took a very conservative approach to the pilfering of prized art.

Outraged personally, she reported David to administration. This led to a formal expulsion. He only avoided prison thanks to the efforts of his father, combined with the art being returned - at least the ones they knew about. He had kept silent on the rest.

By this point David's life trajectory was set and getting expelled meant high-level banking and legal were now out of the question. He transferred to another school and tried to keep his nose clean, but he kept indulging his habit. And it did become a habit. He liked to steal things. The money was never really the reason. He couldn't sell most of it, but he liked pissing off the elites that controlled or owned the pieces. David chalked it up to rebellion against his father and a privileged upbringing. Either way, it eventually stopped being cute and ended up landing him in even more serious trouble.

His family pleaded with him to go straight, which he dutifully promised but never actually did. The only change came when his dad threatened to cut him off. That was too much. The idea that his bank account might suffer forced his hand. He promised to go straight. But only his way. By this point in time, the world had started to come around to the whole "repentant criminals" type of story that was taking things by storm. The Frank Abagnale-*Catch Me If You Can* routine had captivated employers as they suddenly realized what a sexy asset ex-cons (in certain positions) represented. Suddenly, David's criminal shenanigans had made him desirable, and highly employable. Add in his ability to mix with the well-monied and he became an easy sale to some of the largest insurance firms in the world.

Big companies love ex-crooks who "turned it around." David's checkered past now worked in his favor. He gave lectures and held important meetings where he shared his stories (usually embellished far beyond reality) for whatever assembled suits were in the room. They loved having an ex-con in a position of security. Bizarrely, it seemed to make them feel safer. Like having an ex-hacker running your network. The funny part was how easy it was to continue to steal them blind. David loved it.

Today, he was flying out to New Mexico. The firm was considering a sculpture for insurance in some large private collection. They wanted an independent assessment of the security in place. David would check it out, give it a failing grade, and spare his company the trouble. They didn't care anyway. The collector would either be forced to pay a higher premium, or they wouldn't.

Sometimes, if they didn't want to pay the higher premium David would simply sell the details of their security system to a back line source who would steal the piece for themselves. Not bad for a day's work, and he even got to fly business class to do it. Thankfully, they finally had lounges that stopped allowing idiots to come in on their points. David couldn't take another pre-flight, rest up surrounded by cheapos hyperventilating over free food and drinks. But he couldn't leave until he saw her first. Why was she always late? He had told her when the flight would be boarding.

As David grew more and more annoyed, he looked around and spied a brunette with legs to die for sitting near the coffee bar. He walked near to her table. She was "reading" *Vanity Fair* which meant she was really just looking at the pictures. *Smart enough to know she needed to look smarter than People magazine, but not by much* thought David. He sat down and spoke quietly.

"Shhh, don't look up. Pretend you expected me here."

Long legs looked up and gave David a quick once over before dropping her eyes lazily. "I'm waiting for someone."

David smirked. *Like candy from a baby.* "Actually, that's perfect. Don't do anything. And just for the record, please don't get the wrong idea. I'm on a fairly sensitive business trip and I just noticed someone might be following me. I'd rather avoid that if I could. I'll sit quietly if you don't mind."

Again, without looking up but still visibly rolling her eyes she exhaled. "Ummhmm, and what do you do?"

David stopped for the smallest of moments, smiling at his prey just before he took her as his own. "Actually, I'm kind of an art thief but I really shouldn't say any more than that." He turned his head and looked away.

Beautiful legs immediately keyed in on him, as her hand dropped one half of the magazine and she raised her dark, and suddenly flashing, eyes. "You're kidding? Art thief? How's that?" She touched her hair. *They always touch their hair,* thought David.

"Well, it's sort of complicated, but if you're interested why not? Do you want a drink? It would help with my cover."

David was sure it was going to be a very good flight. He got up to get a drink for his future conquest, making his way to the open bar. As he selected the glasses and pulled a fresh bottle of *Stoli* down from the shelf, he felt his phone rumble. Reflexively, David pulled the phone to his nose. A text, from her.

"Can't make it. Big problems. Call when you land. XX"

Typical. It was always the same, which is why he would never commit to anyone fully. Luckily, he had made alternate plans. He re-caught the eye of his catch across the room as she fussed with her hair. He may have to close the deal on her before they took off. It wasn't looking like he'd have much time, unless she was headed for New Mexico too. He scanned for a handicapped washroom. They always have lots of room for action. Plus, the locking door.

As he headed back towards his conquest in couture jeggings, he smiled to himself. Life was good. Extremely good and it really didn't matter what the hell Bunny's latest crisis was. He would have other things to think about, at least for a few hours.

8

MORNING CAME EARLY. Maggie slipped out of the covers, stretching her lithe and almost ageless body very high and then very low. She had never really needed much effort to stay slim. Years of good eating habits had made that second nature but being fit or strong enough to steal things effectively took effort. Today though, she hurt. All over.

Determined to push through, Maggie dropped to her hands. She needed to kick things up a notch, to make up for last night's mistakes. First off was a speed circuit. 30 push ups, 30 leg lifts, 30 squats and 30 walk-outs, all done in 3 sets. It was agony. She thought how it used to be 80 of each. Maybe that explained things. She was letting herself go a bit. After some side planks, a few handstands and 20 fingertip pull ups Maggie was ready to allow herself to eat.

Heading to the kitchen she flipped on the coffee maker as she pulled out a small pan and turned on the stove. Eggs with pre-cut veggies, spinach and salsa were on the menu and she prepared it quickly, draining four large glasses of tepid water as she did. As her food cooked Maggie reached for her calendar, checking off the date. Habits. Always habits.

Maggie stirred the eggs and veggies before sliding them into a bowl. She took her seat at the outside patio table. Rain fell lightly.

Getting nailed for lifting batteries was bad enough, but being caught by Aldo was infuriating as hell. Sure, she wasn't being that careful or particularly creative when she did it. She did rush into it with no prep to speak of. But to get caught so easily was embarrassing. When you spend years getting good at something, only to see those same skills apparently drift away so easily, one might begin to doubt oneself. And lately, Maggie was doubting herself more than ever. She tried to be cool about whether Ivan would reach out, but it was scaring her the more she thought about it. She couldn't decide what she wanted more: to hear from him with a job…or not.

She thought of her father. Nobody really chooses a career in art theft, but Maggie did. Obviously, it required a certain moral flexibility to start out with, which she certainly had, but even with a couple of short prison terms behind her the fact remained that it was still the single best decision she had ever made.

Maggie had followed her father into the trade so long ago and even though he tried to discourage her at the start, he eventually gave in. Maggie's father was the best at what he did. Smart, curious, and always so careful. He never made a move he hadn't checked six ways from Sunday. And he always had an out.

Maggie was a little more reckless at first, but she had been young then. Age cleans you up. But it was so much fun. The travel, first and foremost. You got to go everywhere. Plus, the very nature of the gig meant you usually moved in circles of extreme wealth and influence. Poor folks certainly didn't own art, and if they did, they sure as heck didn't fight over it with other poor folks. But rich people did, all the time.

Maggie stared into the backyard garden as she ate her eggs. She hadn't really ripped off anything significant in years now. She missed the rush, the excitement, and the challenge of slipping in completely unnoticed and undetected, only to leave just as invisibly, except with a million bucks or more in value tucked under an arm. She knew that was probably the main motivation for her to go after Aldo. More about her own ego than Fatima's shabby treatment. Just to do it. Just to work that muscle one more time, especially after such a long lay off. Tempting, but stupid as it turned out. Still, she had to admit it felt good.

Forget the movies and their wild chases or spectacular run-ins with cops or near-misses with underworld baddies. High-level art theft could be as routine as filing your taxes. Do your job right and no one would ever know you were even there. That's what real cat burglary was all about.

Maggie checked her phone. It was ten to eight. She had slept late after her adventures. Now she had a half-shift at the store at nine. Her "normal life" was calling. Maggie brought her dishes in and turned on the shower, pulling off her clothes to get cleaned up.

Art was one of those things that had the potential to go from worthless to invaluable, and then back to worthless again, several times over the course of even a few years. More often than not the value of some items was based more on who had it, and who wanted to take it from them the most, than what it actually was. That's when it really got fun.

As Maggie showered, she reminisced. Spending her youth at her father's side learning the trade. Living a life of excitement most young girls in the seventies could scarcely imagine, or even dream of. She saw Russia, Poland, Germany, and England. She worked in Switzerland, Austria, and France. She broke into the *Sorbonne*, the *Louvre* and more palaces than she could count. She even managed to lose her virginity at the Kremlin, in Catherine the Great's golden carriage no less.

It was a life of cafes, parties, and nights on the town. The planning and organizing for jobs certainly took time but even that left hours each day for wandering cities and seeing sights. Maggie learned each of the world's most famous cities like a local, understanding them for what they truly were: the good, the bad, the beautiful and often the very ugly.

Her mother had died when she was ten, which was just as well. She had left her father when she learned what he did for money. And she never would have supported Maggie's role in it. The divorce left Maggie numb but it was her mother who had left, leaving Maggie behind. If she thought crime was so bad why leave a child inside? But she did. Her mother was always serious and cold, unlike her father who was more open, and light.

The jobs were very rarely dangerous, at least comparatively. Most art is unbelievably easy to steal. It was more the knowing how to do it than the actual doing of it. Knowing where you can be rough on a piece to get it out the door versus how to handle it were some of the more delicate aspects of the crime in question. The physical act of stealing art was fairly simple. Maggie would laugh at the Hollywood movies full of infra-red lasers and pressure sensitive floors and temperature-based alarms. Sure, they existed, but not in most places. The budgets to install such equipment rarely exist and often the art on tap to steal isn't even hanging in a museum or gallery at all. It's stuck in some back storage room, stacked alongside thirty other pieces behind a door with a deadbolt at best. In most cases, if you're smart enough to lift a hinge from a door you can steal a piece of art. You just need to know where it is and have someone willing to pay you for getting it.

Her father had done quite well. He had squirreled away a couple million dollars over the years. Had a few homes around the world. The money didn't last though, and when cancer came it hit him hard. They had done everything they could. Clinics, pills, injections, miracle cures, but nothing had helped. All it really did was sap the resources. By then Maggie was the only one doing jobs anymore. Her father was too sick. But it was inconsistent, and the art game was changing. By the late 80's and early 90's organized crime had moved into art theft in a big way and coupled with the rise of terrorism, some very bad players had gotten involved. What was once comparatively safe became complicated and quite dangerous.

Maggie and her father had always specialized in working the margins. Dealing with collectors looking to get something for a secret estate, or perhaps just hoping to "liberate" a painting from some business rival who had screwed them on a previous deal as a form of payback. Fairly innocuous stuff, not so risky but paid well. Still, the jobs had become less abundant all the time.

By the time Maggie's father died in 2002 he wasn't even half the man she remembered. The face was there, but the memories had gone thin and the sparkle that had entranced her from so very young was long gone. Maggie was almost 41 and all alone. She washed her hair, remembering the feelings.

She kept up the routine. Finding the jobs, arranging the details, and then pulling them. Her reputation was always good, but she was never as capable with the money as her father was. Then "the job" happened. It was rock-solid. Very private, low risk, and very well planned. But it would ultimately ruin everything. And by the time the music stopped Maggie was the only one left without a seat.

In the end, she had lost all her money, any assets she had inherited and was sentenced to six years in prison. The only bright spot was that once upon a time Maggie's folks had happened to do one thing right together: they had Maggie born in Canada. That meant she had the best passport she could ask for when it came to jail-time. Her lawyers got Maggie's sentence commuted to Canada where the prisons were a lot less hell-hole and way more humane. Sure, it was still sitting in a box, but location made all the difference. Thankfully, her behavior behind bars led to early parole. Another reason to shout hip-hip hooray for the Great White North.

Her shower done, Maggie dried off and quickly dressed. She had just enough time to make it to work. She would meet Fati downtown afterward. As she grabbed her jacket and keys her smartphone began to vibrate in her hand. Maggie looked down and her heart nearly stopped.

Why was she calling? Was he too afraid to tell her himself?

9

AS THE BLACK SUV roared out onto the 401 Tranko gazed dumbly out the window. When they had rolled up on him after Bunny drove off, he had been sure it was all over. The doors had opened, and all the guns had gotten out. The fact that he was still breathing meant he had a chance of some kind. Damn that woman. Somehow this was related to her. He just knew it. Obviously, they wanted to talk to him first. They would have killed him otherwise. It was only his responses to whatever it was they wanted to know that would decide his fate from here on out.

Edward Dachshund was not a nice man. Tranko knew of him, but he'd never met him. He had been part of a crew a few years back in South Africa where a competitor had been informed that his business with Dacshund had come to an end. In that case, they had blown up his sewing machines and burned the factory to the ground. Officially, no one knew who the job was for, but Tranko's contacts filled him in on who was driving the whole thing. Tranko rarely went into things without knowing the angles. At least he never *used* to. These days it seemed like nothing was going right.

As Tranko looked around he noted the guy beside him. Big, probably Korean. He had that look. Behind him in the third row was another gun, but he seemed fat and stupid. Tranko snuffed to himself. *Even Dachshund had trouble getting help.* The driver and passenger never looked back but seemed to be arguing in Russian the entire time. That fit. Dachshund was one of those Russian billionaires everyone heard so much about. It was kind of ridiculous really. They were spoken of like mini gods but in most cases, they were simply uncivilized twits who happened to be in the right place at the right time.

In Dachshund's case, it was oil. That's where the money was. He'd done porn and gambling of course. He was Russian, how could he resist? Add in the free-for-all Russia became in the 90's and there was no shortage of bright lights begging to expand his empire for him. Edward was supposedly a small-timer who was smart enough to sit back while the forces around him made his empire huge. Then, when he realized what he had, Dachshund was ruthless enough to kill the lot of them and hire new guys that were loyal to him. That doesn't sound like much, but that talent is what sets the more successful crooks apart. Underestimating Edward Dachshund would be a mistake at the best of times.

The big Ford finally took an off-ramp into Burbank. As the car turned, Tranko noticed that they were being tracked by another SUV. It had been farther back as they drove the freeway, but once they exited it pulled up behind and the mini convoy continued down Alameda. The Warner Brothers lot sat just to the right, with all their giant movie promo posters. It had a surreal quality to it.

The SUV train turned a corner and flowed past several low-slung office buildings and then headed for what looked like an abandoned compound near the back of an industrial park. The cars rocketed toward the fence, which barely opened in time thanks to some sort of remote control. The cars headed for the main building, a large, steel aircraft hanger-looking place and drove inside the one open door.

As the cars came to a stop the men in the front jumped out and headed into an office just adjacent the main door. Tranko remained in the car with his handlers pointing their AK47's directly at him. *Impress the boss, huh?* thought Tranko.

The thugs returned and motioned to the men in the car to bring him inside. As they led Tranko out of the SUV one of the toughs smacked him on the back of the head - a "hey, here it is" sort of message. Immediately, Tranko showed who he was by suddenly turning and breaking the guy's nose. As the large man was laying on the floor yelling and squirting blood out of his nose the other guys circled him and waved their guns. "That's it! That's it!" one of them shouted.

"Fuck you," offered Tranko. He had sat passively long enough. This crew of rent-a-goons were hardly impressive and if he had to wait much longer to die, he was either going to get busy doing it or get the hell gone. This whole thing was getting ridiculous.

"Hold it."

Everyone looked up, including Tranko. There on the top of a rickety staircase leading to what must have once been a warehouse floor manager's office was a man built exactly as wide as he was tall. Tranko found himself smiling as he considered the almost cubist nature of the guy. Even his features were somewhat lined off. You could draw this guy with a ruler.

He had arms that looked like *Popeye's*, but square, complete with tattoos the length of them. And he had a steely, mean gaze that indicated he was used to being in charge. On his head perched the most ludicrous head of hair Tranko had ever seen. It was high, absurdly dark, and so very full. Like Wayne Newton full. There was no way in hell that was a real head of hair. Period.

The man-brick spoke: "You'll come up here to see me now. Thank you." Then he turned and went inside the office, closing the door behind him.

Tranko looked at the troops surrounding him as if to say "So, you gonna back off so I can go?" He wondered why they never searched him for weapons. That was sort of *Bodyguarding for Dummies*, even when it came to mouth-breathers like this bunch. They never even searched him when they first picked him up. These guys were either hammer stupid or awfully confident. Either way, it meant that Tranko didn't have to part with his lucky knife or the ass-gun. He loved calling it the ass-gun, if only in his head. A nice, slick piece he had picked up in Prague that literally fit in the small of the back and aimed down into the crack of his butt. It looked ridiculous but the damn thing held two shots and could beat almost any pat down. Hell of a piece.

Anyway, that didn't matter because Tranko had a massive Desert Eagle stuck clear in the front of his pants the whole time. They never even asked.

The crew parted and Tranko made his way to the top of the stairs. He paused at the door, wondering if he should knock but then felt stupid for even considering it. *He's not showering*, he thought, so Tranko turned the handle and went in.

The office was about 10 by 15, had a broken desk, several shelves full of literal garbage, and two chairs placed in front. There was a ratty couch along one wall that looked like it had barely survived either a fire or a bomb blast along with a single framed picture on the wall. It was a D10 cat, a bulldozer. The carpet was only carpet in someone's imagination because it appeared to exist mainly to trap whatever grease and oil it currently held. All told, the office was a shit hole but what really caught his eye was a picture on the desk. *Dammit!* It was Bunny Levi, Zevon's wife. *What the…?*

"Tranko Lutz."

"Yeah."

"I needed to see you."

"Apparently."

"You don't know me?"

"Should I?"

"You should."

"Are you Dachshund?"

The square man nodded. Tranko kind of recognized him. He'd only ever seen a few grainy photos, but to think he was face to face with the infamous Russian billionaire was kind of a stretch. The nationality was right and all, but he was just so sort of ridiculous looking. *Whatever* thought Tranko, *I guess there's no casting call for bad guys.*

"What do you want?"

"You killed someone the other day. A little Jew named Zevon."

Tranko sighed and looked around again. Now he knew where he was. This was Zevon's studio office. *Damn.* Zevon wasn't connected, was he? His heart began to hammer. Suddenly Tranko started planning how he was going to shoot his way out of the building. Coming back down the stairs was going to be tricky even if he could kill the fireplug facing him. He scanned for other doors. None. Windows, maybe?

"You kill him, right?"

"It was an accident."

"Sure, yes it was."

"No, this really was an accident. One of my mooks hit him too hard. And I never did it anyway. He just died. When I kill someone it's on purpose."

"The little Jew worked for me. He owed me money. A lot of money."

Shiiiittt. Tranko knew what was coming next. He had gone and inherited Levi's debt. *Fuck Bunny Levi. Fuck her.* And he was so going to kill Howie, that idiot. What a useless tool. *Knocking someone out isn't an exact science.* Actually, it is, but only when you're not as dumb as a busted fence.

"I think now you should owe me his money."

"I got nothing to do with Zevon's business."

"Now you do." He tried to cross his arms menacingly, but their shape made it almost impossible to do so. He seemed to be holding his forearms together, like he was treading water or something. Plus, the hair.

"How much are we talking about?"

"Seven million, give or take a few."

"Bullshit. Zevon didn't even have that much."

"The deal was what it was."

"There's no way. Stick it in your ass. I don't owe you shit."

"Oh yes you do."

"No, I don't."

At this point, Tranko shifted his weight. He'd been in enough of these situations to know when something was about to happen, and the talking stage of this little chin wag was nearly complete. He rested his weight evenly and planned in his head which gun he would go for first, mentally running through his options. He watched the square man tense up too. It was nearly on.

"You refuse to take responsibility for the man you kill?"

"I never killed him."

"Your crew then."

"That may be, but I ain't taking on his debts. Get the wife. She's got it all now anyway."

"I don't deal with women."

"You do on this one."

The brick man stood up. Tranko tensed and then got tired of waiting. He pulled his gun.

"You aim a gun at me?"

"Fucking right I do." Tranko was nervous. Something wasn't right here. Dachshund looked almost relieved that he'd drawn his gun on him. It should have been the opposite.

"You shoot me, now? Go on, do it."

Tranko thought again about his options. Once the sound of his gun travelled Dachshund's crew of mouth-breathers would be up and in here like flies on shit, making it almost impossible to get out alive. He didn't have a choice though. He was going to have to do something.

There was knock at the door. Tranko nearly jumped. He had focused all his intensity on Dachshund and had quite literally forgotten about the space behind him. What was going on? He was better than this. Tranko spun sideways, spreading his coverage across the door and Dachshund, who remained perched on the edge of the desk clutching his comical forearms. A voice called through the door.

"Might I come in?"

English accent. Not threatening per se. What the hell was going on?

Dachshund spoke.

"Yah, come."

The door opened and a trim little man in jeans and a button up shirt stood there. He held his hands in the air. He was five-five, at best. He looked at Tranko.

"You're Mr. Lutz? Tranko Lutz?"

Tranko nodded. What was going on?

"May I come in? Would you mind?"

Tranko didn't answer but he stepped sideways, allowing the man passage. The little man entered. He had gentle features, trim hair and an almost schoolteacher-like bearing. Talk about something that didn't belong. The man came in and sat down on the horrible couch.

He motioned to Tranko Lutz. "You can sit if you want."

Tranko still had his gun trained on the man, nearly blushing when he realized it. There was something about his manner that made it seem ridiculous to keep aiming it at him. For the first time since he was a kid, the gun in his hand felt awkward and sort of improper. He shifted and lowered it, wondering what was about to happen to him.

"I've heard about you. You're pretty good at what you do. Fallen on some hard times though. Doing jobs quite beneath you, I'd say."

The world was spinning. Tranko had to sit down. Square man never moved from the desk and Tranko found himself situated in the middle of the two.

"I apologize for our approach. There are certain realities when you deal as we do."

"Who are you?" demanded Tranko.

"I'm Edward Dachshund."

10

TRANKO HADN'T seen that coming. He turned and looked at the square man, the first Edward Dachshund he met. The trim man caught his look.

"That's Stig." he explained. "He plays me."

The confusion on Tranko's face must have been crystal clear because the trim man continued.

"In the circles I inhabit, loyalty is in short supply. The life expectancy of people such as myself is directly dependent on who we choose to surround ourselves with. I'm certain you, of all people, know how challenging this can be."

Tranko nodded, directly considering the weakness of his own recent hires.

"Real" Dachshund continued. "I needed a more dependable form of cover. So, Stig here is me. No one in that crew downstairs has any idea who I really am. They think I'm simply an accountant that works for him. It is an easy feint. I look like a bean counter, no?" Dachshund keyed on Tranko's confusion.

"Often, we have more to fear from those close to us than not. It is an efficient fiction."

Tranko nodded imperceptibly.

"So, why reveal this to you? Bottom line Mr. Lutz is that your actions have caused me a lot of trouble. Mr. Levi owes me a significant amount of money that I need to collect. Now, he claimed to have assets that were going to cover that debt. Finding those assets has become much more complicated thanks to your less-than-careful actions. So, effective immediately you work for me. You will find out exactly what Mr. Levi has and where it is. Then, you will locate it and bring it to me."

"Then what? You kill me? Fuck you, find it yourself."

"I could have you killed now."

"Exactly, so what the hell do I have to gain here? I bust my ass finding shit for you and you off me anyway? Might as well shoot me now. At least I don't have to waste my time looking for imaginary treasure chests."

"You don't think it exists?"

"I don't think what exists?"

"Mr. Levi claimed to have an item of incredible value that would convert into cash and cover his debt off. He even planned to buy his way free of me, though he didn't know I knew that. I think what he had is quite valuable indeed, I just need you to find it."

"What's in it for me?"

"I will pay you. And quite well at that. Mr. Lutz. Look at yourself. Accepting online hit jobs? Seriously? That's the best you can find with your background? Working for me is a far better fate than the alternative."

Tranko knew he had a point. He hated working freelance, especially the way things were today. The number of guys complaining about their personal "anxiety" or "panic" almost guaranteed he'd have to shoot one of them for sure. He needed to hook up with somebody professional, but he wasn't crazy about the situation he found himself in. All deals are tenuous but this one even more so. The likelihood that they just planned to kill him when they got what they wanted was strong. Still, if he was out looking for whatever they thought they wanted he might be able to grab something for himself. Then he could leverage his own deal out of it. It wasn't great but it was all he had. At least for right now.

"Where do I start?"

"Zevon had his Malibu home. You've already been there, obviously. He had this warehouse for stages, an office on Sunset, plus another home. He may have had other places, storage lockers, whatever. You need to find them and go through them. You've got 24 hours."

"24 hours? What the hell am I going to be able to do in 24 hours? This is crazy. I don't even know what I'm looking for."

"That's your problem. I need it resolved now. The wife will be back in the picture soon enough, soiling everything with lawyers and investigators chasing their pound of flesh. Time is of the essence."

And with that, the real Edward Dachshund stood up and headed out the door.

As he turned to look back at Stig, who was still perched awkwardly on the desk, he considered his options. While he hadn't officially accepted the terms offered, it seemed Dachshund was convinced he had, and he really didn't have anything better to do anyway. When they had grabbed him, he was only on his way to unload the truck of crap they'd boosted from Zevon. Might as well do this for a bit. He stepped toward the square man.

"Looks like I'm in the band after all Stig, I.."

Like a bolt of lightening Stig moved, shooting out a massive fist, hard and fast, into Tranko's gut, knocking every ounce of wind from him. Then he drove his fist up and into the area beneath Tranko's jaw. Almost immediately, Tranko went down to the floor and found himself looking up at the massive, square man with the bushy eyebrows.

"Do not ever call me Stig again. You make that mistake once and it's too late. Use sir or Mr. Dachshund. That's it."

Tranko nodded. He got it. And that sonovabitch Stig was going to get it too. But not now. Now, Tranko had to get his edge back because he'd be damned if he was going to keep being everyone's whipping boy. It was time to get serious, for real. Dachshund had a pretty good thing on offer. It might be a way off a somewhat pathetic path. At the very least he'd make a new batch of contacts, if he was able to stay alive. Plus, if he could dig up this guy's stash then he might get some leverage of his own. Something he desperately needed right about now.

As he stood, Tranko looked Stig dead in the eye. "That's your one free shot. Try it again and I string you up with your own intestines." He didn't break eye contact, waiting until Stig did so first.

Stig headed out of the office. Tranko heard everyone snap to attention as their "leader" descended the stairs and got into one of the SUV's. Three men jumped in as well, along with the real Dachshund before taking off. Tranko watched from the window at the top of the stairs. Two vehicles remained.

As he turned back to the room he looked around. What a dump. It was a temp office to be sure. What is it with these movie guys? He always thought they had plush offices and stuff. This was a dilapidated warehouse full of rats. How did that make any sense? Like Zev would've kept anything of value here anyway. He needed to find out who he should be talking to. To get a sense of what Zev had. Bunny Levi was an obvious choice, but she'd be looking out for herself, and he hated talking to her anyway.

The door burst open. It was one of Stig's goons.

"Get your ass downstairs. You got work to do."

Tranko chewed his tongue. This was not going to go well.

11

SITTING AT THE DESK in his Santa Fe hotel room, David closed his eyes. He needed to visualize the last few hours. Going through that ridiculous mansion was exhausting. The level of security the moron had put in was over the top. Heat sensors, laser beams, facial recognition software, biometric scans, air movement sensors, you name it. A flea couldn't fart in that gallery without setting off an alarm. He had wall-trips, double-sided rock anchors attached to panic alarms, pedestal blast caps and even magnetic locks, all wired directly to a local security firm and the Santa Fe police department.

Money was clearly no object. Obviously, the guy had watched every Hollywood movie ever made about art theft and then subsequently installed, or invented ways to counter every threat. The tour took four hours! Back-up generators, satellite phone lines, even underground power cables with magnetic door locks utilizing geo-thermal power independent of the New Mexico grid. The security spend was insane. The most offensive part was that it was done to protect a mediocre gallery of cartoon cels. Now that was a crime. David shook his head. *That's what you get when the world starts rewarding pasty internet geeks with umpteen millions of dollars.* Fools that believe a cartoon cel of *William J. Frog* dancing is somehow akin to the *Mona Lisa*. What a moron.

David took notes but writing up a full description was giving him a headache. He would submit his overall take as to the level of insurability of the collection's security and make a recommendation. It would be hard to deny this one, even though the guy did admit to planning on opening the room to public parties and events. That was his reason for the insane levels of security. Thing is, as soon as you let folks in any room a good eighty percent of the security immediately became moot. It's turned off so they can come inside. That was always the conundrum with art. It's most safe when no one gets to see it.

As he worked his notes David looked up and noticed the clock. It was almost 5pm and he had agreed to meet with Bunny back in LA later that night, flight depending. She was all worked up and needed some vitamin David to calm her down. As he typed, there was a knock at the door.

Not thinking it was anything beyond fresh towels or a turn-down service David went and opened it without paying much attention. As he looked up, he came face to face with two great big dudes in black suits and dark glasses. They said nothing as they grabbed and pulled him into the hallway.

"Hey, what the..?"

The bigger of the two gave David a look that made him rethink resisting.

They led him down the hallway, up the elevator and onto the pool deck on the roof. David became concerned he was about to be tossed off but figured at some point they had to say what it was they were mad about. He decided patience would be a virtue, for now.

Furiously he ran names and situations through his head, trying to remember who he might have screwed over or nailed in the New Mexico area. None jumped to mind. What the hell was going on?

As he was being led through the pool area, David noticed another small group of suited men surrounding a big cabana to the right of the deck. The goons took him directly to it and thrust him inside. Then they turned their backs to him, effectively blocking his way back out.

David turned to face a small Asian man fiddling with his smartphone. Was he playing a game? The man never once looked up, even as he spoke.

"You are David Teck?"

David nodded nervously and answered. "Yeah? What can I do for you?"

"Insurance questions."

This was weird. He'd had some rough encounters, but this was his first "abduction quote." He tried to roll with it.

"Insurance questions about what?"

"You do art insurance, no?"

"Yes, well, kind of I…"

"So, tell me about securing and insuring art."

"Uh, okay, plans can vary substantially depending on what you are looking for. For example, if you planned to move your art around or loan it out to fundraisers or similar it would be significantly more expensive than doing a classic, stand-alone security plan. Anytime you move art or sculptures you increase the risk substantially. If the collection is to be placed in one secure location and left alone, save for viewing, that is the most basic. What we usually do is arrange insurance on the collection and then add individual riders relating to an exact event or situation that might arise for each piece of art. Usually, the first approach is to assess each piece of art and then do a review of existing security measures before…"

The Asian man broke in. "I think you give us something a little different."

David tensed. He felt the surroundings turn further against him, noticing the bulges in the men's suits. The extremely private nature of their location didn't help either. No one could see him. This wasn't good. He thought again about getting tossed off the roof.

"I'm not sure I understand."

The Asian man finally looked up from his game. "Mr. Teck, I am fully aware of your, shall we say, extracurricular activities on behalf of certain clients. I personally know some individuals that made use of your services only to get robbed soon after. Coincidences are rare, no? Anyway, my interest in you today surrounds a Mrs. Elfrieda Levi."

David swallowed hard. "I'm not exactly sure what you mean."

"Oh, I think you do. I understand you have a meeting with her tonight. I want to know what it is she's meeting you about. Your firm generally insures only large-scale items or projects. What could Mrs. Levi have that suddenly needs insuring?"

David could feel himself starting to sweat. This was not the way he liked to work.

"Look, I'm uh..you see. I'm sort of… I don't actually know how to put this. You see, I am not seeing her in a professional way, it's more…personal and sort of…"

"Yes, you're screwing her."

David frowns. "Well, you can be crass about it but yes, we are in an adult relationship…of sorts."

"Her husband is dead, Mr. Teck. Now, I'm not sure if you had anything to do with that or not but her husband did leave behind some rather large creditors. That means I want information on Mrs. Levi that I think only you can provide."

Dead? thought David. *What the hell?* He felt quite exposed in the moment, unaware of what was going on, but he knew he had to recover.

"Look, I don't know about all that but I'm fine with helping you however I can. No problem at all. I can talk to you after I've seen her. I don't really know all that's going on but I'm happy to share anything you need. 100% I'm your guy. No problem."

"Good choice, Mr. Teck. I'll be in touch with you tomorrow at some point. Your helpfulness to me will determine your ongoing status."

"Status in what?" asked David.

"In life, Mr. Teck."

David nodded, gulped a tiny bit, and turned to leave the white-sheeted cabana. The two large suits previously blocking his exit moved stiffly to the side. As David quickly walked away, back toward the roof exit, he never once looked back. Opening the elevator door, he spun inside and pressed the 8th floor button in one smooth move. He stayed calm, betraying no sense of anything as he rode down, back to his room. Once inside, David headed directly to his bathroom, dropped quickly to his knees, and promptly threw up in the toilet.

Twice.

12

Standing in Ivan's shop was exhilarating. It had been a solid two years since Maggie had the scent of a real job in her nose. She didn't mind admitting that the premise of working again had her excited and nervous. The adventure at Aldo's place had her doubting herself something fierce and she needed a pick me up. Ivan would do just that.

If only Greta wasn't still around.

Greta was Ivan's assistant and had been for what seemed like forever. She was a cranky, nasty, you-know-what, at least that's how she always treated Maggie. Ivan trusted her implicitly so when Maggie got the text from Greta that Ivan needed to see her right away it was a mixed blessing. First, she had never given Greta that phone number and second, she hated being summoned by her. But it was about work with Ivan, and she was happy to see him however it happened.

Ivan kept a small lock and key shop just adjacent the Pike Place market in downtown Seattle. It was a touristy kind of place but had been Ivan's home for almost sixty years. His father had owned the shop before him. The obvious uniqueness of the site was unmistakable. It was located directly above one of the most famous underground networks in the United States. The Seattle Underground was a network of passageways and basements that had been ground level at the city's origin in the mid-19th century. After the streets were elevated most of the lower spaces fell into disuse, except the few they resurrected as a tourist draw.

The story was that back in 1889 or so a cabinetmaker accidentally overturned and ignited a glue pot. An attempt to extinguish it with water spread the burning grease-based glue. The fire chief was out of town, and although the volunteer fire department responded they made the mistake of trying to use too many hoses at once. They never recovered from the subsequent drop in water pressure, and what eventually became known as the *Great Seattle Fire* completely levelled 25 city blocks.

What the city had done at the time was interesting. Having several issues in mind that needed solving they proposed a new idea. Instead of simply rebuilding as before, they decided that all the new buildings should be brick or stone and that the streets should be regraded to one, or even two, stories higher than before. This would guard against flooding, which had also been a problem apparently.

To do it, they lined the streets with concrete walls, forming narrow channels between them and the buildings on both sides of the street, along with a wide "alley" where the street previously was. Because the steep hillsides of the city already existed, they were used as well. Eventually this led to filling the alleyways in and raising the streets to the new level of about 12ft higher than before. In some places it hit nearly 30ft.

When they rebuilt, original merchants and landlords knew the existing ground floor would end up underground and that their second floor would become street level. As a result, they added very little decoration to the doors and windows of the lower level, but extensive embellishment to what would become their new entrances. Once the new sidewalks were complete, building owners moved their stores to the new ground level, while also carrying on with business in the lowest floors that had survived the fire.

Pedestrians continued to use the underground sidewalks lit by the transparent glass cubes embedded in the grade-level sidewalk above. It all worked great until 1907 when the city condemned the Underground for fear of the bubonic plague. As such, the spaces were abandoned and left to deteriorate or be used as storage. Some went on to become flophouses, gaming halls, speakeasies, and opium dens. Nowadays only a small portion of the *Underground* has been restored for tourists, but the network beneath the streets remains all the same.

Ivan's shop sat above one of the 30-foot sections, having the equivalent of an entire two-story building underground. It was not registered as such, not publicly known, and most definitely not a stop on any tour. Ivan Bosche had his very own *Batcave*.

Just finishing with a customer, Ivan turned to Maggie. He smiled slightly as he walked past her and saw the client out. He locked the door, turned his sign to be 'back in a while' and smiled. Maggie scanned the shop for Greta. Nowhere in sight.

Walking past Maggie, Ivan indicated she follow him behind the counter where they stepped into the backroom. He pulled the curtain across the entrance and then hugged her close.

"My little Vixen. How are you, precious?"

"Ivan, I'm 62. I'm too old to be precious to anyone."

"You will always be my little treasure. I knew you when you were this high, Vixen."

Maggie hated that name. "Vixen."

Her father had been known as "The Fox." He always claimed it was a kind of branding/reputation thing. He had a flair for the dramatic, plus he enjoyed the romance of such a moniker.

Simon Deacon always had an affinity for foxes. As a boy in England, he had worked for a well-to-do family that regularly rode the hounds, chasing the foxes. He was often tasked with cleaning up after the hunts, preparing the tails, cleaning up the horses and whatnot. In that time, he came to appreciate the fox most of all, for the simple reason that here was a large group of grown men getting all gussied up in red outfits, arranging horses, hounds, and parties for the sole purpose of chasing it down and killing it. Secretly, he rooted for the fox and was always a little disappointed when it got caught. So, when his own future came calling, adopting the namesake of the ultimate outsider seemed natural.

Maggie picked up her appellation thanks to one of her father's competitors at the time. A nasty, brutish man that came to the house periodically when she was young, usually with information to sell or trades to make. Maggie always had an uneasy feeling around him and tried to find a way to be somewhere else when he arrived.

One time when she was about twelve, the brute came by the house expecting to see her father. He was delayed so she had to ask him to wait. In the uncomfortable 15 minutes or so she was forced to make small talk and wait on him until her father finally arrived home.

"How are you?" Simon was slightly aware of her feelings toward the man. However, Maggie didn't get a chance to answer. The brute spoke up.

"The little vixen is fine. She has cared well for me."

Well, Maggie hated it, especially because it came from Jean St. Tropez, but it tickled her father enough that he mentioned it to a few friends, in teasing jest at first. Then, as Maggie grew older and began to work in the trade herself it became a natural fit for the role she filled.

After her father died, it was even harder to shake because it became a sort of way to honor him posthumously, acknowledging all that he meant to her. So, Maggie became Vixen, at least in brand name. But it had been years since anyone used it. St. Tropez was long dead which was a blessing of sorts. Now, it was only Ivan who called her that, but he did it with such affection and sincerity that it warmed her. Ivan could call her Vixen anytime.

The two continued into the back room where Ivan turned off the heavy grinding wheel next to a massive, ancient key cutting machine. It looked like it weighed 17 tons, which was the point, as he casually disengaged two locks before easily swinging the entire machine to one side, revealing a hidden staircase heading down through the floor.

As much as Ivan was good on the locks and keys and necessary tools of the trade, his true love was his role as a fence. Ivan knew everyone that no one knew. He was a cipher to most while still being a player of some note. The space beneath his store had held some of the most valuable works of art in history. They never stayed long, mind you. Ivan was about movement and art that arrived was art that needed to be placed. He had little patience for delay, believing first in getting the job done right and then by moving the art out once more.

At the bottom of the long, winding staircase, Ivan led Maggie to the living room in the lower corner. They sat across from each other.

"I have a job for you, it seems a deceptively simple one. Still, it demands a strong heart and professional temperament." Ivan was so formally dramatic. Maggie loved him. "The piece is not too big, about this high." He indicated with his hands about 12in. "It's a small painting. Not too heavy, fragile yes but you can remove it from the frame very easily. The opportunity window is short. It's currently in a residence just outside Moscow. The home has no security to speak of, but there may be others around if the owner is not. You will need to get in and out clean, and then get the piece to a pre-arranged drop location as soon as possible. Then you will have to leave the country."

Maggie was thrilled. "I'm sure it will be fine. No issues. Thank you so much. It means a lot."

"Shhhh, wait little Vixen. I'm not offering this out of pity. You're still the best at what you do and in this case your age offers a very valuable asset when it comes to pulling off this particular repatriation."

Ivan always called what they did 'repatriation.' He never said steal because he didn't see it as stealing. In most cases, the art they took had been stolen many times already. It was so far from the legitimate hands already that even when it ended up in a museum collection it was still ill-gotten gains. According to Ivan, art could never be purchased anyway. It belonged to everyone but was simply possessed at different times by different individuals. How long they possessed it was open to change at any time.

"You will need to fly to Moscow. I will prepare measurements and a few other items for you. Let me know of any other needs you may have. The dates are mid-week next, so you will have to hurry. Will it be a problem to get away?"

"No, I can do it. Will the piece be crossing any lines?"

"Eventually yes, but your drop will be in Moscow. Getting you back could be tricky if anything goes wrong. You have to careful little Vixen. This is not an easy job."

"How much is the gig?"

"Only $15,000. I'm sorry."

"Ouch. Times really are tough. It'll help though. How do they pay?"

"$5,000 up front, the rest to me upon completion. I got them through two secure contacts. They don't know me or you."

"Always preferable."

"I'm sorry I haven't been able to give you more work. It's been hard. I don't hunt it down like I used to anymore. So much unseemliness in the trade these days. And Greta says I'm too old. That I need to slow down more."

"I always appreciate what I get. Thank you, Ivan."

Maggie hugged him and they made plans to meet up once more prior to the weekend. It was a 4hr drive back to Vancouver, but it was late. Maggie decided on a hotel instead. As she checked in and moved her bag upstairs, she smiled. The excitement of a gig always put a grin on her face. She forgot how much she lived for the raw excitement these jobs provided. Truth be told, she'd have done the gig for free just to have something to do. Still, the fixed expenses would eat up a fair amount of the profit. Planes and hotels were not cheap. Even art "repatriators" were getting squeezed in this economy.

The phone in her purse began to buzz wildly. Glancing down at the phone Maggie picked it up. A text, from Fati.

As Maggie read, she sighed. What had Fati gone and done to herself now?

13

FATI FIDGETED nervously on her seat. The lounge at the Fairmont was busy but not obviously so. Lots of customers but still lots of room. Fatima had found a private corner, she liked being tucked away, and waited with her boxcar. Stirring the ice obsessively, Fati felt silly for being so nervous waiting to see Aldo. She was a grown woman for heaven's sake. She hadn't been this nervous about a meetup since high school. She couldn't believe she was doing this.

As she looked around, Fati comforted herself in the surroundings. It was a lovely lounge, and the view of the planes taking off was very relaxing, at least for her. She peered out the window closest and marked the private plane area of the airport. That's where Aldo would come in. She watched the small jets come in and out, trying to guess which was his. Each time she watched a large black car leave the area she hoped it was him coming to meet her.

Fati had grown up privileged. Her father worked hard and by the time she was born he was literally above it all. The days of down and dirty work were done. By then, it was all meetings and deals and negotiating. The shipping business was very exotic to her, and Fatima had enjoyed the excitement of receiving packing crates from far off locales. Her father would be setting up some trade route or shipping contract and spy something he liked, say a handmade hobby horse in Portugal. Then, he would dutifully have it packed up and shipped home. It was his way of sending little "I love you" notes to his only daughter. Fati enjoyed getting them but cared more about her imagined image of him carefully placing the item he had found in a perfectly chosen box and surrounding it with packing straw, tying it down, and then addressing it officially to her. She knew in her heart that he had others do this but in her mind's eye it was father doing it all and she loved him for it.

The difficult times came when she was away at school. Father had sent her to an expensive boarding school in Connecticut. Fati was unaware at the time, but the shipping business had hit some snags and her father was over-leveraged. Loans were called and when two ships sank within weeks of each other a massive problem arose. Her father had been self-insuring, not uncommon at the time but risky when you were a comparatively small operator. Combined with his existing debt loads and a negative market turn, the family's fortunes took a serious hit. So serious that Mario Bello was never really the same again.

Her father became cynical, less whimsical. That made it all the harder when her mother died. Fati had continued in school, got fair marks, and eventually graduated but the excitement of the family was muted considerably. Her father retained a portion of his business, nowhere near what he had originally had, fighting tooth and nail to keep even that. She didn't know it then but the only reason he fought so hard was because he considered it her inheritance. It was the protection he had promised himself he would always give her.

She was twenty-four when she married Anthony. Anthony was bright and kind. He was a good man and he loved Fatima completely. He advised her father on certain moves, options, and languages in contracts. He was a lawyer, and talented enough that in the end he not only secured his father-in-law's position but allowed it to grow substantially. Mario Bello already loved him for marrying his daughter. He adored him for securing what business had remained.

When Fati's father passed, he left everything to her but instructed Anthony to take control. And he did, turning the fraction Mario had fought to retain into a lynchpin of control that saw him broker deals no one thought possible. The fortune grew and Fatima was happy.

Children were an ever-present desire. They tried for years but this was before the days of doctors and the tests done today. But Fati had never been one to think she deserved whatever she wanted, deciding it was probably God's will. She never adopted because she was fearful someone would come and take her baby away. She would not risk her heart in the meantime.

Anthony died suddenly, at the young age of 45. It was so unexpected. He was healthy, strong and did everything you were supposed to do. He just died, as people sometimes do. Fatima was alone now, and the business fell to her. Not that there was much to do. Anthony had constructed it in such a way that most of the day to day functioned without significant effort. A foundation was set up and the controlling interest was aligned with a team based in New York.

Anthony had promised her father he would ensure her lifetime protection and he had been true to his word. The business churned along and left more than enough wealth and protection to care for Fatima several lifetimes over. Personally, she didn't need much but she enjoyed not worrying. Being an only child, she was always comfortable alone but as the years passed, she found herself trying more and more to replace the sort of psychic comfort Anthony had provided her. Fatima missed having a body to lie next to.

The years since were a steady stream of bad choices. Either they were bums interested only in her money or they were unambitious louts who wanted a mother. It was tiresome, but Fatima was nothing if not an optimist who tried to see the best in others.

Aldo had seemed different. Very different. The way they met was odd. Fatima had signed up for one of those hoity toity executive dating services. She had gotten so tired of the types looking for a bank account versus a relationship, figuring maybe if the man already had wealth, it would be less of a problem. It wasn't. The ones that supposedly had money usually didn't. They were just good at looking like they did. And the few that truly did have wealth spent more time negotiating terms than trying to fall in love. No one was easy or fun to get to know. It was like a wrestling match where both parties circled each other looking for weaknesses before they pounced. In fact, Fati had all but given up before she met Willy.

Willy was a nervous man. Really nervous. He always seemed to be shaking, even when he wasn't. Eventually, it became annoying but the first couple of times they went out it was charming, at least in a sort of funny way. Fati didn't really connect with him romantically, but she did find him nice to talk to. He listened so well, showing more interest in Fatima and where she came from than any other guy. She'd even introduced him to Maggie, who thought she was crazy to date him, but the three had a nice time. At the very least, Fati thought she might have found a new friend.

After getting together on and off for a couple of months via a show here, a movie there, dances, and special events he finally invited her out for an intimate dinner late one night. This was out of character for Willy. He was more of an early supper kind of guy. Anyway, when she arrived at the restaurant Willy had a friend with him. He introduced her to Aldo Neto, and then bizarrely melted into the background before disappearing outright for the rest of the night.

Aldo was a dream, literally. The man was tall, well-built, and handsome. He was a shade older than Fatima but wore it so well. Distinguished, confident and sincere. His skin was perfect, and just begged to be touched. Fatima even had to catch herself as she almost involuntarily stroked his face. She didn't even know him yet!

But what happened to Willy? Why Willy brought him was always a mystery to her. He said they did business, and that Aldo was visiting, but he just sort of sat back before leaving them alone. He didn't seem angry or even disappointed. Just gone. He didn't ever call again either.

Fatima knew she had to take a certain blame for how things turned out. Willy couldn't hold a candle to Aldo. She couldn't take her eyes off him. Even the way he spoke English was attractive. His voice had the deep tones and warmth of an evening news anchor. It was like he was deposited from the gods above.

And he was rich, so rich. Not one of those fly-by-nighters claiming to have grabbed the brass ring. Aldo owned several brass rings already. A billionaire several times over, he walked with the confidence and assurance of a titan yet didn't wave it in anyone's face. At least until the other night. Fatima grimaced. Why was she here again?

When they first dated, he never even discussed money or business with her. And she was fine with that. They talked about art, or music or current events or whatever. He was interested in her life. Her friends, what she did, what she liked. He was interested in her.

Fatima fell hard. Too hard probably. Aldo's one problem was his lifestyle. The man was almost always on the move. Fati had travelled with him twice. The finest hotels, private jets, the works. It was not completely foreign to her, but it was still impressive. Not to Aldo though. To him, it was expected. Simply the way things were done. And things were perfect up until that darn dinner. She flushed remembering it.

Where was he? The waiter came over and she ordered another boxcar but added a club soda as well. She didn't want to get full-on tipsy. Why had she even agreed to this? He screwed up, not her.

He had called her. Multiple times in fact. She had ignored them all. Until the last one. She finally answered. Wanting to hear him squirm, Fatima finally relented and let him speak. He claimed that the dinner party was a sort of test and that the only one who passed was Fatima. Her heart leapt at the idea, but she didn't show it. She wasn't sure. Why should she trust him again?

Aldo begged her to meet with him. Here, at the airport hotel, tonight. He said it was important. And that she would not regret it. Fati gave in. She thought about telling Maggie but figured that would be a bad idea. She knew what Maggie would say.

The waiter returned with her drinks and placed them down on the table in front of her. He paused, and then handed her a note, folded over. He spoke. "A gentleman called for you and asked to leave a message."

Fatima sat up straight in her chair and hesitated before opening the paper. Taking a deep breath, she unfolded it and almost immediately began to cry.

14

"He loves me, Maggie. The dinner party, all the women…it was a test. I was the only one who passed. By telling him off, by leaving, it showed him that I was "the one." Fatima sighed to herself, reimagining her bad memory as a newly vindicated one.

"He's a jerk, Fati. Period." Maggie bent down and slid her cleaning rag across the shiny horse's extended front leg.

"Aldo said he misunderstood our relationship. And to be fair, maybe I did too. I'm just an old romantic. Emphasis on old." Fati answered without looking back. She was on tippy toes trying to dust around the top of the Wurlitzer military band organ. "I can't be looking at things like some 21year-old hoping for magic. The way you date today is…I don't know, just not like…it's different now. Not like before."

Maggie wasn't hearing any of it. "Not that different. Fati, he's playing you. And he only wants you now because you told him to go pound sand. Rich guys hate being told 'no.' They literally can't handle it. You do not want to play with someone like this. He's not worth it."

At that, Maggie stood up and surveyed the sparkling ring of horses. Beautiful. She loved it here, on the carousel. Cleaning it was almost more fun than riding it.

She reached out and rubbed *Bingo's* ears. "Horse 18" was his official designation, but *Bingo* was supposedly named after some guy that helped bring the rickety, old carousel to the museum back in the early nineties. It was here where she first met Fati, actually. She volunteered with the original restoration work committee on getting the vintage carousel back into shimmering shape.

The story went that the carousel was in a bad way when it arrived at the museum, but over the years, and thanks to a ton of effort, it was fully and lovingly restored to its former glory. Maggie came late to the process, almost by accident. Fati had been one of the first "Friends of the Carousel" who helped make it happen, arranging to bring the pieces from the old Playland location where it had fallen into disrepair after fifty years of use. Maggie had just been on a random walk one day when she happened upon the park and saw the crew working away. She got talking to Fatima and was impressed with her devotion to something so whimsical. She also just liked her energy. She was a pip.

Afterwards, they would meet up every week or so, whenever Maggie could get away, and work together on the restoration. There were a ton of professionals doing their things. Artists, welders, carpenters, and more. Everyone pitched in. Maggie even got to do some line painting and sealing on a few of the horse's saddles. It was great fun. And through it all, her and Fatima became fast friends, spending more and more time together. It was like finding the sister you never knew you had. Fati was funny, and naïve, but always bright and sunny. She just made Maggie smile no matter what. That even now, years later, they still got to come back and spend time around the carousel was a treat.

The carousel itself dated from 1912 and was made by the C.W. Parker company in Kansas. They called them Carry-Us-Alls because apparently old C.W. hated the term "merry-go-round." Guess you can call them whatever you want if you're the guy building them.

This carousel was #119, or the 119th one made by his company. Maggie's favorite horse was always *Scampering Dawn* because of the frilly flowers in her colorful bridal, plus the name "Scampering." The museum always needed volunteers and when the chore in question was something so pretty, well, that was a no-brainer. They both knew they'd be coming back to Deer Lake Village for as long as the museum would let them.

"I'm not getting any younger, Maggie. I want to have someone. I don't know, just to be with. To do things with. Is that asking so much?" Fatima waved her long duster in the air.

"Of course not," answered Maggie. "But playing this guy's game isn't smart either. I just don't get a good vibe from him. And why all this from a note anyway? You switched your feelings on him pretty fast, no? Besides, I thought he was supposed to meet you at that bar? What was that about? Can you trust anything this guy does?"

Fatima walked over and leaned against the horse Maggie was cleaning. "He was coming to meet me, and then weather forced his plane to re-route back to Seattle. He apologized. I have a tendency to be dramatic. You know that." Fatima smiled at Maggie.

Maggie wanted to stay serious, but she knew her friend. "Yes, you and drama are well-acquainted."

Fati bubbled over. "Look! We're getting together tomorrow on his yacht, down in Coal Harbour. He said his man brought it up from California a few weeks ago. We're having dinner on it. You should meet him. Come with me."

Maggie took a deep breath. This would be a bad idea on several levels. She had no real desire to meet Aldo Neto until she had a chance to check him out some more. She was still burned up about their last meeting. Not that he knew they met, but she would know and that was enough. Maggie needed to have a few more details in place before she was willing to go toe to toe with him.

"I'll pass. Look, you're a big girl. I can't tell you what to do. But I can say 'be careful.' This guy has messed you around once. Don't let him do it again."

Maggie hated arrogance, but even more than that, she hated arrogance from a fake. It's bad enough to make someone feel small because of who you are or what you have but to do it when you're not even what you claim to be? That's just slimy. And low. In most cases, payback was a waste of time, but Fati had really been hurt by this clod. Maggie wanted badly to pass on the humiliation to this Brazilian big shot. And she wanted Fati to see it. Whether that was going to happen or not was an open question. But Fati did offer a nice suggestion without realizing it. *So, Mr. big shot had a yacht, huh?* Of course, he did. Which meant maybe there was a quicker way to get more detail on Mr. Neto than Maggie first thought.

15

BUNNY LEVI lay back on a cushioned table with her legs splayed wide in the air. Her feet rested in plush stirrups, with electric lime green, and absurdly long, toenails just screaming for attention. She was completely naked from the waist down, a Filipino woman seated at eye level between her legs, head down and working away. Bunny dangled a massive *Slurpee* cup from one hand, with a long, wide, flexible straw. Half-full of frozen margarita, Bunny sucked away on the alcoholic slush like her life depended it, flinching every so often as the small lady toiled away on her lady parts. *A Brazilian wax performed by a Filipino.* The thought would have made Bunny smile if she could have moved her face.

The indignities of aging had been creeping up on Bunny for a while now. She was 46 but trying to look 26. Things weren't going well. Her life had not been an easy one, at least in her estimation. Born in Kansas, she couldn't wait to get out. By the age of 16 she had finally managed to run away from home once and for all. Determined to find her way to a "real" state Bunny figured entertainment was the best way to go. In practice, that either meant stripping or becoming a groupie for a band willing to travel out of state. After a few dead ends she finally hooked up with a group called *Love Locker*. Bunny lived with the band all the way to Cleveland. Then she jumped ship and took up residence with a "promoter" based there. She still wished someone would have mentioned that Ohio wasn't a real state either.

A full series of shitty jobs and/or relationships later, Bunny finally managed to hook up with a football player. She always had a killer body, along with a complete willingness to use it for almost anything whatsoever. While this pleased the football player, and a good many of his teammates as well, it was not desirable to Bunny. But she got over it when a team road trip finally got her to L.A. When she arrived, Bunny knew the City of Angels was the only place she ever really wanted to be.

The sun shone all the time and surface beauty was legitimate currency. For a hot young girl in her early twenties, it was the place to be. From then on, she only rode in expensive cars and ate in fine restaurants. She never paid for food, clothes, drugs, or much else. All it cost was a little sexual degradation every now and again. For her, there were far worse ways to live. Like on a boring-ass farm for instance. Bunny Baffle was home and she absolutely loved it.

But the other shoe started to drop. It was gradual. A faint line here. Maybe some skin flakes or two. She was getting older, and without a locked in situation things could get ugly, literally, pretty damn fast. Bunny's party life took on an urgency she hadn't previously known. Aging? That was for old people. Bunny found herself becoming desperate. Willing to say 'yes' to things she would not have considered months before. But she had to. This was a crisis that wasn't going to end well. It was just going to end. And she did not want to be alone and broke when the music stopped.

The trouble was when she set her sights on marriage the guys around her noticed. Suddenly they weren't so interested now. They had lots of time for party girls, but not a moment for someone looking for more. The mantra was "nothing serious, ever." And now that they knew what she was after Bunny would have to get creative. A kid was always the best shot. Get the right guy to knock you up and you have an insurance policy to die for. Unfortunately, Bunny seemed to be infertile. She used to brag about never getting pregnant. Now it was an actual problem.

She had done everything she could to get herself knocked-up, but nothing worked. She ate tubs of honey and cinnamon and elevated her legs after sex so much that guys thought she had vertigo or a weird fetish. She used cough syrup to thin her cervix mucus and acupuncture too. Nothing. Nada. And she had some real catches on the line that slipped away. Just one of them would have set her up for life. But Bunny never even missed a period. She went for tests but there was never anything specifically wrong. In fact, there was no actual, defined reason that she could not have a baby. It just never happened.

Bunny twitched and spat a shot of frozen margarita into the air. "Hey, fuckin' watch it down there. That hurt."

"Sorry, sorry." Replied the follicle technician.

Age was catching up quickly. She started having to hide money away just to get the "jobs" done. Boob job, tummy tuck, butt-lift, tattoo removal (from the band days) eye lift, neck smooth, you name it. And it was getting expensive. So expensive that she didn't know how much longer she was going to be able to keep it up. She'd seen the women that got the cheapie plastic surgery. That terrified her. So far, she'd been able to keep with the best. Sure, it took selling off the various gifts and whatnot received over the years, but she had to do something. Getting a job as receptionist at the best plastic surgery clinic helped. They offered the services at cost, which was almost too good to be true. The competition to get the job in the first place was fierce. In fact, the only way she even pulled that off was by being willing to make out with the owner's wife in front of him. Never underestimate the levelling effects of perversion. Anyway, Bunny did all she could to slow the effects of aging and just when she thought all was lost, Zevon Levi came in.

He was a client of Janderson Fell and was in the office for, of all things, a butt lift. For whatever reason, Zevon was obsessed with his ass and the way it looked. He had a huge gut and jowls but somehow that didn't matter. He wanted an ass that would stop traffic and everything else took second to that.

He asked her out three times, and even then, she probably never would have gone with him, but Bunny herself was recovering from a nose peel and an ear pull which meant her entire head was wrapped in some form of bandage and gauze. For Zevon to keep chasing her with that in play meant something. He offered dinner at some private club he was a member of. That meant a meal she might not otherwise get to have. In the end, Bunny said yes to a free lunch. What did she have to lose?

As the days turned into weeks, Bunny continued to heal at the expense of Zevon Levi. She never could have gotten dates looking like the mummy she was, but he didn't seem to care. Accordingly, she was content to live the good life on his dime until the latest scars healed. Plus, he never touched her. To be fair, he really couldn't while she was healing. Still, it was perfect.

The wrinkle arrived on their last date. Bunny's bandages had finally come off and Zevon had promised a weekend away at some top-line, plush spa in Malibu to celebrate. Bunny knew what was up. He figured it was time to "seal the deal." She went to dinner, fully expecting to drop him like a hot rock, but got drunk on sambuca and sambuca always made her do stupid things.

She started feeling sorry for him. And he was so excited about her fresh looks. He praised her beauty, wrapped in bandages so long. He gushed over her features, her eyes, everything. He was so sincere. So in love. Bunny wasn't. Not even a little but she did feel sorry for him. She decided there was little harm in providing a goodbye hump. Why not? He had treated her pretty good. It was the least she could do. Plus, the sambuca. Besides, once it was over, she'd move on with as clean a conscience as she was ever likely to have.

Only this time she got pregnant.

Of all the times to suddenly be fertile. And she might have taken care of it except she wasn't at all sure she'd ever be able to do it again. This was likely her one shot at total life insurance, which meant Bunny grabbed it with both hands. Within six weeks she was Mrs. Elfrieda 'Bunny' Levi. He made her go Jewish, which didn't matter to her all that much. But his friends went ape about it and she got a huge party and tons of cash as gifts. It was totally worth it. She didn't really have to do anything other than memorize a few lines and pretend to like his awful mother. There were no specific rules that she could find on being a good Jew in Hollywood so that meant she could pretty much do whatever she wanted. Bunny Baffle became Bunny Levi and boy did she go to town.

Once the kid was born the deal was set in stone. With the money locked in she needed to look for a way out. She would have the steady income of child support plus something for her needs. It was time. She knew enough about Hollywood to realize that being married to a D-level movie producer was pathetic, whereas being divorced from one was simply good business.

She had lined up her plans, got all the papers in order only to get suckered in by sambuca again, which by this point must be considered as some form of legitimate fertility drug because this time Bunny had twins. Twins! Now she had three kids by this moron and going out on her own got a whole heckuva lot harder. So, instead she waited and bided her time, until the kids got old enough to be sent out on their own.

But Zevon didn't stay pliable. Or passive. He got mean. He didn't feel like rolling over and playing dead in the divorce. He played hardball. Rough lawyers, harsh investigators, the works. He even found out about her yoga coach and his "sessions" with her. He was aiming to cut her take down to nothing. That's when she ran the ad.

She never wanted to kill the vengeful asshole. That was never in her best interests. He was much more valuable to her alive than he would have ever been dead. He couldn't earn if he was dead. But that stupid mouth breather she hired screwed it all up and left her a widow. Which wasn't all bad except now she'd have to fight the kids for the cash and assets, all while playing the sad, bereaved widow left behind. The game wasn't over by any stretch, but it had gotten a whole lot more complicated.

"Okay, you done. Do you want balm?"

"Yeah. I want some friggen balm. It feels like you used a cheese grater down there."

"You want eucalyptus or orange grove?"

Bunny sucked on her straw. "Orange grove."

Now she had to navigate the whole dead husband thing. Organizing burials, services, insurance, the whole nine yards. A pain in the ass really. Plus, the kids were coming home for the funeral. There was money, several million she figured, but nothing like she'd always imagined he had. She certainly couldn't live like she had been. As long as he kept filling the tanks with cash things were sweet. She had loads of free time to get to know some other horse to jump on with Zevon footing the bill, but now? Now she had limited funds to land a new ride which meant she needed a plan. She needed a plan more than a wax, that was for sure. But this was the first Wednesday of the month which meant if she let things go any longer down there, they would need a guide with two machetes just to get close.

As Bunny sat up and pulled her gown back down over her legs, she spied the clock. It was already 6:30pm. She was supposed to meet David by 7:45pm at the house. He was losing his crap over something that happened in New Mexico. She smiled knowingly. He wouldn't tell her over the phone.

Anyway, she would have to get moving if she was going to make it in time. Traffic was horrible by the evening with the Lakers in town and she'd be damned if she got stuck in the Valley after dark again. Only rookies made mistakes like that.

16

AS A GOON opened the door to the SUV, Edward Dachshund — already seated inside — cast a glance up. He saw Tranko Lutz looking down from the office window. Stig arrived, crawled in and sat down beside him. The door was slammed shut. Leaning in close, the square, squat man asked. "You think he buy all that?"

Laughing ruefully, Dachshund turned away to gaze out the window.

"It doesn't really matter, does it?"

"Then why in hell we bring that idiot along? He's gonna be trouble."

"Look, you know as well as I do that Levi is dead, and we have no idea where he stashed it. The squeeze on the operation in Moscow is coming. I can feel it and we're going to need something to bargain our way out. And if I don't find some breathing room we're done. The Booli Brothers have made serious trouble for us. We have to find out where it ended up."

"What do you think? You think this asshole figured things out with Levi?"

"Who knows? It's possible. I tend to think that's why he killed him. Either that or he really is that stupid, which he very well could be. Bottom line: we need him close, for now. Besides, the minute we get something concrete on where it is, we kill him. No issues."

"I'd just as soon kill him now." offered Stig.

Dachshund smiled. "Have I ever steered you wrong?"

Stig dropped his face and looked at him, eyes wide open yet still somehow dead. "It would only happen once."

* * *

Tranko was ushered into another SUV by the remaining thugs. He looked at his handler. "So where do you guys expect me to start?"

Handler thug answered. "That's your problem dipshit. Boss says you need to start looking around for stuff and we need to stick with you."

As the vehicle pulled away, Tranko spun through his options. He could take them to the truck of stuff he boosted from Levi's place but that would be stupid. He hadn't really had a chance to look at it himself yet. And considering the way things were going maybe there was something there after all. He could also haul them over to Levi's beach house. He knew what was there. Nothing. Best idea was to figure out what these guys already knew, just in case they had some intel that he knew nothing about.

"You guys already checked his rental space out, right?

"What rental space?"

"It's some massive warehouse in the Valley. I heard he's got a ton of stuff in there. I was gonna go there myself," Tranko lied. He had no intention of going there because Levi never rented the place. He was cheap. That's why he was storing it at home.

"So, what is the place?"

"It's how these movie producers make their money, you know, renting junk to other productions and shows. Just the sort of things they use for filming movies or TV shows."

"Ok, so we go there."

* * *

Standing inside the decrepit, musty warehouse handler thug seemed disappointed.

"What is all this shit? I see no movie things."

Tranko laughed. "What'd you think they kept in here, George Clooney?"

The group was not impressed. Tranko tried to explain. "It's the kind of stuff they use in making movies: fake walls, desks, chairs, furniture, set decoration, anything you might have in a house or office. They build sets and keep all kinds of things here."

"What about those wood cages with the padlocks on them?"

"Like I said, furniture, desks, things like that. They use 'em in filming."

"It looks like a giant thrift shop, but with garbage."

"I guess it kind of is. That's moviemaking, at least on this level."

Tranko smirked. He knew places like this all over the Valley. He could waste these guys' time for hours while he tried to figure out an angle for himself. Or some idea to get away.

A commotion alerted the group to a large truck outside. As a unit, the thugs slowly moved back, subtly circling the truck, without really looking like they were. Tranko was slightly impressed.

The guy inside the truck, however, looked like he might be taking a personal washroom break right then and there. As they approached, the guy brought the rig to a halt and rolled his window up, leaving a mere half-inch of space to speak through.

Handler thug stepped forward and tapped on the window. "Hey, who are you?"

"Look man, I'm just a delivery guy, okay? I got no issue with whatever…this is."

Tranko had a thought.

"Maybe this guy can give us some ideas about where Levi keeps stuff."

Before anyone could answer, Tranko stepped up to the window and motioned for the guy to lower it. The driver did as he was instructed. Cautiously, he craned his neck to look around, clearly nervous about what he had stepped into. Tranko tried to put him at ease.

"Don't worry, man. Nobody is going to hurt you. We just need to know what you're doing here."

"I'm just driving truck. Returning items to the lockups. I'm a driver man. I don't know nothing."

"Anything," said handler thug.

"What?" said Tranko.

"I don't know anything. 'I don't know nothing' is a double negative."

Tranko rolled his eyes and turned back to the driver. "Whatever. You work in film long?"

"Yeah, forever basically. I've done lots of shows."

"For Levi?"

"Who?"

"Golem Pictures."

"Sure. Yeah. Not all of them. Just the last year or so. They're so friggen cheap but there's not much work out there."

"I need to know where his specific stuff is. You know offices, storage lockers, trucks, whatever right. He must have stuff."

"I know about the corporate office on Sunset."

"Can you take me there?"

"I guess, sure."

Tranko looked at the guys standing around.

"Okay, he's gonna take me to Zevon's office on Sunset. We'll take a look around and see if there's anything there that might twig to what your boss is going on about. I'll ride with him. You guys follow behind."

"But I gotta unload this."

Tranko fixed the driver with a look that made him go silent quickly.

Handler thug spoke up. "What if this is a waste of time?"

"That's the point. We ought to be able to find out quickly what he knows and what he doesn't. Once we're sure either way we can get rid of him."

The driver turned white as a sheet and looked horrified. He began to hyperventilate.

"No, no. Not THAT," said Tranko. "I just meant go talk to someone else."

And with that, the whole group mounted up and headed off towards Sunset Boulevard.

17

ONE OF THE best parts of being a professional thief was having the knowledge of what the business truly entailed.

Most people think organized theft is some exotic, edgily glamourous profession. They usually picture *Ocean's 11*-like capers that, were they genuinely attempted, would cost far more to stage than what could ever be conceivably stolen. And they are always far more cinematic than realistic.

Then there's the fear. Most people wouldn't get within a dozen miles of anything truly risky or dangerous. Average folks talk tough, but fear is a natural mechanism to keep most of them on the straight and narrow. It's only when a riot or some sort of mass-chaos event happens that people suddenly get brave enough to steal. You need stones to go it alone. Or a drug habit.

Maggie had taken the Seabus across the harbour to North Vancouver and now walked from Lonsdale Quay, down the boardwalk and toward the Burrard Drydock area. She strode with purpose.

Movie crimes always featured fancy maps and detailed models. Maybe deep-cover insiders too. Actual, real-world heists? They rely mainly on large amounts of mundane research and leg work. The kind of things that would bore average people stupid.

That was just fine with Maggie. Boring was where the money was made. Learning what levers to pull and which buttons to push. Boring was where the best secrets lay bare.

Like carpet cleaning.

Who cares about carpet cleaning? Talk about boring. Nobody thinks twice about something as mundane as that. But on every yacht, everywhere in the world, are some of the most exotic and expensive carpets that money can buy. And when that fancy floor covering gets dirty, someone has to get it clean.

Maggie smiled to herself as she approached the *Jimena*. It was a beauty, though a little small in terms of the "bigger is better" yachting world. She guessed maybe 200ft or so.

Jimena? That poser. El Cid's wife? Really? thought Maggie.

She hoped Aldo had bought it named already, though the idea that he fancied himself a modern day El Cid certainly fit. What an egoist. Still, Aldo had a nice set-up to be sure. As she approached the gangplank, Maggie adjusted the lanyard around her neck so that it would be clear to see. The logo for Eco-Orange Carpet Cleaning was almost as bright as the actual sun. It would not be missed easily. She called out to the person cleaning the windows to one side of the entrance. "Is the 2nd Officer around? I'm from Eco-Orange. Just need to check all the carpets and make sure they were done right."

Contacts were everything in this world. And knowing the gal to call when it came to yachts in town was priceless. Annie had been an organizer for things like this for years and she loved to show off her connections to the rich and powerful. Sure, her job was organizing all the "little people" that kept the uber rich pampered and fed but she revelled in it all the same. She loved going on and off their vessels like she belonged to the world they inhabited. More than once she had even toured Maggie around.

This time though, Maggie was a little late. By the time she called Annie the carpet cleaners had already come and gone. It was far easier to snoop around a boat when the work was in process, but she had missed her window by a full day. Still, it wasn't a big deal for Annie to get her on a boat to do a "managerial walkthrough," making sure the work that was ordered had been performed correctly. It did mean that privacy was not as easy to come by, but Maggie figured it wouldn't matter. No one paid much attention to older women anyway. And if they thought you were a talker, they were only too happy to slide away and leave you alone. Perish the thought that you might waste some time chatting up an old lady. Whatever. It should give her enough time to case Aldo's floating playhouse, at least a little.

* * *

The 2nd Officer was quite nice, a woman named Stefanie. Maybe Maggie was the one being "old school" by expecting a guy. The world was changing, a bit. Stefanie was very friendly and very professional. She took Maggie's (fake) name and noted that she was on board, alerting her to the rooms that were open and those that would stay locked. She indicated that if they personally found issues with the carpeting in the locked-off areas that they would be sure to contact the company directly.

As Maggie made her way around the lower deck, she marked things out in her head. At the bottom of the stairs was a sort of inside/outside club setting with a wet bar and a day head with a shower for rinsing off after swimming. She noted the tender storage, the boat for coming ashore without a large dock, and the hatches. She assumed the main engines were positioned aft of centre and that more to the middle were the guest quarters. In this case there was one VIP stateroom (locked, of course) and three double cabins, all with ensuites. They were nice, if not particularly memorable. The bow section contained the crew accommodation, but she'd go there last. Didn't want to risk interacting too much without being able to make a quick exit.

She also avoided the galley and the mess for the most obvious of reasons: no carpet in those areas.

The main deck had a lift as well as a staircase connecting the floors. Forward of the foyer was a library. *Who'd have thought Mr. fancy pants read?* snarked Maggie to herself. She moved around the outdoor seating area and took in all its sofas and amenities. Just beyond the main foyer was the formal lounge. It had tons of natural light coming in through the full-height windows. Two long sofas and multiple armchairs faced in around various small coffee tables, while to the aft there was a games table for after-dinner conversation. Lots of room for his ladies and other assorted sycophants, Maggie supposed.

The formal dining area seated 10 and was situated right beside a set of massive sliding doors that opened onto the ocean itself. There was a crewman / bartender at work prepping things at the lounge bar. Maggie smiled and he offered a wave in return. She studied the carpet.

The 2nd Officer had indicated that the upper deck was off-limits, which meant that was Aldo's private area. They usually had a large Master suite to the aft so he could have his Bond villain-like views of the sea. She would have liked to get up there but that seemed out of the question. She spoke to the bar man.

"In port for long?"

"No, just a few days. We came down from Seattle, before that Port of San Francisco and LA. But I think we're headed back soon."

"Tough life." Maggie chided.

The crewman smiled. "It has its perks, for sure. But when you're working, you're working."

Maggie leaned in.

"Tough boss?"

The bar man smiled, cocked his head to one side and gave a look as if to say "Well, aren't all billionaires tough." But he never said a word. Tight-lipped crew proved little more than crew that wanted to keep their jobs. It certainly wasn't all that strange.

As Maggie turned to head out onto deck something deeper in the lounge caught her eye. She immediately turned and headed toward it. The bar man noticed her gaze.

"Quite something, isn't it?" he said.

Maggie just stared at the painting. Who was this Aldo Neto fellow? Was he kidding? She simply could not believe her eyes.

18

BUNNY LEVI uncrossed and then re-crossed her legs as seductively as she could. They weren't particularly long. Sort of short, not stumpy though. Totally proportionate. She remembered one girl from cheerleading back in the day who was obsessed with showing off legs she didn't really have. No one said anything. They let her act like the fire hydrants she was stomping around on were attractive vs. the comic relief they presented as. Bunny snuffed to herself, picturing the midget hooker from *Total Recall* but replacing the character's face with that of teenage memory. All the while, Bunny continued tugging and adjusting her skirt, giving ample opportunities for insurance boy to pretend not to notice what she was doing.

Eventually, she locked in on her look, going for a *Sharon Stone cold stare* thing, aiming it right at him. Maybe she wasn't 25 anymore but all guys try for a quick glimpse under the skirt, and if you can catch them looking, they're yours. Bunny stared at David Teck, waiting as he paced back and forth in front of her, shifting in her chair with faux discomfort, all the while engineering an appropriately subtle panty peek-a-boo. *C'mon chump, you know you wanna, c'mon, c'mon.. gotcha!*

David turned beet red when she caught him looking. He always looked. He couldn't help that. But usually, he was way cooler about it or at least the one in control. But not now. Not this one. He cast a scornful look at her. She was trouble. Bunny had thrown him completely off his game and he didn't like it.

"You're not taking this seriously. This is…serious."

Bunny rolled her eyes. "Well, you're not making any sense."

The fury boiled in David's head.

"They threatened me, Bunny. And it was all about you. How do they know about you? How did they know about me? Who the hell are they?"

"I'm sure I don't know."

"Do you, though? I think you do. I think you know exactly who they are." David leaned against a wall and let his arms drop to his sides. He gazed out the patio doors and across the Pacific.

"The guy knew that my firm was insuring art for you. He knew that you and I were…together. He knew that."

Bunny cocked her head to one side. "Together? What does that mean?"

David looked back to her, even more confused. "What do you mean 'what does that mean?'" He knew that we had, you know."

"We had what?" Bunny demanded.

David fixed her with a look and held it. Bunny responded by letting cold eyes settle on him, then breaking into a half smirk.

"Oh, you mean the other night? Ok, that was fun, kind of, but together? I don't think so. And I don't think you thought so either. And how 'bout we skip the whole "I'm a gentleman" routine you're pushing here. You don't buy that any more than I do."

"Do you think they did?" asked David.

Bunny sighed before zeroing in on her iPhone, tapping away at some game.

David began to pace again. "Yeah, you're probably right. Damn it! I need to know what's going on here. I don't like surprises. Surprises always mean trouble."

"I think we need to focus on what you're actually doing here."

David stopped and waved his hands in the air. "Of course. Let's get into that. Your husband just died. Murdered it would seem. In his own house. This very one, in fact. So, it was a robbery gone bad, they think. You're sad he's gone and supposedly had nothing to do with it."

"I didn't!" said Bunny.

"Of course not. But right now, you are more interested in getting a big insurance payout on some works of art gone missing."

"That's what insurance is for."

"Of course, it is. And if it would've been just some items getting ripped off it would have been no big deal to cut you a check, but now there is a murder investigation to contend with alongside a pretty sizable insurance claim."

"Zevon dying proves this is real."

David's eyes grew wide. "Sure, it does…but it also invites more scrutiny. Something we never talked about before."

"It wasn't my fault."

"It doesn't matter whose fault it is. The reality is that this has become a bigger deal and somehow there is a group of Chinese thugs involved."

"Chinese. How do you know they're Chinese?"

"I don't know. They seemed Chinese."

"That sounds kinda racist."

"Racist how?"

"Everybody from Asia look alike to you?"

"Go to hell, Bunny. I insure art for a living. I'm used to looking at shapes in detail. Chinese faces are typically round where Japanese faces are longer, more ovoid. Also, Japanese eyes are often angled upwards where Chinese eyes are usually angled down. In contrast, Koreans often have smaller eyes."

"That sounds like profiling."

"Of course, it's profiling. A profile is what anyone starts with when describing someone or something. It's a generalization designed to serve as a placeholder until more detailed information is available, like say the exact name and address of the scary bastards that might just decide to try and abduct me again."

"Still sounds kinda sketch."

"As a final clue, the Triads are big into art theft when it comes to paying debts for drug transactions. Triads are Chinese organized crime. So, not racist. Just smart."

"Ok, genius. What do we do now?"

"I need you to think about anyone who might know about your insurance claim. Anybody you mentioned it to or whatever. And for God's sake do not tell anyone else about this. Keep it quiet. It's hard enough keeping the media out of this. They love dead movie producers."

David kept the last bit to himself. He knew if this was a Triad deal then there might be way more money at stake than even Bunny realized. He still didn't trust her, but she didn't seem to know anything about the crew in Santa Fe. Her husband was into more stuff than she realized. It would be a real trick to find a path through this one.

"C'mon, I want to show you something," said Bunny.

Standing in the hallway with her arm outstretched, she motioned toward David.

He tried to brush her off. "Bunny, I've got to figure some things out."

"I know you do," Bunny nodded, "but I just wanted to show you some other art in the bedroom back here. Maybe I can get your thoughts on its value."

David watched as Bunny turned and walked away, headed for the semi-privacy of the back rooms. He had a lot on his mind right now. Without a doubt, Bunny Levi was a sociopath. But David was allowing himself to get pretty worked up, and that never helped anyone. Besides, maybe clearing his head a little wasn't such a bad idea. David took a deep breath and headed off in Bunny's direction toward a back bedroom.

19

FATIMA PULLED the curtains aside again. She scanned up and down the street.

"I don't see him. It's almost time."

Maggie spoke up. "Fati, come on. He's sending a car. He'll get here. You don't have to worry. He should be the one who's worried."

Fati smiled. Maggie always made her smile. She was so confident and in control. She was everything Fatima was not.

"Thank you for going with me. I know you didn't want to."

"I'm perfectly fine going. I'm just not all that impressed with someone who seems to be jerking my best friend around. You know that."

Fati went back to the window again.

"I know, but really it's my fault. I'm overly dramatic at the best of times. If I was a little cooler about these things, then maybe I wouldn't get myself so worked up."

The two friends waited in Fatima's living room. A huge home for one person, it somehow captured Fatima perfectly. 1920's Mediterranean Revival in style. White walls, loud contrasting elements, small fountain, lots of palms, yet still kind of kitschy. It was almost out of place in the neighborhood as its size doubled most other nearby homes.

Fati's husband had almost completed it before he died, creating a sort of obligation for Fatima to finish after his passing. She mixed in some Spanish Colonial architecture along with Italian and Venetian Renaissance. Her finished home came out overall as thoughtful, tasteful, and cultured, and still finding ways to present as somewhat childlike and even a little gaudy. In short, it was Fatima to a T.

"The car's here. Let's go. Let's go."

A light rain was falling as the chauffeur stood outside in Fati's driveway. Beside him was an elegant, two-toned Rolls Royce Phantom. He held the rear suicide door open with one hand, as the other shielded rain with a large umbrella. Fati and Maggie slipped inside the luxurious saloon.

As habit, Maggie surveyed her surroundings. Aldo had splashed out on this one. Personalised and illuminated treadplates, embroidered headrests with "AN" stitched on them, full pile carpeting, aluminum drink holder, the works. It smelled heavenly, which she attributed mainly to the handsome young man driving them. He had to be using something a few steps up from *AXE* body spray.

She looked over at Fatima, who sat beside her. She was oddly calm, almost regal. It was like she was returning to a time or place where things finally made sense. Fati grew up with wealth and it was familiar to her. Certainly, more so than Maggie. But it was also her relationship to it. Maggie's approach was adversarial. She was a thief, after all. But Fatima's was not. She was part of it. She was protected by it. It was her security blanket through her youth. And not in a bad or usurious way. She was a child whose surroundings were what they were. Sitting in this car, being whisked about in luxury was normal for Fati in a way it would never be for Maggie, no matter how much money she might have. Fatima was a creature of different surroundings. It was exciting to see her experience it, even a little.

* * *

As the two women made their way up the gangplank of the *Jimena* Maggie finally caught sight of their host. Aldo stood at the top of the entry, smiling broadly, and calling out to Fatima.

"Oh, my lovely. Finally, yes. You are here."

Aldo was dressed well in linen pants and shirt, loose but still properly fitted, with several gold and silver chains around his neck. His hair was slightly tousled from the wind on the water, but it made him more approachable, less perfect. As Maggie got closer, his age also became more apparent. He didn't seem to have had work done, but if he wasn't using hair dye Maggie would be stunned.

Aldo embraced Fatima, kissing her on both cheeks, before turning.

"And this is Maggie, of course. Fatima talks of you often. So glad to finally get a chance to sit with food and get to know you."

Maggie smiled, a little uncomfortable at the attention, especially considering her own meeting with him the night she was trying to rob him. *Does he know?* she wondered.

"Please, come. My chef has prepared some lovely little treats to start us off. He even did my mama's *brigadeiros*. And drinks of course. Please, please. Let's move this way."

Aldo led them aboard, ushering the ladies into a covered outdoor lounge area with soft seats and amazing views. The hazy rain clouds of a cool evening on Coal Harbour did not seem a likely partner for Aldo's outdoor heaters, cashmere throws and attentive charm, but somehow it worked all the same.

* * *

Maggie hated that she liked him. Bad enough when it was just surface meetings, like a throw-away "hi" or "hello" here and there when he and Fati first dated. But now, after spending real time with him, in his place, she saw what all the fuss was about. Aldo Neto was downright wonderful.

The exact opposite of arrogant, Aldo was funny, self-deprecating, and thoughtful. He wasn't aggressive or pushy, didn't once try to put Fati (or anyone else) down. He treated his onboard crew with respect and kindness. Contrasting all of this with the image Maggie had built up in her head was confounding. Maggie wasn't usually this far off on people. Was she being blinded by her friendship to Fatima? Did she just react emotionally to it? Maggie hated when she did that. She prided herself on being able to suspend that aspect of her femininity when the situation called for it. Maybe she was simply wrong about him.

Aldo broke into Maggie's thoughts.

"Maggie, you seem lost in your head. Tell me what is so deep inside?"

Maggie smiled. His attention was very flattering. For whatever reason when he turned his focus toward you it felt special. No wonder Fatima fell for him.

"It's nothing Aldo. Just enjoying the evening."

"You are too kind to lie to me. I know what you think. How can this old fool chase my friend around and try to steal her away? What's wrong with him?"

At this, Fatima giggled as Maggie smiled.

"I was married, yes. Quite young. And I loved her very much. But I put business and material success first. We divorced many years ago. It was and remains my shame. Aline is a wonderful woman. She remarried and had a wonderful family. A wonderful life. Her husband was good, successful man. Her life worked out. Me? I had a little trouble growing up. I was a…rascal, maybe you say?"

Maggie's face gave away her previously negative thoughts about Aldo.

"Ha! Yes, I know. You worry for Fatima. And you always should. She is a flower of great beauty and grace. She needs her protectors. But I have found that I need her too."

Fatima's eyes grew wide as Aldo praised her.

"She lights me from inside. I feel the joy that I felt when I was young when we are together. For an old man like me that's not something I ever expected to see again. I cannot lie. It surprised me and made me wonder what to do. I was confused. And my…things…can sometimes make this sort of heart and feelings area difficult. There are so many that pretend to like me but are more in love with dollars and duvets. I love easily but not deeply. I wanted, needed to be sure. I never, ever wanted to hurt you, dear Fatima. I do so adore you."

Fatima, on the verge of tears, shifted in her seat. "Oh, Aldo, you know that's just…I'm so…not young and…"

Aldo stopped her. "Don't say that. We may be older in years but young in heart. The body ages one way but the soul another. The age of a soul only increases its beauty, but you must be seeking it. You, my lovely, do just that. I have little doubt that as beautiful as you are today, it will pale compared with tomorrow. That is why people should choose to spend their lives together. To make each day together the best it can be."

Fatima's eyes opened wide.

"Aldo, I've got a home. I've got friends here. I can't."

"Don't. Not now. This is not a question for now. My feelings for you are...intense. *Brasileiros* like me are all passion. It can run away with us. Look, it's getting chilly. Come inside the cabin. We will have *quindim* with warm coffee. It's so good. You'll love it. Absolutely."

As Aldo made his way into the main lounge Maggie watched Fatima closely. She was clearly unsettled but again, far calmer than she would normally be. She spoke to her friend.

"Fati? Are you OK?"

Fatima turned and looked her right in the eye and nodded. Then she smiled as she took Maggie's hand and pulled herself up.

"Coffee and *quindim*?" asked Fatima.

"Coffee and *quindim*." agreed Maggie.

As the two stepped into the lounge Maggie remembered her surreptitious visit the preceding day. Her eyes shot to the other side of the room, directly to the painting on the wall. Aldo was preparing the seats facing it.

"Come, over here. The heat vent is just by our feet. It will make it perfect."

As the two ladies walked over to Aldo, Fatima could not take her eyes from the painting.

"That picture. I know that. I saw it once as a little girl. It's called... what is it called?"

"*Storm on the Sea of Galilee*. By Mr. Harmenszoon van Rijn. Rembrandt for short."

Holding a cushioned chair for Fatima, Aldo looked over at Maggie as she spoke. "You know this picture, yes?"

"I do," said Maggie. "An oil on canvas, painted in 1633. It is considered one of Rembrandts most famous pieces. A masterwork."

Aldo smiled. "I love this painting. For obvious reasons, to have such an image on a boat is appropriate, no? But I also love the image of Christ's calm surrounded by the others' fear and panic. It is a lesson in many things beyond simple beauty." As Aldo sat down, he grabbed a small decoration from the center of the table and began to fiddle with it, rolling it from hand to hand. Fatima broke in.

"That is not the original work, is it?"

Maggie, still staring closely at the piece, spoke, "In 1990 there was a robbery at the Isabella Stewart Gardner Museum in Boston. Twelve original works of art were stolen, the most famous being Vermeer's *The Concert* and Rembrandt's *Storm of the Sea of Galilee*. It was the biggest art heist in US history. In 2013, the FBI said they knew who was responsible, but that they could not release a name while the investigation was ongoing."

"Oh, my goodness!" exclaimed Fatima.

Maggie continued, "There have been absolutely no mentions or signs of the painting since. Not even a hint of a trace of it."

Aldo smiled as he watched Maggie staring into the painting. "Maybe I am the great master thief that lifted this fine work, yes?"

Maggie turned and looked straight at Aldo. "Where did you get this?"

Aldo pushed his toy to one side as he cut a small slice of his *quindim* dessert. "I printed it, well, I had someone print it. On the computer. It is also an…uh, inside joke you would say."

Fatima, by now completely confused, looked around. "I don't understand."

Maggie shook her head and began to laugh. Loudly, and with sincere release. Aldo smiled as well, even as Fatima struggled to catch up to whatever was going on.

"I still don't understand," pleaded Fatima.

Maggie finally stopped laughing and turned to Fatima. "Look there, on the painting. Do you see that one person there, near the bottom?"

"Yes."

"That's the artist. The artist put himself in the picture."

"That's Rembrandt?"

"No, that's Ankur Patar."

"Who is Ankur Patar?" said Fati.

Maggie leaned back in her chair. "Ankur Patar is an illustrator who used stock photography to re-create Rembrandt's famous piece. It was all done for an ad campaign. For *Adobe Illustrator*, I think. He put himself into the picture, like Rembrandt had done on his. Aldo's picture is that picture."

"Well, it's a photocopy of that picture. Even if I owned such a remarkable piece, I wouldn't ever want to risk having such a special picture on a boat at sea. What a tragedy that would be. Also, gauche. Very show-offy."

As Fatima and Aldo continued to laugh about the fake Rembrandt, Maggie finally took notice of the tchotchke Aldo was fiddling with. It was an Imperial Fabergé Egg. Only fifty-two individual, jewel-encrusted masterpieces were made for the Russian royal family between 1885 and 1917. They were valued at more than a million dollars each and eight of the original fifty-two were still missing. Except for the one resting inside Aldo Neto's neatly manicured hand.

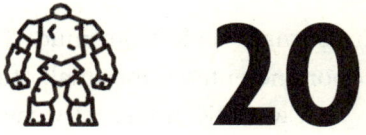

20

WHEN YOU ARE 6'5"and 265 pounds, cramming yourself into cars is a chore at the best of times. And when you're being made to sit in the middle seat it's even worse. Tranko did not enjoy being a cocooned passenger, but he had little choice. These guys were not letting him out of their sight. But he would get his chance. He'd make sure of it.

The props guy was named Saverino. He was an oily little bastard who seemed more interested in his next paycheck than anything else. To be fair, that did describe everyone in his immediate vicinity.

As the SUV headed past the Saddle Back Chop House on Sunset, Saverino, perched in the front seat called out, "There, that building there. Just on the side."

As the big vehicle slowed to a crawl, Tranko leaned over and peered out the window. Nothing special. A little two storey walk-up. Pretty non-descript. He barked out a command, "Can we find a place to park this thing? I'd really like to get out."

They pulled into a red zone and the rough crew got out. Tranko, handler thug, oily Saverino and another. The driver stayed put.

"You guys stay here, okay? We don't need to freak out the regulars inside." Tranko pointed to Saverino. "You, come with me."

Handler thug protested. "I don't think so. I'm coming too."

"Do what you want. But if they clam up inside it's because of you."

As the trio headed in handler thug shoved Saverino ahead of him, indicating that he was to lead the way. Inside was nothing grand, just a collection of doors and a filthy carpeted staircase. Saverio headed up the stairs.

On the top floor he came face to face with panel glass door that read *Golem Worldwide Pictures* with a logo that looked like a giant rock man made from mud. Tranko followed Saverino through the door and entered the small office.

It was OK, not exactly cheap looking but not over the top either. A couple leather couches, a chair and a table. A magazine rack on the wall. Hollywood trade papers bursting from it. The reception counter was deserted. There didn't seem to be anybody nearby. As Tranko turned himself around he gazed at the framed movie posters that decorated the walls. One, two, three, six, eight. Eight posters of movies he had never even heard of before. He didn't even recognize the stars on them.

"Rob Stewart? Who the hell was that? And he was the name in *Rocket Point*. Dag Lundgren? A brother or cousin of Dolph maybe? Cheech Tong? Was that a fucking joke? It was like they were trying to fool someone into watching the movie. Tranko was fascinated. Saverino tapped his shoulder.

"So, uh, this is it. Can I go now?"

"Hang on a minute. I'm getting my bearings, okay? Where is everybody? Who's supposed to be here?"

"I don't know. I mean, I've only been here a few times. Usually there's a lady at the desk. I just had to pick up something. I never worked out of here."

Tranko wandered behind the reception desk. There was a half-full coffee mug. It wasn't warm but it wasn't old either. Someone was here, just not right now. He headed for the large door that was likely Levi's office and tried it. Locked. He turned and tried the adjacent door. This one was open, and it led to a small boardroom that had a table surrounded by about twelve high-backed leather chairs. The walls were covered with the same weird movie posters, although he did finally recognize one name. Tom Sizemore in *Death Drop*. He didn't know about the movie, but he heard once that Sizemore could drink. He respected that. As he turned around a voice spoke.

"Can I help you?"

Lutz turned to see an odd little woman in a loud sack dress staring at him. She had huge breasts, both aimed straight down, but in opposite directions. She wasn't old but certainly not young either and was either from another country or spent weeks at the tanning salon.

"Can I help YOU?"

Tranko's brain had locked. *Tanning salon.*

"Yeah, I…"

Internally, Tranko realized he didn't exactly have a good reason to offer. He had killed the guy that owned these offices. Now he was showing up at them. To what? Take over? This was probably not the best idea all the way around. He was really going to have to get his head out of ass at some point today. Saverino stepped in.

"I worked props on *Firedrop*. Just wanted to see what was happening, y'know, with everything."

"Did you have a check coming? Is that it? 'Cause I don't got no checks. The payroll company has got them not me. You guys have gotta stop hassling me about those damn checks."

"No, I just wondered if Ben knew whether the next one was gonna go off or not?"

This stopped her spiel for a moment, as she moved closer to the men. Then, reaching past them she closed the door to the boardroom and effectively moved them back into the waiting room. She returned to the front of her desk and grabbed a clipboard.

"Ben isn't in today. He said he might come by later, but no one knows what's up. When Zev croaked it kinda put everything in a tailspin. No one knows what's gonna happen."

Tranko stood quietly. He was trying to think of an angle or a way in. Saverino spoke again.

"I've got a few offers, things I'm considering but I wanted to make sure Ben was cool with that. He told me to check with him before I accepted another gig."

"Yeah, yeah, I know it's slow and you all gotta work. I do too. You wonder about me? What the hell am I supposed to do? Nobody's writing any checks for me, are they? We might have to close this office. No one knows what the hell is going on. What am I supposed to do?"

Tranko stared at her. He thought Hollywood was supposed to be about image. Who in their right mind would ever want this thing greeting them when they came in the office? He figured that Bunny must have forced the guy to hire her, just to avoid any late-night hookups.

"No, this whole thing is going down the tubes it is."

Tranko spoke up, "So, who's the boss now? Y'know, who's second in command? Who did Zevon work with?"

She turned her head with a pivot. The breasts stayed in the same position. Maybe it was a sweater underneath, or something.

"Ben of course. Ben did everything. He's going crazy right now. He has no idea what's going on. We were going into prep you know. It was all lined up. Now it's all up in the air. Ben doesn't know what to do. We could lose Gary Busey!"

Tranko looked at Saverino. "You got his number, right? Call him."

"I got his cell. I can call but he hates when you waste his time. I mean, he's probably out scouting for a big show right now. I don't wanna piss him off. He's a good guy for work. Well, he was."

But Tranko wasn't listening anymore. He looked around again. This place. It was perfect. An absolutely perfect setup. Just normal enough to avoid suspicion but really easy to do whatever the hell you wanted. No wonder Dachshund was dealing with Levi. This crew was the best cover a guy could have. Tranko looked at the receptionist. "What's your name, sweetheart?"

"Jodi Bone. And lose the sweetheart schtick. You ain't that tough, butterfly. I got Teamsters that hassle me. You ain't nothing."

"No hassles. My name is Lutz. I'm gonna give you my number. When Ben comes by or calls you tell him to call me. Tell him that I want to help him out. I want to help you all out. I was one of Zev's partners. A sort of background partner, and there's no reason we can't keep making movies and doing some work. We all gotta eat, right?"

"Damn straight." said Jodi. "Eat we must. You leave me the info and I'll see that Benny gets it. He's a good kid, whip smart. Just kinda freaked out right now with the whole dead boss thing. If you can help keep things going that'll be great. I'll call him now."

"You do that." Tranko turned and headed out the door, looking back to make sure Saverino came with him. He glanced past the old receptionist and caught sight of something completely out of place, especially in an office decorated with cheesy movie posters. He pushed back past Jodi and walked into what seemed like a photocopy room.

"What are all these?" He asked to no one in particular.

Stacked all over the room were paintings, old classic-looking paintings, at least twelve of them. Some gilt framed, others on canvas and little more, all leaning against the wall and looking like so much junk. He never would have noticed but what had caught his eye was the first painting he saw. It was upside down. Tranko didn't know art at all, but he knew this one. His mother had a tiny, framed copy of it on the wall of her kitchen when he was a kid. He'd always ask about it and she'd talk about it like it was the real thing. She loved that stupid painting. And now, here he was, face to face, with a large version of it. *The Last Supper*.

"They're all fakes."

Tranko turned and looked right at the woman dressed in maroon drapes. "What?"

"They're copies. We get them painted for the films we do. Guys just churn 'em out so we can use 'em in the movies for background. If you have a rich guy or a big deal baddie, they always have fancy art around. They're set decoration."

Tranko considered this. Fakes. Pretty good fakes, though. And from the little he knew about art it might be enough to be another sideline for crafty Mr. Levi. Was this the stuff everyone was looking for? Turning away from the paintings, Tranko made a mental note. He would get these picked up. He sensed he was on to something, but he just wasn't sure what yet.

The trio headed back out to the street where the SUV was waiting.

"Can I go now?" asked Saverino.

"Your truck is still back at the warehouse."

"I can get it later." Saverino was jumpy. He wanted out. Tranko understood why but he needed to hold onto him a bit longer. He pulled him away from the guards.

"You guys go get his truck and bring it back here. We'll wait over there." He motioned towards a small café across the street.

Handler thug was not impressed but he complied. Tranko turned to Saverino. "Come over here and let's get something to drink. You and me, we need to have a talk."

21

MAGGIE STOOD outside the Tourist Hotel in Minsk. The air was humid but pleasant as fluffy clouds hung low. Maggie eyed the various tour busses parked near the entrance with their legions of silver haired vacationers moving on and off. In the distance sat a massive block of 5 to 6 storey apartments. Maybe not the view the average tourist lifts their camera for, but it was Belarus. Maggie looked to her left and spied a sign for the Partinzanskaya metro station. She would be checking that out in detail later. First, she needed to get herself onto a bus tour.

Working a gig in Russia seems easy on the surface. You fly in, find passage to where you want to go and pull it. But if you want to avoid capture — and you certainly do in Russia — you had to take things very slow and methodical. It takes more time, obviously, but it usually ensures protection from being trailed (as in watched) and provides rock-solid alibis. These become critical in case you get stopped for any reason whatsoever. In practice, most people getting tagged in country get caught out of sloppiness. Do your work, and spend the time, and you will almost never get noticed.

Which was why Maggie was staying at the Tourist Hotel a whole country away. Offering a restaurant, free WiFi plus a TV and fridge in every room made it the perfect cover for a tourist on a budget. It even had tourist in the name! They had a restaurant, billiards room, and the Belarus Shopping Centre about a 100ft away. There was even a movie theatre nearby. And Maggie would visit them all, just long enough to grab pictures, tiny souvenirs, and valuable receipts, all noteworthy in officially establishing her presence there.

The next bit would be somewhat trickier.

Maggie needed to get on a tour bus to Moscow, but it was important not to book such a trip in advance. That would be tracked. Showing up unannounced on the day and sliding your way onto one instead often meant no paper trail, which was critical. Most operators were too lazy to update manifests that were barely skimmed by lazy authorities. The biggest risk was not getting a seat.

To overcome that, Maggie placed her trust in a pair of universal truths: first, that older people on vacation are almost always getting sick in some way or other and second, that greed is a truly international vice. She approached the first large bus with blue lettering down one side.

"Hi, I'm trying to see if you have any spaces for the excursion to Moscow. I didn't book in advance, but I was hoping maybe I could get a seat."

The sleepy-eyed driver looked down from his seat with a confused face. "*Au cham idet rech?*"

Maggie's Russian was weak, but she understood him. *What are you talking about?* Maggie smiled and turned, looking for someone else. A tour guide emerged from between two other busses.

"Hello, can I help you?" in perfect English.

"Hi, I didn't book but I was hoping to find a spot on your tour into Moscow? Are there any openings?"

The tour guide smiled in a way only someone practiced in the craft of maneuvering cranky, ill-tempered visitors about foreign countries could. "Of course. I don't have anything on #12 here but we do have another leaving the property in about four hours that has several openings. The trip is wonderful. Four days in total, with incredible little stops along the way, completely guided of course plus an express ride back later. Can I mark you down?"

"You wouldn't have anything more direct? I'm anxious to spend some time in Moscow."

"Well, I've got a bus leaving tonight that is an express. Sort of a "midnight ride" theme where you can sleep through the night and arrive in Moscow for the late morning. The return trip is fast though. It comes back at 11pm the same night."

"I think that would be perfect."

"Excellent. Follow me and let's get you a ticket."

* * *

As the bus pulled away from the front of the hotel Maggie's mind wandered. She thought about Fati and the dinner with Aldo. She thought about the egg he so obviously waved in front of her, almost daring her to notice. A multi-million-dollar *Fabergé* egg that was probably stolen, while he acted like it was a paperweight to play with. And all after the fake-out with the painting. Yet he was so charming, so…normal seeming. But he wasn't. Aldo Neto was misdirection and obfuscation. Just when she thought she was getting a handle on him he would shift off in another direction and make her question trusting him in the first place. It gave Maggie emotional whiplash. And to be fair, as much as it infuriated her it was also immensely intriguing.

Fatima had agreed to sail down to Los Angeles with Aldo. He claimed to have some important overseas meeting he'd be flying off to from there. Fati was set to head back to Vancouver once he left. The yacht would be staying in LA to get prepped for a move into warmer waters somewhere. He had some bucks, that much was clear. And the kind of money he represented only came about in a few ways. You inherited it, you had a massive, operating business throwing it off or you were crooked as a dog's hind leg, meaning you stole it. Maggie was convinced of the latter but had to admit she had no real idea.

Fatima, on the other hand, was totally entranced by him. And that was her main fear. She didn't want Fati to get hurt, especially by someone who seemed like such a predator. But she was a big girl and she got to make her own decisions. The issues surrounding Mr. Neto would have to wait. Maggie was back to work now, and she needed to keep her eyes on the prize. She adjusted her tiny travel *MyPillow* against the large glass window and closed her eyes. Eleven hours was a long time to be on a bus. She might as well sleep through as much of it as she could.

22

DAVID WINCED as the pool cue poked him in the back. Again. He turned around and glared at the guy, who looked surprised but unfazed.

"Uh, sorry dude. It's tight in here. My bad."

Your bad is right, thought David. The Hinano Café was a dive bar alright, and David hated dive bars. At least the ones that always seem to become famous for being small and not particularly nice, which in his opinion, was all of them. It was no secret that David preferred expensive, and expansive, lounges and restaurants. So, finding himself perched on a vinyl stool, leaning on a deck-wood ledge and facing a painted wall was not his idea of fun. Getting a stick in the back every few minutes was only icing on the dislike cake. But he had no choice. Vinny Dyce considered Hinano's *his* place, which meant that meeting anywhere else was simply not an option.

David turned his head and stared at the staining on the wall from the 1983 flood. He laughed inside. What should've destroyed any other business suddenly became a selling feature because they were smart enough to hang a picture of a "lost shark" swimming in a 4ft deep lagoon that used to be the parking lot. What a joke. Or genius.

Hinano's original owner, Joe Oarson, opened the doors in 1962 after returning from a somewhat bizarre adventure in Tahiti in 1959. According to Vinny, young Oarson was a punk, bartending on Catalina Island when he ran into some sailors looking for another guy to sail to Tahiti with them on their 30ft yacht. Up for adventure, Oarson dropped everything, went to Tahiti and wound-up spending all his down time at some local island place called Bar Hinano.

One day, a movie crew came through Tahiti looking for locals to act as extras and Joe got himself cast in *Mutiny on the Bounty* with

Marlon Brando. Between that and a few other things, he eventually saved up enough money to return to the States and open his own Hinano on Venice Beach which he ran for twenty-five years. Vinny was just a kid back then who got caught stealing beer from the back room. Instead of turning him in, Joe gave him a job sweeping up every now and again. And while it didn't exactly turn Vinnie's life around it made him loyal to the place. And that loyalty endured long after Oarson had sold out and moved on.

David stared down at his burger and Fritos. Where was Vinny? He was supposed to be here a half hour ago. David picked up a corn chip and pushed it inside his mouth. It was damp with burger sweat. Might as well eat, he thought, as he glanced around at the décor. A captain's sign that used to be a rudder from an old boat. High-top tables lined with hatches and thick rope. Even the physical bar was wood pulled from an old boat deck. Plus, famous people.

Vinnie always jabbered on about Billy Idol hanging out here. And Jim Morrison before him. David thought there were movies shot on site as well. Though, in LA, that could be said of most places. David took a bite from his burger. It was actually pretty good.

Eventually, a somewhat bloated guy appeared with skin so pink and legs so skinny that he looked more like a can of Spam walking in on toothpicks vs. an actual person. Long, stringy hair on top only completed the comical look. He could have been a character in *SpongeBob*. Vinnie made a beeline for David.

"Davey T."

"Hey Vin. Where were you? I've been waiting."

"Couldn't be helped, my man. Had a little jam up that required my attention. Can't put a clock on problems, am I right? Hey Stu, *Topa Topa*? A pitcher? Thanks."

The bartender shook his head side to side. Vinny raised his hands in a *What? C'mon!* gesture before turning back and sliding onto a nearby stool.

David rolled his eyes and reached for his water glass, stopping himself and pulling his hand away just before touching it. He wiped sauce from his fingers with a paper napkin, addressing Vinnie without looking at him.

"Is this something I need to be worried about?"

Vinny grinned. "Worry? It's why you talked to me in the first place." His long, straight hair hung over his blotchy face like a beaded curtain. "You wanted intel. I can provide you with what I got so long as you got my cash and will agree to…eh?" Vinnie opened his eyes wide and cocked his head to the left, towards the bar. David breathed out.

"Yeah, yeah. Of course. Here." He handed over $200 in folded $20 bills. "And yes, I'll cover the tab off too."

"Cool, man. Cool. Righteous." Vinny turned and raised his voice toward the bar. "Did you hear that, Stu? He said he'll cover me off. Now can I get some *Topa Topa*? Yeah?" The bartender sighed and began to pour a pitcher.

David looked right at Vinnie. "So?"

"So, your man Levi was into some shit, I can tell you."

The bartender arrived and placed the pitcher in front of them with two glasses. Vinnie immediately started to rub his hands and lick his lips. He poured a pint for himself and another for David. Then he took a too-long pull on the glass, closing his eyes to better savour the golden nectar flowing down his throat. Vinnie exhaled, just before breathing deep once more to find enough oxygen to speak.

"Russian mob. Local crew. They were laundering money through him. Using his dog shit movies as switchbacks to wash their cash. He'd get a small cut of the action while they propped up his movies, but his main thing was to use it to get the banks on-board to make things legit. They never risked their cash, 'cause mob, right? And Levi was just praying for a hit or something to maybe help cut 'em loose."

"OK, what else?"

"Art. The dope was that somehow, he got his mitts on something big. Like huge."

"Huge how?"

"Like a big deal piece."

"What?"

"I have no idea."

"What do you mean you have no idea? How does word get around that he had something big, but no one knows what it is?"

"Look man, the word is the word. Grapevine told me that Levi got or was about to get something so big even he didn't know what to do. He reached out about it to a few folks, which, I guess, is how word started moving. It was a stolen piece for sure. But what it was I haven't got a clue. Thing was, he def didn't tell the Russians about it. Problem was somehow they found out but not from him and they were pissed. I bet they killed him."

"Maybe. Yeah, maybe they did kill him." David took an angry bite of his burger before looking at Vinny as he continued to chew. "That really doesn't help me." He looked at the burger again. *Damn, this burger is good. Like In N' Out good.* "I need to know what he got himself into."

Vinny slapped him on the back. "C'mon buddy, y'know I got you for anything I find. If I score more, I'll hit you up. For sure. You look after me, I look after you."

But David wasn't listening anymore. He was staring again. This time at a picture on the wall. It was a shot of Jane Fonda and Jack Lemmon from *The China Syndrome*. They were sitting in front of the same old fireplace located just across the room from the Hinano bar. *Zevon was in the movie business* thought David. *Did he end up with something he shouldn't have because of a movie?* David still didn't understand what exactly he was thinking but he knew that he was closer to an answer than before. Maybe Zevon found something and it got him killed?

23

SERGIEV POSAD was home to one of the most revered monasteries in Russia, the UNESCO-protected Troitse-Sergeiva Lavra, making it an obvious tourist attraction for anyone visiting the Moscow area. That was solid gold good luck for Maggie. Additionally, Sergiev Posad was the only city in the Moscow region to be officially included on the Golden Ring route, which meant it was connected directly to Moscow by a ring of trains and busses. Accessing the city meant about a three hour round trip, which gave Maggie a tight, but eminently achievable, window for the heist.

The tour bus she had ridden from Belarus came to a stop near the Yaroslavsky railway station in Moscow. Maggie hit up the host and indicated her desire to "see the monastery at Sergiev Posad" versus travelling on with the pre-arranged stops for the group. She then received advice on how to go her own way. Obviously, this was advice Maggie didn't need, but asking for it would provide further alibi coverage should something go wrong. Released from her tour group "obligations," Maggie found her way to the train station and bought her ticket for the ride in to Sergiev Posad.

The Golden Ring express train stopped in Sergiev for exactly one minute, which meant Maggie had to get off quickly or miss the stop. That was fine. But it also meant she had to get back to the same stop with lots of time to spare after the lift or risk missing the express back to Moscow. That was a big deal as she had to catch the same Moscow tour bus she had come in on before it returned to Belarus. Missing anything can be overcome, but that kind of mistake was where red flags got raised and people started "looking" for you. A huge no-no in the business Maggie was in. No, she'd have to stick to some tight timelines to make it all work, but she wasn't worried.

It was exhilarating.

The pressure, the adrenaline, the excitement. Maggie loved it all. The idea of running along a wire without a net had a way of focusing the mind and exciting the senses. Whenever the activity you're engaged in truly challenges your abilities the outcome is thrilling.

As Maggie watched the train slowly pull away, she ran the plan over in her head once more.

Find Ulitsa Parkhomenko Street, address 344 and then apartment 1203. Get inside, nip painting, return to train station with enough time to catch the return express back to Moscow. That meant she had just under two hours to find and grab the painting, get back on the train and get herself to the drop-off point with enough cushion to leave the painting and rejoin her original tour group for the return bus to Belarus. Easy as pie.

Sergiev Posad, apart from its role as a monastic tourist attraction, also served as something of an administrative center for the district. That meant that a lot of government and party bureaucrats called the place home, making it likely that the painting Maggie had been sent to rip was being kept by some crooked government official or other. Valuable paintings or artifacts were sometimes used as gifts or tests for the people they were presented to. The idea was to find creative ways to protect items that upper-level people accumulated. Then, by "gifting" them or asking lower echelon members to hold onto them, the gifter either secured loyalty or ensured compliance. There was often a dual nature to things like this, in Russia or elsewhere.

Maggie had little issue with lifting the piece and getting it moving once more. She didn't know the reason why it was being stolen and she didn't care. Her concern was simply the how. She had been given the address, basic location details and a final drop-off point. And because this drop-off was located in-country it became far easier as there were no borders to navigate. In the repatriating-of-art business this was about as easy as it got. Worrying too much about the person you were stealing from was a waste of time. That kind of distraction only lead to trouble no one wanted.

The piece Maggie would be "liberating" was called *Tod und Feuer* or *Death and Fire*, one of the last pieces ever completed by the

German artist Paul Klee. In fact, the year he died, 1935, saw Klee suffering with intense fatigue, skin rashes, throat problems, breathing issues and severe pain in the joints of his hands. The painting itself was simple in design, suggesting an almost hieroglyphic style. Even the features of the face, if viewed from different angles, very clearly spelled out the word "tod," German for death, at least twice. It wasn't a big piece. About one and a half feet square. Without the frame it should be an easy lift. Maggie had thought the painting was still on display in a Bern, Switzerland museum but that was never a guarantee. Reals and fakes moved around the world with surprising regularity, with "experts" routinely authenticating the fakes while dismissing the originals. Mix greed and corruption with good, old-fashioned ineptitude and you got the current state of the professional art world.

As Maggie headed off on foot she took note of her surroundings, relating them to the map inside her head. She had an iPhone but never used the maps or device in any way other than to establish whatever backstory she had decided to go with. Only idiots travel with tracking/listening devices. For now, she had hidden her phone in the bag of someone she met on the bus to establish her location as being there instead of where she was headed. She'd get it back the next day.

Maggie did whatever computer mapping and searches she needed on public computers or disposable smartphones. The tech was great to use but only when you were careful about it. Following a *Google* map to a future crime scene was just stupid. Memory was the only safe way to get places. That, and maybe a paper map that could be torn up. Looking left, Maggie saw the street sign she was looking for and pushed forward, adjusting the backpack on her shoulder as she went. She didn't notice the man watching her from a block away. Nor did she see him begin to follow along behind.

* * *

The apartment was humble by North American standards but clearly the home of a government official of some note. Nice, newish furniture, modern books, larger, flat-screen TV and even an individual heater. The steel entry door provided the first challenge, but Maggie dealt with it quickly, picking the lock in short order. It helped that the hallway had a bend in it, effectively creating a sort of private area to work unobserved.

Once inside, Maggie scanned the common areas, looking for the Klee. She couldn't see it displayed on any wall, making her believe it was being "held" for someone. She started opening cabinets, and then closets before finding her way into the bedroom.

Nothing.

Was her intel wrong? Was she in the wrong place? Her anxiety started to rise. Had this whole thing gone a little too easily? Was it a set-up of some kind? Maggie had to stop and focus. She was letting her mind play tricks. *Keep hunting* she told herself. *You'll find it.*

Now in a side bedroom, Maggie dropped to one knee and peered under a bed. Piles of something. She reached under and slid out a stack of items. A laminated world map, a foam core of some concert poster, several framed family photos and one Paul Klee.

Maggie held it up, looking at it carefully. It was the right size. It seemed to be the piece in question. It was inside a bulky frame though. She reached inside her backpack and pulled out the multi-tool she bought at the Tourist Hotel. Flipping open the pry attachment Maggie laid the painting face down on the bed. Studying the back, she noted where the staples were attached and began popping them out, careful to not damage the burlap canvas. When that was done, Maggie slowly pried the spline from around the painting, removing one of the major pieces between the frame and the stretcher bar. With that done, she pushed the canvas from the frame and went to work on slipping her tool underneath the edge of the canvas, between it and the frame. Often, they were stuck fast due to time. They were never glued.

Slowly, the canvas started to come from the stretcher bar. Maggie stopped, listening for noise of any kind. Total quiet. She would have to hurry. Time spent in enclosed, single-exit spaces made her nervous.

Finally, the canvas came free of the framing. Maggie grabbed a small, rubber tube from her bag and inflated it - creating a pliable, straight inner core. She carefully rolled the painting around it, taking care to not damage the image in any way. Once rolled, she slid the painting into a slim, hard-core tube that nearly fit inside her backpack. It jutted out by a few inches. Bending over to replace the items under the bed, Maggie reached as far as she could putting everything back in place.

Then she heard something.

It was a key in the lock of the apartment door. Maggie needed to get ready, and fast. Someone was most definitely coming inside.

24

FOR BROTHERS, they really didn't look that much alike. Rael Booli was tall and handsome, while Sauf Booli was not. Their noses were different, their eyes were different, and even their features appeared to come from different people. The only real similarity was when the two happened to walk beside each other. It was uncanny how they appeared to move in concert. The way their bodies floated, sort of moving up and down at the exact same points and to almost identical rhythms, was kind of hilarious, especially when they looked so dissimilar. One tall, one short. One fit, one fat and yet somehow, still the same. Seeing them walk together was the best, and only real visual, proof that the Booli Brothers shared DNA of any kind.

They were arms dealers, at least, that was what they called themselves. It wasn't the original plan, of course. They had been sent to the best schools, educated in all the right places, and even found themselves meeting all the right people. It was no accident. Their father's uncle demanded it, even though the two had very little interest in work of any kind.

They were the only sons of a wealthy but slightly disgraced sheik. Their father had a reputation as being the dumb one in the family. As such, the brothers generally spent most of their time hanging around and showing off. For their friends. For women. For whatever. Motivation was not strong in them. But when their father died in a boating accident their stricter, more respected uncle stepped in, and he was determined to make something of them. The brothers resisted as much as they could, but when the taps of wealth were threatened with closure, they chose compliance instead of rebellion. It was more lucrative, of course, but not near as much fun.

For a while they lobbied to get sent to the USA to study, knowing it would be harder to monitor them there. But that never panned out. They did admit that they preferred life overseas. The European way appealed to them, and they liked the ability to splash money around in London and Paris, partying all the while. Life was pretty good, most of the time.

But their first arms deal was a mistake.

At the urging of their late father, the brothers purchased some land in an area of Albania that had seen some conflict. Their father's idea was that having at least some water access via the Adriatic Sea would eventually make sense to some other future buyer, and because the area was decidedly war-torn, he picked a large holding of slightly beachfront land super cheap. And he was right, sort of.

It was several hundred acres that eventually saw the brothers offered much more for it than they paid. What they didn't know, their father included, was that the site held an underground missile storage silo that had been constructed by the Soviets in the eighties and then abandoned for whatever reason. The reality that several warheads had been left behind was revealed only when they visited the site prior to completing the sale. And while the missiles had been deactivated, certain hardware elements remained in place. They simply needed re-arming to be effective. Determined to act like they knew all along what they were doing, the Boolis faked confidence about the "treats" contained in their sale to the group that turned out to be terrorist sympathizers, certain they would be able to acquire the means to fire the rockets at some point. Accordingly, they paid the Boolis a significant premium for the chance. So, while the brothers originally thought they simply had a magic touch in picking real estate, they realized the actual trick was the underlying "product" that happened to be included.

Luckily, being devoid of morals (or sincere intellect of any kind) they jumped into their new trade with zeal. The Booli Brothers quite liked the idea of selling weapons and tanks and bombs to whomever wanted them. And each subsequent deal led to a better reputation for them and further opportunities. The brothers were apolitical in that they favoured no nation or cause over another. Obviously, their sympathies lay with Islam but that was merely a family requirement. Their uncle would allow nothing less. To close a deal, they would sell anything to anyone.

Trouble hit when the war on terror ramped up. Prior to that it had been business as usual for most of the world's arms dealers, but when the USA got smacked on 9-11 there were big changes and suddenly it became very difficult to be an arms dealer. The easy-as-pie paydays they had previously enjoyed became slim margins and dodgy deals. Suitcases of cash were replaced with bartering and trading, in all manner of goods and services.

As underground as the whole arms dealing world was already, it became even more entrenched, morphing almost overnight into one of favors and promises versus immediate, hard cash. Anything that moved could be tracked, so ownerships had to be transferred without directly trading anything. It was too risky. The arms world became a grand game of "off the books *Monopoly*". You knew in your head what you owned or traded day to day but to anyone out of the loop looking at the board of assets and who held them, nothing was ever out of place. Everyone kept the cards they had and the exchanges that took place were agreed upon with handshakes and nothing more.

It was around this time that the brothers found themselves tiring of the game. They wanted out and they needed one last big score to settle accounts so they could slip away into the shadows and live appropriately debauched lives. Arms dealers have a hard time enjoying kids and in-laws and at least one of the Booli brothers felt his internal clock ticking very loudly.

Then the big score presented itself.

A branch of Al Qaeda had scooped up a mess of items in the big move from Iraq to Syria that was done sometime when the UN weapons inspectors were touring the country back in 2004. It was sort of an inside joke as to the ridiculous rules the inspectors operated under. Like in a *Benny Hill* program, they would get word of the group coming and move things just out of sight long enough to move it back as the inspectors walked by, except now with a UN seal of cleanliness attached. As a result, there was a huge cache of weapons that technically didn't exist that went into semi-secret storage. Like the famous scene from *Raiders of the Lost Ark*, they were hidden deep inside a massive warehouse and forgotten. At least until the Boolis got a line on them years later.

The score was a big one. Huge. If they could get the material, and move it, they could set themselves up for good. The issue was money. They had some, but not enough. They needed something valuable enough to swing the deal, to keep the players onside. Amazingly, the opportunity came to them, just as in their first big deal, by accident.

For years, the story of the missing Vermeer painting captivated the underground arms world. This was mainly due to its value, and the fact that crews knew if it showed up anywhere at all it would be in their world first.

Publicly, *The Concert* was valued at $300+ million but the hotness of the picture, and the inability to move it anywhere easily, made its top out trade value a solid $200-$220 million.

Which was exactly what the Boolis needed.

And one night of boozing it up in a Monte Carlo casino dropped *The Concert* into the brothers' laps. They had a contact for someone claiming to have the stolen painting. If they could get it secured, they could then trade it for the arms, make the sale and disappear forever. The plan was simple but solid. All they had to do first was get the painting before it disappeared beneath the waves once more. They had a name. He was an American. And they were determined to meet the man known as Zevon Levi, face to face.

25

ONE OF THE KEYS to being a good climber is balance. People watch climbers scale walls and can't figure out how they seem to glide up sheer faces with little or no visible hand holds. Balance, and strong legs. Another key is the right footwear. Having shoes that offer a tough, slip-free soul that wraps around the foot helps a ton too. Maggie had both.

Things like this always crossed Maggie's mind when she was in the throes of some stunt or other. In this case, she was propped on the exterior wall outside the 4th storey window of the small apartment she was robbing. A slim case dangled from her shoulder carrying the incriminating item.

She shifted her weight slightly, re-setting for another few minutes or so. Hopefully the little cleaning woman busily tidying the apartment didn't have a lot to do today, or that today was "clean under the bed" day. She would have to trust her luck on that one.

Maggie had left the window open just enough to hear the old matron working away. She was vacuuming now. Finally! A sure sign that she was almost done. Maggie was glad. She was getting tired hanging out here. One of the tricks is to use the legs, of course. The legs are the biggest muscles. People always make the same mistake of thinking climbers are climbing mainly with their arms or with their hands. A good climber uses their legs more than anything else.

Which she did, perched - and balanced - on a small edge of concrete, set somewhere between an upper cornice and a thin antennae wire, of some kind. Russian buildings, at least these ones, were so stark and boxy in nature. Not a lot to hold onto. And they didn't even have balconies. Not that there was that much to look at around the area. All Maggie could see were some large trees and another long block of flats. Thankfully her colors blended with the side of the building. Unless someone was looking closely it was doubtful anyone would see her.

As Maggie did the mental equivalent of twiddling her thumbs, she turned her head left and then right, only to lock eyes with an older gentleman, leaning out of his apartment window, less than 10ft away from her. Apparently, he had decided to get some fresh air and instead came face to face with someone hanging out where they shouldn't be. His face registered shock at the sight of her but he said nothing.

Maggie looked back at him, wondering what she might do. Then she did the only thing that seemed right. She smiled and cringed her shoulders just a touch.

Surprisingly, the older fellow smiled back, before indicating with his hand in a way that Maggie took as on offer of help.

"*Srednja zhena*" said Maggie, which was Russian for "mean wife."

The old man nodded his head knowingly, before motioning with his thumb towards the inside of his own apartment. "Srednja zhena."

Now it was Maggie's turn to nod in agreement.

At this point, Maggie heard the door of her apartment close, looking back inside just in time to see the lock snap shut. She turned and smiled at the old man before lifting the window once more and slipping back inside. It was time to get moving.

Taking a quick, last look around, Maggie reset her face and calmly stepped into the hallway, heading straight for the stairs and out. The slim case holding her day's prize rested between her left arm and shoulder.

* * *

Out on the street, Maggie checked her watch. She had about 22mins to get back to the station and catch her return train to Moscow. If she missed it there was no way she'd make it back to the bus tour in time. And while these were not insurmountable problems, sticking to the established timetables and schedule was always better than deviating even a little. She reset her backpack on her shoulder with the small, slim case stuffed mostly inside and upped her pace some more, taking care not to run but moving almost as fast as if she was. Maggie needed to get to that station, no matter what.

Again, she missed the focused eyes of a man in dark overcoat standing in the shade of some large trees. He watched her intently as she crossed the street, dropping his eyes only to make a note in a book before he continued along after her, down the street.

* * *

As Maggie dropped down into her plush coach seat, she let loose an obvious exhale. She'd made it! Back on the train just in time and now headed straight to Moscow where she would rendezvous with the bus tour and get back to her hotel in Minsk. Then, a few light days of touristy stuff to maintain the fiction of the trip and back home. Of course, there was still the handoff of the stolen Klee to complete, but that was an easy one. Ivan had set a storage locker as the drop. Total no-brainer. As Maggie felt the train begin to edge from the station, she cast her eyes out the window, looking at the landscape. She took a deep breath and let it out. It would be so nice to decompress for an hour or so.

"Pardon me?"

Maggie looked back to the aisle, and then up, coming face to face with a handsome gentleman standing over her. "Yes?"

"Would you mind if I sat in the seat opposite you?"

Maggie smiled. "Of course not. Please, help yourself."

And with that, the man removed his dark overcoat, folded it over his arm and took a seat, just as everything went dark when the train disappeared inside a tunnel.

☕ 26

TRANKO LOOKED left and right, crossing Sunset as he dialed his cell. Saverino trailed just behind him. The number rang and rang. And rang. Finally, a voice picked up.

"Chief?"

"Yeah, Stewie. Where are you?"

"Going north on the 101. Almost to Toluca Lake."

"You got the van from Howie?"

"I'm driving it. So yeah."

"Good. I'm gonna need you to swing around and get back here. But you gotta do it fast. 8000 block of Sunset. Call me when you're close and I'll give more detail. But now, okay? You got 20 min, tops."

"C'mon. No way I'm getting back that fast."

"Make it happen."

And with that, Tranko hung up, pulled open the door of the café and strode inside, with Saverino trailing just behind.

Standing inside, Tranko took a wide look around. Another overly hip, designed to within an inch of its life, café slash restaurant. Everything matched where it should and did not where it shouldn't. Every surface was perfect, every view was curated and designed. No way was anyone getting a cup of their coffee for less than $19 bucks.

"I love Tesse. Their Blue Crab Simplissime is absolutely divine. It's sort of a deconstructed crab cake, looks a little like mashed potato but when you start eating it just goes on forever when you…"

Tranko turned toward him and stared until Saverino realized he had crossed a line of sorts.

"…but they, uh, probably have good coffee too, I think."

Tranko sighed loudly. Finally, a host came over and guided the duo to a table near the window on the street. Tranko successfully ordered coffee for both, but only after a mini standoff as to the style in question.

"Coffee. Two."

"Drip, espresso, macchiato, latte or cappuccino. Now, to your preference we also offer oat or almond milk along with various infusion shots."

"Black is fine."

"Drip or decaf?"

"Just coffee. Regular coffee."

"So, drip?"

"Are you really gonna make me say it?"

"Well, I guess drip it is then."

As Tranko rolled his neck, loosening his muscles and focusing on his hands, Saverino piped up, "Were you serious about all that stuff back there? Are you going to get some productions going?"

Tranko, impatient with events, finally took the time to really look at Saverino. He was older than he had realized. Must be in his late forties. Balding, but with a ton of flowing hair shooting out from beneath the now bare skin on top. He dressed like a twenty-year-old but certainly wasn't anymore. Probably an ex-rocker. His face was lined. Not heavily, but his look was earnest. Tranko smirked inside. These film people were children.

"Yeah, I might have some contacts to make things happen. You never know of course, but we can see."

Saverino seemed to accept that. He turned and looked out the window. As he did the drinks arrived. Tranko breathed his in deep before taking a sip. It smelled pretty good. He took a drink. *Damn! It tastes pretty good too.*

Saverino broke in.

"You know, I've helped out on some low budget projects before, in a sort of production manager way. Like what Ben does. Just smaller scale of course. If you're looking for someone like that, I'm totally available."

"What do you do?"

"I'm props. Assistant props. I've done lead a few times on smaller shows. I was supposed to get the next show actually."

"I thought you were just driving a truck."

"I was. I mean, show's done so I gotta get the stuff back, right? Better that I do the job than hire another guy. Like, I'm good with budgets and organization."

"Yeah, okay. Well, I've got a truck coming over here with some stuff in it. I need a place to put it for a while."

"Full truck? Like a cube van?"

"Yeah, maybe three quarters full."

"Well, we could keep it at that first place I met you at. Where all the other guys were. That's our lockup area."

Tranko shook his head. "No, I want to keep this stuff separate from that. Is there any room across the street?"

Saverino looked puzzled for a second. Then his eyes lit up.

"There is a big room we do the full production reads in. It's not busy now with nothing starting. Maybe we could put the stuff in there for a bit. But Jody has got to okay it, right? I mean, it's not my place."

"How do we get the stuff in?"

"There's a sliding door out back of the building. Just off the road that goes up. There's no direct access but we could hand things over the edge of the railing. Access is a pain but it's LA, right? As long as nothing is too big it should be easy."

Tranko sat back in his seat. This might just work, he thought. But could they get things loaded in before the other guys came back with the truck? His cell phone chirped so he answered it.

"Yeah? Okay. Go to Miller Drive, just off Sunset to the right. Yeah. And then stop just behind the buildings below you, to the left. We're going to unload, fast. I know, I know. Just do it."

Tranko turned back to Saverino. "Drink up. We're done here. Let's get across the street and talk to Jody. I want that stuff unloaded ASAP and put away." Tranko motioned to the server for a bill, which was dropped off promptly.

"$22 bucks. Guess I was off by three." He dropped $25 on the table and the pair headed out of the café and back across the street.

* * *

As they lowered the last item down the bank and into the rear area behind the office, Saverino grabbed it fully, hiked it onto one shoulder and headed into the office building. Stewie called out to Tranko.

"Hey Chief! That's it. Truck's empty. What you want me to do?"

Tranko, who was standing down below looked up at Stewie. "Just take it back to the guy, okay? I'm not paying another day's rental on that piece of shit. Then you go home and wait for me to call, okay?"

"Got it, chief." And with that, Stewie pulled the sliding door down, secured the latch and ran around to the driver side. He hopped in, fired up the cube van and roared away. Tranko took a deep breath. Stewie was the lone bright spot on the LA crew. They had history, which meant something. But he was also solid when he needed to be.

He knew the Russian goons would be back any minute, so he double-timed it inside the building. He came face to face with Jodi Bone.

"Okay big fella. We got your stuff in. And you got me working actual labour. I don't do that for nobody. You owe me now. I'm going to need some details on things pretty fast you know. I mean, I got people hassling me for checks right and left. I can put 'em off but not forever. And Ben's a good kid and all but I'm starting to worry he might not be able to handle things. You really up for this? Film's a tough business."

Tranko smiled. *Film's a tough business? Try being a merc some day, you silly bitch.* "No problem. I'm going to deal with a few things and then I'm gonna come back and go through all this stuff. It won't be here for more than a few days. A week tops."

"People always say that, then I end up babysitting their crap forever. And when I finally get sick of looking after it and dump it, they show up whining and crying about me losing their stuff. I ain't a storage locker you know? We have to get this place set up for..."

And suddenly, Jodi stopped. And just stared for a moment.

"Well, look at me. I was going to say get things set up for Mr. Z. Guess that ain't really happening no more, is it?"

And Jodi Bone moved away from Tranko, walking back to her desk inside the office. Tranko turned and went towards the front entrance and down outside to Sunset. Saverino was already there.

"I think I see my truck. See? Over there?"

Tranko nodded seeing the van parked a few spaces down. He glanced at the traffic moving to and fro down Sunset. Then he marked the big SUV of goons headed right for them. There was no way he was going to get this crew of assholes off his back for more than an hour or so at a time. He needed to get some serious distance, fast. Tranko winced. He knew what he had to do. The only question was how much this was going to hurt.

27

AS THE TUNNEL receded and light returned to the train Maggie glanced at the well-dressed man seated across from her. Older, mostly grey, but still attractive. Sitting very balanced. Not slouched. He had an almost military bearing. His jacket was folded neatly beside him. His fingers adjusted the glasses on his face. He was wearing tight, driver gloves.

Why was he still wearing gloves?

Immediately, Maggie was on alert. This wasn't right. She tried to keep her energy in check, but it wasn't working. She had allowed herself to be surprised and it was surely reading on her face. She struggled to get control of her inner emotion. She needed to be ready for anything.

"You've had a busy day?" offered the stranger.

"I'm sorry, pardon me?" Maggie lied, pretending she had not heard him. She was busy running potential sequences through her head. *He attacks me in my seat, maybe he waits until I look away, he threatens me, maybe he has confederates on board.* Maggie looked up and down the train as casually as she could, trying to spy anyone paying too much attention to her or her opposite seat mate.

"There is no one here but me. You needn't worry about that. And I'm more than a handful, I promise."

Maggie was in deep. She'd been made. This guy clearly knew more than he should, and she was stuck on a train going 80 mph through the Russian countryside. Her options were dangerously limited.

The stranger folded his gloved hands into each other and rested them on his lap.

"You don't need to be afraid. I'm simply here to pick up the item that you, ahem, rescued a short while ago. Simply pass it to me and I will be on my way."

Maggie took a deep, but slow, breath. The man was refined, at least that was how he was acting. He didn't seem to be in the mood for making a scene. That much was clear. Although assassins like things quiet. She tracked her eyes across his body, looking for the sort of bulge that would give away a firearm of some kind. Her eyes landed on his carefully folded coat. She watched his hands very closely.

"I'm sorry, who are you?"

The stranger smiled. Bad, bad teeth. Instantly, he was far less attractive and way more, scary.

"Why don't you call me Manheim."

"Okay, Manheim. I'm not sure who you think I am and what I'm supposed to have done but I really don't understand what this is all about. It's very *007* exciting and all but I'm at a loss. Should I call an attendant? Maybe they can help you find who you're really looking for?"

And for the first time, Manheim became irritated.

"No games, please. Don't insult me. Or you. I know who you are and why you are here. You want attention about as much as I do. Now, hand me the Klee and I will be on my way."

Maggie had a choice to make. He wasn't going to let her fake him out. He knew exactly what she had taken, and he probably had backup. If not on the train right now, at the very least somewhere near the station. Maggie was committed to the drop and you never, never missed the drop. Ivan was clear on where the painting was to be placed and if she changed it up in any way that could lead to serious consequences. This kind of art theft had a lot of moving parts and if a single part is upset, all hell could break loose. Maggie simply could not give up the painting.

She looked to the clock on the back wall of the coach. There were at least forty minutes to go before they would reach Moscow. More than anything, Maggie needed time.

"Okay, Manheim. I have the Klee, but you must know as well as I do what my instructions on what to do with it are. And giving it to you, or even someone like you, is not part of them. I like my head exactly where it is right now. I'd rather not offend my employers."

At this, Manheim seemed to soften, if only a little. He was markedly less irritated.

"How do you know that I am not the one you are supposed to drop your parcel with?"

"Because that wasn't my instructions."

"Your instructions have changed."

"And how exactly would I know that? If I was told to hand it to you I would. I'm a simple pilferer, Manheim. I have no taste for all the intrigue. If you are who you say, then get a message to my employer and have them direct me how you want. Is that too much to ask?"

Manheim broke into a very creepy smile.

"Then the message that I would give you should be a very clear and simple one, shouldn't it, my little vixen?"

Maggie's breath immediately caught in her throat. *Little vixen? How does he know that? Ivan? Is this from him? Has he been compromised? Killed?* Maggie's heart began to race. She felt exposed in a way she had not felt in decades. Completely unprotected. She was deep in the heart of Russia and feeling very alone.

But she had to do something. And at this point, her life likely depended on it.

"Ok, Manheim. You win. I'll give it to you. But here? Right now?"

"Yes, now."

Maggie shifted slightly in her seat, creating extra room beside her.

"Could you sit beside me then? I'd rather not advertise that we are passing something, and that camera behind me marks you even worse than me."

Manheim looked up, past Maggie.

"I don't see a camera."

"Near the roof latch, upper left? Do you see it?"

Manheim darted his eyes up and down before grunting something that approximated agreement. He shifted himself over beside Maggie, leaving his folded overcoat on the seat where he was. Now, directly beside Maggie he turned to her. "The Klee?"

Maggie reached to her side and slid the tube out. Slowly, and keeping it along her body, she slid it into to Manheim's gloved hands.

"It's yours. Now what?"

"Not so fast, little vixen. Open it."

Maggie did as she was instructed, slowly opening the tube, and sliding the rolled painting out just enough to allow a glimpse of the artist's genius. And the second Manheim's eyes fixed on the painting Maggie struck him, directly in the windpipe with the side of her hand. As hard as she possibly could.

Manheim leapt to his feet, before falling sideways to the floor and struggling for air. Maggie slid the Klee back inside the tube and in a single, deft touch replaced it in her bag even as she moved across the seats to place herself between Manheim and the gun that was most certainly hidden inside his folded overcoat.

As Maggie let her weight rest on the coat she felt the steel beneath, but she wasn't finished yet. Maggie started screaming.

"Oh my God! Somebody, please help him! He's choking!"

With Manheim hitting the floor and Maggie screaming it was mere moments before the entire train became an uproar. But Maggie wasn't done yet. She reached up and pulled the emergency stop lever. Suddenly, an alarm sounded, just as the train began grinding to an awkward stop. Screaming and chaos were everywhere, except for Maggie who used the distraction to slide the gun from inside the jacket to her backpack. She didn't have a lot of time. She would have to get off the train before anyone effectively identified her. She cast her eyes in the direction of the "camera" that wasn't there. But Manheim bought it, which was all she needed. As she took a last look around, she caught sight of Manheim's horror-filled eyes. She may have broken his windpipe, and if she did, he wouldn't last long. But this was her or him, and Maggie was not giving up yet. She had to get to Moscow some other way, and she had to do it without knowing who might be chasing her. She turned back to the aisle and headed through the panicked crowd, slipped out a side door down onto the track and was gone.

28

ZEVON LEVI stood inside the cage. Made up of 1x4 pieces of unpainted pine, sixteen feet high and stapled together with a chicken wire covering, the lockup was constructed deep inside a decrepit one-time, dump truck box manufacturing warehouse. The air was stale and sort of dirty, but that was mainly from lack of movement. Standing inside any old warehouse meant the only way air moved was by assist from a giant floor fan or two. Musty was the name of the game.

Taken alone, the lockup was nothing special. Thrown together in an afternoon by the production carpenters, it did the trick. There were six of them in total, one for each of the departments needing a static location to store stuff that would be used in whatever was currently being filmed. Camera had a lockup that was mainly for extra gels and some consumables, plus boxes of original negatives and now, tapes. Props had one. And construction. And locations. Only set decoration had two.

Set dec needed two large lockups to store the various pieces of furniture and decoration used for filming on sets. Usually rented from high end stores, the furniture needed to be protected from damage and/or theft. It also helped to keep things organized during the run of a production. They were secure, but not in any kind of Fort Knox way. Just a padlock on a hasp that, in an emergency, could be pried off with a screwdriver.

And it was here that Zevon Levi stood, hidden away inside the lockup located farthest from the front of the warehouse. Set Dec Lockup #2. And in this lockup, alone, he gazed into the face of transcendent beauty.

He always marvelled at how it was smaller than he guessed such a thing would be. Maybe as big as a mirror one might hang in a hallway or at a front entrance. But still it radiated something so pure and important and real.

The painting was a singularly captivating image of a classic old parlor, where one man and two women were intent on making music. The standing woman held a sheet of written music and raised her hand to beat out the time for her companions. Turned just away from view sat a gentleman sporting a fancy sash. Maybe he was a soldier in a militia of some kind.

Zevon took a deep breath and let his imagination take flight. The figures in the painting were focused and preoccupied with their task: they did not look at each other, and appeared unaware they were being observed. Lying on the large table to their left was a lute, while a viola da gamba rested on the floor. Or discarded? Questions were created. Were they instruments to be used next? Were they played and rejected? Zevon would never know.

And the light! Vermeer's famed attention to light and all its reflections. The sparkles off the women's pearls, the golden threads of the man's sash almost shining. The white silk skirt, and even the Persian carpet, spread heavily across the table.

Zevon's eyes finally left the interior of the work and rested on the whole. The lost painting, noted by many as the finest of Vermeer's work. *The Concert*, hidden deep inside a cheap LA warehouse and being stared at by the lowest of B-level movie producers, was the most famous missing painting in the world. And it was still missing, technically. It remained on the lam from the 1990 heist that took it. Lost to the entire world, save Mr. Zevon Levi.

And he was happy.

Not because the painting was stolen. Or even that he had it. Or that it was even valuable. Those things all played a role of course, but the internal, swelling happiness that he felt had nothing to do with dollar signs or bank accounts or even the blush of ownership. It was akin to clutching an ancient roman coin. Of knowing that the item resting in your hand had travelled centuries, millennia, through time and almost miraculously ended up on your palm, and that by simply holding it you joined a line of individuals linked by a single thread. You had touched something, become part of something, that few recognized as mattering. It was illicit. It was wrong. But, for now anyway, it was his. And that filled Zevon up.

He took another deep breath, studied *The Concert* for a few moments longer and then slid it back inside the solid wood case housing it and turned away. He stepped outside of the lockup, swung the hanging door closed and replaced the humble padlock into the hasp with a click.

Hiding in plain sight. Vermeer's masterpiece and yet Zevon Levi could not display it anywhere. It had to remain invisible. Unnoticed. And the idea that he would soon be parting with it forever broke his heart.

* * *

It was no coincidence that a teenage Zevon Levi found himself running through the streets of New York with $65,000 worth of diamonds in his pocket. Talk about a way to earn spending money in the summer.

New York City's famous Diamond District was home to more than 4,000 jewelers and wholesalers, all congregated in Midtown Manhattan. Entire streets dedicated to small jewelry stores and exchanges selling gemstones, fine jewelry, diamonds, and other precious artifacts. This had become Zevon's summer playground.

The job itself was easy but very stressful. Hired thanks to his father, Zevon would run diamond or other precious gem pouches between dealer shops. He was inconspicuous, fast, and very trustworthy. The thinking was that no one pays attention to a young boy running, and absolutely no one would think such a boy would ever be carrying anything of significant value. And because Zevon was small for his age, the fiction became even more believable.

Most days, young Zevon would sprint between shops delivering gems to facilitate deals or trade handwritten messages that dealers would not trust to phone calls. Zevon learned the value of personal information, and discretion, at a very young age. And while the diamond world itself never fully drew Zevon inside, the people he met, and the contacts he made, would contribute greatly to the life he would eventually enjoy as an adult.

And it would also lead to a very strange telephone call, almost fifty years removed from his youth.

Now into his sixties, Zevon received a message from someone claiming to remember him from his runner days, and that he needed to get together with him quickly, privately, and quietly. But it must be absolutely in person. ASAP. Now! As a somewhat respectable movie producer, Zevon was initially skeptical, but also extremely curious. Anyone calling "from the old days" deserved a listen. He agreed to meet.

The meeting produced a man much older than himself. Eighties at least. The man spoke of a younger brother who had recently passed. No names of any kind were exchanged. He relayed that his younger brother was an individual who "bent" the law every which way, yet almost never got caught. Somehow, his younger brother had come into possession of something extremely valuable but also complicated to handle. And after approaching his older, more legitimate brother for assistance, he had died suddenly before anything could be done. Now, some years later and facing a regular world without his younger brother's underworld know-how, he remembered the name of the most trusted, connected individual from his youth: Little Zevon, the diamond runner. He didn't even know about the movie business. He knew only of Zevon's impeccable standing within a community dedicated to the currency of secrecy and handshake trust. And he needed both, desperately.

He didn't want money. He didn't want favors. He didn't even want to know details of what he had. His only requests were that the item be accepted, no questions asked, and that it never ever be traced back to him or his family. He also asked that under no condition should it ever be turned over to the police or authorities. Zevon pressed him, worried about his own liability or risk in stepping forward but a sharp look from the octogenarian made his feelings about law enforcement clear. He spoke softly but with force. "No one knows what I have, and my brother is dead two years. There is no one looking at him or me." Zevon agreed to his terms, and they shook hands. The old man went out to his car, returned with a large burlap-wrapped something and handed it to him. He thanked him, turned, and left. Zevon never saw or heard from him ever again.

And just like that, Zevon Levi became the sole owner of the most valuable missing painting in the world.

It was fun, for a while. Like any secret first learned. Just the idea of having something special that no one knew about was exciting. What Zevon hadn't counted on was the stress that eventually arrives as well. First, from the fear that someone might know he had it or at least possibly find out, and then second, that here was this insanely valuable item that he owned but was incapable of exploiting in any useful way.

He couldn't brag about it. He couldn't hang it. He couldn't throw parties around it. He couldn't even donate it to a gallery for a showing. And really, what fun was there in having something you couldn't tell anyone about?

For almost two years he held the secret close, content to know in his heart what he had and how special it was. He would visit it every now and again, keeping it hidden inside a secure room within his home.

But then times changed. For whatever reason, his film packages weren't working the way they used to. The distributors were paying less and the numbers to build the projects were not adding up like they once did. Suddenly, the kind of talent that used to sell a flick was becoming harder to come by. And the ones that could sell a film to distributors wanted more. Much more. It seemed all at once, but it was incremental, and absolute. Zevon was having money trouble.

He couldn't get the financing from banks he was used to. And the rates they offered were killing him. Eventually, the friendly banks stopped taking his calls and the unfriendly ones wouldn't take a meeting. Zevon got desperate and turned to other, less than credible financiers. He reasoned that he wouldn't need them for long. Just a hit or two and things would rebound.

But things didn't rebound. They just got worse.

Now Levi was struggling to balance one crooked investor off another. Pay off the old one with the new one's investment. Keep the balls in the air, no matter what. That meant the deals became riskier and the partners sketchier.

In general, the film industry existed as a gift to money launderers of all stripes. The amount of money floating around, the high use of cash, the completely off the wall purchases and expenditures. Film-making just naturally leant itself to that kind of thing. But Zevon was having trouble satisfying the various parties he had crawled into bed with, and he needed a way out.

It was time to make *The Concert* work for him.

And thanks to his new friends the Booli Brothers, Zevon thought he saw light at the end of what had been a very dark tunnel.

29

MAGGIE HAD LEFT the train in the distance. Whether it was still stopped or not, she didn't know or care at this point. And she didn't know what happened to Manheim either. She didn't stick around. Maggie continued to move forward.

After jumping from the train, Maggie slipped into some trees where she could hide. There couldn't be video of any kind showing where she'd gone. It would be too easy to track her down already. There was a ticket, but she had used a fake ID for that. Still, even in Russia there were plenty of smart phones around and it only took one to record. She passed through the trees and around some bushes, taking a path separate from the line of sight near the train. Thankfully the weather was cooperating. Rain was a constant threat at this time of year and when it started, it took a long time to stop. She wasn't dressed for harsh conditions. Immediately, Maggie started hunting for a roadway.

She guessed that she was about 50 miles outside Moscow. It could be further, but she wasn't sure. Between the chaos onboard and her efforts to get away unnoticed she was flying a little blind. She had not planned for this. Maggie looked left and right, straining to see the movement of vehicles. She needed a road.

Maggie had checked the maps originally, and the train route was somewhat parallel to a roadway. There was some deviation but if she didn't get turned around, she was likely to hit a roadway at some point. Maggie adjusted her coat. The wind was blowing stronger now. Rain was coming. The only question was when and how hard would it fall? And would it make getting a ride even more difficult?

Her issues had compounded quickly. Manheim's attack on the train clearly meant she was being followed and there was no way he was the only one. It was likely there were others on the lookout for her as well. And any one of them coming across her could lead to big problems getting safely out of country. Maggie quickened her pace, looking around and listening with as much focus as she could muster. Was that a road across the way? About a half mile? She started to jog.

Her mission had been compromised. That was reality. How she did things now mattered more than ever. Maggie could feel her panic rising. She needed to calm down, fast. She needed her head back in the game. She started box breathing. One deep breath to the count of five, then hold for the count of five, then exhale for the count of five, then hold on empty for the count of five and repeat. She could feel her anxiety begin to subside. She looked ahead. It was a roadway. It might be too much to hope for a road sign, but this was a good first step. By car, in the most direct way possible she could get back to Moscow in a half hour, but she needed a car. First step was to get to the road.

Hitchhiking in Russia is not out of the ordinary. And even seeing tourists do it is not a huge surprise. The Russian word for it is *avtostop*, which literally means "car stopping," basically the only word locals understand when it comes to getting rides for free. Average locals might say *poputka* but it would be fairly clear that Maggie wasn't from the neighborhood.

Also, certain areas would be less expected to see hitching than others. She hoped her recent proximity to the churches and missions of Sergiyev Posad would make her presence less of an issue. Maggie would mention them if she needed to, mainly to keep the tourist fiction alive. She finally saw a car in the distance. Maggie stuck out her thumb and watched as it buzzed right by. *Darn!*

She flipped her head around looking for more. Nothing yet. She wasn't sure what direction she should be walking in. No point going farther away. If only there were sign somewhere.

Maggie touched the small of her back. The knife she had picked up was still there. It wasn't *Lola*, that treasure she had left back home. Overseas airport security was ruthless on stuff like that, and she never flew checked luggage when she went overseas. Too much complication. She picked up her insurance blade at a tourist stop. It wasn't the sharpest, but it would do the trick in a pinch. Another car was coming, and this time Maggie smiled when she saw what it was. No way would the driver of this machine not stop.

And stop it did.

As Maggie walked up to the passenger window of the rusted old, army green van she smiled and waved. The driver reached across and manually rolled down the window. Maggie spoke first. "Hello. *Privet. Ya lublu tvoyu buchanku.*"

Immediately, the young driver burst into a huge smile and started to laugh. "*Bukhanka? Vy govorite pau-russky?*"

Maggie put her hands up in surrender, admitting quickly that she didn't speak Russian, except for a little but he loved the *bukhanka* line so much he waved her inside. The van the young man was driving was an old 1960's UAZ-450. Because of the way it looked it was usually referred to by those that knew it as a "loaf of bread" or a *bukhanka*. The only reason Maggie knew was because she spent a few months living in one for a summer during the seventies. She asked him if she could get a ride. He smiled again and pushed open the door so she could crawl up and in. Once she was set, the driver threw it in gear and the clackity engine roared off once more.

The van had two front doors, a single-wing on the right side and a double-wing at the rear. It was full of stickers, empty Red Bull cans, instrument cases and sound equipment, all arrayed across the most garish dirty, orange shag carpet you ever saw. Maggie loved it. She turned to the young man.

"Do you speak English? She asked hopefully.

"*Net, nou, nemnogo.* Uh, a little?"

The young man was maybe mid-twenties, with shaggy long hair. He was skinny with tattered jeans and a black band shirt that read *Kino* on it. His wallet chain ran from the back of his jeans to his side pocket. He had several tattoos and most of them appeared self-administered. He wore multiple earrings and had the brightest of blue eyes.

"What's your name? I'm Maggie."

The young man blushed a little but smiled again. "I'm Luka. Hi, hello." Then he struggled a bit, appearing to figure out in his head what words to use as he tried to speak in English once more.

"Uh, where to go? *Khodba?*"

Maggie leaned her head, and in the most, gentle, and pleading way possible asked. "Moscow?"

Luka brightened up immediately. "*Da! Ya toze.* Umm…me too."

Maggie felt the tension drain from her almost immediately. She hadn't felt this relieved in hours. She wasn't out of the woods yet but right now she had a solid shot of a least getting to the drop point in less than an hour. Assuming Luka's *bukhanka* held together, which, if you knew them like Maggie did, meant that was no guarantee. Luka waved at the dashboard, indicating to Maggie.

"*Muzak? Pank?* Punk?"

"*Da*" said Maggie.

And the loaf-van continued forward, smoking and rattling its way across the Russian countryside, headed towards Moscow.

30

AS THE SUV glided in towards the curb Tranko breathed deep and then let out as much air as he could, slow and long. He needed to relax and let his body release as much tension as possible. The big vehicle was ten feet away and closing. He needed to time this perfectly.

Just as the SUV got close Tranko took three steps and tossed his body into the air, directly in the path of the slowing vehicle. He was working as hard as he could to get at least his hip above the hood line. If he could do that, this just might work. Success!

Tranko's hip cleared the hood just enough to let spin him over sideways in the air and come crashing into the front windshield with his butt. His legs almost rolled up and over the roof but due to the slowing speed, followed by a panicked stop, Tranko came to rest splayed across the now badly dented hood.

Damn! he thought. *That still really hurt.*

Thug #1 jumped out and immediately started cursing at Tranko in Russian as the other guys began to mill around and create a scene. Tranko was still trying to catch his breath when he heard the sound he'd been waiting for.

A siren. A police siren.

Tranko had made the cop car almost a quarter mile away. He saw him coming and he knew if he timed it just right his little performance would occur exactly in front of LAPD's finest. At least if this one was willing to admit he saw anything instead of turning his head and driving on. But in this case, he did see, and he was stopping. Right on cue.

"What were you trying to do? Jumping in front of me? This is your fault, not mine! I didn't hit you. You hit me!"

Tranko just groaned. He wanted to laugh but it was still a little too painful. The chirping of the cop's siren caused the main thug to pause in his recriminations for Tranko and spin around.

"Ah, no. C'mon. Not these guys." He walked toward the advancing car waving his arms and shouting. "NO. No, we don't need you. Everything is fine."

The cop pulled across the near lane and left his lights on. Then he exited his cruiser.

"Is he okay? Could you please stand back? Sir, I'm going to need you to move over there."

The officer had his hand on his weapon but had not drawn it at this point. The Russian goons were starting to disperse and turn away. They did not like the direction this was going.

Tranko raised his head. "Hey, could I get a hand?"

The police officer came to him. "I think you need to lay still, sir. I'm not sure what's been injured. I'm going to get a paramedic here. You just hang on."

Now it was Tranko's turn to wave him off.

"No, it's okay. Really." And with that, Tranko slid himself off the hood onto the ground. He grunted a little when he landed but managed to raise himself to full standing height. He started to brush the glass crumble from his pants. The cop continued.

"Look, I really think we should get someone to take a look at you. And besides, I'm going to need information from everyone here… starting with you." The cop pointed at Thug #1 who turned a light shade of red.

Tranko started to do some stretching, making a big deal of working out his back.

"Look, officer. It's all my fault, really. I was kind of messing around with my friends here. They did not do anything wrong. It's all on me."

The cop wasn't buying it. He stared at Tranko suspiciously. Thug #1 did the same.

"We're stunt men. Literally. This is our production office here. I saw my friends coming in the SUV and they were pulling up to the front and I was just going to show off a little, but I screwed it up." He pointed to the busted windshield. "That's gonna come out of my paycheck, unfortunately. It's a production vehicle. We were supposed to go on a location scout."

The officer turned and looked at the main thug. "Is that true?"

The thug seemed to consider his options before answering. "Yeah, location scout."

Tranko dug in with gusto.

"Hey, officer, I'm really sorry about all this. You got way more important things to be doing with your time than refereeing idiots like us screwing around. Clearly no one was hurt, and the only damage done is going to have to be dealt with by us. No insurance on this one. I'm happy to come downtown with you and answer some questions. Here's my ID. I can verify who I am and all. I just don't wanna jam the other guys up on this one. It's my screwup. I gotta own it." The main thug's eyes opened wide. *What was that mudak doing?*

The cop looked at Tranko for a long time. Then he looked back and forth at the main thug and the others leaning against the SUV. He knew something wasn't right, but he hated paperwork. He also didn't need someone else calling this in and making it look like he didn't do his job.

"Well, if you're willing to come in and answer a few questions I think we can sort this out."

Tranko smiled. "No problem, officer. Happy to help."

As Tranko walked towards the officer's squad car the main thug started to protest. Tranko raised a hand to calm him. "It's okay, Dimitri. I'm fine. No problem at all. I'll just go downtown and get all this settled off. Tell Mr. D. that I'm going to get back to him as soon as I can, and I'll make things right. No troubles."

The glare from "Dimitri" was so sharp it could cut glass. He was furious but there was absolutely nothing he could do at this point. If he pushed things the cop would want information from him too and that wasn't going to be good for anyone. No, Tranko had gotten him good.

Tranko smirked in the henchman's direction. *Fuck them* he thought. *I need some space, now back off!*

The officer opened the rear door to squad car and ushered Tranko inside, slammed the door after him and turned to get in the car himself. Tranko was careful to direct his middle finger to the entire gang of thugs as the cruiser pulled away.

Driving down Sunset, Tranko rubbed his side. His hip really hurt. Dumb stunts like that were for guys a helluva lot younger than he was. Still felt good to do it, mentally at least. As the car began to pick up speed Tranko began to run through things in his head. He was going to hear from Dachshund but that was to be expected. He was also going to have it out with "Dimitri" at some point. That ass was absolutely going to get kicked. But he had to get back to the production office ASAP and go through the contents of the truck. Somehow, he knew there was something back there worth finding. And he couldn't take the chance of letting someone else find it first.

31

MAGGIE AND LUKA sang at the top of their lungs and could not quit laughing and smiling as they did. Toto's *Africa* blasted from the house-sized speakers in the back of the van as they sang along to the 1980's hit. It was ridiculous, and fun, all at once. Luka might not speak English all that well, but he had clearly memorized more than his fair share of American pop lyrics.

Maggie glanced out the window. They were on the outskirts of Moscow now, rolling along the Yaroslavskoye Hwy. Maggie watched the greenery of the landscape give way to the concrete buildings and towers. Traffic was steady but moving quickly. She figured they would hit central Moscow in fifteen minutes or so, and then she could focus on getting to the drop location and dumping the Klee.

Maggie was still worried about Manheim. She was certain she hadn't killed him, which meant he would more than likely still be after her. The only consolation was that it didn't appear he was being assisted by any government agents because if he had been, she'd have faced at least a couple of instant "road checks" along the way. As she and Luka covered the miles, she hadn't noticed any cars following them either. Whatever group Manheim was with didn't appear to have an official capacity. At least, that she could tell.

Which was a relief. Moscow is tough enough on its own.

The Kursky train station was where Maggie would have ended up if she'd been able to stay on board, but the detour scotched the neatness of that. Still, Luka would be getting her nearby anyway. She had asked him to take her to the Atrium Mall and Shops, which was somewhat adjacent to the station. The bus tour was set to depart back to Minsk from the mall and she would be able to access the drop location Ivan had arranged. Things were going to plan, at least so far.

She checked the time, noting she had roughly forty minutes or so to meet up with the bus tour.

"Almost there." Luca said with a smile.

It was cloudy, but the city still managed to impress. It always did. Maggie had not been to Moscow in at least twenty years, but the memories persisted. She wished she wasn't so pressed for time. Just to walk through the grand metro stations was a treat, with their luxurious finishings, intricate molding, giant chandeliers, and beautiful paintings. And how in true Soviet form, the farther the stations got from the center of the city the less decadent and far more blandly homogenous they became. Maggie smiled at the thought of running through the station with a very special young man once, but the memory suddenly turned sour, and she pushed it away.

As the van pulled to the side of the Garden Ring road and finally came to rest near the front entrance to the Atrium Mall, Maggie fixed her coat and reached for her bag. She turned to thank Luka, but he had already jumped out of the driver's side and rushed around to open the passenger door for her.

"No, no, let me."

Maggie smiled. He was really a sweet young man. "Thank you, Luka. You really saved me. You have no idea."

Suddenly, Luka's face registered shock and horror. He turned and ran around to the back of the van. Maggie watched as he ripped open the back doors and was tore furiously through various bags and boxes. Finally, he appeared to find something and raced back to where Maggie was left waiting on the curb. He had a smile on his face as he proudly handed her a piece of paper.

Maggie looked at it. It was a photocopied poster for a concert. She recognized one of the Russian words on it. Noise, *shun*. The other she wasn't sure. She held it out to Luka and pointed. He said "*Vosstavat*..uh, get up?" and then raised his arms in the air. She looked back at the one-sheet, all modge-podge and visual noise intercut with guys on motorcycles and leather jackets.

"Rebels...Rebel Noise!"

Luka smiled broadly. Then he pointed to the paper and then to himself. "Us. You see us play maybe?"

Maggie understood. It was a poster for Luka's band. He stood there, so skinny and young and innocent. A boy-man getting by in a brutal country just trying to be something. She smiled and stepped forward, hugging him so spontaneously it even surprised her. Maggie wasn't really a "hugger", but this kid just brought it out. "I would love to see your band. I don't know if I ever can, but I will keep this."

Luka smiled at Maggie as he stepped back to the van, blushing a little, before closing the doors and heading around to the driver side. He paused for a moment, took a last look at Maggie, raised a finger just above his eye and then jumped inside and drove away.

Maggie took a deep breath. The souls that you meet. Back to work.

She headed into the mall. Maggie had scouted it out briefly before she left on the train. Ivan had indicated a mailbox outlet, giving her details of a box number and where a key would be left for her to open it. Maggie remembered where the food court was, on the fourth level. There was supposed to be a coffee shop there. And she was expected to find a little storage locker place there were you could rent a place to put your stuff inside. Maggie was to find and rent locker #2323, place the Klee inside, lock it and then take the key and drop it into a small fountain nearby.

But there was no locker #2323. There were no lockers even. None at all.

She walked around the food court several times, convinced she must have missed something. Nothing. Had they been removed? Was she in the wrong place?

Convinced that she must be on the wrong floor, or that there must be another food court Maggie turned back towards the illuminated map of the mall in the center of the tables. It was only then that she saw what she should have seen before. There, sitting four or five tables away was Manheim, staring at her. Maggie felt a lump form in her throat. Granted, it was a public place, so he wasn't likely to do anything severe here, but it still wasn't the best result to all that had transpired. Manheim motioned for her to come over. Seeing little other options, Maggie complied.

As Maggie took a seat opposite Manheim he spoke, "I'm certain you'll understand if I decide to keep my distance from you." His voice was raspy, and sore. She had hit him pretty hard.

"Well, it could have been worse, you know."

Maggie didn't have much to lose at this point. Might as well play it tough.

"I know what you're looking for. It isn't here. There is no #2323. There are no lockers. Now just hand over the painting and get out of here. You've got a bus to catch."

Manheim was far too informed about things he shouldn't have been for it to be a fluke. Clearly, Ivan had been compromised. Or more likely, that shrew he let work with him. But Maggie couldn't understand why Ivan would provide false specifics. Had he double-crossed her? Was something else going on? Was Manheim even going to let her get away?

"I should beat you for what you did to my throat. Maybe another day."

Dumbfounded, Maggie reached inside her bag and slid the covered Klee out, handing it to Manheim. He opened it, confirmed it was what it was, and then stood up. He turned, appearing to be forming something to say, but seemed to think better of it. Manheim walked away, joining a crowd, and quickly disappearing from her view.

Instantly, Maggie felt naked. She had been made in the worst possible way and now she was alone, in a Moscow mall. She needed to get back to that bus tour ASAP. There were no guarantees now, and without even the painting, no leverage of any kind. Maggie knew her odds of surviving the next twenty-four hours were fifty-fifty at best.

32

MODELED AFTER THE *Villa dei Papiri* in Herculaneum, Italy, the Getty Villa just outside Malibu, California was constructed in the early 1970s by architects who worked closely with its founder and benefactor, J. Paul Getty, on all aspects of design and construction.

Getty was the American-born, British industrialist who built the Getty Oil Company in 1942. Already the son of a rich oilman, J. Paul himself grew to become the richest living American, and the world's wealthiest private citizen, with an estimated $6 billion fortune at the time of his death. In 1976 money no less. He was known as a savvy businessman, a demanding taskmaster and a ruthless dealmaker.

And, for whatever reason, he became obsessed with Roman architecture.

Eyebrows were raised in both art and architecture circles when Getty set out to build an exact replica of an ancient Roman villa on land that he owned overlooking the Pacific Coast Highway. And while he never once set foot on the property, or even saw it with his own eyes, the incredible realization of his vision somehow spoke to the odd relationship between those with truly uncountable wealth, and the often unique or even bizarre ways they find to dispose of it.

What better location for Zevon Levi to arrange an introduction between himself and the Booli Brothers? Grand but personal, exclusive but not exactly closed off. And private enough for them to meet but public enough to avoid drawing any unwanted attention.

Either way, Zevon figured it was the best place to meet his potential saviors for the first time. Arriving early to their appointment, Zevon scouted what he deemed to be the best spot for them to gather, the outdoor amphitheater. The seats were largely unoccupied, save the odd tourist eating a bag lunch or resting from a tour. In total, they would be visible from all sides, but not likely to be noticed as anything out of the ordinary.

At least he didn't think anybody would notice them.

When the Booli's SUVs arrived, their speed was the first clue something was up. The cobblestone entry road forced most cars to crawl up the driveway. Apparently the Booli team didn't worry about such niceties. Their seven-vehicle convoy raced up the road and almost took out the parking attendant waving desperately at them to stop.

"Uh, do you have a reservation?"

The lead driver, dressed like a secret service agent in dark suit and sunglasses simply stared at him, saying nothing. Before the flummoxed attendant could ask a follow-up question, a well-dressed man exited one of the chase cars and walked straight up to him, smiling and with his hand extended.

"Hello, I'm Bashir. I'll be handling the details." He shook the attendant's hand and immediately turned and waved for the convoy to continue forward, which it did. As the swarm of SUVs whipped past the booth, Bashir placed a soft but firm hand on the somewhat stunned attendant's shoulder. "Absolutely no problem at all. I think this will work out perfectly." He walked him gently back to his post.

Slightly off-kilter himself, Zevon didn't notice the heads turning all around him. Eventually though, the sheer volume of bodies leaning, fingers pointing and raised eyebrows caused him to look and see what was up. It couldn't be a presidential visit, but it sure looked like one. No less than fifteen dark-suited men had fanned out across the entry pathway, acting as silent, yet intimidating, heralds for whatever was coming.

Zevon began to walk up the amphitheatre steps, incredulous at the spectacle taking place and feeling more than a little sick to his stomach at the realization that the arriving chaos would almost certainly include him.

"Zevon Levi!" a voice called out. "I am seeking Zevon Levi!"

Zevon opened his mouth to speak but nothing came out. He could feel the eyes of those assembled begin to turn his way. He lifted his right arm like a slightly embarrassed school child asking to be excused.

"I'm...uh...me... Zevon.." His voice trailed off, even as Rael Booli, emerging like a butterfly from within the cocoon of dark suits, amplified his arrival further.

"Zevon Levi? Ha ha ha ha ha! Wonderful, wonderful! Sauf! Look, look. He is here!"

Zevon felt trapped. Literally everyone in the Getty was locked in on the spectacle unfolding just above the amphitheater. He wished he could crawl inside a hole. Not that anyone would lose sight of where he went. The loud, bright colored silk shirt and shiny gold shoes would have marked Rael a mile off. Absolutely nothing about the man was subtle.

Until Sauf emerged from the protective detail.

As unassuming as Rael was in-your-face, Sauf looked left and right before stepping up to Rael's side. He nodded a greeting in Zevon's direction.

Zevon came forward, looking left and right himself. "Are you kidding me? I asked to meet here to draw less attention to us, not more."

Rael smiled, big and broad, and then swooped in on Zevon, spinning him around and slipping an arm around his shoulder like a car salesman.

"I ask you, Mr. Levi. Is it not sometimes easier to hide within a hurricane? When there is much going on, people do not notice details all that much." At which point Sauf came forward.

"And my dear brother would not get to make a scene, which he so enjoys."

Rael smirked at his brother and refocused on Zevon. "I cannot say my brother is wrong, but I cannot say I am either. No matter. We have come to meet, and I cannot think of a better place to stroll and talk than through the halls of such a magnificent edifice, at least for Los Angeles. History here is a lot newer than back home."

As the three men, Zevon, Rael and Sauf, began to walk together the accompanying retinue of security and handlers fanned out, staking various positions, until there were only five remaining to shadow the men from a respectful distance. They walked along the gardens of the outer peristyle, discussing.

"We are grateful for this meeting," offered Sauf.

"Indeed, we are," agreed Rael, "but we do need to know that you actually have what you claim to possess."

Zevon smiled. Finally. This he knew about. Making deals. All of life was deal-making, from beginning to end.

"I can and will take you to see it, eventually. But only once we have decided what the real interest is from you and your plans on how you want to handle things should we decide to move forward."

Sauf spoke first. "Our interest is very real. And I think you will like our proposal."

Zevon smiled, but his eyes must have suggested he was skeptical. Rael picked up on it immediately.

"You question inside whether we are serious, I know this. I can tell."

"Easy, Rael," cautioned Sauf.

"Look at this watch, look at it." Rael shoved his wrist in front of Zevon's face. "This is a *Philippe Patek Nautilus*, full ice. Bums don't wear such things on their wrist." He took it off and pushed it into Zevon's hand, urging him to examine it.

Amused, Zevon studied the watch and began to smile. He looked over to Sauf, who betrayed nothing. Then he looked back to Rael.

"It's beautiful, do you always use this specific one as a test or do you have others?" Zevon's eyes glinted at his casual insouciance.

"I don't follow."

"You want to know that the person you are dealing with is a man worthy of trust, but also that he is not a fool because not being fools yourselves, why deal with such a man?"

Standing to the side, and certain Zevon could not see, Sauf allowed himself the slightest of smiles.

Zevon continued. "Let's just say the pearl of great price buried in my field is exactly what it presents as, unlike your extremely well-made fool detector."

Now it was Rael's turn to smile. And he burst into a huge one. "Ha ha ha ha hahaha! I love this man! I love him so much! What did you see? Tell me, what tipped you first?"

"It wasn't easy. The weight is very good, and the presentation obviously is perfect. But the Calatrava Cross on the back. They never mess with that, and when I expect to see four balanced points and instead see three points plus a diamond, well, that tells me this is something else entirely."

"Who says Arabs and Jews can't be friends? Look at me, Sauf. Look at me, I'm in love with a Jew!" Rael reached over and hugged Zevon, who gently, but firmly, pulled away.

"OK, OK. But let's get serious on this. What are you imagining here? A straight purchase?"

By this point the men had come all the way around the reflecting pool and re-entered the inner peristyle. As if on cue, Bashir approached and interjected, "Gentlemen, a room has been prepared." He turned and gestured with his arms toward a side room.

Rael, Zevon and Sauf entered the separate museum area as Bashir closed the large double doors behind them.

"This is private?" asked Zevon.

"Bashir took care of it. We won't be bothered."

Sauf took a step forward. "This is a very good deal for you. We don't even need to take possession of the piece. Once we have confirmed it's real, you simply store it and ensure its safety. It must remain with you and cannot be disposed by you unless first cleared by us. For this service we will pay you $5 million."

Zevon nodded. "And this has value to you?"

"It does. We will use the existence of the piece as a form of guarantee for other deals. Most of the time we would have no need of the physical painting. Knowing it is secured is enough. But if those deals go sideways or otherwise require full payment, then you would agree to sell us the painting at an agreed upon cost."

"Did you have a number in mind?"

"$25 million."

"No, not enough."

Silence. Sauf turned and motioned to Rael. The two walked to the far side of the room, deep in discussion. Rael was animated, arms waving and gesticulating. Sauf was compressed, arms wrapped around him in thought, his head and eyes cast down. The brothers returned to Zevon. Sauf spoke.

"Did you have a number in mind?"

Zevon breathed through his nose. "The public value is $350 million. Assuming even a reasonable underground sale, that could go for $150-$200 million. I want $125 million."

Sauf laughed out his nose. "No way that gets even $125 million off market. Maybe $75 million. Not more."

Zevon spied a nearby chair and sat down, exhaling comfortably. "This is a very useful piece for you gentlemen. I'd focus more on the $7.5 million you're paying to make use of it instead of the $100 million you might have to pay to buy it. That's a great deal."

The brothers look at each other and headed back to the other side of the room. More discussion, more arm waving. Then silence. They just stared at each other for what seemed an eternity. The brothers come back over to Zevon.

Sauf held his right hand up in the air, as if asking for a pause. Then he dropped it and stuck out his hand to shake. "Deal."

Zevon accepted the presented hand, shaking it back. "Deal."

Rael immediately clapped his hands together in excitement. "Alright! Yes! Now, let's get serious. Tell me this place has a giftshop? I freaking love giftshops."

33

DAVID STOOD in the living room of the doublewide trailer, gawking at the *Mona Lisa* on the wall. Next to it was a Degas, and just underneath that, a Renoir. The other wall held similar jaw-dropping masters. Rembrandt, Picasso, even a Dali. It was like being inside the greatest museum collection ever assembled, only to notice a collection of Troll dolls displayed with equal care and affection alongside. A trim little woman sat on a massive couch to one side.

"*Monsieur and Madame Édouard Manet* is one of my favorites, really. It's just such a perfect piece. Real art, real intrigue, real life. Incredible story really. Do you know it?"

David looked at the odd picture, noting the tear line down the one side. He knew the story. He also knew it was better to have her tell it than him.

"No, I don't."

The woman sat up, excited to share. "It's a double portrait actually. It shows Manet and his wife Suzanne. They were friends of Degas, at least Édouard was anyway. I love the way he has him lying across the couch, almost bored. He must have seen him do it sometime. You can't make that up. Anyway, Degas did the portrait and gave it to Manet and the story goes that Manet was fighting with his wife about it because he didn't like how she was portrayed or something, so he slashed it out of anger or spite. Eventually, Degas visited and saw the destroyed painting and absolutely lost it, cursing out Manet for his crime and taking the gift back. He intended to restore it but never did, which sort of suits because his friendship with Manet never recovered either. So much drama from some paint on a canvas."

"That's pretty crazy," offered David.

"They certainly were," answered the small woman.

David shook his head. He knew he was in for it when he got her details. Abigale Mountbatten, a Fresno, CA. nursing aid/artist who just happened to paint some of the best "fakes" in the art world. But not illegally. Abigale didn't try to pass off her work as the real thing. Far from it. She took great pains to let everyone know her paintings were not the works they thought they were. She just liked doing it. And to be fair, displaying them in a trailer park sort of made her point for her.

"So, why'd you want to see them anyway?" asked Abigale.

"How do you get them so close to the originals? Are you working from closeup pictures or what?"

Abigale preened a bit. It was nice to be regarded for your skill. And it had been a while since someone was around to praise her abilities, at least as a painter. Might as well soak it up a bit.

"They're all different really. Usually, I see the original in a museum or on a trip somewhere. The curators, guards and administrators can be quite helpful if you show the right attitude and respect. I've been let into galleries after hours and even allowed to get up close to the pieces. Way closer than they ever let regular tourists go. Sometimes they even let me take pictures and as long as I'm careful they give me plenty of freedom. Then, working from the pictures and my own memories I go to work."

"How long does it take?"

"Anywhere from six months to a year. Depends how busy I am at work. Some days I'm just so tired I can't. But the painting perks me up. It's a release."

"They really are amazing. How many have you got?"

"Lord, I don't even remember now. Some are in the garage out back. I put a few in the main clubhouse too. The other folks like seeing 'em that way. I get tired of them sometimes. That's usually what gets me to paint a new one."

David loathed being in such trivial surroundings, not to mention having to be generous towards someone as unremarkable as this. In David's mind, to copy was the lowest form of anything. A machine copies. Humans are supposed to be unique. But he had a purpose for being here.

"Why'd you come all this way, anyhow? You don't seem the type interested in a tour of my little hobbies."

David cleared his throat. Maybe he wasn't hiding his contempt as well as he should have.

"I wanted to see you more than the paintings really. I told you my work, art insurance. But my interest is the work you've done for film companies."

Abigale smiled and waved her hand. "Oh that? Well, it sounds a lot more exciting than it really is. The first time was an accident really. I was displaying one of my paintings at a community event downtown, probably the *Mona Lisa*, and some guy came up to me asking if I'd consider renting it to some film company. They only offered $50 or so but I figured why not, what could it hurt?"

"What could it hurt?"

"Exactly, as it happened though it was some sex movie or such. Not a porno thing but lots of naked people jumping up and down on each other. If I would've known that I'd have either said 'no' or asked for more money."

Abigale waited for her joke to land but seeing David ignore it, she went on.

"Anyway, that guy was a set decorator and somehow my name got passed around between others like him. Movie making seems to be kind of a small world. Every few months I'd get a call from someone asking if I had this painting or that one, offering to rent it. A few I had, others I just painted because they asked. Only one big movie though, a Robert Duvall one. I just love him. Anyway, they actually paid me to paint *Black Iris*, the one by Georgia Okeeffe? I worked for two and half months on that one. Took time off work to do it 'cause they paid me. Always a rush with film folk. Anyway, after all that they never used it anyway. Got an autograph from Robert though."

David tried to keep his eyes from looking bored. He hated having to interact with the rubes.

"Yes, that's quite something all right. What I was getting at, was there any work you did for a producer by the name of Zevon Levi?"

Abigale moved from the couch, heading for her kitchen. "Doesn't ring a bell. Tea?"

"No, I'm fine. How about Golem Pictures? Based in Los Angeles?"

Abigale prepared a massive mug of tea for herself. "They're all in Los Angeles one way or another. At least that's what I found. Can't say Golem Pictures rings a bell either. Maybe, but maybe not."

David was annoyed. It had been a long drive and he hated wasting time this way. "Are you sure you never made any pieces for them?"

Abigale reseated herself and creased her brow, looking down and to the side, like she was really digging deep. "It's certainly possible. I know I had a spell there, maybe a year or so, where I kept getting calls for these heist movies. Always the same. Lots of big shots with fancy art on the wall stealing stuff from each other. I was painting so much it was becoming like a job. At one point, they even introduced me to a kid and got me to teach him a few things."

David perked up. "A kid?"

"Well, to me he was a kid. Twenties maybe. Art school. Really talented, way more than me. I just showed him my process, right? The grid system for copying. Then, the things to look out for. Brush strokes, color tints, the right paper. Little tips that might make a difference when you are trying to make it look as close to the original as possible."

"Do you remember his name?"

Abigale took a deep breath. "You know, I really don't. But hang on now. I might still have a contact number or something." She went to a cabinet, took out a notebook and began flipping through pages, forward and back. Eventually she seemed to settle on a pair of pages.

"Best guess is this guy. Denny Cooper. I'm sure this is him. Red hair, quiet but sweet. Loved to paint. Really. He helped me a ton during that period. I never could have done it without him really. And he learned fast. Like really fast."

Thanking Abigale profusely, David headed out the door as quick as he could, desperate to shake the stench of Fresno and get back on the road. Denny had an LA number which meant he was more than likely still there. And if he had a line on Zevon, there was a chance he'd have some insight into what David was thinking. Maybe, just maybe, Zevon Levi had figured out a way to make some serious bucks fleecing rich idiots with flawless copies of priceless originals.

And even if he didn't, it was certainly something David was more than willing to do. David pressed the accelerator hard as his BMW took the 126A exit to the 99 South. The sun was setting in the distance and David still had a three-hour drive that he planned to complete in slightly more than two.

34

MAGGIE TOOK a deep breath as she pushed the bell. It was late, almost 2am, but she didn't care. Ivan would see her. He had to.

The last thirty hours had been intense. From Manheim's appearance at the mall all the way to the current Seattle sidewalk, Maggie had felt like she was walking across the sky on a ribbon of glass that could shatter at any moment, sending her plummeting to the earth below.

On the ride back to Minsk the bus had slowed and eventually made an interminable stop at the Russian border, convincing her she would be removed at any moment. That feeling stayed all the way through boarding the plane at Minsk National and beyond. Maggie had held her breath the entire time expecting to be stopped, escorted somewhere private, and finally made to disappear.

It was a feeling she remembered from years ago and did not like one bit. Not at all.

Ivan needed to explain. He was the only one who knew where she was. All the way back to the United States, when she wasn't watching for signs of attack out of the corner of her eye, she was planning what to say to Ivan. She needed to know what he had done. Why he had done it. She felt betrayed but she didn't know if she really had been. She needed to face him. It dug at her so deeply that she changed her return ticket to land in Seattle instead of heading directly back to Vancouver. No matter how much she wanted to sleep in her own bed she needed to see Ivan's eyes first.

No answer. She pressed the bell again. Harder.

When her plane had finally crossed back over North America, Maggie had allowed herself some measure of calm, though she still eyed every passenger acting strangely, and even a few acting just a bit too normally as well. Anyone could be there to take her out, and when you feel like a secret has been exposed you tend to move about as if you are naked, convinced that everyone can see inside you, that your secrets have no cover anymore. She needed to get back to her inner sanctum and reset. To find that place of calm center.

But she had to confront Ivan. There would be no peace without facing Ivan. Without hearing him explain what happened.

Still no answer. She pressed the bell again and held it.

Maybe Ivan had been compromised? Maybe somebody got to him? The waves of doubt and confusion undulating in Maggie were threatening her anger. She needed to get back to that. Anger was allowing her to focus on getting some answers. She needed something to focus on instead of being afraid. She needed to see Ivan.

Finally, the lock in the door started to move. The door was being opened.

Stupid, nasty Greta. *Darn!*

Maggie did not want to see Greta. Maggie never wanted to see Greta. And as the door opened wider, she realized she had another reason not to want to see her: the image of grumpy Greta wearing a teal *Little Mermaid* bathrobe and *Pluto* slippers. Now that was a surprise, and something one can't unsee.

"Where's Ivan? I need to see him, Greta. Now!"

"He's not here, but you should come inside. This isn't a good street at this time of night. Come in."

Maggie stepped in through the door and waited as Greta locked it behind her, then turned and pushed past Maggie, leading her deeper into the shop. As she moved, her slippers began to flash with little colored lights. Greta caught Maggie noticing them.

"So what? I like the Disney stuff, ok? Sue me."

Saying nothing, Maggie followed. They went behind the counter, into a small office with two chairs. Greta sat down and motioned for Maggie to do the same.

Instead of complying, Maggie made the effort of standing purposely, trying to throw off as much disdain as she could without speaking. Recognizing Maggie's protest, Greta rolled her eyes slightly, but decided against significant comment on the mini-tantrum Maggie was throwing.

"I know you're pissed, it's okay. Just sit down. Let me fill you in."

Frustrated, and still very tired, Maggie gave in and sat down. Greta pulled a vape out of her robe's pocket and took a drag. The area around her head exploded in smoky vapour. The room instantly smelled of warm cotton candy.

"He didn't want to do it, but he wasn't given a choice."

Maggie said nothing. She just stared at Greta, willing her to say more.

"They were very specific in wanting you for the lift. And they were equally specific in what they wanted to have go down. Ivan defended you, totally. He wouldn't have agreed to anything if there was any real danger to you at all. You know that."

Maggie fumed. What was she talking about? And where the hell was Ivan? Maggie had questions but she didn't want to speak just yet. Better to let some more silence pry stuff from the silly twit in the bathrobe.

"You don't realize how much he protected you."

Hearing that line, however, made it simply impossible for Maggie to keep quiet any longer.

"Protected me? I was the one in Russia with my butt exposed, not him. And, apparently, I had zero knowledge of what was going on, at least if I'm to believe you, which I don't. I could have been killed so easily and no one would have done a darn thing to protect me."

"You were never in any real danger. You were protected."

"How can you say that? How can you know anything about it at all?"

Greta sighed and took another long drag from her silver tube. The comically teal robe mixed with wafting smoke gave her the look of a short, squat Christmas tree just starting to catch fire. Maggie would have laughed out loud, if she wasn't already so angry.

"Maggie, the whole thing was a test. They wanted to know if you could be trusted for a bigger, more dangerous job. Believe it or not, you passed it with flying colors, at least according to them. Be damned if I ever would've believed that."

Maggie sat dumbfounded. *A test? For what? And where the hell was Ivan?*

"They particularly liked it when you smacked their guy in the field. Showed 'em you had the edge they were looking for."

Smacked their guy in the field? How did she know about that?

"How did you know about that?"

"They told us. Well, they told Ivan. We both laughed about it. I've had to deal with that smug asshole a bit before and wanted to hit him plenty. Couldn't have happened to a nicer guy, in my opinion."

"I want to talk to Ivan."

"You can't right now. He's out dealing with something. But he'll be back in the morning."

"I'll wait then."

"Suit yourself." Greta turned and walked away, talking as she went. "You can sleep in the back room. There's a cot. It's okay. Pull the sheets in the morning. I'm not cleaning up after you."

And with that, she exited through a rear door and was gone.

Maggie found her way into the room and surveyed the cot. It wasn't much but it would do. She was exhausted and needed a somewhat restful sleep, even though she was convinced that would be impossible. Ivan had left her exposed. That would not be easy to forgive. Maggie laid down and closed her eyes. She figured she'd rest just a moment before prepping properly for bed.

Too late. Within seconds she was sound asleep.

Back in her room, Greta pulled out a cell phone and dialed a number. She waited as it connected.

"She's here. Yeah. No, she's pretty ticked off. Okay, whatever you want, but I warned you about this. Fine. Night."

Greta turned off her cell and sat down on the bed in her suite, kicking off her *Pluto* slippers. She laid her head down on the pillow and stared at the ceiling. She mouthed a single word.

"Bitch."

And with that, rolled onto one side, closed her eyes, and went to sleep.

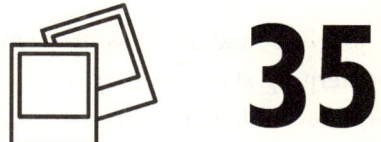# 35

ALDO WATCHED as the man seated at the desk studied the pictures. His round, pale face was serious but not near as worried as Aldo would have been looking at such shots. A briefcase sat off to one side of the man's desk, open and with even more photos spread askew plus a small jump drive. Aldo stroked the fabric of his pants as his left hand rested comfortably on a folded knee. The two men were alone, and the room was so quiet you could hear the ticking of the small desk clock located between them.

"Yes, well then. The sins of our children. Not much you can say or do. You either let them fail or you clean it up. Everything is as you've said. I've done my part. You have been officially recommended for the trusteeship post. Now, there are others that will be named as well, but you have the inside track. Unless something unforeseen happens, you should assume the position within the next few weeks or so."

"I don't like unforeseen," Aldo responded coolly.

"Maybe not, but I can only do what I can do. I have used all the influence I have to ensure you receive the votes. And they are solid. I called in plenty of my own favors to make this happen. They won't let me down. The only thing that could happen is some outside appointment or similar that muddies the water. Then other parties will start using their own leverage. We're safe here though. My leverage is based on their weaknesses, a lot like my son's apparently, and I consider those bonds to be much harder to break. You'll have your post, and with all its royalties intact.

Aldo nodded. He better get it. Aldo had been working towards this position for a long while now. It was going to be extremely useful, not the least of which in how he should be able to get back at that Russian bastard for blocking his interests in Belarus.

Neto had successfully won himself a prime position in an emerging shale oil play in Belarus. He had effective control of the entire field, which in a comparatively short time would lead to an absolute gusher, in oil and therefore money. He still required other businesses to park the proceeds he would receive from his more questionable affairs but adding up the costs to get the field in Belarus into production, mixed with the money it would eventually toss off, he was in a strong position. Or at least he would be eventually.

Getting into horseracing in America, not to mention a series of land developments in Dubai, had hurt him tremendously. That, plus the damage the world economy tilting sideways did to his main businesses and holdings. He needed this play in Belarus and Edward Dachshund was blocking him. By choking off that deal, it put everything at risk for Neto. He was in a cash crunch and exposed in ways he did not enjoy. He needed some breathing room.

The UN post would be a godsend. The access to heads of state alone was worth millions, but the backroom opportunities were almost limitless. He tried not to look eager about the turn of events, but it was hard. This was very good for him. Very good.

The man looked up from the photos. "You will see that this… embarrassment…goes away?"

Aldo waved a lazy hand in the direction of the man's desk. "Like it never happened. But I would be more concerned about his future behaviour, no?"

"Ay, yes. What can I say? He shames me with his actions. I would blame myself for spoiling him only I didn't. I'm sure it's still my fault somewhere down the line though."

The office phone buzzed.

"Mr. Dragic, can you come to meeting hall three? The delegation from Austria has arrived."

The man stirred. "Apologies. I must attend to this. But be assured. News of your appointment will come in a matter of days. Now, I have your word this will not leak?"

"As long as I'm installed properly you and yours have nothing to fear."

"You will see yourself out then. I am needed down the hall. We will be in touch." And with that, the round, pale man Aldo nicknamed "tragic Dragic" was gone.

Aldo gathered the contents of his briefcase back together and locked it. He stood, removed his coat from the adjoining chair, and lifted it across his arm. Picking up the briefcase he considered how light it was considering the weight it carried. Leverage could move anything, including his personal empire, which should hopefully be back on track sooner than later.

As Aldo left the paneled office, he caught sight of Dragic entering another room. They made eye contact but said nothing. Quickly, Dragic disappeared inside. Aldo stopped, watching the door he entered. Something about the unspoken exchange unsettled him. Aldo was always confident, assured but his personal monetary crisis had unsettled him. He needed to get his cool back. And the look he had just received from Dragic suggested all he thought was good might not be. Dragic was up to something. There was no way he was just rolling over and taking this abuse.

Would Dragic double-cross him? It was possible, of course. Anything was possible. But as an official he was comparatively clean. Aside from his offspring, the man appeared disciplined in his sexual tastes and never ran specifically afoul of governments or international laws. By most standards he was as crystal clean as you can get. Something that could not be said for most billionaires. He laughed inside as he considered himself a billionaire. *Is one still able to be considered a billionaire when they owe at least that much and more?*

The racetracks were a sinkhole and the Dubai properties had left him stressed for cash. The only area that might pay off were the oil fields but because of Dachshund they were tied up. It killed him but he had zero leverage in that area. He was trying to get something on the Dachshund front but there were no guarantees. The UN post would provide concrete opportunity. He could slap some enviro-tax or other that could only be lifted if certain things were done. Like his contracts being released. Or maybe a human rights crisis? He could even wave a red flag at the US war machine and get them on Dachshund's scent. But he needed the post to do such things. For now, he was running on debt. And although you could run a long way on debt, the current economic climate meant that banks were tightening up more than ever. It was not a great time to be struggling.

His phone buzzed. It was Fatima. A text.

"Aldo — thinking of you. Can't wait."

With a love heart emoji.

Aldo smiled. Fatima was a dear. A true lady. He thought back to that night in his Vancouver condo. First, she had made a scene, which basically ended the entire party. A few of the other women felt emboldened by her huff and brought the entire evening crashing down. Aldo laughed out loud. She was worth the effort. Definitely.

Aldo replaced his phone inside his jacket and fished out a second, smaller one. He hit a speed-dial and waited while it connected. A page came by. Aldo stopped him.

"Excuse me? Mr. Dragic was meeting with the Austrian delegation, and I was supposed to join them. Is it in that room there? Aldo gestured to the room Dragic had just entered.

"No, I'm sorry sir. The Austrian delegation is in meeting room three. I can guide you there."

"That won't be necessary. I know the way. Many thanks."

As the young page headed away, Aldo turned and spoke into his phone.

"Hello? You have it? In your hands? Excellent. No. I want you to prep it for her. Direct to her house. Yes. I'll send a note. Perfect. And when that's done, I need you to dig deeper still on Mr. Dragic. He's meeting with someone right now and I need to know who. Right now! Yes. Good man."

Aldo clicked the phone closed, paused, and stared again at the closed door down the hall, thinking about what he might do. Suddenly, his face brightened into a smile. He touched two fingers to his left eyebrow, making a sort of casual salute towards the now unseen Dragic. Only then did Aldo confidently turn his back to the door and begin the long walk down the carpeted hallway and away.

36

MAGGIE PUSHED on the gas pedal, but the *bukhanka* just wouldn't move. She heard the engine roaring, but nothing happened. Looking to her left she saw Luka and wondered why he was letting her drive. She tried to ask him if he had the emergency brake on, but he just kept smiling and laughing. It angered her, especially as she kept trying to get the van moving forward by waving her arms. Looking back at Luka to ask for help, she saw it was now Manheim sitting in the passenger seat. And he was smiling and laughing. Knowing something wasn't right, Maggie decided to fly overhead and have a look around. Hopefully she could figure out where she should go.

"Maggie? Little vixen?"

As Maggie hovered in the air, above the countryside, she realized the van was gone. Only the train remained, but it was derailed. There was smoke and fire farther on. She tried to fly toward the flames but heard a voice.

"Wake up. I'm here now."

Shaken awake, Maggie slowly sat up on one elbow. She had been asleep, and dreaming, but a voice had called her awake. Ivan's voice. She rubbed her eyes, seeing him sitting next to her cot.

"What time is it?" Maggie asked.

"Still early. I'm sorry. I should have let you sleep, but I know you probably have words for me. And that sooner is better than later, no?"

Maggie slid up to a sitting position, wrapping the blanket around her shoulders. Ivan looked at her with warm eyes.

"I'm very angry with you." Maggie stared at him, willing her words to penetrate deeply.

Ivan took a deep breath, looked down to one side and then raised a single hand in acknowledgement. "Yes, and you should be. I am guilty, without question. But there were...ah...extenuating circumstances. Things I was not able to say."

"I trusted you. You! And there are darn few people in the world that get that from me. How could you expose me like that? How could you play me? You played me, Ivan. You know how serious this is, don't you?"

Ivan sat silent. His large frame humbled by age, seeming so much weaker, and less imposing than Maggie's memories. His eyes remained cast down. Ivan knew betrayal, and his role in causing it. He spoke without looking up.

"I cannot offer excuses, only details. You of all people know the world in which we move. It is often...complicated."

Maggie nodded her head but continued to frown at Ivan.

"I can only tell you what happened. I got a call. A job, to liberate the Klee. And I was directed to hire you specifically, no one else. Now, that immediately made me suspicious, and concerned. For you of course, but myself too. This was not, uh...normal."

Maggie's frown began to loosen. She leaned in to listen.

"I pushed back. I asked where your name came from, and why that mattered. The man gave me nothing. He just said it again. Hire you to get the painting."

Maggie exploded.

"So, you just gave in? You agreed to set me up for whatever was going on?"

"No, no. Never. I refused. I refused the job outright. Told the man to go away. But he wasn't having that. He began to list...things...he knew about my business. And my past. And my current reality. He was...well-informed. And he indicated that I did not have an option to decline the commission. And then he showed me why."

Maggie began to speak. "Oh Ivan, I..."

"My son does not know me. He is unaware of both my profession and my existence. I watch after him, in my way and have done so for many years but it is only one way. He lives his life but one totally ignorant of me. I will never know him. But that's okay. I made my choices and I had to protect him when I did. That was a pain from long ago that I cannot pull up now. Anyway, this man knew about my son and threatened involving him if I did not go along."

Maggie looked down at the floor.

"But even then, I pushed back. I could not put you at risk. I could not offer you up in his place! You are as much a daughter to me as flesh and blood. He assured me that it was not an attempt to harm you or put you at risk. He was auditioning you for something else."

"Auditioning?"

"He was directed to find out if you could handle the job in question, and that your performance would dictate if they took things further. I protested, arguing that you could not go in fully blind. And the risks. It was unfair. But he assured me that you would never be in danger. You were free to fail, as that was their test, but you would not come to any harm, no matter what happened."

Maggie remembered striking Manheim in the jugular, and the fact that he never actually struck back at her in any way, even when he caught up with her.

"I wanted to tell you. Truly I did. But I had to protect my son. And for the record, I did have backup for you in Russia that they knew nothing of. I trust you enjoyed the ride with young Luka?"

Maggie couldn't stop herself from smiling at the memory. Luka was a plant. She really should have known better. "Who is he?"

"The son of a good friend. He's a good boy. Not professional, but he had instructions to get you where you needed to go and who to call if issues arose."

Maggie pushed to her feet and walked over to a small table, still clutching the blanket around her. The dawn light peeked through the louvered windows.

"So, what now? Did I pass their stupid test? And what makes them think I even want to take their 'big job' anyway? Heck of a way to hire someone. First, they threaten you, make you lie to me, send me on a wild goose chase and then act like I owe them a favour?"

Ivan reached inside his jacket. "Well, they did pay, and this is yours."

Maggie turned from setting up the kettle to boil. Ivan reached out and handed her a large envelope.

"It's more than they promised. $25,000. That's all yours. They were exceptionally pleased with you and the way you handled a situation that was effectively blind. That's where I was when you came in early today. I had to meet with him to get that and the details of what they want next."

"What if I don't want to do anything with them? I can't say I'm a huge fan of how they do business."

Ivan stood up and went to the window, pulling the blinds up and letting the morning sun flood the small room. "You might change your mind when you hear this. Remember that big heist back in the early 90's? At the Gardner in Boston? He has a line on the Vermeer, and he wants you to snatch it."

Maggie stopped and looked at Ivan. "*The Concert*? Really. What does he have?"

"I don't know exactly. He wants to speak to both of us about it. Are you in?"

Maggie breathed in and out, twice, and began shaking her head from side to side.

"You are a troublesome old coot, aren't you? Fine. I'll have a meet-up with what's his name. When do we do this? And what is his name, by the way?"

"10am, at Lowell's. He calls himself Manheim."

37

THE COFFIN was formed in smooth stainless steel and painted the brightest shade of pink imaginable. The interior lining was inviting, faux fur, and done in a luxurious zebra-print style. Tiny LED lights, mounted inside the casket, rotated through an ever-changing series of colors and strobe patterns. Gaudy did not even begin to describe it, though a wealthy pink flamingo might consider it an appropriate final resting place.

"I don't think so."

The thin man with the John Waters mustache nodded sharply and then gestured to his right.

"Now, this one is more rugged and traditional. Cut from recycled old growth timber, lined with a lumberjack cotton and featuring hand-carved, solid birch handles that conform to most natural grips."

"Too Canadian."

Bunny was getting frustrated. Not that she expected coffin shopping to be a blast or anything, but it was going on a little longer than she had expected it to. Who would have thought there could be so many options when it came to selecting your last piece of furniture?

The showroom at Bulger & Sons Mortuary was more expansive than she had expected. There were at least thirty caskets on display in some form or other, not to mention an urn garden with water feature plus a coffee bar located alongside a massive drapery wall. She assumed it was to choose coffin fabrics, perhaps? Something else? Discount car dealers looked subtle next to this kind of blitzkrieg setup. And Franz, the guy helping her, was a real piece of work. He suited the surroundings, presenting more as a didactic fashion designer than some somber mortician.

"Would the 1920's film star package better suit your needs? Very art deco and retro while providing an air of design sophistication. Very Rudolph Valentino."

Bunny stared at the black and white coffin. *Who the hell is Rudolph Valentino?* It was pretty swish, not that Zev would care. Still, the funeral should be well-attended and making it look as flash as possible would do two things. First, it would make it clear how sad she was that he was dead, which was important in case anyone wanted to try and pin his death on her in some way. And second, if anyone of note happened to show up, she would look pretty good presiding over the whole thing. Like it or not, a funeral is a big-deal party and if you do it right you can get a lot of things accomplished, more for the living than the dead.

"I don't mind that one. Can we put it on the list of considerations? I'm still not certain we are going full casket but if we do that one is definitely in the running."

"Of course." Franz checked a box on his iPad before turning back to Bunny.

"Have you chosen a final resting place yet?"

"He wanted Hollywood Forever but I'm still looking into that."

Founded in 1899, Hollywood Forever Cemetery in Los Angeles was the final resting place for hundreds of Hollywood luminaries. Restored impeccably over the years, the cemetery was even listed on the National Register of Historic Places. Add to that, it was one of the only cemeteries in the world with a cultural events program. People visited it like a theme park. They hosted outdoor film screenings, concerts, literature events, lectures, and even live podcast tapings. People did sleepovers in the cemetery. It had even hosted the largest *Dia de Los Muertos* event in the United States. And Zevon was insistent that when he died, he wanted to be buried there.

"It's the best real estate in L.A. Location, location, location," Zevon had said.

Being located on fifty prime acres in the heart of Hollywood certainly proved Zevon right on that count, and if nothing else, Bunny would honor this request. She had to. Besides, his other request would be much harder to pull off. Being buried alongside Bugsy Siegal or

Toto from The Wizard of Oz was not going to be easily accomplished. Bunny figured she'd cross that bridge when she came to it.

"It's wonderful there. I go some weekends just to see the peacocks."

"We'll see. I'm not sure yet. There is just so much to do."

"Of course, of course. Did you still want me to get you that brochure on headstones? It might help with your needs?"

"Sure."

Immediately, Franz turned and zipped away, leaving Bunny alone in the massive space. Bunny looked left and right, before sitting down on a Greek columned bench, located beside a casket display bearing the name *Viva Zapata!*

Bunny had problems. Big problems.

She was on the wrong side of forty and her meal ticket was dead. Zevon wasn't perfect but he was a good provider. The divorce would have been fine. She would have done okay but with him dying it threw everything into chaos. His will had cut her out hard. He was still mad when he re-wrote it. But the bigger problem than that was the debt. He was leveraged in ways she never realized. The last week had been a shit-show of revelations as one accountant after another informed her of how little remained. Zevon had debts everywhere, and a lot of folks were cruising around looking to slice off whatever remained for themselves.

David was supposed to smooth things along on the insurance front. She wouldn't have invested so much time in him otherwise. But then he started getting twitchy. Bunny didn't know what was up, but she had to do something. Hiring Kwan and his other actor friends to scare David in New Mexico seemed to do the trick. It was certainly safer than using a thug like Tranko. He was to blame for the mess she was in anyway. At least a bunch of theatre geeks weren't likely to accidentally hurt someone. She just needed to know if he was keeping anything from her. At this point, it didn't seem like he was. She figured some muscle might loosen him up enough to spill. However, when he didn't offer any information up the peace of mind provided was momentary. It meant he was as blind as she was, and as he wasn't making the insurance dough come any faster, she wondered at even keeping him around. Still, throwing him off balance wasn't all bad.

Bunny flipped her fingers lazily along the *Stairway to Heaven* windchimes displayed next to her. Why did things always have to be so complicated?

Franz returned. "This should provide you with a wonderful cross section of what we have on offer. And please know, I can get you anything. Let this be a guide only. We can accommodate any ideas you may have."

Bunny offered a fake smile. "Thanks."

"Is there a reception being planned?"

Bunny adjusted herself and rose to her feet. "Yes, we've arranged for the rooftop of the Roosevelt Hotel."

Franz was impressed. "An excellent choice! Well, again please know that we can help with rentals of all kinds, from grieving displays, bell ceremonies, candle pyramids, life circles, you name it. Just call me. I'm your personal "Forever After" assistant. And call anytime. I take my work very seriously."

At that, Franz offered his card, an impossibly thin piece of granite, shaped like a headstone and laser-etched with his contact information. Bunny accepted it and headed off.

Exiting to the rear of the facility, Bunny turned and started down the steps to the parking lot, nearly tripping as she dug inside her purse looking for keys.

"You better watch it. Simple accidents can have serious consequences."

Surprised, Bunny looked up and straight into the face of Tranko Lutz.

"You and me. We need to have a few words, Mrs. Levi."

Bunny looked left and right.

"Where's your car? What are you driving?"

Tranko looked her square in the eye. "Well, I just got out of jail, so it looks like you're going to be giving me a ride. Good?"

"Oh yes, Mr. Tranko" answered Bunny as sarcastically as she could. "Why don't you hop right on in?"

38

"I'LL HAVE Joe's Scramble." Maggie ordered at the counter. Ivan had already asked for the crab omelette, a staple of Lowell's. The Seattle institution had been serving the public in one form or other for almost 100 years. In the early 1900's, it was as a combination coffee/peanut roaster and cafeteria called "Manning's." It only became Lowell's in 1957. Maggie glanced back toward the old sign hanging in the main arcade of The Pike Place Market and directing customers inside. She had always liked seeing the little blue neon fish they had swimming across the bottom.

Ivan and Maggie then made their way to the third floor, a literal "seagull's view" of the Port of Seattle. Maggie slid into a seat first, Ivan beside her.

"Where is he?" Maggie asked.

"He'll be here," assured Ivan.

Lowell's was a great place to eat, so long as you got a seat early. Even late morning meant the tourists would start showing up and by then the place was a madhouse. It had been ages since Maggie had been. She only wished she could enjoy it.

Almost immediately, their food and drinks arrived. Maggie took a long pull on her grapefruit & lime Mockito. She absolutely loved real mojitos, but it was just too early for alcohol so the virgin-version would have to do. She scooped a spoonful of eggs and chewed them down. So good! Only then did she realize that she had gone almost twenty-four hours without eating proper, cooked food. Too, too long.

As Maggie took another bite, she gazed out the window toward the Pier 57 Ferris wheel on Miner's Landing. At night, it was lit up and sparkling, but come early morning, it looked a little like a sleepy party-girl that needed a lie-down before it could even consider roaring back to life once more. The owners of the pier had wanted to bring a Ferris wheel to the city back in the eighties, much like the Santa Monica wheel farther down the coast. It never really took off though. Then, sometime around 2013 or 2014 interest was revived and they got it done. At 175 feet high, the Great Wheel of Seattle was now the largest such structure on the West Coast.

Ivan sat up in his seat, gesturing forward, and called out, "Manheim!"

And all Maggie could do was imagine how perfect it would be to drop Manheim from one of the gondolas at its very highest point.

Ivan shuffled from his seat and stood to greet Manheim, but Maggie didn't even raise her eyes. She simply continued to eat. She had no intention of offering pleasantries of any kind.

"Ivan, Ms. Deacon." Manheim spoke, bowed slightly and then offered a crooked smile.

Maggie snuffed in his direction, ate some more food, and took another drink. She was not making things easy.

Taking the snub, Manheim re-adjusted and then seated himself directly across from them.

"Did you order food?" asked Ivan.

"I won't be here long enough. My purpose is clear, yes?"

Ivan nodded his head, deferring to the man. Maggie, however, continued to ignore him.

Manheim continued, "Though it would seem my presence here today is not entirely appreciated?"

Instantly, Maggie turned her blazing blue eyes towards Manheim. It looked like she was about to tear into him, either physically or verbally. But instead of doing either, she simply held her look, locking eyes with him for a moment as she took a sip from her glass. Then, dropping her eyes, she said nothing and simply returned to eating her breakfast.

Catching the non-exchange, and desperate to shift gears, Ivan interjected, "It was an early morning, I'm sure we are all quite tired. Maybe it's best if we discuss details?"

He cast a hopeful look in Maggie's direction. She continued to eat, choosing to ignore him now as well.

Manheim wasn't having it.

"No, I don't think I'll be discussing any details if your "little vixen" isn't even interested. I get that her ego is bruised but I'm the only one who was injured during our exchange the other day. She should be thanking me for how things went."

Hearing that was just too much for Maggie. Instantly, she dropped her fork and knife onto her plate.

"Listen Manheim, or whoever you really are. You're playing games with me. I don't like it when people play games with me. It means I can't trust them and when I can't trust someone, I don't want to have anything to do with them."

Ivan's eyes start to grow. Slowly, he turned toward her, almost pleading. "Maggie?"

Maggie looked toward Ivan and continued, "And don't 'Maggie' me. I'm not done being ticked off at you either." She turned and aimed herself at them both. "You two 'gentlemen' don't seem to have a problem when it's my butt hanging out in the field. You play your little games but I'm the only one putting myself at risk. And you getting injured? Don't make me laugh. I could have killed you if I had decided to hit harder, which I most specifically did not. You came up on me in the middle of an operation. What in the heck did you think was going to happen? I'm a professional and you tried to change the rules mid-game."

Manheim started to stutter at little. "We, we, uh...Well, we had to know..."

"You had to know what? If you could trust me? I was bringing the Klee to you. If you would have given me a real drop, then you would have seen that I can deliver. But you had to get tricky and futz around with things. Why? What was the point? And why would I ever want to work for you again?"

The table was quiet. Ivan had cast his eyes downward and Manheim simply sat silent. Everyone appeared to be taking things in.

Still full of righteous indignation, Maggie pressed her point forward once more.

"Well? Why would I ever want to work for you again?"

As those at the table remained still, only Manheim stiffened slightly. Slowly, he reached into the inside pocket of his jacket and pulled out a single sheet of paper that had been folded in three. Carefully, he opened the 8x11 sheet to its full size, smoothing it down on the table in front of him. Then, turning it over, he pushed it directly towards Maggie.

"Do you know what that is?"

Maggie looked at the paper in front of her. It was a photocopy of Vermeer's *The Concert*.

"It's a Vermeer."

"Yes," said Manheim, "But do you know about it?"

"The Gardner heist? Of course. Ivan said you had a line on it. And that you need me to get it for you. But do you even know where it is? No one else has even seen it for more than thirty years."

"Recently, it has surfaced in Los Angeles. And the circumstances for…ah, retrieving it are slightly complicated. More complicated than simply going and getting it."

"Then what are you asking me for? I'm a straight up grab-artist. I don't do cons."

"Your ability to change direction and adjust is what we need. It's why you were tested the way you were. This is an extremely delicate operation."

Maggie leaned forward on her elbows, almost crossing the table. "The flattery is nice and all but why would I even consider doing this for you?"

Manheim reached forward and pulled the piece of paper back. He refolded it into the same form it had when he pulled it from his jacket. Then, he reached inside the same pocket and removed a pen, with which he proceeded to write on the folded paper. Complete, he then slid it back towards Maggie.

Maggie accepted the paper and looked at what Manheim had written out. $2 million.

Disbelieving, Maggie snapped back. "Are you for real? There has got to be a catch. Nobody pays this much for a simple grab."

"As I said, it's not 'simple,' it has complexities. My employer is willing to pay for the right person. And we believe that person is you."

Maggie looked down at the number on the paper. $2 million. That would fix a lot of problems for her. It would eliminate all her outstanding debts and leave plenty for a solid, real retirement. No more working scrub jobs to make ends meet.

"Can I count you in?" asked Manheim.

"I'm thinking," replied Maggie, as she took a long pull on her Mockito. Maybe she should have asked for alcohol after all.

* * *

As the cab pulled away from the front of her Hunter Street house, Maggie Deacon walked with heavy feet towards her front door. She had only been gone a few days, but somehow it felt like months had passed.

The rain falling around her in that interminable Vancouver way somehow read more comforting than usual. It was good to be home. Stowing her carryon suitcase to the side, out of the rain, Maggie pulled open the screen door and readied her key. Only then did she see the package hidden just inside the outdoor space. It was a parcel, about as big as a large coffee-table book, but not heavy at all. Picking it up, Maggie opened the door and pulled it, along with her suitcase, inside.

The swirl of the day was beginning to recede. The early morning with Ivan, the breakfast with Manheim and the offer. So much going on. She just needed to relax. To get free of the last week.

Standing at her small dining table, Maggie pulled off her wet coat and rubbed her face from the dampness. She looked closer at the package and saw it had a card attached. Opening it, she instantly recognized the handwriting. It was from Fati.

> *Maggie –*
> *Aldo saw this on his travels and told me he thought of you. Asked me to drop it by your house when you came home. It's a little "caveman" for my liking but I know you understand art better than I do. Hope you like! See you soon,*
>
> *Love Fati*

Pulling open the package, Maggie almost collapsed in shock. In her hands, fully framed, was the painting *Death & Fire* by Paul Klee, just like the one she had stolen in Russia.

And now it was in her hands. As a gift. From Aldo.

Maggie took a deep breath. Could things get any more complicated?

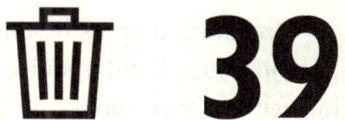

TRANKO RIPPED into the grilled cheese sandwich with his teeth. He was so hungry that he didn't even care about the bits dripping down his face and chin. Bunny Levi, sipping on a vanilla shake, screwed up her face as she watched him.

"You're disgusting."

Tranko ignored her. He was more intent on getting as much food inside him as possible.

Crouched on the cement steps of Hollywood High School, Tranko stuffed his face as Bunny Levi stood nearby staring at him. They were just across the street from the In N' Out burger at Sunset and North Orange.

"How much are you going to eat, anyway?"

Tranko grabbed a handful of fries from the takeout bag, shoving them in his mouth. Then he took a deep pull on his extra-large pink lemonade.

"Until I'm full. Thanks for this, by the way. Appreciated."

Bunny looked annoyed and disinterested. "Whatever." She turned toward the high school itself. "You know Sarah Jessica Parker went here, right?"

"Who?" Tranko quizzed, as he pulled open the greasy wrapper and bit deep into his second grilled cheese.

"*Carrie Bradshaw? Sex and the City?*"

Tranko spoke as he chewed. "What's that? Like a band or something?"

Abject shock registered on Bunny's face. "Seriously, how old are you actually? A hundred?"

Tranko rolled his eyes and continued to eat.

"C'mon. I've got things to do. Tell me what you wanted. And I don't want to see food when you speak."

Breathing deep as he took a final, long drink from the red palm adorned cup, Tranko stifled a burp, paused momentarily to center himself and then spoke.

"I think Zevon had something really big hidden nearby, I think you know about it, and I need to know what it is."

Bunny crossed her arms. "Don't you think I'd know about it if he did? Clearly, he never told me anything about that. If he did, I'd have it by now, hmmm?"

"Maybe you know something about it without realizing it."

"That makes no sense."

Tranko got to his feet, balled up his garbage and pitched it towards a nearby garbage can. He missed the steel bin by two feet.

"Damn. Look, he had to have something. Why'd you hire me to grab all that stuff anyway? You must have thought something in it was worthwhile."

Bunny just looked around at nothing, pursing her lips.

"Well, why did you?"

Bunny faced him dead-on. "If you recall, all I wanted you to do was scare him a bit. Maybe into thinking someone was after him. You guys grabbing all that stuff was supposed to be cover for the thing, duh? It was your idea, lunkhead."

Tranko stopped talking and tried to think.

"So maybe the art? There was something in the art that had value?"

Bunny didn't like Tranko moving in this direction. The last thing she needed was him getting any sense of her potential insurance payout. She needed to move him off that scent.

"Zevon didn't have any taste. He almost always paid lots of money for junk no one else wanted. Trust me, I looked at that "collection" of his plenty. No one wanted any of it."

"But did you see all of it? Was there anything else? Maybe he kept it somewhere else?"

Bunny froze inside. What if Zev did have something of value? Something big? She couldn't let this clod know about it.

"Kept what? Like a secret *Mona Lisa* or something? If Zevon would have had something like that, he would have hung it in the center of the room and made every single person that ever entered the place tromp over and gawk at it. And then he would tell them how expensive it was and how difficult it was to get and blah, blah, blah. He never would have shut up about it."

Tranko dropped himself back down to the steps and rested his arms on his knees. He stared off into nothing, trying to comprehend something he wasn't quite sure even existed. "There's got to be something."

As Bunny totted around on her heels a sinking feeling began to take over. What was Tranko getting at? He must have a hunch about something. What if that idiot Zev had squirrelled away actual precious art? Maybe that's what David was sniffing around for? Maybe David was just lying to cover what he already knew existed?

"You went through all that stuff in the truck, right?"

Tranko was rubbing his head with one hand. "Yeah, we loaded it all into a space on Sunset. Zevon's offices. I didn't see anything that tweaked. It was just movie junk."

"Why were you there? What did you take there?"

"The stuff, all that crap we loaded in the van…"

"To Zev's main office?"

"I needed a place to put it so I could look at it."

Bunny turned her own deep shade of pink and exploded.

"You jackass! You absolute moronic, asshole!" Bunny was stomping her feet she was so mad. Tranko would have laughed if he didn't get the sense something was really, really, wrong.

"What?"

"What? Are you fucking kidding me? What? You don't see this? Mr. "I'm-a-big-time-professional-tough-man" doesn't get it?"

Tranko said nothing. He just raised his French fry-oily hands.

"Ok, stupid. Go with me on this. Guy gets his home broken into and surprises the thieves, who KILL him…"

Tranko winced at the memory.

"…and then they take off only to drop everything they just stole AT THE PRODUCTION OFFICE OF THE MAN THEY JUST KILLED!"

Tranko's eyes go big. "Oh, fuck. Yeah, right…"

"Yeah, right! You idiot."

Tranko got to his feet. "Look Bunny, I'll get the stuff. And get rid of it. Trust me."

"Trust you? You will not. You need to stay the hell away from that place. There is still a police investigation going on. Do not go anywhere near that office, no matter what. What is wrong with you?"

"But..."

"Are you kidding? You're going to argue? I swear to God you are the dumbest sonovabitch I've ever met. You need to get away from me. Just go. GO!"

Bunny knew she needed to get to the production office. There was something in that pile of crap that stupid Lutz took, and she needed to find it first, before Tranko or David figured out what it was.

As Tranko lumbered down the sidewalk Bunny yelled after him.

"Hey! Pick it up!"

Tranko turned and glared at her.

"What?"

"Pick it up. Your garbage, stupid. You threw it at the can before and missed. Pick it up and put it away properly."

Sighing deeply, Tranko Lutz walked back to the crumpled bag lying beside the garbage can. He bent over, snatched it up and dropped it in the can, staring directly at Bunny the whole while he did it.

"Good?" he asked sarcastically.

"Good," answered Bunny, "Just because you're an idiot doesn't mean you get to litter. We're not animals, you know."

Tranko wanted to answer back, badly. But all he could think about was how stupid he was for ever getting involved with the titanic little scrag in the first place. It was his own fault.

Seething, Tranko resisted the urge to pick the entire garbage can up and throw it into traffic just to prove he could. Instead, he turned and walked away, fishing around in his pocket for his cell phone. He needed to get a ride.

As Bunny watched the big man head away, she thought about her next steps. She knew she had a funeral to plan, plus a reception. But that would have to wait. Right now, she needed to drop everything and get her tiny hiney to that production office, pronto.

40

MAGGIE HATED re-organizing the parcel room. It was dark, airless, and there were spiders. She hated spiders. But she had just taken more than a week off and this was always the trade: clean the parcel room. The job itself wasn't bad. It's not like it was all that busy. Parcel counters at department stores were no longer the hub of activity they once were. Online shopping had seen to that. Now, they were mainly the quick option to return something in person, or just a place for the much older to come and feel like things were still the way they always were.

Maggie always knew this job was not going to last. Times were changing. She swept the dust off the top shelf, rubbed a damp rag across it and then began putting the alphabetized parcels back in place.

The offer from Manheim stuck in her brain. She couldn't agree to work for that jerk, but she also couldn't exactly agree to passing on a $2 million payday. That kind of money could ensure a comfortable future, versus an unsure one. Yes, she had her father's house, and selling that would probably get her enough to live on, but she would still have to buy another place or rent. And in Vancouver that wasn't going to be easy. Prices were insane and rising all the time. The money would make things much easier.

But could she trust him? Not likely. He had already worked her over with this job, though she did get paid. Her cash position was healthier than it had been in ages. Maggie placed the last of the "c's" on the top shelf.

And then there was the painting. The Klee. It was the exact one she stole in Russia, that much was clear. And now it was a gift from Aldo. Did Aldo know Manheim? Did he buy it from him? Was it a forgery all along? If it was the original it could be worth serious coin, meaning her worries about taking Manheim's offer were a waste of time. She could sell the stupid Klee as is and maybe get enough cash to walk on any job for good.

Maggie bent over and moved the step stool to the far end of the shelf, stepping up and starting to remove as many parcels as she could from the "d" to "g" area, careful to keep them in order.

Her mind drifted back to her years in Europe, her 20s and 30s. The excitement, the events, the lifestyle. It seemed like a million miles, and years, away. She liked the life. It was fun and she hated to leave it. But she had to. It sort of killed her father, and it likely would have killed her too.

But she had never learned how to do anything else. Not that she wanted to. But where in the real world do the skills of a cat burglar fit? Certainly not in legal areas. No, her life became a series of blue-collar, low-to-no skill jobs and barely making ends meet, especially once her father died. She never begrudged spending the money on trying to help him. He fought her on it. He told her to let him go often, but there was no way she was going to do that. How could she ever live knowing they had had the money to try and help him but had chosen not to. No, that regret was non-existent, but the day-to-day frustrations of not having a safety net underneath was tough.

She could say "yes" to Manheim.

But he was a bastard. She knew she couldn't trust him. Ivan too had become suspect. Not totally, but he was compromised for her. He would have to be involved, of course. Could she trust him? She had to. He wouldn't double cross her again, would he? That nasty old bag working with him certainly would. Maggie was conflicted.

So, what if she said "yes?"

She could lay her must haves on Manheim: a percent of the money up front, or expenses at least. Ensure she had a safety net around her as best as possible. It would be fun to do a real job. Not something like Ivan's last few, little snatch and grabs that relied on outside planning. This would be her own job. Something she controlled and set up herself. That would be exciting. More exciting than this.

Maggie coughed as some dust got caught in the fan and clumped in her face.

"Maggie?"

It was Grace. Her supervisor.

"Yeah Gracie."

"Can we talk?"

"Of course."

Maggie put down the cleaning rags and faced Grace. Grace was about ten years older. She was tough as nails but a sweetheart, at least to her. She had worked the catalog counter for almost thirty years. Raised two kids and survived a husband. She could be specific, and a little dictatorial, but it was her castle. She had earned that.

"Maggie – I....we have to start adjusting shifts and it's just...."

Maggie could see she was having trouble getting out what she had to say.

"It's okay Gracie, just say it."

"They're cutting us back. All of us. I mean, I'm not surprised. The counter has been a dead zone for a few years now but I thought we'd get a little....longer."

Maggie breathed in.

"What does it look like?"

"9am to 5pm is becoming 11am to 3pm...and they want me to cut hours and lay people off. Eventually me too." Grace started to cry.

"Hey...don't."

Grace turned away and rubbed her eyes. Maggie sort of stood, not really knowing what to do. Eventually she moved forward and put her arm around Grace, hugging her.

Composing herself, Grace sniffled.

"I'm sorry. I shouldn't. It's not professional."

"You didn't do anything. Nobody did really. Things change, I guess."

Gracie nodded. "I'm going to try to keep you on the schedule as much as I can. I want to try and let all you girls share as many of whatever shifts we have left. I just..."

"Hey, Gracie. I know you'll do your best. Look at me. I just hit you with a mini vacation. I can't complain about anything."

"Oh you." Grace smiled as she swiped at Maggie.

"I was going to ask for fewer hours anyway. Maybe it's time I took up some more leisure activities. That should make it easier for you."

"You're just saying that."

Maggie smiled.

"Let me get this parcel room ship-shape for you, and then we can go over the schedule. It'll work out as best it can."

Gracie reached over and hugged Maggie. She looked like she was about to say something, but she appeared to change her mind, and kept quiet. She exited the parcel room. Maggie turned back to her work and took a deep breath. *Guess that's another point in favor of taking the Manheim deal. And what if that Klee is real after all?*

41

BUNNY'S REAR END bounced up and down as she struggled inside the impromptu storage area of the production office. Her grunts were as numerous as they were distracting. She was getting more agitated the more she struggled. She screamed at no one in particular.

"Uhhhh ghunah! Are you fucking kidding me? Hello? Can I get some help? Jody!"

Bunny was caught between several pieces of furniture, two pedestals and several plywood sheets. Realizing she could have been more deliberate in how she pulled things out stung a little, but she didn't know what she wanted to see before she started trying to decide what to see. She yelled again.

"Jody! Jody! Help me now!"

Jody Bone came swinging around the corner, sporting an exaggerated look of frustration on her face.

"Mrs. Levi, I said I'd help. You just needed to wait a second. I was taking calls."

"I didn't want to wait. Can you pull that thing off my shoulder and prop it up? I just want to pull this out."

Jody stepped into the chaos and propped the offending piece of flotsam along her back, all while helping to support some other pieces threatening to box Bunny's efforts in further. No matter. Bunny was relentless about digging forward.

"I can see this goddamn box holds something but I can't....get....it....free...THERE!"

Suddenly, the large, plywood box gave way and slid about a half foot, just enough for Bunny to regain her somewhat less tenuous footing and relax. Finally able to right herself, Bunny adjusted her chest, brushed hair from her face and tugged her skirt back down.

"Good. Perfect. Now help me drag it out."

Jody and Bunny leaned into the 5ft high crate and slid it out from the assembled mess it was contained within. Now in the open, Bunny turned to Jody.

"I need to open it somehow. Do you have one of those pokey things? Like a hitter?"

"A hammer?"

"Sure, get that."

Jody headed back down the hallway in search of a tool while Bunny surveyed her collection so far. One sculpture of a naked man with an oversized ass, two paintings, one of a flowerpot on a table, the other of some guy staring at the wall with a guitar on the floor behind him, one heavy, overly designed Persian rug or something and the current box of who-knows-what-it-was she had just hauled out.

Tired and perspiring, Bunny spoke out loud, and to no one in particular. "I swear to God, I cannot imagine ANY of these things has value."

Still, she knew she had to try. Something was going on and it had to have something to do with the stuff taken during the robbery. At the very least she had to figure out what it was before someone else did. Like that lunkhead Tranko. Or horny David.

Jody returned with a tiny desk hammer.

Bunny screwed up her face. "That's not very big."

"I keep it in my desk. To bang in picture hooks."

"It's smaller than my hairbrush."

"It's all I've got Mrs. Levi."

Sighing, Bunny rolled her eyes in a manner that said 'whatever' before stepping to one side and trying to physically mime how she planned to open the box she had just dragged clear.

"How would I do this? Maybe hit it here or something?"

Now it was Jody's turn to screw up her face. She wasn't a huge fan of Bunny Levi, but she was the boss' wife, and her having a soft spot for him meant she also had a tiny soft spot for her.

"I could try to pry the top open. Maybe that will show us something?"

Shrugging her shoulders, Bunny seemed to agree with the idea, so Jody stepped forward and attempted to pry the wood cap open from one end. Eventually, the piece started to lift, allowing Jody to remove the small claw and use the hammer end to begin pounding the nails out of the way. This provided more leverage to push against the top cap.

Finally, the efforts of the two women resulted in the 4ft wood cap popping of the plywood casing. Both peered inside.

"I can't really see anything," said Jody.

"I can't either. Maybe we need to lift it up, sort of pull it out? I just want a quick look at it."

"If we grab on each side, we can slide it up."

The two stood at either end, together lifting the contents inside as best they could. There was what appeared to be a burlap rag covering part of the piece, but it slid away as the painting finally came free of its case. It was heavy but they grunted and fought and eventually pulled it out enough to clear the edge of the crate. The ladies placed it back on the ground once more, leaning it against the box it came in.

Jody just stared.

"What is it? Is it valuable?"

Bunny cocked her head to one side and then the other.

"I don't know. I mean, it's looks like something, right?"

Jody was unsure but answered anyway. "Sure. It could be something. Like art-art."

The two women stood motionless in front of the painting, trying to discern the importance and value of a painting that depicted an old-timey group of men being tossed about the ocean in a boat.

Jody broke the silence first.

"It looks famous to me. Like, how a famous painting would look."

"You think?"

"I could Google image search it if you want."

At this, Bunny stopped. If it was valuable, she certainly didn't need anyone else confirming it, especially some nudnik from Zev's stupid production office. Better to get it out of here first.

"I think I'll just get this stuff back to the house. Then I can have our insurance guy look at everything. That would be best."

Jody looked around at the remaining pile of goods.

"Are you going to be able to carry all this? It's kind of odd-sized…"

"Yeah, it'll be fine. Are there any guys hanging around we can get to load it up though? That'd be easier."

* * *

Watching Bunny's tiny Fiat pull away from the building on Sunset was almost comical. Packed floor to ceiling, with items poking out here and there, Bunny's car looked like a cartoon. Between the rug hanging out the open passenger window, the naked man sculpture leaning beside her in the front passenger seat (with the large ass rubbing her hand as she shifted gears), and the three paintings half in and out of the rear hatchback and strapped to the headrests inside, Bunny's car looked ridiculous. But it fit, and Bunny Levi was headed somewhere to tease out what her efforts had recovered. But where? Taking them back to the Malibu place would be crazy, right?

As Bunny's car drove down the strip another car, parked farther back and slightly away, took notice of her departure. The driver smiled, shaking his head from side to side before starting his engine, pulling out from his spot, and following along after her. David Teck smirked as he watched Bunny and her carload of goodies, bouncing along down the street. Things were starting to get very interesting.

42

TRANKO RODE shotgun in the F150. They were headed to Stewie's mom's place.

"Why are we going to the valley?"

"I gotta take something to my mom."

Tranko asked, but he didn't care. He mainly needed some mental breathing room. He had to get a sense of where to go from here.

Tranko's thoughts didn't get much time to roam before his phone started buzzing. Looking at the display confirmed it was the Russians. Sighing, Tranko debated whether to answer it or not. But he wasn't a chickenshit. Rip the band-aid off was more his style anyway, so he flipped the phone open.

"Yeah?"

"Your little stunt bought you alone time. Did you do anything productive with it?"

Tranko closed his eyes and gripped the door handle like he might squeeze juice from it. *Edward Dachshund? No, I wasn't gonna forget about you.*

He swallowed hard and answered. "Yeah, maybe. I'm thinking that the ex-wife knows something. I can't figure what yet but I'm getting closer."

"Get the answers quickly. I'm not inclined towards patience. We had a deal."

Tranko's face registered serious frustration. "Well, if the deal was that I give you help and your hired ass-clowns get to slap me around then there was no deal, right? I don't put up with shit like that. So, I'm thinking we really didn't have a deal."

Silence from the other end of the phone. Tranko wanted to speak, if only to check if they had been cut off. He resisted the urge.

Finally, Dachshund responded.

"Your tough talk is expected but sort of wasted, no? You know the kind of man I am, and you know that stepping sideways on me will not go well for you. I don't do threats. So, deal or not, you know what I want, and you know what waits for you if you don't provide it. And do I really have to remind you that it's also more lucrative for you to help me?"

Tranko weighed his options. *What waits for me? I know full well what waits for me.*

"You have my number. When you know more, use it."

And with that, Dachshund's phone call clicked off.

Tranko took a deep breath and started drumming his fingers on his knees.

"Stewie, how long is this gonna take?"

"Not too long. I just told my mom I'd bring her new rocker by today. I've already blown it a few times. I can't break any more promises to her."

"Rocker?"

"Rocking chair. A glider-kind. Not old school. The kind that, sort of rocks without going up and down. More back and forth, but smooth."

"Whatever."

"Like a porch swing, but inside…and in just a single chair."

"Ok, whatever."

Silence ruled as the truck flew down the freeway. Tranko stared back out the window. He was thinking about the first day. When they were supposed to "scare" Levi. He was trying to remember the stuff they had decided to haul out.

"Stewie, what did you see when we were at Levi's place? What did you load out?"

"I don't know. Stuff. Some fancy things. Like paintings, art things. I think we grabbed a giant TV too. In a box. Mainly stuff from the garage and a bedroom."

"But how did we decide what to grab? Why did you take certain things over other things?"

"'Cause you said so."

"What do you mean?"

"On the way over you told us "We're going in the front door, make a ton of noise, lots of yelling and threats and then once the guy is secured, we should take some stuff.""

Tranko nodded but remained frustrated. "I know that part. But what did I tell you to take? Like, specifically?"

"Well, you didn't say specific stuff, Trank."

"I know I didn't. So, what did I say?"

"You said, 'get the fancy stuff' and 'look in that door off the kitchen.'"

Tranko nodded, "I did say that didn't I?"

Stewie continued, "Yeah, so I went in that door and there was stuff piled all over in boxes, but I started looking for things that seemed expensive or important kind of."

"What was in there? That room, I mean?"

"Garage. It was a hallway from the kitchen into the four-car garage. No cars though. Just full of stuff. Like art and statues and fancy furniture and shit."

"Did you see anything…big?"

Stewie looked confused. "Like huge?"

Tranko rolls his eyes. "No, no. Like a big deal. Important. Something that looked like…something important would look."

Stewie screwed up his face like he was really trying to cast his mind back. Then he shook his head from side to side.

"I don't know, Trank. Who can tell on that stuff? One picture looks like any other but 'cause some smart folks say it's like famous or something then it's a million bucks. I don't even really know what a million-dollar painting is. I mean, If I had that kinda money I sure as hell wouldn't buy some painting with it. There was a friggen awesome couch though. It wrapped around kind of, like if you were sitting on one side and a chick was sitting on the other, you'd be looking different ways but if you turned around, you'd be right beside each other and…"

"The couch don't matter, Stewie. Somewhere, in that mess, I'm thinking, is an expensive painting."

"Yeah? Wow."

"Yeah. Wow," answered Tranko.

"What would you do with a million bucks, Trank?"

Tranko looked over at Stewie and smirked. He turned back, not willing to answer. So Stewie offered his own thoughts up in place.

"I know what I'd do. I'd hire Kid Rock to do a private show at my old high school for everyone I ever went to school with, even the assholes. And we'd have a massive party with food and free booze and free weed for everyone."

Tranko began to laugh. "You're kidding."

"Why would I be kidding? That'd be so fuckin' cool. Total throwback shit. People be all 'wow, dude, you know Kid Rock? And I'd be like 'yeah, no big deal.' That'd be awesome."

Stewie's smile grew as he imagined the scene he had just created inside his head.

Tranko looked at him. "And if you had some money left over what about that?"

Stewie stopped and looked thoughtful for a moment before answering. "Municipal bonds. You can get some serious returns on municipal bonds."

"Municipal bonds?" said a shocked Tranko.

"They're a great way to preserve capital while generating interest. They're tax advantaged, have a way lower rate of default. Plus, they're liquid as fuck."

Tranko looked at Stewie like he was an alien. Stewie caught the look and protested.

"What? I'm not supposed to know things?"

Tranko shook his head and turned back towards the passenger window. Bunny Levi told him to focus on that garage. She had to have a reason for that. Tranko knew she was holding back on something, and it was time find out what that was before it got him killed.

43

MAGGIE STARED deep in the painting. She focused hard on the visible word *Tod*, German for death. She repeated the picture's title out loud, almost mantra-like, to herself as she held the painting in two hands, leaning at her worktable. "Death and fire, death and fire...." Maggie liked puzzles but she wasn't crazy about potential secret messages being sent with "gifts."

Sequestered deep inside her secure basement room, Maggie had been prepping for the LA job, deciding what she needed to take and sketching out basic plans. But she had been distracted by the Klee finding its way back to her. It was the same, and real no doubt. She absolutely considered selling it, but profiting would be somewhat tricky to say the least. Certainly, Ivan could move it for some money, though a fraction of its value. But who cared? It didn't mean anything to her specifically. And maybe if she could move it along then she could avoid even getting involved with Aldo and Manheim again. That was an upside, for sure. But in all her years, and her father's as well, Maggie had never kept a piece for herself. It was a very minimalist approach to the "ethics" of stealing things in the first place, but it meant something to her. And she didn't want to break practice on something like that.

But Fati complicated things.

While her instincts told her to steer far clear of this entire gig, Maggie couldn't ignore the reality of Fati's involvement with Aldo. And an escalating, ever-more serious involvement at that. She had fallen for this man. And while love can always be separate from the harsher realities of life, the world that Aldo certainly appeared to travel in would not be hospitable to Fati.

But who was Maggie to decide that? Fatima was a grown woman. It wasn't Maggie's place to decide what was or was not right for her.

She stared at the painting until she could take no more. Sighing, Maggie placed the compact piece to the side, purposely sliding it away from her. She would come to a decision on it eventually, but for now it would have to wait.

She was going to do the job for Aldo but not because she trusted him or wanted to work with them. It was mainly because it might give her a sense of what was really going on. Plus, there was the matter of the original encounter in Aldo's penthouse and the fake-out on-board his yacht. He was playing with her, and as much as that drove her personally insane, it was also quite exhilarating. She hadn't felt this electrified in years. But Fati.

Maggie moved over to one of the shelves and searched around for something. She couldn't shake the notion that Fatima had been targeted by Aldo solely to get to her and, love or not, as far as Fati was concerned that just wasn't fair. If Aldo really did target Fatima as a way to get to Maggie, he needed to be stopped. Hard.

The only problem was she didn't know how she was going to do that. She also didn't know how she was going to steal the painting, either. Fati needed some level of protection before she got in too deep.

Taking a couple of bins down from a shelf, Maggie rummaged through them looking for two very specific items. One was a magnetic tape measure while the other was a small bottle of lighter fluid. She found one, but not the other…yet.

Maggie knew why she never told Fati, or anyone else, about her past "career." First off because it was safer, especially with regards to the compromising position such knowledge would put them in. But mainly it was because most normals already had trouble with "free thinking" about anything.

People watched movies and talked tough but when push came to shove, they conduct themselves in highly controlled and very careful accordance with perceived rules and accepted norms. And that meant when introducing something legitimately illegal, they either got squirrely as heck or over-compensated by pretending they were Al Capone or something. It wasn't a surprise really, but years of learning from her father and seeing her own realities come to pass had taught Maggie just how much people could handle. And the answer was not very much at all. Maggie guffawed to herself. There was a reason pharmaceutical companies sold even more drugs than street dealers did. People seek numbness over knowledge.

Maggie pulled out a couple of climbing harnesses and began to check them for wear and tear. Pulling at buckles, studying them, deciding on their suitability. Readying for a job wasn't so much about planning every little thing so much as prepping for a myriad of eventualities with the goal carrying the least amount of gear or unnecessary add-ons.

And the LA job was not an easy one.

Complicated by the fact that they didn't even know where in the city the physical painting was currently located, she would be truly flying blind. Sure, Manheim seemed confident that they would have more info once she was on-site, but it still presented a difficult set of circumstances.

One of the first things Maggie had done was start ruling out the kind of places it was not likely to be. Locations like museums, art galleries, or any sort of professional entity dedicated to showing such things were obviously off the table. This was as underground as stolen art got, and it had been missing for decades. That meant if it moved at all it would be floating around in very secret or anonymous areas. And that meant places like private mansions, storage lockers, or even being "on the move," as in trucks, vans or even boats as stronger possibilities.

It also made physical theft easier, even as the trick of finding it would be increased dramatically. Maggie approved both harnesses for use and placed them in a specific spot on the floor, arrayed with other items and tools already chosen. She stood above the assembly and surveyed her collection so far: Two harnesses, two thin ropes, coyote spray, finger ring knife, black clothes, oversized clothes (for shedding), two masks, duplicate IDs, fake IDs, fake business cards, mini blackjack, two slim knives, lighter, fluid, light, sunglasses with reinforced lenses, bodysuit with panels, fold-out backpack plus a handful of steel marbles. She needed a few more things but her kit was looking tight already. Maybe she could bring *Lola* along after all?

Crossing borders wasn't that hard. Air travel was of course trickier. Most stuff got checked, but so long as it was disassembled in the right way, nothing would even tweak security. You just had to place the right parts alongside whatever complimented the narrative you want security to buy best. Create a story that the guy running the security scan can complete in his own head and the camouflage job is done before you even get there.

Maggie looked at the old clock on the workbench. Almost 6:30pm. She was supposed to meet Fati for drinks at her house. She didn't want to go. What was she going to say? You couldn't tell your best friend she was making a mistake, even if she was. She wanted to avoid the discussion altogether.

To the job. Focus on the job, Maggie reminded herself.

She had needed a cover story for the trip itself. The potential to be in LA for longer than a day or two complicated things slightly, but an extra-long weekend planned around an appropriately "normal" gathering limited uncomfortable questions and greased the wheels to keep things moving forward. She glanced to her left at the online printout from the *Crochet Guild of USA* and the details surrounding their first ever California convention. It bugged her that she was having to resort to such obviously "senior" cover stories, mainly so that it instantly bored whoever might choose to look a little deeper. She had come a long way from the weekends at *Studio 54* and similar, that was for sure. Beyond that, her surface cover was basically complete.

Maggie had specified a certain amount of money up front from Manheim to cover the expenses of setting up in LA and getting herself ready. He balked at first, wanting to arrange things himself, but Maggie wouldn't hear of it. The necessity of paying your own way whenever possible was critical in when it came to covering one's own butt. Always set your own terms. And get a hotel room. She smiled at hearing her father's words inside her own head.

Glancing at the clock, Maggie took a deep breath. She had just enough time to get upstairs and clean up before heading over to Fati's. She was in no hurry though. She had absolutely no idea what she was going to say.

44

BUNNY STOOD at one end of the expansive living room, hand on hip, surveying the assembled items of "art." Three paintings, two medium-sized sculptures, one larger (the big-assed man) and a box of smaller items plus a wide, Persian-looking rug now unrolled and laid out across the space. Still sweating from her efforts lugging the contents of the Fiat into the Malibu house, Bunny dabbed at her brow with paper towel. She hadn't done heavy lifting like this in ages, at least outside of a gym. Looking around for her water bottle, Bunny grabbed it, popped the cap, and took a generous drink. Her mind schemed. There had to be something here. She just knew it.

Walking ever so slowly back and forth, Bunny attempted to intuit just which of the items arrayed before her were of significant value and which were not. She had absolutely no idea what was truly quality, but knew it was critical to figure that out. She couldn't trust anyone, but she also didn't really have a way to tell for herself either. Obviously, she could look things up on Google but what did that do? So, what if the item seemed valuable? How did you even know that the item you're looking at was the actual item pictured? Bunny kept pacing, trying to think of what to do. Her head hurt, a lot. Why did things like this have to happen to her?

Her head was a minefield of problems and issues to be dealt with. She had the upcoming funeral, the arrival of her kids (always tricky) and then the actual reading of the will. How was she supposed to figure things out without help? Bunny stared at the items in front of her, but her vision was indistinct. She was lost inside her head, until a voice from behind shook her back to reality.

"That's quite a collection, Mrs. Levi. Were you wanting insurance on each of the pieces individually, or would you prefer grouped coverage?

Bunny turned and there was David, leaning against the front entryway with his arms crossed. As ticked off as she was at him sneaking in on her, he was probably the one guy who could do something to help at this point. She still couldn't trust him, but she would have to make do with what was available. And Bunny knew she was good at that.

"Well, Mr. Big Shot? Why don't you tell me what I have here?"

Slowly, David moved towards Bunny, talking away as he crossed the room toward the collection of assembled "items of note."

"My professional, cultured opinion, I assume, is what you need, yes? Because suddenly I am valuable enough to be…trusted?" David smirked as he made his comments.

"Don't be an asshole, David. You know I need your help."

David stopped, seemingly preparing to yell something out, but held it in and twitched his head from side to side instead, appearing to mentally will an explosive burst of anger away. His eyes, however, blazed as the next stream of words come out.

"Help…you? Yes, help you. Like the help I got after my little gang threat the other day? What exactly did you do to help me then? You sort of laughed it off, making me think that perhaps you had something to do with it. I haven't ruled that out at all."

Bunny held his gaze tight, betraying nothing.

"But I can't prove it. At least not yet. And then there's the reality of the already messy business you wanted MY HELP with in the first place that now, for some reason, includes a dead husband. Again, I'm not entirely convinced you didn't have a hand in causing that either. But still, I'm supposed to help you?"

Bunny shook her head and found a chair to sit down. Looking bored, she unscrewed the cap on her water bottle and took a small sip before speaking.

"David, you've benefited personally from our little get togethers and you will also benefit from the plan we originally set up. Yes, things have changed somewhat but that's how it goes. That bunch of stuff over there is a big chunk of what those goons took from the house on "the day." Now, you can focus on things that have zero importance, or you can do what you claim to know how to do, which is tell me whether anything over there is valuable or not."

Chastened, but only slightly, David kept his head high as he directed his gaze toward the assembled items. Walking closer he stopped and peered intently. He touched some items while seeming to carefully inspect others. He studied the images in the paintings and touched the surfaces of the sculptures. He poked around in the box of smaller items, fishing things out, studying and then replacing them. Through it all, his face betrayed no indication of what he was thinking or seeing. It could have been gold bars, or it could have been literal feces. Bunny could discern neither from his mannerisms. Finally, David returned to her vicinity and plopped down on a nearby stool.

"Well?" prodded Bunny.

"Those," said David, pointing at the sculptures, "are cheap copies of nothing at all. They aren't even trying to be famous anythings. Just sculpture for the sake of shape. Furniture store nothings."

"How do you know they're cheap?"

David frowned at being challenged. "Really? Well, first because I know a lot about things you have no idea about, but also because you could physically lift them. You hauled all that stuff into this room. Had those been actual sculptures versus throwaway tchotchkes made for taste-challenged housewives there would be no way in hell you could even move them. That, and they were clearly not hand-made or carved in any way. Injection-mold dreck if you ask me."

Bunny was annoyed. "So, it's all junk?"

"The rug is nice. Probably worth a couple grand or so new, but certainly nothing fancy. The paintings, however, now there's a different story."

Bunny's demeanour instantly changed. She felt an excitement rising in her. "Really? Tell me."

David looked surprised. "Don't tell me you don't recognize those images? I mean, I thought that's why you dragged them in here in the first place. Most high school students learn about those even if they aren't paying attention. Other than the *Mona Lisa* they're some of the most universally famous paintings in the world."

"No!" yelled Bunny.

"Yes." Intoned David, looking at Bunny, slightly confused by her excitement. Lazily, he leaned back a little and pointed with his index finger.

"That is a painting of *Storm on the Sea of Galilee* by Rembrandt, that is a painting of *Still Life Vase with Twelve Sunflowers* by Vincent van Gogh, and that is a painting of *The Concert* by Johannes Vermeer. All famous and mostly all missing.

Bunny looked at David expectantly. "And…..what are they worth?"

David screwed his face up and flipped his hands around. "Hard to say, really. The market for high-quality, display copies is not that established. It's more about how much someone wants it and what someone is willing to pay if they…"

Bunny broke in. "What did you say? Copies? I thought you said they were famous?"

David stood up. "Well, they are. Really good copies of very famous paintings."

"You said they were by Rembrandt and, and van Gogh and…"

"No, I said they were 'paintings OF such and such by so and so.' That's totally different. Good God, you didn't think you had the real works of art, did you?" A mocking smile crept across David's face.

"Why not, I mean… I don't know what Zevon spent his money on…"

David couldn't believe his ears. "Bunny, the originals of these are either in museums or missing. The sunflower one is in Germany, at least last I heard. A version of it, the fifth I think, sold for $50 million but that was years ago. The storm picture and the concert one had both been stolen way back in the 90's and haven't been seen since. *The Concert* alone is worth more than $350 million. No way your husband had this kind of art 'sitting around.' You can't be serious that you thought you had nearly $400+ million of art in your living room?"

"I didn't know what I had, jerk. That's why I asked you. Besides, you said two of them were missing. Maybe those are them, and no one has found them until now." Bunny stuck out her tongue at David.

David started to laugh. "Sure, that's what happened. International manhunts for years, all searching for the missing masters but no, here they were all along, hiding out in some D-list movie producer's beach house the whole time. Zevon Levi, international art aggregator. It's ridiculous on its face."

Bunny stormed into the kitchen to refill her now empty water bottle, all the while seething at David's mockery of her. How did she ever let herself be attracted to him? Admittedly, she was using him, but she still liked him a little bit. Suddenly, Bunny had a serious thought.

"What if you're lying?" She turned on David, looking right at him.

David turned and looked at her. "Huh?"

Bunny continued, "What if you're lying? You could tell me anything. I'd believe you, Mr. fancy art guy. But you lie to me, tell me they're worthless and then take them or sell them yourself..."

Now it was David's turn to roll his eyes. "C'mon Bunny. Don't be dumb."

Bunny walked towards him. "It's not dumb. You make me think I have nothing here and then you offer to get them "tested" or "checked" and then I never see them, or you, again. Those stupid paintings could very well be all the cash I get outta this stupid marriage and I'm not letting some snake oil creep screw me out of my rightful share."

David shook his head. "I'm not lying to you, Bunny. In fact, I've spent the last few days chasing something down. Seeing all this, it makes quite a bit of sense now as to why your husband even had those around. I found out that..."

"Found what?" A loud, powerful voice cut David off mid-sentence. Both he and Bunny looked towards the open patio area to the rear of the house, hunting the voice.

There, standing just outside the nano-door perimeter, was Tranko Lutz, looking very large and very threatening. He was also pointing a very big gun directly at the pair. Neither one offered up an answer.

Tranko spoke again. "I said, 'found what?'"

45

FATI HAD PREPPED for Maggie's arrival. She had the sandwiches cut her favorite way, funeral style, which meant in fours. She had the teal teapot that Maggie always liked plus round sugar cubes, just to be silly, even though Maggie never took sweet in her tea. It had been too long since they had shared a tea together and Fatima was excited. Focused on her fussing, she begged Maggie to excuse her.

"Oh! I almost forgot the most important part. Almond Roca!" Fati stood up and headed away from the pool deck to reclaim the missing treat.

Maggie smiled. She loved Fati. She was everything a friend should be. Sincere, caring, fun to be with, and a genuine good person. Maggie knew that she wasn't as good a person as Fati was and it bothered her. She didn't like lying to her about her background, but she really didn't have a choice. Besides, it wasn't exactly lying when you just never brought it up. She never had to. Who would even think to ask a question like that in the first place? Fatima retuned with a Costco-sized bucket of foil-wrapped Almond Roca treats.

"I was going to put them in a pretty little bowl, but you know I can't stop once I start eating them so we may as well keep the whole bin nearby."

Fatima sat down again at their shared table. Immediately, she began pouring the tea and trying to decide which two sandwich cuts to start with. "Do I want the cucumber or the smushed ham? Or the egg salad? Hmmmm?"

Maggie took her tea, added a spot of milk, and stirred it, just before breathing in the warm scent. The aroma was so nice. It reminded her of cold mornings and toasty insides. She took a tiny sip and felt the heat fill her up.

Fatima was excited to begin chatting.

"I know it's only been a week or so, but it feels like ages. So much has happened. You did your big trip to Minsk, I did the little mini cruise. Say, I didn't even ask, did you like the picture from Aldo? He was so insistent that I give it to you. He said he saw it in a little shop and just immediately thought of you. Isn't that so nice? I know he's buttering you up for me, but I still appreciate it. Oh my God, we haven't even really talked since dinner on his yacht. What do you really think about him, Mags? He's a handful, I know, but he's just such a dream at the same time, no? I'm such a motormouth. Can you tell how excited I am? It's just been too long since we did this."

This was what Maggie was dreading. The conversation was going in the direction she knew it would. She couldn't lie to Fati, but she couldn't tell her the truth either. Heck, she didn't even really know the truth. At least not yet. So, instead of engaging she weaved.

"The painting was a sweet gesture. I appreciated it. Where did you eventually cruise with him anyway?

Fati leaned back in her chair with a broad smile and opened her arms and hands wide.

"Oh Maggie, it was so much fun. We sailed up the Sunshine Coast first for a few days before cutting out to sea and heading back down. We stopped off in Oregon for a little bit and then in San Francisco for one night, LA for two. I got to see Elton John in concert! With that crazy piano of his! This was before Aldo had to leave for overseas work."

"What did you do once he left?"

"I stayed on board for another day before my flight home. It was so much fun. His boat was going to continue down to the Panama Canal and cut through. He said they would be moving it to the Caribbean for the next season. But he might send it all the way to Casablanca and then in towards the Mediterranean. Isn't that exciting? Casablanca. Doesn't that sound incredible?"

Maggie smiled. "It does, Fati. It sounds wonderful."

"I wish you could have come. How was your trip? You always pick such exotic places. I mean, Belarus? I just can't imagine. Who goes to Belarus?"

Now, that was a loaded question for sure, but one Maggie was more than ready to deflect. Obviously, her actual stories of climbing in and out of windows, stealing art, fighting on trains, and driving a bread bus through the Russian countryside with a wannabe rock star would not do. She would have to offer the "sanitized version" instead.

"It was quite fun. Independence Square in Minsk was incredible. The old art and sculpture really knocks you down when you see it. I traveled the countryside a bit, you know me. I like to live as a local, sort of. Not really one for tourist spots per se. I stop here and there and try to see what life is like. This is weird though. Believe it or not, I saw Lee Harvey Oswald's place."

"Lee Harvey who?" Fatima was totally confused.

"Oswald. He shot John F. Kennedy? Well, the one they *say* shot Kennedy. He supposedly lived there for a couple years. I came across it by accident. I had this cab driver who loved to talk and when he found out I spoke English he decided to practice. From there on in, he wouldn't shut up. He jabbered constantly. And somewhere inside the waterfall of words he started going on about Lee Harvey Oswald living in Minsk back in the day."

"You saw him?" Fati asked, eyes wide.

Maggie laughed. "No Fati. He's long dead. Jack Ruby killed him before he even went to trial. Anyway, it's not exactly a tourist attraction. It's a private residence and not open to the public, but you can supposedly see his apartment from the outside. I would never have known but taxi man was all over showing it to me. He even made me get out of the car so he could point out the exact unit he lived in and get a picture. Here, look."

Maggie was proud to show off the pic because everything she had just told Fati had indeed happened. There really was a cab driver who wouldn't shut up and he really did insist on taking her to Lee Harvey Oswald's apartment. It was nice not to have to lie.

Fati looked at the pic on Maggie's cell phone. She appeared to study the apartment intently, like she was looking for something.

"I don't think you're going to actually see him," teased Maggie.

'Oh," said Fati, looking a little sheepish.

Fati handed the phone back. "You always do such interesting things. And you know so much. I don't know anything about anything. I'm such a fool."

Maggie waved her hand. "Oh, you. You're not a fool."

"Oh yes, I am. I am so completely sheltered and dopey. You know I am. You've seen the world. I know I'm the one who had the rich family and all the fancy education and trips and such, but you understand so much more. It's sort of like I read the brochure of life while you went and lived the book, or something like that."

Maggie teased Fatima. "Dopey? Really?"

Fatima cocked her head to one side and held up her index finger and thumb, leaving a slight space between them. "Okay, naïve maybe. Little dopey."

Both women laughed out loud, enjoying the moment and each other's company.

Fatima lifted a small sandwich and took a nibble. "You think I'm crazy, don't you?"

Nodding her head in the affirmative, Maggie sipped her tea and then began unwrapping an Almond Roca. "Crazy as a bedbug, I'm sure." She was thinking they were still playing.

But Fatima had turned serious. "About Aldo. You think I'm crazy, don't you?"

Here it was. The talk she didn't want to have but absolutely had to have. Maggie looked at her friend.

"I don't think you're crazy. I think you're incredible and wonderful and better than any guy deserves....and I just don't know about this one."

"About Aldo?"

"Yes, Aldo. He's just so…"

"Sophisticated?" offered Fati.

"I was going to say potential *Bond* villain." Maggie deadpanned.

"Maggie!" responded a shocked Fatima.

"Ok, that was harsh, but come on honey. He just plays the big shot almost too well. And I know, have known, guys like that and, not that he is like that, but guys like that can be…well, they can…"

"Do bad things?"

"Hurt you was more my point. He could hurt you without even realizing or caring. And I don't want that."

Fatima smiled. "This is 'big sister' stuff again."

Maggie blushed a little. "I'm not trying to be 'big sister'."

"Always looking out for me."

"I just want you to be careful. He came out of nowhere and you just never know what his intentions really are."

Fatima stopped midbite, her happy warmth suddenly chilling. "Intentions?"

Maggie had crossed the line. She didn't plan to, but she had. She would try to explain.

"Yes, intentions. You don't know if he's after your money or something about your family businesses…or…"

"He's already rich Maggie."

"Okay, but those types are sometimes great at looking rich so they can sink their hooks into some poor widow's bank account…"

"Poor widow? Now I'm a poor widow?"

"I didn't mean you. I meant…"

"Well, I am a poor old widow. So, the suave playboy wants my money and not stupid old me, hmmm?"

"I didn't say that."

"Sounds like you did." The tension increased between them.

"Fati, you're overreacting. I'm not saying anything beyond 'be careful' with this guy. You're falling hard for him and if you let it go too far without knowing more, he could really do some damage."

The blood had drained from Fatima's face, and whether it was her own insecurities or even a slight sense of personal confusion surrounding her own feelings for Aldo, Maggie's caution had hit a nerve. Fati lashed out.

"Maybe I'm not made to be alone like you are."

Maggie sat up in her chair.

"Alone, like me? What does that even mean?"

Fatima pushed on, harder, "You are so confident and so 'I don't need anyone,' well, maybe I do need someone. Maybe I can admit when I'm lonely and need a companion. Going through life by yourself is no fun at all."

Pinched, Maggie felt the need to pinch back. "Alone is how we started and alone is how we finish. And not needing the attention of some womanizing piece of Eurotrash is something I'll never apologize for."

Maggie regretted the words as soon as they came out of her mouth. She had got caught up in the moment and bitten back too hard. Immediately, Fatima got up and left the room, slamming the door to the patio area behind her. Maggie stayed motionless for a few moments, trying to decide whether to chase after Fatima or just let things cool down. In the end, Maggie went with the latter and headed out of the house.

Sitting in her car and preparing to leave, Maggie re-ran the conversation in her head. Why did she have to make such a big mess of things between her and Fati? It wasn't necessary. Not at all. Why was she so bad at having female friends? Why?

Giving in to the knowledge that she had ruined the evening tea, Maggie started her car and pulled away. As she went to turn out of the driveway her phone registered a text. Glancing down, she could tell it was from Ivan. Picking up the plastic brick, Maggie tapped into the message:

Ivan: strong lead on location. Time to move.

She breathed deeply. They must have found the painting and that meant things would be getting very real, very quickly. Maggie sighed and pressed the accelerator forward, thinking *Los Angeles, here I come*.

46

"OH MY GOD, put that thing away. Seriously? Are you kidding?"

Tranko moved slowly towards the pair. He did not lower his weapon. He asked a question instead.

"What am I looking at Bunny?" He motioned toward the assembled items in the middle of the room with his head. "What am I looking at?"

David, confused by what he was seeing, looked back and forth from Tranko to Bunny to the gun Tranko was holding. "You know this guy?" he asked.

Bunny looked directly at David and sighed audibly. "He's just being stupid." Cocking her head to one side, she raised her voice and yelled in the direction of Tranko. "YOU'RE being stupid!"

Tranko took immediate exception to her accusation. "Stupid? You've been lying to me. You had this stuff all along. I'm trying to get my ass out of the sling with the fucking Russians and you've had the goods all along. Bitch."

Tranko motioned with his gun for David to move away from his perch and closer to Bunny. David responded quickly but with some confusion, dangling his arms awkwardly like a sort of emasculated T-Rex. Tranko kept talking at Bunny.

"This is why you wanted to get rid of me so bad. I freakin' knew it. I knew it! You were hiding something." Tranko shook his head slowly from side to side.

But Bunny had heard enough. Slamming her water bottle down on the counter she turned on her heel and strutted directly, purposefully at Tranko, getting right in his face.

"Hiding something? Are you joking? Hello, stupid? Hello? YOU had this stuff in your truck. Not me. Do I really have to remind you of that? And then you decided to stash it in the last place it should ever be stashed? Zev's production office? You do remember that genius decision was yours, right? I went and got this. No one is hiding it from you, you moronic asshole."

Tranko's look turned sheepish. His gun arm drooped slightly. Bunny didn't seem to notice, or care as she continued.

"Maybe you should tell me where you found all this stuff? I sure as hell didn't know anything about it. I assume it was in the main garage or something when you first grabbed it. So why did you take it? Maybe there's something you're not telling me, hmmm? Well, c'mon big man with your big gun. How about you telling me what I have here? I swear to God, the men in my life are absolute fucking idiots!"

Faced, Tranko's gun arm dropped lamely to his side. "Hold on now Bunny, I just…"

Calculating the entire time, David saw an opening and piped up.

"Bunny, I think we have to tell him the truth."

Now it was Tranko and Bunny's turn to swing their looks toward David.

"What are you talking about?" Bunny's eyes went wide as saucers, pleading silently with David to close his trap.

Realizing that he had officially placed himself "on stage", David took a quick, deep breath, forced his spine straight and screwed up his courage. The effect left him standing a good two inches taller.

"Bunny, he's right. Yes, these are indeed valuable pieces of art. I authenticated them. My name is David Teck. I'm a…consultant for high-end art. These pieces were likely stolen years ago and spent most of their time floating on the black market. Somehow her husband got his hands on them and voila. Now we have the problem of how to move them. We can't just sell them to some art gallery. Obviously, you and Bunny have some sort of…relationship so maybe you can be the one to front the sale of these pieces and get some cash for all of us…"

"Us?" Tranko grunted as he looked toward Bunny. "Who is this guy?"

Picking up on some of what David was throwing down, Bunny did her part.

"David's right. We do seem to need each other in this case. You said the Russians are giving you grief. Take one of these pieces to them and see what you can get for it. Then maybe we can negotiate on the rest of them. There's a lot of money at stake here."

Tranko looked at David. "How much?"

David pursed his lips. "Maybe a few hundred thousand? More, less? Hot art is notoriously hard to value."

Tranko stood quietly. He was thinking. Deciding what he wanted to do next.

Finally, he spoke. "You want me to take one of those things?"

David looked to Bunny. Bunny looked to the art and then back to Tranko.

"Yeah. We really have no choice. You already screwed up the first part by killing Zev. This is your chance to fix things."

"How do I know you're not lying to me?"

Back in control, Bunny sashayed herself into the kitchen and leaned on the marble countertop, looking right at Tranko. "You don't. But I'm letting you take whatever piece you want and show it to your contacts. You go see if there is a deal to be made. I'm the one taking a risk. If you leave with it, and it's as valuable as he says it is, it's not like I can say you stole it and then come after you. It's already stolen. That means you're in control now, not me. I can't even guarantee you'll come back."

Tranko had to consider this latest development. He was certain Bunny was lying to him again. That was a given. Plus, this new guy raised plenty of alarm bells himself. But he didn't really have a choice either. And getting to present something to Dachshund might finally get that problem off his back a bit. It would at least show he'd done something. And if it turned out to be valuable, well, he could either get some cash for himself out of it or get the hell away from the Russians in general. It wasn't a horrible idea, as things sat.

"Which one should I take?"

"That's up to you," offered David, "All three paintings are quite special, each in their own way."

"What if you're trying to trick me into taking the junk one?"

Bunny came from behind the kitchen island and walked toward Tranko, swinging her hips the entire way. "Well, I guess you're either going to have to make that guess for yourself or maybe now you've got to put a little trust in me." Turning her head, she barked, "David! Which one should he take?"

David, staring directly at the three paintings, moved his eyes from side to side. "If it were me, the one that has the most potential value is the Vermeer. It's arguably the most famous of the three. Take that one and see what they say."

"Vermeer?"

"*The Concert*. The one with all the instruments lying around. That's your best bet."

Tranko walked toward it. "*The Concert*? This one?"

"Yes. I think that's the best one."

Tranko looked at it for a beat. Then he paused to look at the other two displayed adjacent.

"I think I'm gonna take all of them."

Bunny freaked out. "What?! You can't take all of them! What are you doing?"

Tranko raised the gun at Bunny once more. "Bunny, see this thing in my hand? This is why I get to do what I want to do. And what I want to do is take all of them. I don't trust you or this clipped loser you're currently dragging around. And word to the wise, buddy: lying is all this piece of trim knows, so I'd watch my back if I was you."

"You jerk! I can't believe you!" Bunny rushed at Tranko but stopped short when he raised his weapon a tad firmer.

"Ah, ah, ah. Behave now. Or things can get much worse. Remember, I'm the screwup you can't trust. You wouldn't want another mistake getting made, would you? Especially a permanent one. You, handsome Dan, grab that one and carry it out to the front. Let's go. Bunny, you can get that furniture blanket over there. C'mon, let's move you two."

Frustrated and angry, Bunny complied as both she and David assisted Tranko in loading the three paintings into the box of Stewie's waiting truck. Once the pieces were secured, Tranko walked toward the front entrance where Bunny and David were standing.

"Look, I'm gonna be straight with you, even though I know it's better than I ever got from you. If there is anything to these smears of paint, I'll make sure you get some too. But first I need to cover my ass off, from them and from you. Once that's done, then we'll talk about a share for you. *Capiche*?

Bunny looked confused. "*Capiche*? What? What is that?"

Tranko's face dropped, and his eyes opened slightly wide, as if to say 'really?' "It means, 'you understand,' right? In Italian, get it? That's what it means."

Bunny crossed her arms and sneered at him. "Then why didn't you say that?"

Tranko stopped, looked to the sky, and wondered when the world so completely passed him by. He hopped into the passenger side and told Stewie to get going. The truck tore out of the driveway and away, leaving Bunny standing alone and David leaning against the open front door frame. Bunny wheeled around and yelled at him.

"Why didn't you do anything? You let him take everything!"

David moved slowly and calmly, rising to a full stand. "He had a gun."

"So what? You basically got him to take it all. It's your fault!"

David smiled peacefully. "Bunny, they're knock-offs. I told you that. Good knockoffs, but still fakes. Your lunkheaded friend might very well get himself ventilated when he shows up with those things. We just made our problem, his problem. We got the better deal. I promise."

Bunny stood silently, rolling her left foot around and around, almost spinning the stiletto heel on its own.

"So, what now?"

"Now we go and find the guy that painted the fakes."

"What's that going to do?"

"You don't paint something that detailed from a picture on the internet. The artist had to have access to the originals and we're going to find out when and where. Are you coming?"

Peering out through her expensive extensions and comically enhanced eyelashes, Bunny nodded in agreement. "Ok, I'm in. But we're taking the Aston Martin. It's about time I learned how to drive that goddamn thing."

47

"I HELD UP MY END," said Zevon, forcefully, but still quiet enough to avoid undue attention from those seated nearby.

"I'm not suggesting you didn't. It's just that circumstances are kind of complicated right now and a little flexibility would be appreciated. Sincerely appreciated." Rael Booli took a long draw on his elaborate drink before leaning back in his chair and touching the large tree branch just above his head.

Al Capone built the Raleigh Hotel in 1939. And while he sold it only a year later, it remained just as infamous as he ever was. One of the most iconic Art Deco resorts in the entire US, the swimming pool alone rated a cover shot on *Life Magazine*. The place had been a film and television backdrop for decades. And deservedly so.

From the open and spacious lobby to the retro-inspired gray couches, the scene at the Raleigh was subdued, tacky-classy, and just edgy enough for the high-end happenings of South Beach. Powder-blue armchairs hugged glass and gold coffee tables amongst impressive floor-to-ceiling columns and the lobby-adjacent Euro coffee shop. For a neighborhood loaded with swish hotels, it has remained the place to be for decades.

Zevon tensed, breathing deeply in through his nose. He reached for his drink, Perrier and pineapple, and took a sip. Tiny bubbles popped near his nostrils.

For a moment, the two men, seated beneath the decorative tree in the center of the pool bar, said nothing. It took Zevon to break the impasse. He leaned forward and shout whispered at Rael.

"What happened? You said this wasn't going to be a problem."

Rael shifted uncomfortably in his chair, rocking back and forth, turning his head side to side as if looking for an answer to the question in front of him.

"It's not a problem. It's simply a difficulty. Making money for everyone is never easy, you understand." Rael's regular cool was tempered, to say the least. He was not his normal, effervescent self, at least from Zevon's point of view. He had been summoned here by Rael's brother Sauf, who was nowhere to be seen. Now Rael was trying to act his usual self, but something was up. Zevon was getting worried.

"Are you saying you have to buy the painting then?"

Rael put both hands up, in mock 'I'm innocent' style. "Whoa, whoa. I'm not saying anything like that. They just need, want to see it. They need to know it's for real."

Zevon tensed himself and spoke quickly, under his breath. "You've seen it, you know I have it. You know it's real. Why is this suddenly an issue? What are you not telling me?" He watched Rael take another long drink from the bright yellow straw.

Rael paused while he swallowed. "It just is, okay. This doesn't have to be a problem."

"Where is Sauf?"

Immediately, Rael began to shift in his seat again.

"He's...with them. He agreed to stay with them until this all got sorted out."

At this point, Zevon's personal safety radar went crazy. He even raised his voice. "Rael, you said this meeting was a casual thing. You said everything was okay. What the hell is going on?"

Rael looked left and right, and then back to Zevon. He was annoyed to be drawing attention. His tone changed immediately. "Look, you knew the risks when you came on board with this. You've been paid well for your end, up to now. I'm simply asking for a favor so that can continue, that's all."

A waiter walked by the table. Both men dropped their voices and leant in closer still.

"What favor? I'm doing what I've always done. The painting is secured. I had a special place built for it. Nothing could be better protected."

"They want to see it. That's it."

"Well, I don't have it here, obviously. It's back in LA."

"That's fine. They'll see it there. They just need to see it."

Zevon couldn't shake the feelings rising in him.

"What's really going on Rael? Are these men coming to take my painting?"

"In a word, maybe. Probably yes."

Immediately Zevon stood up from the table.

"That's it! I'm done, if you can't be straight with me, then I'm out of here."

Rael reached for Zevon, gently patting him, trying to calm him down. "Come, come. Sit down. Down. Come now."

"Why?"

"Because I asked you to." Rael fixed him with a hard stare.

Zevon re-took his seat. Rael Booli looked down. He picked at the plate of food in front of him, selecting a radish and mashing it together with a pickled shallot then popping the pair into his mouth.

"Zev, they want the painting."

"Then buy it."

"I know. But you see, I don't have the money. That's the problem."

"That's your problem."

"No, it's your problem too, you see. I guaranteed the deal with your painting. I've paid you, a few times I might add, for this privilege. Thing is, our other money got a little hung up and during this ah, period of uncertainty, they wish to hold the painting in their possession vs. mine."

"You mean my possession?"

"You are, how you say, splitting the hairs, no? Anyway, we are in the process of putting this all together. It will not be a problem in the end. They just need to have the painting for a while until they are happy then it goes back to you, and everything is good again."

"What if I say no?" Zevon crossed his arms, desperately trying to look tougher than even he knew he was.

"Well," said a resolved Rael Booli, again digging at the shallots and radishes in front of him, "then we have a problem."

Zevon nodded his head, relieved that his message was finally getting through. Rael began to speak.

"Do you know Mandela? Not the man. His wife. Remember her? The wife of the statesman Nelson Mandela. President of South Africa.

She became political too, eventually. But in the beginning, when he was still jailed, she sort of become famous....infamous, for what was done to people that betrayed the cause. Far more brutal than her husband she was. Women are like that, I find. We play at being tough and hard while they really are. Probably something to do with carrying a baby inside and then pushing it out. Anyway, she gave out necklaces to her enemies. Necklaces made of rubber tires filled with petrol. Can you even imagine that? Putting a tire around someone's neck and lighting it on fire? Then, and this is the part that really gets me, she'd stay and watch. Really! She'd watch them scream and suffer. It took a long time for them to die. Long minutes. An eternity for the person in the necklace I assume. Just horrible. Horrible."

Zevon sipped his drink. His stomach was churning.

"Now, I am no Winnie Mandela. I don't have the stomach for that kind of thing. Hell, even Sauf would rather avoid such things, and he's the rough one of us."

"That's good." Zevon allowed.

"But these people, Zev. They are like Winnie. They are just monsters, really. And while I like their money, I am not always fond of the way they do business. Now, you and I are in business with them. It's not nice but only at this specific point in time. It is the way it is, and we must find a way through. So, right now the idea is for them to come to Los Angeles, get your painting and then hold it until I can get the rest of the deal together to complete our deal. When that happens, you get your painting back, we all make some money, and no one has rubber tire necklaces. Good, no?"

Zevon gulped. Literally. He had read about it in scripts mostly, and seen it in movies, but he'd not actually done it himself. Until now, that is. Zevon gulped.

"When are they coming?" he asked.

"You head back to LA. It'll be a few days unless I get lucky. Maybe I bring an end to this before, you never know. But otherwise, they will reach out to you within a few days. From there, just do what they say."

"And who am I supposed to expect?"

"A man will call and set things. His name is Edward Dachshund."

48

MAGGIE THOUGHT to herself how all seedy motels are not created equal. First, there are the ones trying hard not to be seedy. They try to clean themselves up, bit by bit, but just never seem to get the job finished before another part slips backward again. Then there are the motels that are seedy simply because the neighborhood around them is seedy. In that case, it's not technically their fault but they will never be able to shake the label due to the neighborhood realities that constantly weigh them down. Finally, there are the genuine, truly seedy motels that know exactly what they are, embrace it and go about their business as such. This was exactly the kind Maggie was looking for.

The blue cab made its way through Los Angeles proper, turning onto Wilshire Blvd.

Maggie had already checked herself into the Sheraton Gateway by LAX, where the crochet convention was taking place. She received her assigned room, got a cute welcome bag, and even wore her crocheted lanyard through the lobby and up to her room, making sure that whatever security cameras she could find got good, clear shots of her as she wandered the hotel lobby and pre-convention floor. The facilities were lovely, but they would never work for the task at hand.

Maggie needed a proper base of operations. And she was headed for it right now.

The Sheraton was merely the cover story. Her reason for travelling to the USA in general and being in Los Angeles in particular. Her main cell phone was also left in the hotel room, plugged in, and stationary, providing minute to minute "proof" of her whereabouts for the entire long weekend. On her way out of the airport Maggie had purchased a couple of burner phones at a nearby 7-Eleven. They would work for handling any necessary communications over the next little while. It was always smarter to have something that popped up on the grid only long enough to disappear before it got noticed.

The cabbie dove through two lanes of traffic, came to a sharp stop and then aggressively u-turned into a nearby motel parking lot. "This is it, The Stardust."

Maggie looked out her window. The neighborhood was somewhat transient, obviously on a major thoroughfare and devoid of any baseline attractiveness whatsoever. There was garbage strewn about the property, but not so much as to be disgusting. Just depressing, and ugly. Weeds grew out of pavement breaks while a mix of barely-held-together cars mingled with the odd flashy or expensive cousin.

The Stardust was perfect seedy.

"That's great, thanks." Maggie handed cash to the driver and stepped out of the car. Slinging her backpack over one shoulder, she headed for the front office. The place wasn't that bad, really. In its day it was probably quite nice. An attractive motor hotel for families on vacation, which the remnants of a decaying, and listing, swimming pool slide testified to. Once upon a time this spot was the real deal. Now? Probably a land holding for some investor who never visited and likely had a rule about not being bothered about anything whatsoever related to it. The manager would either live on site for free, or with a reduced rent, and spend his days studiously ignoring whatever problems crept up as much as possible. Maggie opened the door to the office and went inside.

"You have any rooms?"

The mid-forties man seated behind the rickety counter was watching a small iPad leaned against an ancient dot-matrix printer and a large plastic bucket. He didn't move, but looked up, over the top of his eyes, right at Maggie.

"Yah, I got rooms. Whatcha want?"

"Just a double. For a few nights. Maybe a week or so."

Watching her intently, the man spoke without blinking. "$125 plus tax per night, or $600 per week. No housekeeping by the week. You get new sheets and towels dropped at your door every seven days, but only if you strip the beds and get your dirty towels out before 7am."

Maggie surveyed the surroundings.

"So, you want room?" The man asked, slightly annoyed.

Maggie nodded. "Yeah, give me a week to start."

Only now did the man stand up, stopping to tap the screen and pause the show he was watching. He lifted various piles of paper, hunting for something before finally finding what he needed. Pushing it towards Maggie her told her to fill it out.

"I need a credit card and two pieces of ID."

Maggie busied herself with filling out the card. "I'm going to be paying cash, if that's okay."

The counter man stepped back slightly, and then spoke. "No credit card means you gotta put a deposit down. $350 or no room." He put his hands in the air, as if to say, 'not my call, just the rules.'

Maggie finished writing her details and then reached into her shoulder bag. "Here's for the week, plus the deposit." Maggie counted out $600 plus $350 and slid it toward the man. "I need a receipt for payment."

Nodding, the man grabbed an aging, tri-copy receipt book and filled out the bare minimum, confirming that he'd received $950 cash from Maggie with $350 as a deposit. He scrawled a signature and pulled the pink sheet out of the book and handed it to her. Maggie responded.

"If my room stays secure I probably won't need my deposit back." She held eye contact with the man.

Nodding, he turned and grabbed a key from a board. "#13, it's lucky. Just down the way, last unit on the end."

Maggie nodded herself, offered a tight smile and headed out. He hadn't asked her for ID. She didn't think he would. He knew the game. Cash deals meant "don't bug me or ask stupid questions." He played his side perfect. For her part, Maggie's room was now officially occupied by Noni Gersh from Sacramento. At least, that's what the card she filled out said.

Making her way down the building, Maggie found her room. The key opened the door easily and she stepped into her new home away from home. The smell was expected. That slightly sour combination of old dust and cheap cleaning solution. The room itself was better than she expected. Mainly clean, furniture somewhat matching. The bathroom was old and small, but the grout was cleaner than 50-year-old grout should be. That was a bonus. She wouldn't have to close her eyes when she took a shower. The carpet in the room was dark and old. She wouldn't be taking her shoes off anytime soon, but again, not as dirty as expected. Whoever did the cleaning in this place took a certain amount of pride in it. Not likely the desk jockey. Maybe a wife, or a relative.

The bed was old and the cover tacky, but it was solid enough to sleep on. And thanks to being located on the end of the building, unit #13 had three windows. One on the front, beside the single-entry door facing the parking lot and another, over the air conditioner, on the side of the room, looking into a breezeway. Finally, a smaller one, located at the back of the room, in the bathroom. Three ways out, just in case.

Maggie sat down on the bed. She planned to check in with Ivan in the next hour or so. She was hungry though and thinking that a short hike for some food might be in order. Looking around she noticed a buzzing noise. It was a mini fridge. Clearly from the mid-eighties, the faux-wood sticker-siding on the fridge was peeling off, but when she opened the door, it was cool inside and seemed to be working tip top. The interior had gone the faint yellow of aging plastic, but it was clean. That meant she could get some actual vegetables and greens to have on hand. She hated eating gas station fare even though it was sometimes unavoidable. Not this time. She could hit a grocery store and have some grub worth eating.

Opening her case on the bed, Maggie took out various items and began to set things in drawers and prep her space for occupancy. Once done, she grabbed one of the burner phone packages and tore it open, starting the process of powering it on and running through the setup procedure. If she was going to call Ivan, she would need a phone to do it. She figured now would be a good time get out and explore the immediate area a little. She had already spied a large bus stop, on both sides of the street, as well as a taxi stand near a large office building just a few blocks down. That would let her come and go without drawing any attention directly to the motel she was in, preserving her baseline anonymity. That, plus a good hat, were crucial elements of day-to-day movement in an increasingly trackable society.

People always thought the way to fight the system was by going "off-grid", but that was a lot harder nowadays than it used to be. If you got too far off the grid you stood out like a sore thumb, especially in a society that demanded smart phones and credit cards. The wise traveller kept a foot in both camps and used the weaknesses of the digital society against it, for example by parking a cell phone at the LAX Sheraton. If the powers-that-be wanted to track the "little old lady from Canada who came to crochet in LA" they would 'see' someone keeping pretty close to her hotel room. And that kind of narrative was solid gold for keeping snoopy big brother at bay.

Maggie stood up, grabbed her mostly empty backpack, zipped it closed and prepared to head out. Confirming her key was in the pocket, Maggie grabbed her khaki bucket hat and put it on, pulling it low across her forehead. As she reached for the door handle to leave her room she stopped suddenly. The handle was being jiggled from outside. Someone was trying to open her door. Surprised, Maggie moved slowly toward the door, trying to use the adjacent window to see who was trying to get in. Careful not to disturb the heavy drapes she twisted her neck for a better view, finally seeing the outline of a huge man she absolutely did not recognize. He began to knock on the door.

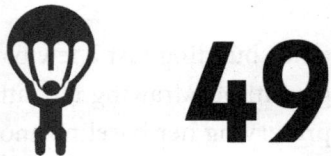

49

ON NOVEMBER 24, 1971, a man boarded a large passenger jet going from Portland to Seattle. Once in the air, he threatened to detonate a bomb unless he was paid a ransom of $200,000 cash. Once the details were negotiated with authorities on the ground, the man had the plane land and released all the passengers and most of the crew, in exchange for the ransom money, now split into two large bags. Once he had the cash, he got the plane to take off again and directed the skeleton crew remaining to fly him in the direction of Mexico, telling them that he would show them where to land when the time was right. Then, at some point over the continental USA, he disappeared into the rear of the plane where he strapped a parachute on — along with both bags of cash — opened the rear door and jumped.

He was never seen again.

It remains the only unsolved hijacking case in the history of commercial aviation.

Dubbed D.B. Cooper by the press, the bold airborne thief ended up becoming something of a folk hero thanks to the almost unbelievable and decidedly bizarre nature of his crime. Stories were written, books were published, and even a few movies got made. Eventually though, like most things suddenly interesting or momentarily exotic, time ticked off and memories faded. The larger world simply forgot. At least until the nineties, when one young man discovered the incredible true story for himself.

His name was Denny Cooper. He was a soft-spoken and noticeably quiet boy. An only child, his father had left not long after he was born. Growing up, Denny spent a lot of time alone as his mother worked two jobs to keep them going. Not terribly big or athletic, Denny stayed out of sports and kept mainly to himself. Once, as a treat, his mother brought home a book about drawing. It was a "teach yourself to draw" kit that included note paper, a few pencils, plus some plastic guides. For whatever reason, something clicked. Denny realized that he loved to draw, anything and everything. He clearly had natural talent and coupled with hours upon hours by himself to practice, he developed legitimate skills very quickly.

Denny got better and better. Pretty soon there was nothing he couldn't draw. Cartoons, landscapes, faces, architecture, anything. He would copy whatever he could get his hands on. Magazines, newspapers, posters, photographs, whatever tickled his fancy. His quality was amazing. By high school, one art teacher even encouraged him to try painting, suggesting he pick some famous masterpiece and try to re-create it. Taking the challenge, Denny painted the *Mona Lisa*. It was so good that the school auctioned it off to raise money for the art students to visit a gallery in New York. Denny was overjoyed.

Sitting in his hotel room, feeling chuffed about his role in getting the art class to the big city, Denny was working the TV remote control when he saw a commercial for an old movie coming on later that night. Originally released in 1981, *The Pursuit of D.B. Cooper* wasn't exactly a hit (or even really that good) but it became instantly fascinating to high school student Denny Boyle Cooper. Here was a charming rogue (played by a youthful Treat Williams) keeping the authorities on the run as he fooled everyone to get what he decided was owed to him.

And he had the same friggen name as Denny.

Immediately, Denny started going by D.B. and did his very best to channel the easy cool exemplified by the criminal portrayed in the film. Desperate for an edge, the quiet young man suddenly had a persona he could embrace which, buoyed by his artistic talents, saw his profile and opportunities escalate in kind.

Denny came out of his shell more and more. He seemed to sparkle like never before. He was still quiet, but somehow radiated a confidence via his skills and the internal dangerousness he cultivated, a la his new favorite folk hero.

At first, Denny had trouble trying to monetize his talents. He took graphic design at a city college and tried working for advertising firms, but he usually ended up clashing with the people in charge. He liked doing things his way instead of how they wanted things done. That meant he didn't usually stay hired for long. The pattern continued until a friend found himself working in the film industry as a set painter. Hearing that production was looking for someone to paint a landscape exterior for the wall of a Greek restaurant, the friend suggested Denny for the task. D.B. got the gig and did such a good job of it that the director changed the entire scene to include more of the amazing background Denny had painted. That break would lead to another and eventually a somewhat steady stream of work in film and television.

Along the way, Denny was sometimes called upon to copy a famous master for some project or show. It was never a big deal. Usually, production was going to have someone smash, damage or steal a "famous" painting, so he was asked to make it look good enough that it might fool the folks watching. Fine detail didn't matter. But Denny was a perfectionist, and he would spend hundreds of hours extra on works that were barely noticed on screen. His efforts were not noticed or significantly appreciated by the people paying him, but he did win one very important fan.

Fat Teddy Adonidas.

Fat Teddy was a bookie, who ran in Hollywood circles. And when marks wouldn't pay their debts, he'd often end up with their cars, or their houses, or their art, or whatever they had to trade, at pennies on the dollar. This allowed him to sell and recoup his cash. Once, he ended up getting a famous painting that, personally, he kind of liked. Committed to liberating the dollar value, Fat Teddy agonized over selling it, until he saw some examples of Denny's work. He hired Denny to make a copy he could keep for himself, which gave him a dark idea. It didn't take long before Fat Teddy had hatched a whole new sideline of selling counterfeit art to Hollywood morons.

Denny knew what Fat Teddy was up to, but he didn't care. He was getting good money for work he enjoyed and was removed just far enough to side-step any real risk. Plus, he loved the genuine outlaw aspect it brought to him. Finally, he really had become a D.B. Cooper worthy of his own legend. At least until Fat Teddy crossed the wrong dude one weekend and found himself laid to rest in a shallow grave near Bakersfield. At least that's what the gossip was.

Denny laid low after that, accepting work or commissions only from people he already knew and trusted or who could at least be personally vouched for. By that point, he had a saved enough to buy a small condo in the valley with enough space for a private workshop. He had no mortgage, so even when his income dropped dramatically, he could still make a go of it without too much trouble. His life got quiet again, but Denny was happy. He was losing the need to be a D.B. Cooper-style outlaw. He had a sort-of steady girlfriend which, along with two turtles and an old car, meant life was pretty good for now.

But he would not be happy to know that David Teck and Bunny Levi were standing at his front door.

David craned his neck, trying to see in the side window beside the door. "Do you think he's here?"

"How would I know?" Bunny moaned. "Just knock, stupid."

David didn't even look at her as he spoke.

"How about you shut up, hmmm?"

David raised his fist and banged on the door three times, then waited. Nothing. He knocked twice more. Still nothing. Stepping back, David tried to look up or around the house, searching for open windows or shadows or any indicators of life or movement of any kind. While he did, the front door of the attached condo opened, and a man's head popped out. He had heard the noise and wanted to see what was going on.

David noticed him but paid no attention. He banged on Denny's door again. The curious man spoke to them.

"If he's not answering he's usually out back. He has a garage off the laneway. That's where he works."

David thanked the man and grabbed Bunny by the arm as he pulled her down the walkway and around to the back of the complex.

Emerging from the side walkway, David and Bunny could see an open car garage with movement deep inside. As they got closer, David spied a slim man in jeans, Chuck Taylors, and a paint speckled t-shirt bending and reaching. By the time they came to the mouth of the garage, he could see what the man was working on: a hideous, tie-dyed version of *Napoleon Crossing the Alps*. Somewhat stunned by what he was looking at, David stared at the face in the painting, trying to make it out. It certainly wasn't Napoleon, at least as far as he could tell. The horse belonged to Napoleon and the uniform was his too, but the face just wasn't right. Bunny spoke up.

"Why is Adam Levine dressed all old-timey on a horse?"

"Adam Levine?" said David.

"The lead singer of *Maroon 5*." Bunny started to sing a little of their hit.

The man in jeans turned around. "Uh, yeah?"

David spoke up. "Is that really the *Maroon 5* guy? Adam…."

"Levine," offered Bunny.

The slim guy shrugged his shoulders. "Uh yeah. Not my taste, but folks want what they want. Who are you?" Denny eyed them both suspiciously.

Producing a badge from his pocket, David came on strong. "Are you Denny Cooper?"

Startled, but staying calm, slim answered. "Who wants to know?"

"My name is David Teck and I'm an insurance investigator. We've gotten some information that you may be involved in passing off forgeries as the real deal. That's a federal crime, as I'm sure you are aware."

Denny took a long pause, saying nothing. He eyed David carefully, and then Bunny too. Finally, he answered. "Yeah, look I don't know exactly what you mean. I just paint stuff. I don't know about anything else."

"But you do copy famous artworks, yes?"

"I've done copies, sure, for movies and TV and stuff. And sometimes for people to hang in their houses but I don't forge things or mess with insurance stuff. No way."

David pushed his way into Denny's workspace. Framed canvasses leaned against the wall, different sizes, most painted, some not. Landscapes, people, places and more. Shelves bulging with different paints, brushes and containers lined the remaining walls while various drop-cloths and rags hanged across saw-horses and easels of varying shapes and sizes. The only lights in the room were standing on legs, easily movable and directed only where they were needed.

"You know, you can be charged as an accessory to insurance fraud..."

"Listen, I don't take to threats from loudmouths with fake badges. I paint. What people do with their painting once they buy it is their business, not mine. I asked a lawyer."

David stared at him, saying nothing. Bunny was getting agitated. David was worried that she would screw things up by speaking. He willed her to keep her mouth shut.

Denny looked back and forth, getting more nervous as the silence mounted. He spoke again.

"Do I need to call someone, like the police?"

David smiled. "You sure you want to do that? Cops don't like murderers too much."

Denny stepped back dramatically. "Murder! What the hell are you talking about? I didn't murder anyone!" He started pacing around, agitated and tense. "This is bullshit!"

Bunny looked at David, trying to understand what he was up to. He felt her gaze but chose to ignore it. He was working now. He had painter boy on the line. Time to reel him in.

"So, you're telling me you had nothing to do with the murder of Zevon Levi?"

At the mention of Zevon's name Denny stopped pacing, turned, and looked at David. Raising his arms up and clasping his hands across the back of his head, Denny breathed out slowly. Then he sat down on an old chair with the back missing.

"I saw that. That Zev died. That's awful. No, I didn't kill him. Obviously. I mean, why would I?"

David slid a crate over to where Denny was and sat down across from him.

"I think you need to tell me how you knew Zevon Levi and what exactly you did for him."

Denny looked up into the ceiling and let out a huge sigh.

"Alright. I'll tell you the story."

50

THE KNOCK at the door shot through Maggie like electricity. Nobody knew she was here. Who could it be? Was she already being followed? She had been careful to cover her tracks and keep an eye for tails.

Maggie cocked her head as she moved back toward the door. Instinctively, she slid the fingers of her right hand toward the small of her back, feeling around for *Lola*.

Darn. She wasn't there yet. Maggie hadn't unpacked her from the hairdryer. Long ago Maggie had learned the best ways to beat airport security scans was by disassembling items and putting them either inside or alongside other, related items. Mainly things that don't trigger the stiffs at security. Whenever possible, she always tried to have *Lola* with her, she just wasn't ready for primetime quite yet. She could see the shadow of a large man attempting to look through the curtains alongside the doorway.

He knocked again.

Maggie screwed up her face. What was going on? Who was this guy? He was huge. Massive. Easily 350 lbs. Maybe more. He looked Samoan, but she couldn't be sure. Who the hell was he? And why was he knocking on her door? She hadn't even established herself at this location yet. No one should even know that she was here. Was he with Manheim? If that jackal had her followed, she was going to go nuclear on him. Maggie did not like having eyes over her shoulder.

He knocked again but this time added some words. "Melvin! Come on buddy. Let's go!"

Now Maggie was really confused. *Melvin? Who the heck is Melvin?*

Doing some fast calculating, Maggie looked left and right, noting several items, and locking in on them. First, she grabbed a water glass from the nearby table. Then, she grabbed the desk chair with her right hand, sliding it into a spot where it would be an obstruction once the door was opened. Based on the light outside, it might even be in a slight shadow too. That would give her something that could be moved or shifted as a surprise should the big man decide to push through the door. It's not like the chair would stop him, but Maggie didn't expect it to. It would mainly provide some visual confusion, plus be available to shift things by kicking with her foot or pulling with a hand. Little movements are often all it takes to pull someone's notice away long enough to make something else happen, like smacking a large mook upside the head with a water glass.

Prepped as well as she could be, Maggie snatched the door open with force. She did it so quickly, and so aggressively, that the abruptness startled the large man, causing him to stumble back a half step. Maggie noted the lack of aggression. She wasn't out of the woods yet, but it was positive. By now, she could see how big the guy was. Maybe even 450 lbs. Maggie kept the door half open, with only half her body visible. In her hidden hand she held the water glass from the desk. Not a perfect weapon but it would do some damage if it had to. She kept it loose in her fingers.

"What do you want?" Maggie asked.

The big man stared at her, clearly surprised.

"Melvin?" was all he could muster.

"I don't know any Melvin," answered Maggie.

The new look on the big man's face was almost heart breaking. It seemed like he might cry. His massive frame almost immediately slumped, and he turned to leave. Taking two steps, he stopped, deliberately turned himself back around and slowly faced Maggie again.

"You don't know where he went do you?"

Becoming more curious by the minute, Maggie softened her tone, but only slightly.

"Look, I really don't know this Melvin guy you want. I just checked in here. Maybe someone at the front office knows him?"

The mountain of flesh sighed heavily. "It don't matter. It's all my fault. He told me to be here two days ago with the bike and I didn't do it. I was stuck helping my sister move her place. I tried to come but I blew it. Sorry to bug you." The big man turned to leave again.

"Bike?" Maggie inquired.

Giant man stopped, and angled his massive head to one side, indicating to his left, in the parking lot.

There, strapped upright on a cheap, homemade trailer was a cherry red early 70's Honda CB750 motorcycle. It was attached to an ancient, and frighteningly rusted out, Ford Escort.

Maggie knew the bike. Her father had one. She even rode it a few times herself in Italy. She couldn't believe what she was seeing.

"That? Over there?" she indicated.

Big man nodded his giant head. "Yup, Melvin was gonna buy it off me. We need the coin."

The impulse was instant. Maggie wanted the bike. This was a sign. It might even be from her father, in some weird way. She was having a hard time playing it cool.

"It runs?" she asked.

"Yeah, of course. Those things are bulletproof. It's in great shape. New motor two years ago. Less than a thousand miles on the new one."

"You rode it?" asked Maggie in disbelief.

"Naw, my sister did. I tried once but bikes ain't my thing. Her helmet and stuff is there too."

Sometimes called the world's first superbike, the Honda CB 750 was released in 1969. It was the first commercially available, modern 4-cylinder motorcycle from a major manufacturer with cool bells and whistles like an electric starter, flashing turn signals and better brakes. Plus, it could go fast. Really fast. As in 120 mph fast. As a market bike, it sold better than anyone could have guessed.

The engine was a fearsome 736cc air-cooled inline-4, kicking out 68 horses at 8,500 rpm, 44 lb.-ft. of torque at 7,000 rpm. The specs were mind-blowing for the time, but the best part was how easy it was to use. It wasn't hard to ride, everything worked as it was supposed to, it was reliable, and it was comfortable. And it looked sharp as heck.

Maggie could barely contain herself. "How much do you want for it?"

"Twenty-two hundred. Cash."

All Maggie wanted to do was scream "sold." That bike would be perfect for getting around Los Angeles. Way better than an Uber, that was for sure. She could get into, or out of places far easier. Plus, she really wanted it. Like a lot.

"Hey, what's your name?"

"Mica." Answered the massive mound of flesh. "I got the ownership papers. It's mine to sell. For real."

Maggie walked out to the small trailer and checked out every inch of the motorcycle. Nice shape, few paint chips but otherwise looked pretty tight. Even the chrome looked good. "Can you start it up?"

Mica nodded, crawling onto the trailer and causing it to heave with so much effort that Maggie feared it might break the hitch connecting the car with it. Mica reached a finger down and flipped up the choke, fished a key out of his pocket, put in in the bike and turned it on. Maggie watched the bike controls light up. He reached over and turned the fuel on and then pushed the starter with his thumb. It fired up like it had been running all day. Maggie was even more impressed now. Mica revved it a few times and flipped the choke off. The motor didn't display any roughness at all. It was in phenomenal shape.

"Look Mica, I'm interested. Would you take two thousand for it?"

Mica's eyes lit up. Happiness instantly covered his face, making him appear younger still. Maggie originally guessed him to be late twenties. When he smiled, that number dropped further. Mica turned off the bike and pulled the key, almost tripping himself as he stepped down from the trailer.

"Seriously? Like, you want to buy it?"

"Yeah. Seriously."

"Sold then."

"Hold up a second." Maggie said. "I don't have the money here. I have to get it. Can you come back in a couple hours?"

Mica appeared to panic. "You're not gonna leave, are you? Like Melvin?"

Maggie smiled. "Mica, I'm staying here. I want the bike."

"That's awesome. Okay, great. Wow." And then suddenly, Mica started laughing.

Maggie just looked at him. Eventually, he noticed her watching him and offered an explanation.

"It's just, Melvin was only gonna pay me fifteen hundred. He told me nobody wanted it. But we needed the money so bad I had to sell it to him. But Melvin wasn't there, you were. And because of that I got more!"

Maggie smirked at the large, immature man-child. "Listen honey, it's not a great idea to tell someone you were going to take less money. It might make them feel like they made a bad deal."

Mica's face dropped. "I didn't mean that. I just…I mean…"

"No sweat." cut in Maggie. "I get you. Melvin was kind of cheating you. This is a great machine. And you're still giving me a real deal."

Mica came over and shook her hand. Maggie's hand disappeared inside his fleshy meat mitt. Soft hands, she thought. Good skin, not much work on them. He really was a boy.

Of course, Maggie had lied about not having the money on hand. She had all of it and more. But you never tell a stranger in a strange town that you have access to any cash on hand. Maggie instructed him to either drive around a bit or go get something to eat while she went off to "get" the money. Mica opted for the restaurant two doors over, strolling awkwardly down the street towards it. Maggie stood and stared at her soon to be purchased motorcycle. It really was beautiful. She couldn't wait to sit on it.

Checking the time, Maggie realized she was past due checking in with Ivan, not to mention figuring out what she was going to say to Fatima. She hadn't left that awful situation well, not to mention skipping town before settling things out with her best friend. It just wasn't right. She knew she had to do something, but she wasn't sure exactly what that was. At least not yet.

Maggie turned and went back to her room. She'd get the money ready for Mica right now, and once that was signed and done, she'd go for a ride on her new motorcycle. Absolutely nothing clears your head like a good ride in the California sunshine.

51

SOMETIMES, Tranko couldn't believe how smart he was.

The Long Beach antique market was a sea of almost a thousand second-hand vendors, all crammed together in 300 sq ft squares, gridded-out across a 20-acre expanse of open pavement. People moved to and fro between the marked-off stalls, peeking, poking, and picking at anything on display that struck their personal fancy. The human traffic throbbed and pulsed, moving in a constant flow, providing a perfect out-in-public cover for what Tranko had in mind.

No way was he going to meet Dachshund and his crew in some out of the way place. If the paintings had any value, they'd more than likely kill him on the spot and simply take them. And if they were worthless, they'd probably do the same. But no way that was going to happen here.

Once a month LA residents flooded the parking lot of Veterans Memorial Stadium near Long Beach City College to snoop through aisle after aisle of antique furniture items and other assorted junk: rotary phones, vintage signs, old jewelry, classic sports equipment, millions of porcelain figurines, and tons more. Food trucks and numerous drink concessions rounded out the experience, providing attractive smells and tasty treats, thus ensuring any patron's ability to spend the entire day poking around while staying happy and fed.

Getting a stall could be tricky, especially if you didn't book in time, but Tranko had figured out a workaround. Finding a stall that he believed would offer him the most personal protection, along with multiple escape routes, he had approached the seller already in place and made a one-off deal to "display" his three paintings just long enough for a meeting. Obviously Tranko had no interest in selling them, but by looking like he was selling them, Dachshund and

Co. could come by and view them with a minimal amount of risk to Tranko's well-being. He was hiding in plain sight, which was always a better way to go.

And reflecting on the inherent genius of his plan made Tranko smile.

It was a beautiful day. The sun was shining, and he finally saw his chance to get out from under the Russians. Once they saw the stuff in question, he'd cut a deal with them and get the hell out of the city altogether. Maybe even the country. He needed to get back to parts of the world where things made sense. Like South America. Or the Middle East. They were all dangerous as hell, sure but Tranko understood the rules of those areas so much better. And he would be dealing with professionals instead of entitled little snags like Bunny Levi. He was fantasizing about going back to being a simple gun for hire focused on watching his own back, instead of trying to wrangle idiots in one direction or another when his solitude was interrupted.

"Where do you want this one?" Stewie walked up carrying the last painting from the truck. The boat-on-water one.

Tranko turned. "Yeah, just lean it by the table there, by the other two."

"It's heavy. The frame is solid wood."

"Quit griping. You didn't haul it that far."

"The parking lot is way the hell over there. And they won't let you cut across. I had to go all the way around and through the main entrance each time," protested Stewie.

As he set the third painting in place alongside the other two a voice from inside the stall piped up, "Hey! You're blocking my stuff from being seen!"

Tranko turned to face the old guy. "What's the problem? I told you what I was gonna do."

The old guy came around the table and surveyed the paintings leaning against his table. "Yeah, sure you did, but you didn't say how big they'd be. Look at this! They're blocking everything! You gotta move them down or something. Maybe stack them."

"Come on, Floyd. We had a deal," pleaded Tranko.

"This is no good. No good at all," fussed the old man.

Tranko rolled his eyes and sighed loudly. "Damnit! Fine. Here's another $50. Are we good? I'm not going to be here all day, all right? You're winning in this."

Floyd looked at the $50 bill in Tranko's hand. He looked back at the paintings leaning there and then back to the money. Then he reached forward and took the money from Tranko's hand and walked into the back of his booth, saying nothing. Tranko faced away from him and spoke to Stewie.

"Now, we just wait for those bastards to show up."

"When are they coming?"

"They didn't say, but I told them when I'd be here. And it all shuts down by 2pm anyway."

"Can I go get a lemonade?"

"Really?" Tranko responded in disbelief.

"C'mon, I'm thirsty. I'll get you one."

"Just hurry, okay? I want you here when they show up."

Stewie went to leave and then stopped. "Hey, can you spot me some cash?"

Shaking his head, Tranko pulled a small wad of cash from his pocket, peeled off a twenty and handed it to Stewie. "I want the change."

Stewie nodded and disappeared into the crowd.

* * *

Tranko looked at his watch. Almost one-thirty. Still no sign of Dachshund or his crew. Stewie was laid out underneath a nearby table, dozing. Beside him were two empty lemonade cups and the remains of a Canadian poutine and a half-eaten hot dog lying in a stained, and already decomposing, recyclable tray. Tranko stretched his arms above his head, flexing his biceps. Then he cracked his neck both ways. He'd been sitting around all day. He closed his eyes and tapped on his temples, trying to wake himself up. A voice broke his concentration.

"How much for *Storm on the Sea of Galilee* here?"

Opening his eyes, Tranko came face to face with an ancient old woman. Standing tall, she reached almost as high as he was sitting down. She was wearing a faded *CATS* sweatshirt, floral pajama pants and blinding-white, vintage Air Jordans. Her white-as-snow hair was crammed beneath a *Gilligan* bucket hat with an "I hate squirrels" button pinned to the side.

"It's not for sale," he answered.

Annoyed, the woman lit into Tranko, "Then why is it here? Why set it up at all?"

Momentarily forgetting his surroundings, Tranko fumbled, remembering that he needed to play things a little more carefully, especially based on his location and the actual circumstance.

"Uh, sorry, it's just that it's spoken for. I already made a deal."

Continuing to stare at him, as if to determine the truth of his words or not, the old lady nodded her head up and down.

"Okay, okay. But what if they're a no show? Did they pay already? I've got money now. Cash. I know what you got there. *Storm on the Sea of Galilee*. That's a classic. Great copy. I'm a buyer at the right price. *The Concert*? Yeah, that's right. I know my art. I'd buy that one too if we made a package deal. I'm not interested in the Van Gogh rip-off though. Never could get behind his obsession with sunflowers. I hate the ugly things myself."

Resigned to dealing with the woman, Tranko rose to his feet, which somehow didn't faze the small woman. She simply cast her gaze higher, attempting to read him and better suss out her chances of closing a deal.

"It's been a long day. Folks are starting to clean up. You're not gonna want to haul those heavy pictures back home again. Give me a price. Come on. Let's make a deal."

By this point, Stewie had emerged from beneath the table, rubbing his eyes. Tranko however, was getting annoyed with the whole process.

"Look, you can't afford it," he told her directly, hoping to end things.

"What do you know I can afford? You don't know who's backing me. Or who I am. I got money. Try me. How much?"

Tranko smirked. "One million dollars."

The lady stopped and stared at him, "Well, now you're just being an asshole."

At this point the old man who owned the booth, Floyd, re-entered from the crowd. He had a churro in one hand and a coffee in the other. The old lady turned on him.

"What's with this guy? Setting up stuff in your stall and then not selling? What's his game? One million dollars he tells me. That's a dick move, Floyd. Who is this guy?"

Floyd raised his full hands, pleading for understanding. "Ahh Julie, I don't know. He paid me to lean things on my table and said it would be quick. But it's been ALL DAY." Floyd was careful to aim the last two words right at Tranko, expressing his personal displeasure at having to deal with him for so very long.

As the two oldsters begin to get into it, bickering back and forth with each other about Tranko's presence at the market a voice is heard from the side of the stall.

"You got something then?"

It was Stig. Still short, squat and very square wearing ridiculous sunglasses. And surrounded by three more of his mooks.

Tranko immediately ignored the seniors and turned to Stig.

"Yeah, I got something." Then, still mindful of the fiction regarding Stig as Dachshund, he asked his next question carefully. "Where is…he?"

Stig looked at him for two beats, saying nothing. Then he mumbled out an answer, "Don't worry. He's watching."

Stig went over to the paintings and stared at them. He didn't seem to study them particularly, he just stared at them, like a dog or someone without any understanding at all might. He mumbled something out loud, but Tranko couldn't hear it. Stig then appeared to be listening to something. Like a voice that is unheard by everyone else. Tranko noticed a small insert in Stig's ear, running to a cord snaking down his neck and into his shirt. Stig nodded his head and then turned to one of his men.

"Tape measure."

The lackey fumbled around, indicating he didn't have one and then looked to the others. All of them raised their eyebrows, making it clear none of them had one either. Stig turned back to Tranko.

"Tape measure?"

Tranko looked at him and then turned to Stewie, who also indicated he didn't have one. Tranko looked farther afield, turning toward the oldsters.

"Floyd, you got a tape measure we can borrow?"

Before Floyd could answer, Julie the senior flipped a tape measure off the elasticized waistband of her pajamas like a gun fighter pulling a draw, pushing it towards Tranko with five inches of tape already extended.

"If I don't get it back there's gonna be trouble," she cautioned.

Tranko nodded, took the tape from her, and handed it to Stig, who immediately went over to the first painting and measured it, first right to left, then top to bottom. All measuring was done inside the frame. With each measure, he mumbled the results, again too quiet for Tranko to hear. But someone was clearly listening.

He went to each of the paintings in turn, measuring each of them the same way, pausing only to mumble whatever findings he made to his invisible overseer.

Then, he turned and tried to hand back the tape measure to Tranko, who simply pointed at senior Julie. Stig took a step toward Julie and now face to face with the diminutive woman, held out the tape measure for her to take.

As senior Julie reached to take it back, she spoke directly to Stig, "Know this. If you make a deal with *Giganto* over there, I might still be a buyer. You can always deal with me." In Julie's other hand was a business card, which she slipped right into Stig's hand as he released the tape to her. She made a "call me" gesture to Stig and then headed off on her way.

Amused, Stig almost cracked a smile, but turned back to Tranko. "They're all fakes. Good ones I suppose, but fake…"

Tranko couldn't believe it. "How the hell can you tell they're fakes that fast?"

"When stolen they were cut out. Re-frame a cut out, it gets smaller, no?"

Tranko nodded. Made sense. If you knew what a painting was originally sized it would be easy enough to compare the two. He was kind of mad that he didn't think of something that simple first.

Stig continued, "We take them anyway." He indicated for his men to take them. They step forward, reaching for the paintings.

Tranko stepped in front of the group.

"Hold on a second. You want these things I want some guarantees. First, I want to get paid, then I want it understood that we're done. If you can't manage that then you're not taking anything." Tranko looked to Stewie, using his eyes to urge him to step up. Eventually Stewie complied, stepping in beside Tranko, between the paintings and the goons.

Stig shook his head from side to side.

"No, we take them now. Deals get made later, after we figure things. You lied before. That's not done yet."

Tranko held his ground, forcing Stewie to do the same.

Stig looked confused at Tranko and went to speak. Then he thought better of it and opened his jacket instead, showing off a piece in his waistband plus a fully-auto machine gun hanging from a shoulder holster under a massive track suit jacket. Then, he moved his hands around as if to say, *"You really want to do this here?"*

No, Tranko did not want to do that here. Stig had called his bluff and he knew it. Tranko stepped aside, indicating for Stewie to do the same. The men picked up the three paintings and headed away from the little stand. Stig went over to Tranko.

"You will get call. Answer this time, yes?"

Tranko nodded, as Stig followed along after the paintings he had just seized. It wasn't the outcome he had hoped for but maybe there was still something to be salvaged from all this.

As he began to walk away, the cell phone in his pocket began to buzz. Tranko figured it would probably be a good idea to answer it.

52

BUNNY STARED deep into Adam Levine's painted eyes, marvelling at how they seemed almost alive. His lips, curled into the sort of half-smirk that she just loved, were perfect. What was that article about him? Something she saw in *New York Mag* or *GQ* or whatever. Something about him being a douche and not caring or something? Bunny had read it a few years back and become mini-obsessed with him. Of course, she had been married at the time, but that didn't stop her from spending a week or so haunting the Blu Jam diner near Brentwood in hopes of meeting him. That was one of the main benefits of living in LA. The chance to meet someone richer or more famous who might just help you get a little farther up the ladder. It didn't work. She did meet some guy who said he was in *Sweating Bullets* though. Not very bright but he had a great ass. Especially for someone his age.

"Bunny?" asked David, noticing that she wasn't really paying attention.

Bunny lifted her eyes, turned, and faced Denny, spitting out the question tormenting her, "Why is he on the horse again? You said it's like a famous picture or something?"

Denny shifted on his chair. "*Napoleon Crossing the Alp*s was a series of five oil on canvas portraits by Jacques-Louis David. The King of Spain ordered them. I think the idea to do this…version was sort of a goof on that. Maybe a 'king's privilege? Sort of mocking him as gauche and maybe a little douche-y? I don't know. I mean, who hangs a picture of themselves anyway? And one like this? They've either got a great sense of humor or they're a total knob. Not much in between."

"So, he actually hired you to do it?"

Denny paused, looking left and right, acting like he had shared too much. "I really can't, y'know say.…it's just…"

David broke in.

"Look, Bunny, can we focus on why we're here? Denny? Please?"

Appreciative of the focus shift, Denny re-gathered himself.

"So, like I was saying before. I was helping paint some flats for a set near the LA river, just off Alameda. Now, I didn't even know the movie I was working on. I was doing it for a friend. She'd gotten food poisoning and couldn't finish her gig for this new art director that hired her, and I offered to help get it done so she wouldn't get a black eye on the whole deal and lose a payday. It wasn't a big show, total low budget. And the painting was a step or two above house painting. Just some texture work and a little contrasting. Nothing of detail or note. Just a few hours at most."

David remained focused on Denny, even as Bunny's attention began to drift once more.

"Now, I'm not bragging, but I do have kind of a rep for the things I do. Not like famous but folks that know, know me, right?"

David nodded. Bunny played with her phone.

"So, I'm working on this flat and I see the art director come in. She's looking at some samples and plans and stuff and checking out other things when an old guy comes in. Obviously, he's got some juice, 'cause she immediately drops everything and focuses right on him. I'm still working but sort of watching them out the corner of my eye. Anyway, I see that she starts pointing at me and they're talking and looking back and forth. I'm trying not to notice but it's getting hard not to and then eventually they both start walking towards me. Now, I'm getting a little worried that my friend is going to catch hell for having me replace her without telling them or something like that so I'm up in my head, working up a story or reason as to why I'm doing her job and all but…"

"But?" answered David.

"But it wasn't about that at all. The art director smiled and introed me to the producer, who was Zev Levi. Told him what a great 'mimic' I was for production-required art impressions."

"Production-required art impressions?"

"It's a classy way of saying copies I guess."

"And she knew you?" asked David.

"Like I said, people that know, know what I can do. Anyway, he starts asking sort of basic questions and stuff. Like, what styles I'm trained in and what I like to do and stuff. And the art director is just standing there. Pretty quick though, it seems like it's bugging him that she's still hanging around and he grabs my elbow and starts pulling me away, kind of freezing her out. So, she takes the hint and goes back to her stuff. Then it got weird."

Bunny's head popped up from her phone. "Weird?"

Denny nodded. "Yeah. Weird. He's still got my arm in one hand and is sort of guiding me into a back corner of the warehouse where no one is. And he starts looking right in my eyes, like directly. Uncomfortably. And he gets super-serious with his questions."

"Okay," said David.

"Yeah, he starts asking about my 'discretion' and whether I can be 'trusted' and things like that. And he's intense about it. Like, he's trying to read inside my head or something. Anyway, I tell him I am. 'Cause I am. And he says that's good and then he clams up. Doesn't say anything for a few beats. Like he's trying to work up the nerve or something. And let me tell you, I've been asked to paint some very strange pieces. Like intimate things, in person. Like this one guy wanted me to paint him and his lady while they were…you know, doing stuff…but surrounded by mannequins dressed in freaky *Mad Max*-like gear."

David's eyes opened wide, "You're kidding?"

"Wish I was."

David turned and looked at Bunny, nodding to himself. Seeing this, Bunny cocked her head to the left and sneered an exaggerated look back at him. Denny continued.

"Anyway, Zev asked me if I had ever copied one of the old masters. And I said 'sure', but he stopped me and said 'no, I mean really copied one, as in forging one.' Now, I've done that level of work before, but I've never "forged" anything. A forgery is when you try to pass off your work as something it isn't. I never did that. Other people might have done that, but I never did. I do homages to the greats."

A cynical smile crosses David's face. "An homage? Really?"

Choosing to ignore David's suggestion of ill intent, Denny continued.

"So, Zev tells me he's got a job for me. He wants a perfect representation of a classic work. There can't be any differences, or tells, about it at all. He wants the colors perfect, and he wants the brush strokes to match, he even wants the canvas to be aged the same. I tell him that time is his enemy and that's it going to take a long while. He said he didn't care, just that it had to be done absolutely correct. And he was willing to pay."

"How much?"

Denny stopped. He looked inside himself, deciding whether to answer or not. He'd rather not.

David pressed him. "Look, you can tell me here or wait for a grand jury, unless I get what I need from you. Then it might not have to happen."

Denny sighed audibly and answered. "$45k."

"Really?" said David. "Holy shit!" said Bunny.

Feeling the need to defend himself, Denny spoke up. "Look, it took me more than six months. I had to drop everything except that one job. This kind of stuff is not easy. Not if you want to do it right."

"And how did you do it right?"

Denny looked confused. "I don't know what you mean?"

David pressed. "Don't snow me. You can't paint something as detailed and specific as that unless you're in the room with the original. You were in the room with it, weren't you?"

Denny dropped his head slightly, shyly. Then he smiled. A little smile but one that was clearly remembering the experience he had lived and was secretly enjoying all over again.

"Denny, were you with the original?"

Denny looked up and answered. "Yeah, I was. It was incredible."

"How did it all work? What was the protocol?"

Relaxing slightly, David leaned back on the broken chair. "Every week or so, around the same time, I'd go to a certain parking lot and wait for a car to come. When it came, I'd get in the backseat and put on a blindfold. The driver was obscured. Then it would drive for 45 mins to an hour and come to a stop. Then, someone would come and get me and lead me into a place where the original was."

"Do you remember where?"

"No, and I never wanted to know. I knew what I was looking at. That painting had been missing for decades and knowing anything more than I had to know was a total no-go for me. I'll paint whatever you want. I don't care about the rest."

Now interested enough to be paying attention, Bunny asked her own question.

"Where did they take you? You must have tried to guess."

"I really didn't. Like I said, I didn't want to know. It was underground. I know that. The space was smallish, but I didn't need much room really, so that was okay. It was hot. Some days I was wearing shorts and nothing else it got so hot. Plus, it smelled sort of chemically. Anyway, I'd measure things, make notes, paint some bits, and then take my version home to work on for a few until I needed to see it again."

David stood up and paced around, thinking first and then talking.

"And you did this for six months?"

"That's how long it took," answered Denny.

"And when you were done?"

"He thanked me, and I got the rest of what he promised."

"Did you ever see it again?"

"No."

"Not ever?"

"Not in person. There was the show on TV about the Gardner heist. I saw it there of course, but not the real thing."

"How do you think he got it?"

"I have no idea."

"And you're sure it was real?"

Denny smiled. "Yeah, it was real."

David stood up, steeled his spine, and squared his shoulders, facing aggressively at Denny.

"Then I think you're going to jail."

Immediately confused, Denny started to freak out. He jumped to his feet, kicking over the chair that he was sitting on. "What are you talking about? I've been straight with you! What do you mean going to jail? I didn't do anything wrong!"

Once more, back in full control, David calmly addressed Denny's outrage.

"You participated in the commission of a crime. You were certainly in the presence of a stolen item, a knowingly stolen item. You just admitted it, in front a witness as well." He indicated Bunny, who is watching with rapt focus now that tension had spiked in the room.

"Why are you doing this to me?" yelled Denny.

"I'm not doing anything. I'm charged with finding that missing painting. You're a guilty party, maybe not in its initial disappearance but certainly in its continued lack of appearance. If you impede me in any way, then you will be obstructing a police investigation." David lied, and hoped Denny was just ignorant enough not to realize it.

He was.

"I never saw where it was. I had no idea ever. You can't hang this on me."

"Tell me where it is then," demanded David.

"I can't tell you something I don't know. I told you what happened. I didn't leave anything out. Zev is the only one who knows for sure, and he's dead."

Now it was David's turn to sit down. "And that's pretty convenient for you, no?"

"What do you mean?"

"No witness to your crime. Maybe you did have something to do with it."

Denny felt himself getting exasperated. "Look, I told you what I know. I'll go to the station with you. Literally, I'll confess to the whole thing. But I didn't kill anyone. Not ever. I'll swear to that, in court or wherever!"

David knew he had to back off. He wanted the guy riled up enough so he could figure out if he was holding anything back, but he didn't want him jabbering to anyone else about what he knew. That'd be too much. He needed to calm him back down again, put him on ice, just in case he needed him later. He adopted his most soothing tone.

"Okay, Denny. I do think you've been straight with us. I don't want to jam you up either. But you know what a big deal this is. You're sure you don't remember anything else about the original? You can't show me the parking lot you were picked up in?"

"Of course. Sure."

"But no other memories?"

"No, seriously. None."

"You know the painting though?"

"Look man, I got to spend half a year with an amazing piece of history. And I did it nearly every day, all day. And it was incredible. I got to paint a near perfect copy of *The Concert,* and I'll never apologize for that. I don't know why he wanted it or what it was for. Maybe he sold it, maybe he hung it in his bathroom. I don't care. But it was a big deal to him that it be perfect in every way possible. He was fair with me. He let me do my thing and he paid me what I asked. I'm sorry he's dead. Zev was a good guy."

At these words, Bunny felt herself choke up, so she turned away, her eyes involuntarily filling with tears. She didn't like hearing nice things about Zev. It made it harder to hate him. She started primping herself, trying to distract from honest emotion or memories. David rose to his feet.

"Here's the thing. I'm going to follow-up on a few of the things you've told me today. And I will be in touch. In the meantime, I don't want you talking to anybody or thinking about leaving town. You are in this in a big way. If you're smart about it, things will be okay. If not, I don't have to tell you how bad it can get."

* * *

As Bunny and David headed away, around the side of the condo and back toward the front street, Denny watched and waited until they disappeared fully from view. The second they were gone, Denny dug through some junk on a table and fished out a paint speckled cell phone. He dialed a number quickly and put the candy bar sized hunk of plastic to his ear.

"Hey. Look, I just had a visit from some guy that could really mess me up. I gotta talk to him as soon as possible, okay? No, I don't want to hear about later. I need him right now!"

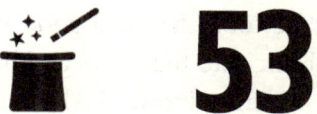

53

ALDO CRINGED as she threw more food overboard.

"No, no, these birds, *rato voador*. You cannot feed them. It only encourages them. They're filthy and they carry disease."

Fati didn't care. She liked to feed the birds, even seagulls. And they certainly seemed to enjoy the attention. She stood at the back of Aldo's yacht, tossing bits of leftovers onto a concrete jetty a few meters out from the stern. The seagulls swarmed it, squawking happily.

The marina at Marina del Rey was one of the largest in the USA. Accommodating vessels up to 150 ft. in length, along with more than five thousand year-round residents, meant this was the place to park when you were floating off California. Its proximity to the private terminal at LAX was a bonus too.

Aldo felt himself getting frustrated. "They will come closer. I don't want them near the boat. Come Fatima. Please don't do this."

Fati turned and looked at him, sort of listening but also with a slightly challenging look. Would he really order her to do something? She was curious. Staring straight at him, she tossed another few bits of food over the side. She almost dared him to comment.

Aldo cringed. He could feel her intention to test him. But his nature as a perfectionist combined with the reality of aggressive seagulls, not to mention the volume of that which they left behind, was starting to override his ability to play it cool. He needed a distraction.

"Do you see that yacht? Rumour has it that it belongs to the magician David Copperfield, but no one knows for sure. He's very secretive, of course." Aldo prayed he could successfully divert Fati's focus from the sea gulls.

Fatima looked towards the yacht. She knew what Aldo was doing and she appreciated it. He was resisting the urge to make a command.

She took that as a good sign. Fatima dropped the remaining food back onto the plates and brushed her hands clean. Grabbing her hat, she turned toward Aldo. "I'm going to have a shower..." and Fati disappeared inside.

Aldo let out a reflexive deep breath as his calm returned. He hated seagulls.

Looking toward the boat he had suggested was Copperfield's, Aldo wondered. Was it really his? Was it a magic boat? He smiled, thinking about magicians and what people believed about them. Copperfield even made the Statue of Liberty disappear. Impressive for sure, but even still, no magician alive or dead could do the kind of magic trick Aldo had learned to do.

Aldo could make taxes disappear. Now that was magic.

Facing the horizon, Aldo looked out across the Pacific Ocean as the waves lapped in.

The concept of a freeport was simple enough. Politicians draw "lines" around a specific place or location. They declare that locale a "freeport" and instantly any item or good coming into that spot exists in a state of limbo. No taxes of any kind. No customs duties. No excise taxes. No VATs. Nothing.

Abracadabra.

Now there were rules, of course. The items stored could get taxed if they were removed from that place and sent to another place. But so long as they stayed there, so long as they remained "in transit," which is what being inside a freeport technically means. Some items have lived their lives for years inside a freeport, changing hands multiple times, appreciating in value, and even being sold over and over. Yet they never leave and therefore never attract any tax.

That was Aldo's kind of magic.

Freeports were nothing new. Their creation and use dates far back in history. One of the earliest examples of a functioning freeport was the Greek island of Delos, in the Cyclades archipelago. The Romans turned the entire island into a freeport around 166 BC, and it quickly became a trading hub for the whole Mediterranean region. Today, the number of freeports around the world ebb and flow. In

2018 there were over 5000 of them. Four years later, a little under 3500. Freeports come and go, but they could be lucrative for sure.

At least that was Aldo's plan when he first bought into them.

He only learned of them by accident. An item he wanted to purchase was being held inside one. Upon going to view it, Aldo found himself falling in love not with the sculpture he originally came to purchase, but with the vault-like surrounding itself. Immediately, he went to work acquiring ownership shares in several critical freeports around the globe, all the while studying and learning the trade.

Aldo was a very good student.

Freeports quickly became the next generation of tax avoidance, that is, legal tax evasion. Wealthy individuals kept their valuables (often precious metals, art, and diamonds) stored in freeports and protected from taxes and tariffs for the length of their storage. Because the taxes and fees were avoided legally this made for good, solid tenants providing large, on-going rental fees. And as world governments leaned harder and harder on tracking the tax status of their richer citizens, more and more of them became regular users of freeports like Aldo's. Win-win.

Obviously, works of art were a natural expansion of the freeport business. Global trading increasingly meant that artworks were constantly crossing borders, and every country had a distinct legal framework for regulating their import and export. Sending works overseas meant hefty duties and reams of complex paperwork, both of which could be easily avoided through freeports.

As an industry, art remains one of the most unregulated on planet earth. Auction houses provide the closest thing to "credibility" the art world accepts, and even they are hardly open or transparent about the way prices or provenances are determined or established. In fact, most of what an auction house does is hidden away from the public and government regulators in general.

Which is something the global art trade prefers.

The key to any freeport is the in-and-out structure. Everything coming in gets recorded in the most hands-off way possible. Privacy and discretion are paramount. But government involvement, and increasingly heavy-handed approaches meant Aldo's clients were getting squeezed harder than ever before. It was easy to see the dark side of freeports. Their potential for money laundering, securing looted or stolen antiquities, actual tax evasion and similar. Aldo never planned for that.

Then he met the Booli brothers.

While the brothers' involvement in the arms trade was something of an open secret amongst those in the know, they simultaneously cultivated enough of a proper front to ensure they retained access to the legitimate side of the business world. And freeports were very legitimate. Aldo had no reason to turn them away.

While the Boolis maintained deposits in several freeports, it was in Aldo's that a fire suppression system malfunctioned, putting him face to face with an angry Rael Booli. He demanded compensation for his water damaged antiquity.

The problem was that Rael would not accept financial recompense. He was far more interested in receiving a favor that Aldo was not immediately inclined to provide. Insurance was the better, and more legal, option but unfortunately an insurance claim in the freeport business was a big deal, and one that had the tendency to dampen prospects should word of such a claim get around.

Aldo was between a rock and a hard place. His regular businesses were already under stress. He had moved into freeports to support them and create new profit streams, but world governments had turned on their high-dollar citizens somewhat, which meant that making money in the freeport game was getting more challenging by the day. Add in a high profile screwup like a malfunctioning sprinkler system and he was screwed.

So, Aldo made a deal. A very good deal. And became a "friend" of the Boolis.

The ability to get an item out of a freeport without it being officially "registered" as leaving was extremely valuable. And it required a certain flexibility with laws and customs. Things someone connected politically could pull off, which was very much in Aldo's wheelhouse. Still, the vast majority of Aldo's freeport transactions remained legal and above board.

But then something happened.

How was never exactly clear, but somehow a deal between the Boolis and a Russian troublemaker named Edward Dachshund resulted in a blow-up between the two parties that resulted in a demand for guarantees. Specifically, for an item that the Boolis claimed to have on site within Aldo's freeport. Problem was it wasn't there, so the Boolis decided to blame Aldo for it being missing.

Now, the Boolis knew it had nothing to do with Aldo or the freeport, because it was never there. Calling in their favor, they used Aldo as a scapegoat and suggested it was his lack of professionalism that allowed the item in question, a supposedly valuable painting, to remain inside its country of origin vs. being shipped to the freeport where it was "registered" to be. They accused him of a "clerical screwup."

Just the accusation called Aldo's trustworthiness into question, which could have been very bad for his business. And even though the Boolis claimed in person to him that they were working things out and getting the painting in question "back", it still left Aldo twisting in the wind. He knew he was being used, but he didn't like being manipulated by the Boolis. Going along with them the first time had compromised him once. Now, he was getting stuck in their unprofessionalism. That simply could not stand.

Aldo needed to get control back and he figured the best way would be find the painting in question himself. He knew the Boolis had screwed up somewhere. Reaching out to contacts in the underground art world, Aldo leveraged them as best he could. He tasked Manheim to the job and set about finding it. He needed to safeguard his reputation within the industry and to protect his already suffering businesses.

But then Fatima. And Miss Maggie Deacon.

Thinking back, he recalled the night he caught Maggie as she slipped into his Vancouver high-rise and attempted to lift a very real van Gogh from him. She was perfect. He needed someone like her to help with this. Manheim constructed the secondary test, the Russian foray. It was critical to understand whether she would have what it took to deal with Dachshund's crew on the other side. Because now it was a race. It was a contest to see who could get the painting back and prove their position within the ever-shifting structure of "power" and who had what.

The Boolis had started the problem. Having the holder of the painting die before anyone could properly locate it only made things harder. But Aldo would not be deterred. Bosche had informed them that the painting had been spotted in Los Angeles, which he needed to be confirmed. He had to beat the Russians to it for obvious reasons, not the least of which was to preserve his ability to claim that he had the panting on site in his freeport all along.

But Fatima.

Now, that was a complication. His interest in her was sincere but the happenstance of Maggie Deacon's involvement, of her being… what she was… increased the level of difficulty ten-fold. His feelings for Fatima were not those of some naïve young man. He was far too old for that, but he did care for her. It was just that those feelings could in no way become subservient to his needs as a businessman. One could never supplant the other.

Aldo turned back as Fatima emerged from the lounge area, hair wrapped in a towel. She walked over, reached up, put her arms around him and kissed his cheek.

"I'm so glad you kept the boat in Los Angeles," she smiled, "It was worth flying back for."

"Well, business sort of forced my hand. It looks like we will have at least a few more days here."

Fatima smiled and looked up at Aldo. "Well, I'm happy to stay for a while. I'm having more fun here with you anyway."

Aldo's head turned slightly as he caught the tart note in Fatima's statement. His reaction told her she had let out more than she intended.

"Well," started Fatima, "I am sort of annoyed with my best friend right now and would rather spend my time here."

Aldo kissed her gently on the forehead. "You are always welcome here, my darling. Always. And who knows? Maybe we will find a way to have Maggie join us before too long, eh? You just never know.

54

MAGGIE STRADDLED the Honda CB 750, and took a long breath of the warm, blowing, sea air. The sun shone in her face as she sat parked at Zuma Beach on her recent purchase. Maggie had pulled off near the public restrooms for a break and to get a sense of place. Now, she was taking in the scene: the sun, the sand, the water, and the endless view just off Westward Beach Road.

Maggie had ridden here for two reasons. One, to try out the bike and see what she could do, while the other was more directly related to the task at hand. Maggie was checking out a lead.

Point Dume was named in 1793 when a British Naval Officer by the name of Vancouver discovered the area. His plan was to name the newly discovered area for a Spanish missionary named Padre Dumetz who was stationed nearby. But in recording his find, Captain George Vancouver misspelled the name, labelling it "Dume" instead of "Dumetz." The mistake stuck and Point Dume it has remained. The only aberration was a brief period in the eighties when a local real estate developer took a shot at upscaling the neighborhood by adding an accent and changing the pronunciation from "doom," to "doo-may", but it never caught on. What did stick though was the area becoming a sort of *Malibu Riviera* thanks to various well-heeled folks buying large plots and building impressive vacation homes. By the time famed late-night host Johnny Carson bought in, the die was cast. The area featured high-end real estate for high-end people. A popular location for film and TV shoots, the famous cliffs have hosted *Iron Man's* house and even the remnants of the Statue of Liberty from the original *Planet of the Apes* twist ending.

Then there's the UFO landing base.

Adding to the glamour of the area is the urban legend that 6 miles off the coast, and 2000 feet under water, sits an almost perfectly oval, yet naturally occurring rock formation that doesn't look naturally occurring at all. Photos appear to show an Olympic venue sized stone pad, supported by carved Greek columns. Some claim the rock formation is an ancient alien landing platform, while others just smile and say "Well, that's California for you."

Maggie didn't care about any of that. She was busy looking for a house. Specifically, Zevon Levi's fancy beach house. This was the right area, and it was her intention to track it down and do some personal recon to get a general feeling of the site.

And if she could get inside, all the better.

Ready to move, Maggie reached up to grab her helmet from the handlebars. She shook her head and chuckled as she began putting it on again. Mica had said that his sister was a huge *Kill Bill* fanatic, and the helmet he included with the motorcycle's sale confirmed as much. The bright yellow background was adorned with the silhouette of a bright pink cat riding along in a bright pink kiddie wagon, and while Maggie was herself unfamiliar with the movie, she was pretty sure she got what the helmet's logo was alluding to. It wasn't her style, per se, but for a melon protector the helmet was solid and fit great. And it came with the bike. If the in-your-face paint job happened to be slightly, or even overtly offensive, she didn't care. Nothing wrong with having an edge.

Maggie started up the bike and rolled away from the beach, heading up the road. She was looking for Birdview Avenue which turned out to be on her left, just past the open beach. She rolled the throttle on the Honda as she made the turn and continued up the roadway.

Keeping her eyes peeled for the address, Maggie struggled to find markers of any kind. It seemed many homeowners made it their mission to obscure, hide or outright eliminate any visible proof of numbered order along the street. Luckily, Maggie had been told to keep a look out for a 3ft. stone golem standing next to a large gate. Zevon had named his production company after the mythical creature, which loosely translated is an animated anthropomorphic being in Jewish folklore entirely created from mud or clay. It was a sort of "mud monster." As a metaphor, the golem contained seemingly limitless symbolism as it could be a victim or villain, Jew or non-Jew, man, woman or whatever. It had been used to connote war, community, isolation, hope, and even despair. Or maybe Zevon just thought a little mud monster tucked out front of his property looked cool. Whatever the reason, Maggie kept her eyes peeled for it as she rolled past the various gates and entrances spread along Birdview.

Then she saw it.

Just as described, a mini monster-man standing guard in the foliage of a landscaped yard directly adjacent a modern-styled, automatic gate. This was Levi's place all right. Maggie didn't stop though, instead gliding by slowly so as not to attract attention.

The gate to Levi's house was set back slightly, just enough room to drive in and use the call box. Maggie noticed at least one camera mounted near the gate. Older system but clearly real. The entire property, at least from the road front, was fenced but with plenty of trees and plants. She could hop it, if necessary, easily. Good climbing trees by fences were sweet as pie for Maggie. She wondered why people never seemed to realize this was a security issue. She continued her ride until the end of the street, which opened into the Point Dume Natural Preserve. This was good. Now she had a built-in reason for being nearby. If questioned, she was simply visiting the preserve. Locking in a good backstory, Maggie brought the motorcycle to rest and parked it alongside the entry to the hiking trails. She took a short walk along them, getting closer to the ocean. She tried to catch a glimpse of the oceanside of Zevon's mansion.

It wasn't working. Even after walking a fair distance, Maggie could not make out which place was the one she wanted. All of them could be accessed from the back, with a little work and some effort, but it wouldn't be clean. And it risked a pretty good fall off a serious cliff. Maggie noted it and walked back to her ride. Throwing her leg back over the Honda, she fired the bike to life and headed back down the street.

As she got closer to Zevon's driveway once more, the gate started to open. Looking around, Maggie spied a classic Aston Martin coming toward her down the street. It was going a little too fast, and moving in sharp, jerky ways. Fast then too slow, then a shift got missed. Eventually, it arrived at the gate and turned inside. Maggie could not see the occupants due to the low roofline and tinted glass. She continued by, watching as the gate slid closed behind the car. So, someone was home at the house. Family? Associate? Lawyer? Whomever it was couldn't drive a stick shift to save their life, that was for sure. Maggie smirked as she revved the bike back toward Zuma Beach. She needed to get into the property at some point and have a look around. From what she saw, it wouldn't be impossible, but it also wasn't going to be easy.

She had a few ideas. The quickest was just to wander inside and have a look, but with people on site that was out of the question. Exiting Birdview Avenue and rounding the base of the cliffs, Maggie looked up toward the houses perched above. She could try coming up from the bottom. Claim ignorance if she ended up caught by someone. Her age and gender certainly helped in that. Totally non-threatening. Maggie stopped her bike and parked it alongside the road.

Nearby, an aging wood staircase snaked its way up the cliff face and into the backyard of one of the overlooking homes. It wasn't Zevon's house but one or two doors down, about a hundred feet or so in reality. Maggie started to climb.

Reaching the top, the stairs converged into a sort of locked cove. Security for the property owner from people doing what Maggie was about to do. However, Maggie wasn't headed for the house owning the stairs. She slipped herself over the side railing and walked along the edge of the property toward the next-door neighbor. This house didn't have a staircase going down, or much of a backyard at all, but thanks to the elaborate construction of what seemed to be the largest personal swimming pool Maggie had ever seen, the foundation created for it made a sort of passable, 6in. wide walkway around the cliff-edge of the property. After a few minutes of careful plodding, Maggie was peeking over the edge of Zevon Levi's backyard and looking into the pool area.

Maggie saw figures moving inside the house. One was a woman, totting around on heels, and the other a thirty-something guy. She couldn't make out faces. Whatever they were discussing was animating the woman. She was waving her arms around and gestured this way and that. The guy seemed to be the source of whatever was driving her. He wasn't moving around much, just talking. Maggie needed to get closer.

The fencing around the back yard was made up of bright white metal slats, and they were darn hot after a day in the sun. They were also 8ft high on the sides. The fence lowered near the view, of course, which was where she would have to climb over. But it would also mean she could be exposed to those inside the house. Then Maggie saw it.

A perfect climbing tree.

The neighbor's tree was just the right height to let her scamper up and drop into Zevon's yard. The only issue would be getting out. There were no trees, or anything really inside his yard that she could use to get back over the same way. Her only chance would be to exit near the view-point, and that was right at the cliff edge, so she'd be navigating a 4ft fence with a 150 ft drop on the other side. Not the best. No matter. She needed in and this had to work.

Maggie dropped lightly into Zevon's yard. Immediately, she looked left and right, ensuring she was not seen. Quickly, she flattened herself against the main building and made her way to a window. Carefully, she looked inside, trying to see the people she had noticed before. Just as she got close, she heard a voice call out.

"¿Quién eres?"

Maggie turned. It was a gardener. He was asking who she was. Immediately, Maggie turned and smiled.

"Hi! I'm looking for my dog. *El perro*? She's little. *Pequeño*?" Maggie made gestures indicating the size with her hands.

The gardener stopped. He didn't appear angry, or aggressive, yet. Maggie noted this and moved closer.

"She dug under the fence, I think? *Cavado?* I can't find her. Have you seen her?"

The man mimicked her actions, also looking left and right, then moved his hands to and fro, suggesting he didn't know anything. Maggie grabbed him gently by the arm and led him right into the posh backyard area. He clearly didn't speak English, but Maggie kept talking.

"Maybe you know the owners. Maybe they've seen little Roofie?"

Maggie continued to guide the gardener along, as he lightly protested, holding a grass rake in his off hand. Maggie started waving at the people inside the massive house.

"Hello! Hi! Hello! Can you help us out here? Hello?"

One of the large glass doors slid open and Bunny Levi tottered out to see what all the commotion was.

Maggie went right into character.

"Oh hello. I'm so sorry to bother you, my little dog...she ran away just as I was walking her. I think she saw one of those little ground squirrels. They just drive her crazy...and off she went after it. I had her on a leash and she just pulled her head out of the collar. I'd loosened it because she had a little sore on her neck, but it totally was my fault and I'm ......"

Bunny's eyes opened wide at the onslaught of information. "I, uh, haven't seen anything." She looked at the gardener. "You?"

The gardener looked around like he couldn't fathom what was happening and threw his arms up in the air. Maggie continued talking.

"I was just trying to get her back and I'm so sorry for even coming in here, all my fault, you understand but when little Roofie gets it in her head to chase something...."

"Roofie?" asked a voice. David Teck strolled out of the house with an interested smile on his face. "Your dog is named...Roofie?"

Maggie stopped, turned, and then faced him. "Yes, Roofie. Because when she barks it sounds like 'rooof.'"

David almost couldn't contain the smirking grin that started to grow across his face.

Maggie continued, "I'm so worried. It's high up here. If my little dear falls I don't know what I'll do."

David looked around. "It is high up. How did you even get back here? Pretty dangerous, no?" He eyed Maggie carefully.

Maggie turned and clapped the Mexican gardener on the shoulder. "This kind man let me in, around the side, he wanted to help." The gardener stared off into the sky, having given up on trying to understand what was transpiring.

Bunny spoke up.

"Well, we haven't seen any dog of any kind in and around here. Maybe you can get Pedro to show you out. Pedro?"

The gardener looked at Bunny as she raised her voice again, waving at the gardener.

"Pedro?!"

The gardener looked at her, trying to discern her meaning, before he nodded his head and smiled.

"Ernesto!" replied the gardener, gesturing to himself.

"Right, Ernesto," said Bunny, "He can show you the way out."

As Ernesto the gardener gestured for Maggie to follow him, David spoke up.

"Did you want to leave a name and a number, y'know, just in case we see your dog?"

Maggie made direct eye contact with David. "Sure, I'm Babs. If you have a pen or something I can write it down."

David took out his phone. "Tell me. I'll mark it down. Now, you said Babs….and it was Roofie, yes?"

Maggie nodded, and then gave him a number before she followed the gardener out of the backyard and around the front to the driveway entrance. She could tell the guy was suspicious. That was fine. She was suspicious herself. She couldn't shake the notion that she'd seen him somewhere before. He was familiar.

After the gardener showed her out the front driveway, Maggie watched the gate close slowly. She had noted basic door and window positions, along with more than a few other important things. If she had to visit again, it would be much easier the next time.

As she walked back down the road to rejoin her bike, Maggie felt her cell phone vibrate. It couldn't be the guy she just met. She had given him a fake number. Looking on the phone, Maggie realized it was a forward from her personal phone, lying on the bed at the crochet convention hotel. It was a voicemail. She had set up her regular phone to forward messages to her burner one. Maggie dialed into the voicemail to listen.

It was Fati. She was sorry about their fight and wanted to talk about things. Now? She was in LA with Aldo and wanted to visit Maggie at the hotel. Maggie's breath caught in her throat as the last part of Fati's message played.

"C'mon down Mags. I'm in the front lobby right now!"

As she closed the phone, Maggie turned her eyes to the sky. What was she going to do?

55

IVAN STOPPED and gazed at the massive structure before him. He took a deep breath. Then another. Finally, slowly, he ascended the cathedral stairs. He moved carefully and deliberately, but it wasn't because he was unsure of his physical abilities. He still wasn't sure why he had decided to come. Ivan told himself it was to see the diBicci, but he knew that was a lie. Still, that lie had gotten him this far. As a pretense it would suffice to push him along a little more.

Ivan passed through the massive bronze doors and walked toward the main aisle. The smells of a church are memorable, even when you haven't been inside one for decades. And Ivan certainly hadn't. At least not for worship. To steal? That was another story. He had done that many times.

Not today though.

As Ivan passed by the holy water font near the door, he resisted the habit to bless himself. It wasn't his place to do such things anymore. He was only a visitor, not a believer. At least, not for a very long time.

St. James Cathedral began its life in 1903 as a plot of land at 9th & Marion, purchased by the diocese of Nesqually and overlooking the other eight hills that made up the growing city of Seattle. By late 1905, Bishop O'Dea had laid the cornerstone of the Cathedral, which would go on to tower over the landscape, ably representing the faithful of the diocese and proclaiming the faith to all who might see her. That sort of imposing presence in the city was no more, as skyscrapers and other high-rises long ago crowded out St. James as a focal point. Still, it was architecture impressive enough to give pause when one came upon it.

Ivan walked past the baptismal area. He knew where he was going. There were no events on, just a few older folks quietly cleaning the church and what seemed a small lineup of five or six near the confessionals. He moved along, turning right at the main altar, and heading for the small chapel to the side.

Up a few steps, and down a short hallway, Ivan entered the chapel. Seeing the chairs arrayed along each side, he moved to one that would afford him the best view of the treasure he had lied to himself about coming to see: *Mary and Child with Six Saints* by Neri diBicci. Ivan took a deep breath, releasing his air slowly, willing the painting to wash over him.

A 15th century painting, a Renaissance altar piece that turned up inside a storage closet at the cathedral herself more than fifty years ago, stared back at him from the wall. Ivan focused his eyes on the ancient composition, searching for a clue as to the reason he came.

It had been at the Seattle Art Museum for more than two years, first undergoing restoration and then as a centerpiece for an exhibit on devotional art or some such thing. He had gone to see it there once. The care they took to restore it was baffling to Ivan. His personal approach to art was obviously coarse. He simply took art when he wanted it, and in rough ways. He certainly didn't stop to appreciate it. To see people put so much effort into something he would steal casually was striking to him. And confusing.

When the exhibition was complete, the piece was returned to the cathedral and put on display, but in the most humble, quiet manner possible; out of the main church, tucked inside a tiny, adjacent chapel frequented mainly by the devout.

Ivan had never seen it here. Until today. Now he was staring at it. And breathing.

To this day, no one knew how the work even came to be in the Seattle cathedral. It was believed to have been a gift to the diocese in the 1930s or '40s. But before that? It became hazy. Provenance from five hundred years prior is a little clearer, but even that didn't answer all the questions of the journey taken.

Ivan knew intimately how complicated the lifetime travels of art could be. He had interrupted many of them. And elongated others.

The painting, done in a heavily gilded style, showed the Virgin Mary seated, baby Jesus in her lap and flanked by Saints Luke, Bartholomew, Lawrence, John the Baptist, Martin, and Sebastian. Each saint was pictured holding symbols hinting at the ways in which they were killed. St. Bartholomew, who was flayed for his faith, carried a knife; St. Lawrence, roasted alive had a metal grill; St. Sebastian, martyred with arrows held one and so on. Horrific when considered, but obviously instructive. Paintings like this were usually commissioned by rich followers and done mainly to propagate the faith. To tell the stories of the church. Most believers were illiterate in the 15th century, so paintings such as this, or carvings or stained-glass windows were used to impress, to educate and, they hoped, to inspire. To get people to examine themselves in the light and experience of others' accomplishments…and their sufferings.

And likely to get more money, thought Ivan. He breathed in and out. He was tired of deceptions. Of lying. He had lived in that web for most of his life now and had spun plenty of his own too. But now it weighed on him. It was too much for some reason. And he didn't know what to do.

This job had broken him. He had been lying to Maggie. Indirectly and overtly. Most of it was lies by omission, as in not telling her everything that was happening or what his own role was in it. But he lied so easily to her that it bothered him. More now than ever before.

Ivan knew of the Vermeer before it was stolen. Through a long-ago friend he knew of the plot to take it that fateful night at the Gardner, and even the grand plan thereafter to move it out of country. And he even knew of the problems that arose and the complications that occurred, ensuring that the contract could never be fulfilled. He had watched as the painting slid underground and off the radar, and during the many, many years it stayed hidden and was forgotten by most.

But he hadn't forgotten it. He had waited. And listened.

He didn't know when exactly Levi got it, or why, but once it landed in Los Angeles his ears heard the waves it made. People think they keep secrets. They almost never do. Everything comes out eventually.

And a painting like *The Concert* demanded to be heard, whether one wanted it to or not.

He knew when the Boolis started using art as guarantees. And he knew when they approached Levi. He also knew when Dachshund and his Russians decided enough was enough and went to hold the Boolis to account. He knew when Levi decided to paint a copy of it and he knew when Aldo tried to save face by blackmailing him to find it, leveraging his only son's weaknesses against him. He knew it all. Ivan was at the center, always. Messages and information were either created by him, went through him, or were heard by him. This was his job. It was what he was paid to do. To know things.

And now precious Maggie was front and centre within the maelstrom he had helped to execute. Ivan rubbed his smooth head, pulling the loose skin on his brow toward his eyes. He stared at the painting. Swirls of color, lines of definition, messages, overt and sublime. All created for peering, bleakly ignorant crowds. Ivan stole art. He didn't appreciate it. Why should he? It was paint on paper. Could anyone creating it possibly take it as seriously as the crowds desperate to view it? Ivan doubted it.

A priest in long black cassock entered the chapel and paused, modestly surprised to see someone seated there. He nodded a greeting.

Ivan nodded back.

The younger man spoke, "Are you here for reconciliation?"

Ivan looked at him, confused.

The young man gestured. "The lineup in the church. Sometimes people wait in here if the priest hasn't arrived yet. Father is there now."

A hint of recognition hit Ivan. "Confession. Is that what you mean, confession?"

The young man smiled. "Yes, we don't really call it that anymore."

"Why not?"

"Well, I guess it's just a more…gentle definition, perhaps? Confession puts the focus on what you've done wrong, while reconciliation focuses more on re-establishing your friendship with God."

"Friendship?" asked Ivan.

"Well, yes."

Ivan considered that for a moment. "God is my friend?"

"Of course." answered the prelate.

"Seems like a downgrade, no?"

The young priest looked at Ivan, confused.

"For him. God," clarified Ivan.

"I don't follow," said the priest.

Ivan rose to his feet. "Never mind. I'm not here for recon-whatever. Or confession. I don't know why I'm here so I should go."

Ivan walked from the chapel, out into the main nave of the church and back toward the entrance. His nose registered the trace smells of incense and hints of burning beeswax. He shouldn't have come here. He knew that now. You mustn't let thoughts like these find their way to the surface. It was bad for business.

As Ivan stepped outside, back into the damp Seattle air he breathed deep, clearing the smells of the church from his nostrils. He reached for the cellular phone in his pocket and dialed a number. He held the cell to his face as he waited for it to connect.

"Greta? It's me. Book a ticket to Los Angeles. As soon as you can get. No, I don't want to argue about this. No, stop. But I have to. Yes. I'm going, whether you want me to or not." Ivan pushed the button to end the call and replaced the phone in his pocket. He resisted the urge to turn and face the cathedral, choosing instead to walk directly away without once looking back.

56

"THERE'S TWO OF THEM."

Bunny wasn't listening as she missed another gear in the Aston Martin. "Just go into third, please!" she grumbled as she yanked aggressively at the shifter handle between the seats.

David stared out the passenger window, oblivious to her lack of interest, repeating his thought. "There's two of them."

Bunny finally found the gear and levelled out her acceleration, taking a deep breath. Then, realizing she might have missed something, barked at David, "What are you on about?"

"*The Concert.*" he answered. "There's two of them. The copy he made and the real one."

Bunny rolled her eyes. "So? I thought we already knew that."

David continued to stare out the window, rolling in thought, as he answered, "I didn't know anything. I suspected plenty. But now I know that your husband had the actual original from the Gardener robbery and he hired that guy we just met to paint an exact copy. I *know* that now."

Bunny accelerated around a corner. "And that gets me money how?"

Audibly, David sighed and turned to face her. "You brought me in for a comparatively piddling insurance claim. Do you even realize how big this could be? That painting is valued close to $300 million or so. Probably more. It's hot as hell 'cause it's still missing from a crime. But clearly it exists, and it must be nearby. You've got to know where it is. Or that lunkhead you hired to kill him knows."

Bunny took instant offense. "I didn't hire anyone to kill him! Scare him, okay? It was to scare him. I never wanted to kill anyone."

"Whatever, that idiot you hired still has the fake one which means he's either still thinking it's real or he's figured out the truth and is on the hunt for the real one. I'm betting that it's somewhere in the house. I mean, it's got to be there. Outside of burying it in some secret location or stashing it in another country but…did he ever show you anything? Mention anything?"

Bunny jerked the car violently to one side, missing a large pothole but dropping one tire onto a gravel shoulder in the process, causing the car to fishtail slightly and overrev. She pressed the accelerator down to correct things. She was getting better.

David was shocked at the violent correction. "Can you slow down a bit? I don't need to die on the way there."

Bunny waved him off. "I can drive fine. I just need practice on this. And I told you before. He never showed me anything. His art was either hanging or sitting around waiting to be hung. No secrets."

"He had acquired the most sought-after painting in the world. Did you know about it?"

"No."

"He paid a guy to copy it. You know about that?"

"No."

"Then I'd suggest there were plenty of secrets between you two."

"Well, I never asked about anything. If I did, he probably would have told me. He always had things going on, crews of people coming around doing things. He had guys from his shows fixing cars or doing shelf build-ins and stuff. What did I care?"

"Was there one person who he leaned on? Like a special assistant? Someone he really trusted?"

Bunny slowed the car down to match the traffic. Awkwardly, but correctly this time. It made her smile. "Maybe Benny. He was Zev's PM on most projects."

"Benny?"

"Ben…can't remember his last name. The production office will have his details. What can he do?"

"I don't know. Give us a clue as to what was going down? Someone had to drive painter-boy back and forth. Maybe it was Ben. You need to talk to him."

"Me? Why?"

"He knows you. Maybe he'll spill something we can use."

Bunny considered this for a moment. "Now that you say it, I could probably use his help on the funeral party. I think I will call him."

"Was he doing anything else around that time? Any big projects or anything? At the house out here? Think! You must have seen something."

David looked forward, slapping the dash of the car with his palms. "I really want to hunt around the mansion a bit too. There's something there. Has to be. I've known tons of these guys. They always make some sort of man-cave where they hide their toys and plot their big ideas. Get a certain amount of money and a good chunk of it always goes into a bomb shelter or a panic room or whatever. That's what they call it for taxes but really, it's just a playroom for boys who never grew up. Are there house plans anywhere? The beach place is newish. They must be somewhere."

"We can look when we get there."

Bunny Levi steered the car up Birdview Avenue and around, slowing to a crawl as she approached a gate. Reaching up to the visor of the car, she pushed a button, causing the gate to open. She nearly stalled the performance machine one more time as she eased slowly into the hidden compound. Before the car was even fully stopped, David had the door open and a leg fully outside.

"Hey!" yelled Bunny.

David was excited. "C'mon! We've got to look around inside." He jumped out and immediately saw a beat-up truck with lawn equipment and grass clippings in the back. He turned to Bunny, gesturing as if to say, *'what the hell is this?'*

"The yard guy. Pedro or Tuco or something. He comes once a week. That's today."

David quickstepped his way to the front door, trying to open it and enter. Locked. He turned and waited impatiently for Bunny to get out of the low-slung car, adjust her skirt and totter over while fishing keys from inside her purse. Finally, she got the door open. David pushed in front of her, immediately heading for the lower areas of the house. Bunny shook her head at him and walked into the kitchen, opening the massive fridge, and fishing out a tiny green Pellegrino bottle. She opened a cabinet to find a glass to pour into. She made her drink and took a sip, wiping the bubbles from the end of her nose.

In a flurry, David came charging back upstairs. "His office? Can you show me his office? There's got to be some clue in there."

Bunny took her drink and led David down a wide hallway to a large back room. The view was of the ocean, and the office was immense. Posters of Zev's direct-to-video/streaming movies hung on the wall. Positioned artfully was a massive glass desk hiding a minimalist leather desk chair behind it. There was a leather couch, a bar, plus a separate blue leather seating area, along with bookshelves holding more DVDs than books.

"File cabinets?"

Bunny pointed to the desk, where a small, matching rolling file drawer was offset slightly. "I think that's it. I never saw any other files. He kept most of that kind of stuff at the production office on Sunset."

David walked around the desk, knelt, and pulled at the drawer. "Locked." he said.

Bunny waved it away. "The key is on the desk. Right there. I found it after they came and took him away. I didn't see anything in them."

David opened the drawers and rifled his way through the cabinets, eventually coming up with a mound of papers having to do with the construction of the house.

"Architect stuff. It might show measurements and stuff."

"What will that tell you?" asked Bunny.

"It's a long shot, but say a room is drawn on the plans as being 20x20ft. Well, you measure the room in real life and it's 15x20ft. What happened to that other 5ft? Either the house plans shifted, and they didn't update them, or somebody walled off a portion and set up a secret entrance to it."

"You can see that in those?"

"No, but maybe I can get clues and that's how to find stuff. Make yourself useful. Go get me a tape measure or something."

David unfolded the architect plans and began to flip them, page over page, looking for indications of anything. Then he started walking around different rooms in the house, getting more and more frustrated by all the windows.

"There's so much glass in here. And it's so open. I don't know where in the hell anyone would hide a secret room. It must be away from the back, more to the street side."

Bunny was starting to get annoyed with David ordering her around.

"Maybe you can settle down a bit. I'm not your assistant here. Technically, you still work for me anyway. And besides...."

David stopped her with a raised hand, looking over her shoulder and out into the backyard. "What's going on out there?"

Bunny turned and looked. "That's the gardener guy, it's nothing."

"There's someone with him." answered David.

Bunny turned the rest of the way around and walked over to the glass wall. She unlocked a catch and slid open the massive door to the outside, stepping into the backyard.

David watched as Bunny conversed with the workman and the mystery lady. She was late 50's? Older? Silver hair for sure but nice body. She was talking a mile a minute. David moved carefully toward the open door, straining to hear the discussion.

"I was just trying to get her back and I'm so sorry for even coming in here, all my fault, you understand but when little Roofie gets it in her head to chase something...."

David stepped onto the back patio and forced himself into the discussion. "Roofie? Your dog is named...Roofie?"

The woman stopped, apparently surprised that someone else was talking to her, before answering, "Yes, Roofie. Because when he barks it sounds like 'rooof.'"

David couldn't believe this. He struggled to stifle a smirk.

The woman prattled on. "I'm so worried. It's high up here. If my little dear falls I don't know what I'll do."

David looked left and then right, beginning to nod and confirming her fears. "It is very high up. How did you even get back here? Pretty dangerous, no?" He zeroed in on the woman's eyes, looking for answers beyond any words coming out of her mouth.

Casually, the woman turned her head and waved her hands about, avoiding David's penetrating stare, instead clapping the Mexican gardener on the shoulder. "This kind man let me in, around the side, he wanted to help me." She smiled directly in the gardener's face and nodded, causing him to smile back and nod as well.

David ignored the pantomime and stared deeper into the woman's face. He had seen her before. This lady was familiar somehow.

Getting bored, and clueless to the subtext occurring, Bunny spoke up.

"Well, we haven't seen any dog of any kind in and around here. Maybe you can get Pedro to show you out, ok? Pedro?"

The gardener looked confused, until he realized Bunny was guessing his name wrong. "Ernesto." He helpfully offered.

As Bunny tried to recover from screwing up the help's name, David drilled in on the woman, looking for tells, thinking to himself *'If she's a fake, she's a pretty good one.'* Finally, as the gardener began to lead the mystery lady out, David saw an opportunity and spoke up.

"Did you want to leave a name and a number, y'know, just in case we see your dog?"

The woman stopped and stared David straight in the eye. "Sure, I'm Babs. If you have a pen or something I can write it down."

Smiling, David took out his phone. "Tell me. I'll mark it down. Now, you said Babs....and it was Roofie, yes?" David began to smirk again, knowing almost certainly that this woman was not named 'Babs' and that the likelihood of a dog named Roofie even existing was near zero. David marked her details down, even as he guessed that she had made those up too. He watched as the woman eventually disappeared from his sight, around the house.

Bunny turned to David. "That was weird."

"More than you know," answered David. She's looking for something. Probably the same thing we're looking for. We were right to come back here. There is something hiding inside this house, and we better get to finding it before someone else beats us to it."

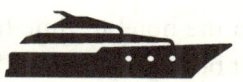 # 57

MAGGIE WATCHED as Fatima attempted to merge onto the 405 freeway and without realizing it, began to hold her breath. Fatima kept moving in the merge lane but was not increasing her speed to match the traffic.

"Hey, I think you might have to go a little faster…"

"I've got it, I've got it."

Maggie felt her fingers dig into the door pull of the Mini Cooper. She didn't like driving with Fatima back home. She just wasn't aggressive enough, even for Vancouver. LA traffic was a whole other planet.

Maggie offered advice, "You really have to be confident, or they won't let you in."

Not looking at Maggie, Fati answered calmly, "Someone nice will give me room."

Fatima continued to putt-putt along, trusting that a space would open in the incessant waves of 405 traffic until, like a miracle, one did. She slipped into the speeding freeway, as all manner of vehicle dodged around her left and right, with no issues whatsoever. Internally, Maggie was a basket-case. But Fatima? Functionally oblivious to the risks surrounding her. The Mini buzzed along.

"I think you could have done surface streets to get back, you know? The navigation shows some roads that go all the way." Maggie pointed at the NAV screen in the little car.

Fatima waved it away. "Probably, but I like trying to use the freeways. It's always quicker if you can use them properly. Plus, it's exciting!" She smiled at Maggie like a mischievous little girl.

Turning back to her seat, Maggie attempted to calm down. It was not easy. She just finished traipsing around the crochet convention with Fatima for two hours, faking interest in all-manner of mundane crochet-ery. And that was after busting the speed limit on the PCH just to get back to the hotel in time to meet up with her in the first place. She had not been prepared for Fatima. And certainly not prepared for her in Los Angeles.

Maggie made a mental note to never, ever use a crochet convention as a cover again. Sure, it would have been fine if she never had to visit it, but the day's events had proven otherwise. An afternoon spent "ooooing" and "aaahhing" over crocheted blankets, shawls, stuffed animals, wall hangings, tea cozies, vests(!), coveralls and God knows what else was simply too much. How in the heck actual people did such mundanity for an entire weeklong event was beyond Maggie's comprehension. Thankfully, the "fastest fingers" contest had already started so she didn't have to lie about not being able to enter it. Even still, Fatima's disappointment at Maggie not competing was palpable.

"I think you could have won. You're so good at things."

"Well, my fingers have been bugging me a little lately. Probably just as well that I missed the cut-off."

Fatima steered the car through traffic, seemingly unconcerned by the breakneck speed of others around her. She would simply wait for an opening and then slide her way into it.

"I think we need CA-90 West. That's just coming up here."

Maggie girded herself as Fatima floated through what seemed like a moving maze of cars. The sight of all these varied machines rocketing around and past their little ride was intense. Yet Fatima was cool as a cucumber the whole way.

"Now, I think I stay on this until Lincoln Blvd. I told Aldo I didn't want a car service taking me around. I wanted a little car to drive myself. It's much more fun."

Maggie smiled weakly. Fun for Fatima, but not Maggie. She was more unnerved riding passenger than walking along the side of a 30-storey building. Maggie preferred control in most situations, and this was not control.

"Isn't it all so fascinating?" beamed Fati, "I love the traffic flying by. Like ants going every which way, or little blood cells in arteries. Have you looked at pictures of the freeways when they are running?

They look like veins in a body, shooting people all over, in uniform little pockets. It's almost like it's alive."

Maggie smiled. She was trying to stay annoyed at Fatima, but it never worked. She just had such an open, interested, and sincere view of the most bizarrely mundane things in the world. She was grateful, always, and appreciative no matter what. It certainly made staying angry with her impossible.

After the crochet torture, Fatima had offered to host Maggie back at Aldo's yacht, berthed in Marina Del Rey. Maggie accepted for two reasons: one, she didn't really have a way of saying no and it was the best way to get the hell out of the crochet madness sooner, and two, she wanted to see what Aldo was up to. Why was he sniffing around Los Angeles, especially after he'd been the one behind officially tasking her with getting the painting? Was he checking up on her? Did Manheim play into this? She had not heard from that weird character yet either, so she figured a visit to the big shot's playground might serve a purpose.

Though it also meant she would have to have a talk with Fati.

Fatima had studiously avoided discussing their fight from days earlier, and it hung in the air around them. Maggie could feel it, and she knew they would have to broach the subject at some point, likely on the yacht. She wasn't looking forward to it. This sort of thing was not Maggie's jam. Having to preserve feelings and emotions and the like was just awkward and uncomfortable for her. Maggie grew up in a sort of British tradition, sort of a "stiff upper lip-bury your true thoughts and feelings deep" sort of thing. No one needed to excavate all that. But Fati was Greek in heritage and loved her drama. Her ability to resurrect all manner of issues and then hash them out emotionally over and over was foreign to Maggie, and not fun. She sighed.

As Fatima veered off the freeway into the final leg of their journey, she exited onto Lincoln Blvd before cutting down Admiralty Way. They followed the marina ring-road around, until finally turning onto a street called Bora Bora Way. It dead-ended in a little parking lot, directly adjacent to where the larger yachts berthed. Fatima pulled smoothly into a spot marked "VIP" and threw the little car into park, beaming widely.

"Wasn't that a blast? Exhilarating! This really is a cute little car. I just love the way it looks and handles. I feel like I'm driving a tiny race car. OK, come on, the boat is just over there."

Maggie and Fatima got out of the car. Before heading over to the yacht, Fatima popped the rear hatch and gathered up her purchases from the convention: a how-to kit for simple crocheting (that Maggie knew she would come to regret at some point in the future) and two little crocheted dolls. One was a black and white *Steamboat Willie Mickey Mouse* while the other was a tiny white dog that somehow resonated with her.

"I just love *Snowy*." She smiled at Maggie as she hugged the little toy.

The ladies walked to the dock and then along until they reached the gangplank for the *Jimena*. They boarded to multiple crew members fussily cleaning and primping the yacht for the afternoon. Fatima spoke to one of the hands.

"Is *El Rey* on board?"

The deferential young man shook his head. "No madame. He is expected soon though."

Maggie gave Fatima a look, which caused her to blush slightly.

"What?" said Fatima, smiling.

"*El Rey*? Really? *The King*?"

"Oh, Maggie, it's just a joke. It's not like he makes me say that. I did it to be funny. You're so silly."

The pair continued onboard and found a shaded spot. While Maggie went to sit, Fatima moved to a refreshment bar.

"Can I get you something, honey? Spring water? A soda? Juice? Whatever."

"A water is fine. With a glass, please."

Fatima brought a glass over and set it down. She took a deep breath and sat right across from Maggie's knees.

"I think we should talk."

Maggie had been dreading this. She thought it was all over her face that she didn't want to have this discussion, but apparently that didn't matter because it was happening. Maggie deflated, giving in to her dread.

"Look Fati, I'm sorry, OK? I spoke out of turn. It's not my business what you do or with whom you do it with. It's not my place. I just…speak without thinking sometimes. I'm sorry. I get protective sometimes. You're my friend and I obviously overstepped…"

Fatima stared right at Maggie, straight in the eyes.

"You didn't overstep. You care about me. I know that. I was being too sensitive. I'm always too sensitive. You know that about me."

Maggie nodded her head. "Yes, but still. It's not for me to say. I should be supportive."

Fatima smiled sweetly. The pressure of not being in alignment with her friend had weighed on her. She leant forward and hugged Maggie with everything she had. Eventually, Maggie surrendered, much like a cat resigned to not being able to escape. Maggie was not big on physical shows of affection. But she did care about Fati. And it was nice. Sort of.

"Oh you!" said Fatima, "I can't stay mad at you!"

Eventually, Fatima released her hug and sat back. Maggie reset herself and spoke up. "Are we good?"

Fatima glowed. "We are good." She then jumped to her feet with a proposition, "Will you have dinner with us tonight? I think Aldo wanted to go into the city. There's some place a friend of his owns that he wanted us to try."

Maggie hedged. "Well, I don't think I'll be able to, actually." That part was true, but then she added a lie. "I was supposed to meet up with someone from the convention."

Fatima put on her best faux pout. "Oh poop. It would have been such fun." She looked left and then right. "Have lunch with us at least? Do you have time for that? I can run you back to the hotel as soon as we're done?"

Remembering the car ride over Maggie offered a compromise. "Okay. I can stay for lunch, but I will find my own way back to the hotel. I want to make a few stops. No need to get you out on the roads again."

"Pffft. It's no trouble at all. I love it. But whatever you want is what happens. Can I be rude and get you to hang out here for a bit by yourself? I just want to get changed and have a quick shower before lunch. I won't be ten minutes, I promise."

"Go ahead. I'm fine," Maggie smiled.

"There are more drinks in that little cooler fridge, and I think some cut up fruit too. Please help yourself. I'll be right back. I swear!"

And with that, Fatima disappeared into the recesses of the *Jimena*.

Maggie turned her gaze toward the water. She breathed in the salt air and started sorting through the things running around inside her head. Levi's house needed another look, that was for sure. The people she ran into were involved, somehow. The guy absolutely was on to her. She also had to find out if there were any updates on finding the exact location of the painting from Manheim. Not to mention doing her own recon and seeing if there was anything else that might be worth digging into. She needed more info on this Levi guy as well. Lost in thought, Maggie was surprised when a voice spoke from behind her.

"You grace us with your presence, Ms. Deacon. How very lovely to see you."

Maggie turned and there he was. Aldo Neto in the flesh. Dark suit, light shirt, with three buttons undone, looking fresh and relaxed as always, and eyeing her directly.

Aware that the game was afoot, Maggie played it cool. "Hello Aldo. Fancy meeting you here."

He made his way over to her and seated himself directly across from Maggie's gaze.

"Fatima said you might be joining us this afternoon. What brings you to Los Angeles?"

Maggie pursed her lips. She could only take so much of this ridiculous fencing. At a certain point, sanity demanded that one simply jump in. And unlike the emotional uncomfortables that Maggie detested, business was business, meaning fair game for confrontations. And for Maggie, such things came quite naturally.

"Oh, come on, Aldo. You know exactly why I'm here. I'm working for you now, apparently."

A smile crept across Aldo's face. He enjoyed Maggie very much. Her fire was attractive and invigorating to him. Momentarily, he wondered what would have happened had he met her first.

"So, we are putting the cards on the table, yes?" grinned Aldo.

"Indeed," replied Maggie, "Why the secrecy, Aldo? Why not tell me what's going on here? With all of it? You could have been straight with me. Or at least straight with Fatima. What are we doing here?"

Challenged directly, Aldo stiffened slightly, but maintained his above-it-all calm. His tone lowered a hair, and he spoke clearly.

"What am *I* doing? It would seem you have plenty of secrets yourself, especially when it comes to your good friend Fatima. Maybe you can explain to her what it is you're doing for me, or is that something you two do not discuss?"

Aldo had her there. Maggie had no plan or interest in confiding the realities of her professional life to Fatima. And now that her and Aldo shared a mutual secret that was as compromising to her as it was to him, it made them partners of a sort. It was not an ideal situation, to say the least.

"We are adults, yes?" Aldo offered, "And some things we keep private for good reasons. I understand this. Of course, you do too."

Maggie wanted to respond. She couldn't let his words go unanswered but engaging directly on this would be a mistake. She decided to parry instead.

"How do I know you're being sincere with Fatima? Can you promise me that my friend is not going to be hurt in all this? How do I know you're not using her to leverage me?"

Aldo considered her words for a moment before answering.

"Would you even believe me if I said so?"

Maggie shrugged involuntarily. He had her there. She answered truthfully. "Probably not."

Aldo leaned back. "Well, then no matter what I say it is not likely enough to calm your fears. But I will offer you this, for whatever it is worth. My interest in the wonderful Fatima is sincere, and completely independent of the business that you and I must transact. I have no desire in...ah, joining the two together. Do you?"

Maggie shook her head no. Aldo continued.

"Then, I would suggest at this stage this is about the best you and I could hope for."

Silence. Neither spoke for several beats. The last sentence simply hung in the air around them. Until things changed once more.

"Aldo!" squealed Fatima, as she entered from the side, "You're back. I was just going to get lunch going for us."

Aldo rose to hug her in welcome. They embraced and then turned back towards the seated Maggie. Fatima looked at Aldo. "Maggie said she would stay and eat with us."

"Well, that would be truly wonderful. Did you have a preference of meal?" he asked Maggie.

Maggie smiled at the invitation and cocked her eye just so. She betrayed the slightest of edge.

"Personally, I tend to like dishes served cold. That would probably be appropriate on a day like today."

Aldo raised both eyes slightly. He didn't expect a shot across the bow, but he respected it. He smiled back and nodded his head in agreement.

"Cold it is, then."

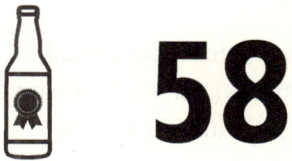

58

BEN LOOKED back and forth, studying the results. He smiled, proud of what he'd done, even though the circumstances were obviously less than ideal. He spied an errant napkin, snatched it from the potted palm it was discarded in, and shoved it inside his pocket.

The rooftop at the Hollywood Roosevelt was as historic as it was gorgeous. Rising twelve storeys above Hollywood Boulevard, the hotel had been the place for memorable after-parties and insider events for decades. Today was no exception. The memorial reception for the not-quite renowned C-level movie producer, Zevon Levi, welcomed rank-and-file members of the Hollywood machine to stop in and say their goodbyes. Or maybe just to confirm that he was officially dead. Hollywood can be cynical like that.

And it was Ben that had made it happen, because he always made it happen, especially when something was tagged as being "difficult" or even "impossible." Ben liked those challenges the best. As his eyes scanned the venue, a waiter walked up.

"The bartender wants more Pabst Blue Ribbon, but I can't find any. Are we out?"

Calmly eyeing the questioner, Ben answered crisply. "In the large fridge of the *Johnny Grant* suite, look on the second and third shelves. And remember to replace whatever you take with extras from the additional cases inside the storage panty, which is located just beside it." The waiter scurried away.

Serving a beer as lowbrow as Pabst Blue Ribbon was a very specific "in-joke" to attendees "in-the-know." One of Zevon's most popular films (which was a relative term) had featured an anti-hero named *Levon Zevits* who was a duplicitous, murderous alcoholic that constantly drank Pabst Blue Ribbon. The characterization was a specific middle-finger aimed directly at Zevon due to a contract dispute with the writer prior to production. It was a combination of arguments surrounding his fee plus access to set.

Angry at the negotiations, the writer responded by mocking Zevon in the final draft of the script. Furious at first, Zevon quickly came to regard the literary "attack" as sort of funny and ended up allowing the insulting changes into the film. *Deathview Window* went on to become a minor cult-hit, due in no small part to a formerly A-list actress' brief nudity, a signature feature of many Golem Pictures. Ben knew that only a few hardcores would even get the Pabst beer allusion, but it was a nice touch to have on offer. At first, the widow Levi wouldn't hear of it, but Ben stood his ground. She relented only after his absolute insistence on the pop cultural importance of it.

Ben continued to patrol the rooftop reception, his eyes peeled for imperfections like tables out of alignment, displays interrupted, or food looking tired, limp, and unappetizing. Pausing to see faces, Ben smiled as he noted the crowd. A mixture of regular crew from over the years, along with day player actor types. Those were the cast members who had bit parts in multiple films, cast for their versatility and willingness to not complain about things like miniscule dressing rooms or non-existent rehearsal time. Inviting run-of-the-mill actors was always good practice. Their need to be seen meant they would show up, making the filling of a room far easier. Ben nodded acknowledgements to familiar faces with curt efficiency.

The bigger names rarely appeared, even though Zevon had seen his share of those too. They weren't big when he had them, of course. It was either before they were uber-famous or long after. Still, the more genuine ones made efforts to come. Corbin Bernsen and Kevin Sorbo both stopped by. Nicollette Sheridan too. Jack Nicholson sent flowers but apparently that was more to do with a bet he and Zev had made decades ago than anything else. For some reason, Weird Al Yanovic was there, bottle flipping near one of the bar stations. Ben couldn't remember what film he did with Zev, if any. Another member of the wait staff approached Ben.

"The finger food pyramid is listing."

Ben sighed audibly, "Take the corresponding pieces from the opposing side, rework the whole thing into two smaller pyramids until the next round of hors d'oeuvres comes out, which should be in less than seven minutes. Go!"

The server hustled away while Ben turned and headed down a row of cocktail tables.

The night was warm, but the breeze made it perfect. The noise of the street was far enough below that it mixed smoothly with the ambient music being played. Decorations were art deco in nature. The widow had chosen a sort of 1920's Hollywood theme. Helpfully, Ben had corrected some of the more egregiously tacky aspects by eliminating them outright or amplifying them in a way that made sense.

Without a doubt, young Ben Savick was a comer in Hollywood. Only twenty-three, he had originally avoided the curse of being tempted by the big three, that is wanting to act, direct or write. From the beginning, Ben was focused on production. And it showed. He got to town at the age of sixteen and accepted whatever job he could find, proceeding to do whatever needed doing better than anyone had ever done it before him. And whether it was stacking chairs, folding tables, or cleaning up some actor's dog vomit, Ben took it seriously. In no time at all he was a personal assistant to a minor producer and was getting associate producer credits on smaller projects.

He was only 19 when he met Zevon Levi. Zev's projects were not the greatest, but he had flow. Where another producer would struggle to get one film in the can every 18-24 months, Zev Levi would churn out 12-14 individual projects in the same period.

Zev had mastered the art of making production pay, first by assembling a core group of people he could travel from show to show. It made him able to offer production services a good 30-40% cheaper than similar outfits, yet still turn a bigger profit than his competition could hope to imagine. Ben soaked it up. Learning from Zev was a master's education in how to situate oneself as close as possible to the "money tap," the flow that must happen for all film and TV productions to exist.

Money always started in the hands of banks or investors, who must be stroked, cajoled, and convinced to steer it towards movie production. Being as close as possible to the eventual "flow" almost always ensured victory, as in getting the most bucks possible. Amazingly, success in this had very little to do with the objective qualities of the film in question. As Zev used to say, "movies that bomb pay just as well as those that don't, and sometimes better." Zevon perfected getting his share, and then went further still, creating new ways to flood even more cash to other areas within his humble empire. Ben learned his lessons well.

He was not prepared for Zevon to die.

Ben took his death hard. By this point in his career, Ben was as cynical as anyone in Hollywood. But Zevon was different. He had taken him under his wing. Ben kind of liked the guy. Knowing they would never speak again was difficult to comprehend or even accept. Losing a mentor was hard enough, but Ben also felt the end of something more personal for the first time. He knew that Golem Pictures would be no more, and that his job was no more as well. He would have to find a new opportunity, and that was scary. Ben knew it wasn't going to be easy to recreate what he had at Golem.

When Zevon's widow reached out to him (at the last minute, of course) to take on assembling the reception event, Ben jumped at it for the chance to honor the life of a man he genuinely appreciated and respected. But he also planned to use it as a living resume for anyone paying attention. Ben stacked the deck in his own favor, inviting as many local producers and connectors as he could find. And while at least half were most certainly enemies of Levi, Ben figured his old boss would understand. He knew the name of the game and would appreciate Ben's wisdom in playing it well.

As the crowds swelled with a fresh push of new arrivals, Ben checked his watch. The gravesite ceremony at Hollywood Forever had ended about twenty minutes ago. He expected the widow and family to arrive anytime. Checking his phone, he confirmed the location of the car service bringing them to the hotel. Seeing it just a few blocks away from the Roosevelt, Ben quickened his pace towards the main entrance of the roof. As he brushed past folks, Ben smiled and nodded constantly. He recognized most people but every now and again there were some that he didn't know. That wasn't odd, per se.

This was film. One day a guy could be taking your laundry at the dry cleaner and the next he was an executive producer with an ass to be kissed. Be nice to everyone, you just never know. Still, the sight of the frighteningly square man filling his face at the sushi table was unsettling. He looked like a character out of *Borat*. Something about the guy just rang alarm bells for Ben. Shaking it off, Ben instead took several photos of the displays and surroundings before continuing to the entrance. Things looked good. Very good indeed.

* * *

David stood next to a large potted palm tree. He was using it for cover, as a place to watch the crowd unnoticed. He skipped the burial on purpose, figuring that people-watching at the reception would be better suited to gathering the sort of information that might help in tracking down the missing picture. David knew there would be someone sniffing around, and funerals were just the sort of place to catch them doing it. Especially when there was free food. David grabbed a shrimp cocktail from the tray of a passing server, tossing the previous one he'd consumed into the oversized pot holding the palm.

* * *

Tranko squinted his left eye and shifted his weight. He was staring at Stig, who was stuffing his face with sushi at the reception. "That fucking pig. Show a little class, you asshole." Tranko's left arm was falling asleep again. He stood up, put the binoculars down and shook it vigorously, attempting to bring it back to life.

Tranko was located across the street, on the roof of an adjacent building. He was watching the whole event from a distance. He had thought to attend in person, but Bunny nixed it. "You killed him. You can't come to the reception. Are you crazy?"

Tranko had reminded her that "he" didn't kill anyone at all. It was one of his mooks and even that was an accident. Bunny didn't care. Apparently, she felt it was taunting fate a little too directly and that it must not happen. Instead, Tranko found his way to roof of the neighboring building. He could watch any outdoor activities easily, though he did have a harder time when people would float in and out of the penthouse suites located around the outdoor area and the famous sign. Plus, he couldn't hear anything. Tranko was terrible at lip reading. He spoke out loud to himself, "God, just watching that guy eat is turning my stomach. Seriously, does he have no nerve endings in his face?"

"Wipe it off. Wipe it off!" shouted Tranko to no one at all.

* * *

Stig and his three goons moved about the event, looking enough out of place to draw some attention. Though no one specifically noticed, most attendees gave a wide berth to them all the same, especially once they were stationed alongside the sushi mirror. Slowly at first, Stig kept pushing more and more sushi into his face, even as his eyes darted about. He liked sushi. A lot. Especially the expensive stuff.

His boss had ordered him to attend the event. To 'make our presence known' was the official request. Stig didn't care. Free food and booze. What's not to like? But even as he ate, he remained focused on the surrounding crowd, looking for faces or names that might be important. He was also supposed to find someone named Ben. He would find him too. But first some more sushi.

* * *

David decided it was time to move position. He started cruising around, moving in and out of the crowd. The amount of ripe, young actresses on-site was lean, not that he could partake if it wasn't. He could not afford to get sidetracked in his mission. Bunny would be showing up any minute and he needed to focus. Ben was his target, and he had been plotting a way to either ingratiate himself or at least have a conversation with him. Problem was, as Ben was the guy running the event, he really wasn't staying in any one place too long. He kept moving. And David didn't want to start questioning him and then lose him to some nonsense distraction. He might have to wait until the end. David walked past a Diet Pepsi fountain, which was apparently some sort of direct nod to one of Zev's personal faves. A Diet Pepsi ice fountain? Really? David shook his head and smirked. What could he expect from a group like this? He stared at a huge man shoving sushi into his mouth like it was a contest. How do you make a funeral reception for a Hollywood producer seem white trash? That's how. David eyed Ben, edging ever closer to the man in charge.

Until he saw Bunny arrive and enter the space with her family.

Decked out in the tightest of black dresses, along with 6-inch stiletto heels and stockings to match, Bunny wore a massive black hat with veiled shade that fell about her face area. Behind that, she wore oversized yellow sunglasses, which, combined with her extra puffy lips, gave her the look of a hornet in mourning.

Trailing behind her were two children, teenagers. Both were red faced with puffy eyes. Older than David had expected. They seemed separate from their mother, like they were on their own, which they probably were. There were a few oldsters around her as well. Likely aunts or parents of Zevon. Bunny didn't seem to pay them any mind, as they simply milled around behind her. It was clear this was her day as much as Zevon's. She took center stage in the middle of the rooftop deck and turned a full circle slowly, allowing all assembled to catch a glimpse. Ben swooped in quickly.

"Mrs. Levi. Did you and your family want to go to the *Gable-Lombard* suite and rest a bit? There is a separate sitting area in there that is private, if you desire." He motioned with his arm in the suite's direction.

Bunny turned to look at Ben. "No, I think I want to be around the people that loved him. At least for right now."

David nearly gagged when he heard that. She was laying it on pretty thick for someone who bragged about weaponizing her divorce against him. *What a bitch.* he thought.

As Bunny primped herself in full view of the attendees, David caught sight of something that immediately made him stiffen. Rising to his tippy toes he spied a woman that had just entered the roof area of the Roosevelt Hotel. He knew her. It was the lady from the beach house. Babs. Whatever was missing-dog Babs doing here?

59

MAGGIE STOOD on the roof of the Roosevelt Hotel and took in the scene. The warm air of an LA summer evening enveloped her. There was just a hint of breeze, enough to make a light jacket worthwhile, but not necessary. She paused, looking at the glow cast by the lower hotel sign, just starting to brighten as the light of the day faded. Maggie walked toward it. Not often you got to see such things up close, at least without much personal effort. She remembered cutting her hand when she had crawled up to the illuminated windmill atop the Moulin Rouge in Paris. But that was on a dare, not a job. Maggie smiled at the memory and listened to the hum of the large sign.

Walking into the event, Maggie tried to stay unobtrusive. She was here to gather info, nothing more. Greta had sent the details, suggesting she might want to attend. Maggie wasn't initially sure she would but thinking about it made her realize it couldn't hurt. She needed to see some of the players, and this would be a good place to look for anything off or suspicious. A crowd was always a better place to observe from. Easy to hide, easy to be missed. Maggie grabbed a small drink from a tray and took a sip. Champagne? Who the hell serves champagne at a wake? Hollywood people. She knew they would never make sense to her.

Greta had said that most of the people in attendance would be associates or friends from Levi's film crews. Maggie didn't have a lot of experience with such people, noting the seeming inconsistencies of the room. You had some people dressed to the nines, others looking like they crawled out of dumpsters, yet everyone had an air of confidence that suggested they knew they belonged there and had a place. Quite a world. As Maggie circled the rooftop, she looked out over the LA skyline, seeing the Hollywood Hills in the background and the city laid at their feet. The hustle of Hollywood Blvd down below was basically invisible unless you went near the edge and peered over. The noise only a subtle background to the chatter of the guests at the event. There was music playing. It was quite a nice memorial, in truth. Subdued, respectful, yet sort of happy too. Strange. Maggie continued to prowl about.

She had done a little research before coming. Apparently, the rooftop was divided between two penthouse suites. One called the *Johnny Grant Suite* and the other the *Gable-Lombard Suite*. Maggie knew who Clark Gable was, and the whole Carole Lombard thing where they hid out whilst having the affair that eventually led to marriage and an inevitably tragic end. But Johnny Grant? That one was a little more earthbound. An old radio personality, he was tagged the unofficial Mayor of Hollywood because he officiated at all the walk of fame ceremonies and basically lived in the Roosevelt. Whatever they knew, they certainly knew about mythmaking, thought Maggie as she snaked her way through the crowd.

Arriving in front of an impressive buffet featuring savory treats, Maggie decided a meal might not be a bad idea. If she had to stand around watching folks she might as well be doing something. Maggie grabbed bits and pieces from various displays and built an impressive covering of treats on her small plate. After spying an open cocktail table just beside the frame of the smaller neon Roosevelt sign, she situated herself with her back to the night sky and the people arrayed in front. Hearing a small commotion of some kind break out, Maggie stood on tip toes, looking over the crowd and straining to raise her eyeline high enough to see where the noise was originating.

She was surprised by a hand on her shoulder.

Starting slightly at the shock, Maggie whipped her head around and came face to face with a smiling Ivan, standing right beside her small table.

"Ivan! What are you doing here?".

Ivan smiled, and then sighed. He said nothing, at first, just looking at Maggie as if he was trying to preserve or remember something long forgotten. He raised both hands in greeting.

"My little vixen. I'm glad you came. I told Greta to get you the details I didn't know if you would come, but I hoped."

Maggie appreciated seeing Ivan, but that emotion was quickly replaced by concern for the job. Ivan didn't go out on jobs. Why was he here? And if he was here, that probably meant something bad had happened. Or was going to happen. Whichever, it was not good.

"What's wrong? Why are you here, Ivan?" asked Maggie.

Almost immediately, Ivan looked sheepish, momentarily dropping his bright eyes underneath his wrinkled brow before returning them to Maggie's view. He looked like he was going to apologize for something.

"Maggie I…ahhh….I had to come see you. I just couldn't let…"

Suddenly, a brash voice pierced the privacy of the pair.

"Babs! How amazing to see you here! Don't tell me little Roofie wandered all the way to the Roosevelt Hotel now? That dog of yours needs a GPS more than a leash, hmmm?"

Maggie froze, trying hard not to look surprised. It was the guy from Zevon's house. The one she was certain had made her before. And if he hadn't before, he certainly had by now. Seeing her there, and now here, was a coincidence way too specific to be real. And yet, offense being the best defense, meant that Maggie knew exactly what she needed to do. Attack.

"Why are you following me?" She spit the words at David like fire, advancing on him physically, her eyes lit up with rage.

This action caught David by surprise. He didn't expect to be attacked. He was ready for any response but that. Momentarily, he began to stammer.

"Follow you? Don't be silly….I am…not….but….I was already…. how do …?"

Seeing him off-balance and struggling, Maggie pressed harder.

"Are you stalking me? Is this some kind of shakedown? Why are you coming at me?"

In disbelief at the turn things had taken, David looked around to see if anyone else was noticing the exchange taking place. Trying to right himself, David attempted some pushback.

"Hold on a minute. You were the one on my property looking for your dog..."

Maggie didn't quit. "Your property? Are you really the owner of that place? I'd be surprised if that was the case..."

David cut back in, "You don't know what you're talking about. Maybe you followed me here! Did you think about that? You're stalking me and..."

"Enough!" Ivan held up his hand as he spoke. David and Maggie turned from each other to face him.

"That's enough. Both of you. Lower your voices."

David cocked his head to one side, looking at the old man. "Who are you?"

Ivan dropped his eyes, and then raised them in a moment, staring deep at David.

"I know exactly who you are, Mr. Teck and I would advise you to calm yourself."

David was stunned. "You know me? What do you know about me?"

"I know you had some problems many years ago that troubled your father greatly. And I know who it was that helped your father make those problems go away."

David looked at Ivan suspiciously. "And who...?"

"Me."

Maggie was speechless, just watching in total confusion what was transpiring in front of her.

Ivan continued, "I didn't know you were specifically involved in this, but seeing you here now makes a form of sense." He faced the pair. "You both need to forget your own squabbles for the moment, as something a little more important is taking place just over there."

As David and Maggie looked uncomfortably at each other, and then back to Ivan, they finally turned their heads in the direction he was gesturing, catching sight of a large man flying into the Diet Pepsi ice sculpture and landing atop two platters of crunchy California rolls. Shouts and screams erupted as the crowd parted for a massive, block-built man now dragging, and pummelling, the food-covered man on the ground.

David spoke first. "Uh, I think I know the guy who landed on the sushi. He pulled a gun on me a couple days ago."

Ivan spoke next, "Well, I'm certain I know the one who threw him. Russian mob. Not local."

Suddenly, into the middle of the fray ran Bunny Levi, screaming and waving her arms. "Stop it! Stop it!" Tables were still being knocked over as chairs flipped sideways and guests dropped plates and glasses in their haste to get out of the way. Ben had also rushed into the center of things but was being held at bay by one of Stig's thugs.

Confused, Maggie looked at Ivan and David. "Would either of you be willing to tell me what in the heck is actually going on here?"

60

TRANKO LIFTED his arms over his head, flexing his biceps as he brought them down toward his head, stretching his shoulders. Twisting his spine right and left, he re-shuffled his stiff joints before leaning back across the air conditioning unit he was propped up on. The memorial party for Zevon Levi continued across the street as Tranko rolled his neck twice around before sighing loudly and bringing the Steiner Military binoculars back up to his eyes.

He hoped that Stig was finally done stuffing his face. It was bad enough watching someone eat but seeing it in 10X magnification wasn't fair. Stig was a pig.

Panning around the distant rooftop deck, Tranko searched for signs of…something. What exactly, he wasn't sure of yet. But something would present itself. It always did. He scanned the crowd, spying the slippery jerk that had been with Bunny at the beach house. He was hiding in a corner by a plant, watching things himself. Tranko noted the spot and planned to return to him as he continued his line of sight around the party area.

Although Tranko's rooftop was about seventy feet from the Roosevelt's, and a few floors higher, his view of things was perfect. In the cool evening, with the lights of the party, he was basically invisible, so there was no fear of being spotted by anyone. His rooftop was dark by comparison, and as the evening light faded to black his cover was assured.

He continued to hunt with his eyes, looking for Bunny. Assuming she hadn't yet arrived, Tranko went back to Stig who continued to eat and drink like it was some contest on a cruise ship to see who could stuff themselves the fastest. "Doesn't Dachshund feed you?" joked Tranko out loud to himself. Then he laughed, because why not?

As Tranko's eyes continued to skim the crowd, they came to rest on a very attractive, dark-haired woman wearing an extremely form fitting black dress. It accentuated every single curve she possessed, causing Tranko to pause his roving gaze. She had an exotic look to her, a very tanned or maybe even olive complexion. Big dark eyes, long hair. Everyone that passed by her turned for a second look. Tranko and his binoculars lingered on her far longer than they should have, especially considering she had nothing to do with why he was there. He didn't care. He was kind of bored and she was amazing to watch. His heart leapt as she dropped a napkin and Tranko immediately started to pray she would bend over to pick it up. Racking his binoculars further to intensify his up-close study of the perfect woman, Tranko traced every line of her body, all the way down to her black high-heels, then up her legs, once around her perfectly proportioned body, arms, neck and...wham! She was staring right at him!

The shock of her look caused Tranko to drop the binoculars and recoil, lifting his head. Feeling instantly stupid, he pulled them back up to his eyes and refocused. Of course, she didn't see him, it just felt like she had for a second. Tranko's heart was beating. Maybe he did need a date. It had been a serious long while.

Returning to his long-distance, inappropriate study of the mystery woman's features, Tranko had simply focused on her face at the exact moment her head turned to the right. Was she saying something? But what? Following her gaze, Tranko panned across the crowd and saw....Stewie? *What the hell was Stewie doing there?*

Tranko had left Stewie in the truck. And he had given him very specific instructions to stay there no matter what happened. Tranko needed the ability to get away fast and getting parking was not good enough. He needed a ride, stopped in the alley, ready to go the second he jumped in. That was his job, but now Stewie was on the rooftop of the Roosevelt where he was not supposed to be. Tranko searched visually for answers, watching as one of Stig's goons shoved Stewie along. *Had they grabbed him from the truck? What the hell?* Tranko watched as the guy pushed him towards Stig, who even stopped dumping food into himself long enough to say something. Stewie shook his head. Stig stepped up on him and grabbed his face with his right hand, shaking it.

Did he tell them I was up here? wondered Tranko. His spider-sense started buzzing, suddenly convinced he was being watched. Tranko turned just as a steel baton crashed down, denting the aluminum housing of the air-con unit he was resting on. *Two guys, sneak right up on me, get on my ass and I nearly get knocked out* Tranko thought to himself, cursing his screwup before turning to face them.

The one guy had an extendable cop baton in his right hand, but the other didn't seem to be holding anything. Both his hands were visible. Tranko didn't see anyone else. His back was now to a closed corner on the rooftop, so he knew no one could be behind him. That was the good news. The bad news was that these guys had the drop on him and clearly intended to hurt him in some serious way. Waiting, Tranko took the opportunity to angle his body, giving baton-man the direct line on him, causing the guy to step forward, which put himself between Tranko and the other man. Tranko waited a beat, hoping the guy would raise his arm to swing the baton. Paydirt!

As baton-man's arm went up, Tranko moved forward, hard, catching the forearm holding the steel rod with his own while simultaneously driving the edge of his hand into the side of the guy's neck. It was a double shot, followed almost imperceptibly with a kick to the shin. Three points of impact are enough to blow the fuses on even the most trained fighter and they did the trick here. The baton dropped to the roof deck just as Tranko spun the stunned fighter around and shoved him low into his partner. Then he dropped to one knee and grabbed the baton for himself, immediately swinging it hard, right into the side of the knee closest to him. The guy went down with a painful moan.

But Tranko wasn't done. Standing up, he rushed the pair, driving an elbow into the face of one while crashing a knee into the face of the guy on the ground, still clutching his smashed-up knee. Swinging his large frame left and then right, with elbows at full point, Tranko caught a jaw, knocking the rear guy unconscious. Turning, he grabbed the man on the ground from behind and fitted him with a sleeper hold, looping his arm around his neck, cupping his own bicep, and pushing forward on the guy's head with his off hand. Nine seconds was all it took. Both thugs, out cold. Tranko did a quick check of their pockets and grabbed two guns. He disassembled one and threw the parts off the roof while keeping the other. He grabbed the baton, slammed it on the roof deck to close it and sprinted off towards the roof access door.

Tranko didn't know if anyone one else was on the way, but if they were, it was doubtful they'd use the stairs. He busted through the door into the emergency staircase and began running down as fast as he could. Even if they were coming up, he was going to be moving fast enough that he'd go right through them if they dared to get in his way.

* * *

The elevator ride inside the Roosevelt did little too cool his temper as Tranko headed up the last few steps toward the rooftop. He strode into the party with a narrow focus, intent on Stig and no one else. Taller than most, Tranko saw above the crowd, spied Stig, and never stopped moving, driving like a shark directly toward him. People in the crowd slipped harmlessly aside.

Lowering one shoulder, Tranko drove his entire body into Stig football-style, catching the squat, heavy man unready and driving him backwards in a clatter through several tables and bodies. Tranko didn't care. He was having it out with Stig here and now. Punching and grappling with each other, the chaos spilled into the larger crowd as people began screaming and yelling at them to stop.

Tranko had no intention of stopping. He wasn't letting up no matter what. The two men continued to crash into things and roll around on the floor as party goers scattered in whatever direction might get them away from the violence. In the middle, Tranko rose from the floor, facing Stig.

"C'mon, asshole. I'll take you down right now. Let's finish this."

Stig, awkwardly lifting his block frame off the floor, set himself into place.

"You talk too much."

The two men ran at each other, colliding once more and crashing through the "ironic" beer fountain to land on a table of finger foods. Ben broke from the crowd and ran into the middle of the two men.

"Stop this! Stop this right now! The police are on their way! I don't know what this is all about, but it must end now!"

Tranko stood up to his full height, staring at Ben and then back to Stig. Stig wiped his nose with the back of his hand and spat some blood out to the floor. In doing, he spied a piece of California roll that jammed itself inside the front lapel pocket of his ridiculously oversized suit jacket. He plucked it out and ate it.

"Fuck you!" he yelled at Tranko.

Stewie came pushing through the crowd.

"Dude, we gotta get out of here. They called the cops. C'mon, I'm good. Let's go!"

Tranko didn't move. He continued to stare at Stig, wanting to put his fist through the guy's dumb face. But he wasn't stupid. He turned to Stewie, nodded, and pushed through the crowd, heading for the exit.

Ben spoke up, "Hey! You can't leave! Hey, someone has got to pay for all this. Stop!"

As Ben shouted after Tranko, Stig's men gathered up and headed for the exit themselves. Sirens could be heard in the distance. Whether they were meant for the Roosevelt or not didn't matter. The excitement was over, and the causes were getting themselves gone. Ben struggled desperately to put the now broken pinata of an event back together again.

"Could someone get pictures of them please? Just send them to me. I'll make sure the police get them." He started trying to right tables and clean up the smashed food with the help of his staff. As he went to lift one table up a man stepped out of the crowd, offering his help.

"That was pretty crazy, huh?"

Ben nodded, speaking without really looking up. He was still in shock. "Uh yeah, it sure was…is."

The man spoke again, "I think you and I should talk. My name's David and I think I can explain a little more about what's going on. Is there somewhere we can get a little privacy?"

Ben stopped fussing and finally focussed on the man speaking. David Teck, smiling his most disarming smile, nodded his head. Ben could see that his staff were cleaning up and the crowd had dispersed. He thought, *Maybe, this guy can shed some light....* before catching himself.

"If you know about this perhaps you should be talking to the police, hmmm?"

David smiled.

"You're not going to want that to happen, I can assure you. Believe it or not, you might just be the one in the most trouble of all right now."

At that comment, Ben swallowed hard. "We can talk over there."

61

INSTINCTIVELY, Maggie began to follow David toward the chaos of the fight. Ivan grabbed her arm, gently stopping her.

"No, little vixen. Come with me." Ivan led her in the opposite direction from the increasing ruckus, pulling her toward the *Johnny Grant* apartment on the near side of the roof.

"In here. Come."

As they stepped inside the apartment, they came face to face with two young women kissing aggressively on a couch while a man stood about two feet away, appearing to appraise them.

Maggie spoke up immediately.

"What the...?"

The women jumped slightly, stopped kissing, and turned, facing Maggie, their eyes wide with surprise. The man also turned to face Maggie, but he seemed annoyed. "You're interrupting!"

"What exactly am I interrupting?" asked Maggie. Ivan stood silently.

The man made a show of his frustration, rolling his eyes.

"They are actresses rehearsing a scene from a new art film I'm producing. Perhaps you could give us some privacy?"

Maggie stepped closer to the trio.

"Any chance either of you girls has seen a written contract from Scorsese here?"

The girls looked at other, and then around sheepishly.

The man interjected, "We are in the rehearsal stage. Final casting is not complete."

Maggie turned and gave him a look. She turned back to the girls.

"Whatever you do, make sure what you do is what YOU want to do. Be grown ups, okay?"

The girls looked at each other and then rose to their feet. One decided to speak, looking directly at Maggie, "You're old!" Each took a hand of the man and all three walked toward the door. The man sneered at Maggie as he passed.

Ivan and Maggie were left alone. Ivan spoke.

"You shame me."

Maggie turned to Ivan.

"I don't understand."

"Those girls, that…man. What he does to them I did to you."

"I think you're being dramatic Ivan."

Ivan slammed his hand on a table.

"I'm not! I used you because I was afraid and because I didn't know what else to do. And you trusted me, but I didn't repay that trust…."

Maggie stared at Ivan. She didn't know what to say, or how to proceed exactly. Looking left and right, she spied a chair and perched herself on the edge, waiting for Ivan to continue. After pacing a bit, he did.

"This….job. There is so much more to it than I have told you. The people involved are….numerous and there is just so much you don't know and I….I couldn't tell you but…I just…"

Maggie stayed calm.

"Ivan, it's okay. Just tell me, okay?"

Ivan acted like a caged animal, a very old, slow moving one, but penned in all the same. He paced in small circles until he spied a straight-backed chair. Ivan grabbed it and slid it over to face Maggie directly.

"I was there. In 1983. The night the paintings were taken from the Gardener. I was part of the crew. Not on site, but behind the scenes. We had prepped everything for weeks. The night came and it went off without a hitch. The problems came only when we tried to sell them. Our contacts, the promises dried up. The publicity was too much. The newspapers made such a big deal that everyone knew about the robbery. Our buyers either disappeared or tried to squeeze us. We had to go underground with everything for a lot longer than expected. Fights ensued and fractures came. Then one from our group, a young one, died. Not connected to it at all. A car accident. Unremarkable. But it broke something. The others involved suddenly wanted out. They were spooked. Believed themselves to be cursed. They ran away, never to be seen again. I ended up with the paintings, all of them but one. *The Concert* disappeared with someone that night. The others I protected and eventually moved, but for far less than they were worth. I never knew what happened to the Vermeer. Until it landed with Levi."

Maggie shifted in her seat. She had questions but Ivan was in a zone of sorts, and not ready to stop. He was talking and she determined it was best to listen, for now.

"I know this game. The shell moving, hiding, playing, manipulating. It is based on lies and promises, on truth and deception. All the players know. Your father knew. And you do too. You are not an innocent. None of us are. But when this painting reached the surface once more, I did not imagine it would create the problems that it has."

Ivan stopped speaking and appeared to be thinking. Pondering what to say next. He continued.

"Levi got it. One of the relatives I think, gave it to him. No money. Never charged him to my knowledge. Just gave it to him. Why him, I do not know. But he did. Now I knew it was back, but I didn't know where or how exactly. I did eventually though, when the Booli Brothers started using art to guarantee arms shipments. I heard through a contact they had secured a massive deal with *The Concert*, but I didn't know how. Or where the painting was. But their deal was shaky, badly prepared. You know as well as I do the paintings are not really the issue. They are simply objects of guarantee, but the Boolis would need this one because they screwed up. There is a man called Edward Dachshund. He is a Russian-Englishman, younger than me, by a decade or so but very connected in the motherland. Mafia. They owed him arms and suddenly became unable to deliver. The UN got a tip, caught their shipment, and sold it to someone else. This put them in bad with Dachshund, who now wanted his guarantee, or else. That is when I found out where the painting was."

Maggie's eyes said *'how?'* even as Ivan responded.

"Aldo was the UN contact. He's connected to very bad people in very clean ways. He is a political player. Very slippery. Owns freeports and the like. Plays games, dangerous ones. He leveraged me over my son and kept it over my head. He has a grudge with Dachshund about something I don't know. He saw this as a chance to make a play, I think to maybe take him out?"

"Ivan, I..."

Ivan pleaded with a slightly raised hand, "No, little vixen...Maggie, I have to get this out. It's important."

Maggie nodded.

"So as Dachshund went to collect his guarantee, Aldo found out and made a move of his own, on Dachshund's other side, crippling his business. Now, Dachshund knew of Aldo's existence but didn't know him personally. Suddenly, *The Concert* is in play as both men need it, but for different reasons. Dachshund wants it to safeguard his missing funds and lack of arms, while Aldo wants it only to deprive Dachshund of his guarantee and force him into default with his creditors, who are big enough in scale to eliminate the Russian entirely. This is deadly serious, and I have dropped you into the middle of these wolves just as they are about to fight."

Trying to process all that she was hearing, Maggie leaned forward as Ivan continued.

"When he asked for you, I should have said no. It was an obvious problem. But I trust you above all and I thought you could do it without becoming entangled. As it got deeper, I realized what I had done but couldn't get you out, not without hurting my son and possibly myself. But your father would kill me if he knew what I've done to you."

At this, Maggie stopped him. "Ivan, I got myself involved with Aldo, long before you even entered the picture. He wouldn't have even known about me if I hadn't...visited... his place."

Ivan looked confused. Maybe he didn't know everything after all. But he still had more to say.

"Be that as it may, I have tossed you into the furnace with them and you don't realize the scale of what is happening around you. That's not fair. I was wrong."

"So why are you telling me now? What changed?"

"My risks have…my boy…he's dead. He overdosed two days ago. He's gone now."

"Ivan, I'm so sorry."

"His life was his own, his demons too. But my curse was an unnecessary stain on it. Were his choices my fault? Perhaps not. But I bear the responsibility of what drove him away. I will never know peace for that. And I don't deserve to. My…choices in life have not been the best. I am a thug really, little more. I take from others. What is that? A trade? Not one someone can be proud of. I think not. I know who I am. There are no illusions for me."

"What does this mean?"

"It means you need to be careful. It's too late to extricate yourself from this but you need to know as much as you can to make sure you don't get trampled by the actions of the giants fighting each other. I've held this information from you for too long. I make this right now. You need to understand what is at play, where things are going and what can possibly be done to protect yourself in this."

Maggie sat still for a few moments. Taking in the words, digesting them. Her emotions ran the gamut, anger, fear, disbelief, sadness… empathy. She looked up at Ivan's tired eyes, seeing them damp with tears. She loved Ivan but she also had to protect herself. As always, the result would rest on her.

"Ivan. Tell me what else I need to know."

62

AS MAGGIE SWAM through the cold water, she worked to control her breathing. LA or not, it was freezing this time of night. Obviously, it couldn't be helped. Timing was everything. She was grateful for her half-scuba suit. She wished it was a full one, but that would take too much room in a carry-on.

It wasn't that late yet, only 8:30pm or so, but the time was crucial if her plan was going to work.

She had arranged to meet up with Aldo and Fati at the Polo Lounge in Beverly Hills at 8:45pm, but cautioned that she would be a little late, suggesting they order the chocolate souffle for dessert as soon as they arrive. That would ensure it was ready in time.

But Maggie knew she would not make it for dinner. Or the special dessert.

This was the only way she could guarantee getting Aldo off the boat long enough to do what she needed to do. Fati had let it slip that the crew was planning a surprise party off-board for a crew member's birthday that same night. The boat would have one or two people left behind, at most. It would be as close to deserted as it would ever be. Maggie continued to paddle quietly through the small waves of the breakwater.

It was a 45min drive from the marina to the restaurant, plus the souffle guaranteed another 45 min more. That should be enough time. She took a deep breath and dove beneath the surface, swimming under water in a more well-lit area of the marina. Maggie surfaced when the shadows returned.

Ivan's confession had presented Maggie with some significant challenges. Not the least of which was how exactly to proceed. She couldn't back out. You can't do that sort of thing once you agree to a job. Especially with the kind of people involved. But she also couldn't abandon Ivan, even after what he had done. Yes, she was furious with him but life being what it is meant she still had to find a way through. And finding a way to get out of this set-up was not easy.

The presence of duelling titans complicated matters severely. It meant that no matter who won, someone was going to be mad and the chance that one of them might take their anger out on Maggie rose significantly. And the dollar amounts in play on this job practically guaranteed an explosive outcome. She needed to avoid that at all costs, while finding a way to protect herself no matter what happened.

That was going to take some creative planning on her part.

Maggie spied the berth holding the *Jimena* and held her breath once more for the final 20ft or so underwater to the boat's keel. The evening was quiet. After re-surfacing, Maggie rested herself near the waterline, using breathing to slow her heart rate, calm down and increase her internal furnace.

She had stumbled across online videos by a guy called the "Iceman." His real name was Wim Hof, a Dutch motivational speaker from the Netherlands who was either crazy or a genius. According to him, cold water therapy was everything and could result in a longer, better life. Maggie didn't know about that. All she wanted was a little warmth right now, so she focused her breathing as Wim taught in his videos. It seemed to work.

At the same time, Maggie strained her ears for sounds, any sounds, indicating movement on the large yacht. It was hard being at this angle. She knew she'd have to get closer to the side.

Moving slowly around the base, Maggie found her way to the anchor, hefting herself up by her arms until she could get her feet onto a hold. Maggie had swim-shoes on, which helped with traction, but she still had to be careful. Nothing was more slippery than an anchor chair spending the bulk of its life in the water. All manner of slime existed on such things.

As she pushed her head closer to the polished wood and brass railings, Maggie could see the boat's evening lights were on. Just enough to be welcoming by the time *El Rey* found his way home again. She couldn't hear anyone, so slowly, carefully, Maggie raised her eyes above the railing, straining to stay in shadow.

Nothing.

With almost no sound, Maggie slipped over the railing and came down on all fours, ready to move. She hugged the deck, leaning into the interior wall and being careful to avoid the camera systems she had spied in her two previous visits to the *Jimena*. Security systems were frustratingly predictable. They usually focused on the most obvious areas, gangplank, boat launch, deck stairs and the like. The attitude was to secure the places someone would usually move. They rarely focused on the places someone would not normally move about in, like low along the deck, over the side or around somewhat inaccessible areas. And nighttime made it even easier to see them thanks to the small red lights indicating their existence.

But Aldo was better than that. She knew she had to be ready for more. He had caught her once. It was not going to happen again.

The lounge area where she had been hosted back in Vancouver was closed off for the night. Only ambient light was visible. This was fine, as she had no intention of going through a doorway. Maggie made her way to the galley. Rarely are security systems put near staff areas, for the simple reason that they are usually working when the master sleeps. He'd rather not be disturbed by the help. Maggie found her way to the service area of the ship and tried the exterior door. Locked. No matter. Kitchens are hot and smelly places. When the crew got a night off, they either cleaned the kitchen or at least aired it out. There would be a port open somewhere for some of the ocean air to enter. *Bingo!*

Maggie spied the open porthole. It was outside the walkway, along the edge of the lower floor. She could reach for it. Worst outcome would be a fall into the water. That would make some noise, but it was worth the risk. The port hole opening was maybe twelve inches. Maggie could fit, it was just awkward.

Sort of the name of the game for a cat burglar.

Maggie stepped over the railing, hooking her foot between the wood and the rail, reaching her fingers as far down as she could.

Touching the edge of the port window she would have to make a leap of a few inches to grab it. The issue was keeping herself out of the water, while also staying in a position to get her body through it. There was no light coming from the galley, so Maggie made a choice to go for it, launching her entire arm though the hole up to her armpit. That should keep her above the water line and hopefully leave enough room to push her head through.

"*Uhhhn!*" The metal of the windows edge pinched her armpit something fierce. Maggie held her tongue, even as she wanted to scream. She was in the port hole up to her shoulder. Turning her head, she could see the window was a little larger than she had guessed. Feeling around with her inside hand, even as she tried to find a spot to leverage her toe against, Maggie found something sturdy and closed her hand around it. Pulling her head up to the window and pushing it inside revealed the contortionist-like abilities she possessed, as she slipped her entire body through the small, vertical circle.

The bruises came later. And they always hurt worse the day after the next day. Wim Hof better be right about the healing effects of cold water. Maggie was going to need it.

Now inside the galley, Maggie made her way back through the crew hallway, listening for whomever was still on board. She had her face covered, so even if a camera picked her up there would be no proof, but she preferred to avoid that issue altogether.

Finally, coming into the main lounge she paused in a corner, pressing her eyes shut and rubbing them for a solid thirty seconds. A little trick to open the pupil and allow more light in, making it easier to see in a darkened room.

When Maggie opened her eyes, she immediately looked to the spot on the wall where the "ironic" *Storm on the Sea of Galilee* hung. Aldo's smart-ass joke to "look" like he had a valuable painting missing from a famous robbery that was really a fake made in a stupid Photoshop contest.

Except there was more to the joke.

Ivan confirmed that Aldo had picked up the real *Storm* only a year or so ago, and that it was something he was personally very fond of. And that had given Maggie an idea.

Boys and their toys. Men were not that hard to figure out. They are almost universally drawn by the playthings that entertain them, and whether that was the main one between their legs or the material ones they covet over the years, the newer the toy the closer they liked to have it to themselves.

Maggie made her way over to the fake painting and began fumbling around it in the darkness. She was feeling for something. A loose edge, a small switch, a button, something. She felt around the edge of the frame, then under the frame. The piece was secured tightly to the wall, but it was decidedly thicker than it should be. There was more to this piece.

Maggie continued to hunt, now sliding her hands over the wall area near the painting and then around the seating areas. It had to be somewhere Aldo could reach it easily without someone else accidentally revealing it. He would never take that chance. Then Maggie stopped. She looked around.

Aldo would never look at the painting here, up close. He would survey it, like the master of the universe he fancied himself. Maggie scanned the room and looked for the best chair, the throne, that Aldo would almost certainly occupy. And she spied it.

The chair he sat in when they visited. The best chair, one that can see the whole lounge, that swiveled and allowed for a 360-degree view of everything. Maggie made her way to it and sat down. She turned to face the picture on the wall, watching where her hands and feet fell. Nothing on the chair was obvious. No switch or button, but there was a side table with a lamp. The lamp had a switch. Looking left and right, Maggie flicked the tiny lamp on.

Nothing. Just a small bit of light. She flicked it off again. Frustrated, Maggie sat back in the chair. She was running out of time.

Staring at the lamp Maggie noticed there wasn't an electrical cord. Clearly it was part of the side table, maybe built into the center pole holding up the structure. She leaned forward and put her hand under the table, feeling around the center pole. She found a small button. Maggie pressed it. Instantly, she heard a small whirring sound, a tiny motor churning. And right before her eyes the fake painting of *Storm* rolled out of sight, revealing the original master work beneath.

She knew it! Maggie was certain Aldo would keep it nearby. She almost leapt out of the chair, racing over to the large painting. Reaching into her suit Maggie flipped *Lola* out. There was no being careful on this one, she'd be cutting the picture from the frame and getting the heck out of there. Spinning the knife into place Maggie reached up, about to slice into the canvas when the lights in the lounge suddenly burst to life.

Maggie froze. *He'd caught her...again!*

She waited for the voice. For anything. Nothing. Slowly, she turned her head and saw a crew member opening and closing cabinets in the back of the bar area. He hadn't seen her! Maggie dropped to the floor in front of the built-in seating, squeezing herself beneath the tables.

The guy was banging and knocking things around in a furious search for...something. Suddenly, Maggie heard a loud "Aha!" as the assistant cook held up a bottle of what seemed like gin or vodka. Whatever it was, he immediately turned around and left the room, flicking the light off as he left. Presumably to return to his quarters and continue drinking.

Maggie went back to work immediately, slicing the picture from inside it's hiding place, rolling it up and securing it inside the waterproof sleeve that hugged the side of her wetsuit. Artwork in place, Maggie went back to the small table and pressed the button, replacing the ironic *Storm* to its position of false honor.

As Maggie made the swim back to her hidden motorcycle, just beyond the break, she mentally marked one item off from her newly created list. "Leverage on Aldo, check." Maggie disappeared into the shadows of the waves as she swam noiselessly across the small basin and away.

63

DIMITRI THREW a tennis ball at the concrete block wall. *Bop!* It bounced back to his hand. He tossed it again. *Bop!* And again. *Bop!* He caught and tossed it over and over, hitting the same spot, almost always seeing the ball bouncing right back into his hand. This particular round of the wall-bounce game had lasted nearly an hour. Dimitri was bored. He didn't want to throw the ball anymore.

Missing the last catch on purpose, he turned and let the ball roll past him as he stretched his arms up to the roof. Dimitri yawned, loudly, and strained to see the plug-in clock resting on the stack of folded cardboard boxes about 20 ft away. 8:32pm. He had been alone in the old warehouse for almost 27 hours now. He was pretty much done with the whole thing.

Dimitri dragged his feet as he schlepped over to his food stash, which by now consisted mainly of empty packages and wrappings ringed by a bunch of half-crushed sweet tea cans. All were one-time products of the 24-hr gas bar on the corner. He dug around in the mess, looking for something unopened or semi-edible. Corn nuts! They would have to do. He ripped the bag open and dumped some inside his mouth, crunching them happily. Finally feeling the effects of his sixth sweet iced-tea, Dimitri felt the need to pee.

Thanks to the abandoned nature of the place, even the bathrooms were non-functioning. That meant Dimitri had to head outside to a self-created spot, about ten feet from the door and inside a patch of 5ft tall weeds, to do his business. As Dimitri relieved himself, he took care to steer clear of the 5gal pail he had already used for a number two. He hoped to be long gone before having to go through that particularly humbling experience again.

Someone was supposed to come by midnight and relieve him. At least that's what Ludis had said. Dimitri stretched again. He had caught some sleep around two in the afternoon, but he was tired again. Maybe a lie down might not be such a bad idea. At least he'd be wide awake when the new guy came. He yawned again and headed back inside the building.

Being part of a crew had its ups and downs. Obviously, it beat having a normal job. The work wasn't hard, exactly. A lot of standing around. You had to get your hands dirty, for sure. But every job had bad parts. Besides, Dimitri didn't have any issues when it came to some of the more violent parts. Almost never did the person not deserve what they had coming to them. And the pay was good. Still, you really didn't have any choices when the garbage jobs came up.

And being a relative junior on the crew meant such things usually got dropped on him. *"Dimitri go here, do this – then sit down, shut up"* or *"Dimitri, pick this thing up and get back here. And shut up."* Dimitri couldn't wait for them to bring in a few more new guys. Then maybe he'd stop being the one on the bottom.

He looked for his tennis ball. Maybe he could set up a target range or something? Anything to kill off the last few hours or so. Reaching around, Dimitri found the errant ball and made his way over to the nest he'd built out of abandoned wood pallets and some folded tarps. He eased his way onto the makeshift bed, propping his legs up just enough to be comfortable, while resting his arms behind his head. Maybe he could grab 45min or so. He yawned again.

Dimitri cast a side eye at the paintings he was charged with guarding. They were leaning together, as a unit, against the far wall under a tarp. You wouldn't notice them if you weren't looking. He had looked at them when he first got bored, maybe a day ago. Didn't make any sense to him why they were so special. Bunch of fancy pants art stuff. Important to someone but who really cared? Just watch them, thought Dimitri. *And shut up!* They looked like old people paintings anyway. Something his grandmother might have had in her apartment, except bigger. He closed his eyes and tried to shut out the world for a while.

Then a noise broke the stillness. Dimitri heard engines approaching outside. He rolled off the pallet bed quickly and went up to the door, drawing his weapon and carefully watching through a small glass window as several dark SUVs pulled up in front. His breath caught in his throat. It wasn't Ludis. It was the boss!

Stig and his men exited their vehicles, and while most of them stood around the trucks, Stig barrelled through the door. Worked up and agitated, he looked directly at Dimitri and spoke.

"*Vy nikogo ne videli?*"

Dimitri stiffened, "No, nobody. I didn't see anyone."

That seemed to calm Stig, but only slightly. Dimitri stood perfectly still. He had no desire to do anything that might make him the focus of the boss' legendary rage. Stig stomped over to the paintings and yanked the tarp off, tossing it to one side. He stared at the pieces, confirming they were still present.

Dimitri turned as he heard another vehicle approaching. Looking out the open door he saw a third dark SUV pull in and stop. He watched as the boss' accountant stepped out and walked toward the warehouse, stepping in through the door. He nodded at Dimitri and stood silently to one side, hands clasped, waiting patiently. Stig turned, noticing his entrance. He nodded at the thin man, then turned and faced Dimitri.

"*Ukhodi!*"

Dimitri didn't need to be told twice. He left the building immediately, closing the door to the warehouse behind him. Stig and Dachshund were now alone in the gloomy space. Dachshund's face went from placid calm to serious intensity, while Stig morphed from barely controlled anger to a focused outburst as he punched an empty oil drum with his bare hand. It had been balanced on a pile of wood, just to his left. The crashing noise was so loud it caused the men outside to jump and reflexively move toward the building. Then, thinking better of it, they pulled back. The boss was mad, clearly.

As Stig stood over the fallen oil drum, Dachshund spoke, "Got it out of your system yet? Do you need to hit another one maybe? Want to break something? What in the hell are you thinking? You got into a public fight…at a funeral? Are you fucking insane? You're supposed to be me to the world. You can't act like this."

Stig looked at Dachshund and mimed something with his hands, attempting to speak and then thinking better of it. Instead, he cast his eyes down.

"Oh good. You feel sorry now? People, cameras, everywhere and you decide a punch-up in the middle of a memorial is a great idea? What the hell, Stig? What the hell?"

Stig nodded his head and flipped his hands up and down, wanting to explain but unsure whether there was any point to doing so. Dachshund pressed him.

"What happened in there? Tell me."

Stig, making his face look as penitent as possible while still trying to stand up for himself, spoke, "That guy, Tranko, he attack me. Just ran into me. What could I do?"

Dachshund barked back, "What you could "do" is not allow a brawl to happen."

Stig's eyes went wide. "I didn't! What…you want me to play dead? He come at me. I push back. Harder."

"You had men with you. You couldn't put a stop to it?"

Stig shook his head and flexed his apartment block-sized shoulders.

"He's big, tough fighter."

"Is he tougher than you?"

Stig looked up, rolling his eyes. Insulted.

"Maybe I should hire him and fire you, then?"

Stig faced Dachshund head on, looking frustrated and annoyed. He looked like he wanted to scream but said nothing, raising his hands in the universal style of *'what do you want me to do?'* He dropped his hands and slumped off.

Dachshund looked away. Walking over to the paintings he slid each of them free, making them visible against the block wall. He studied them silently.

"These were the ones pulled from the home of Levi, yes? Originally, I mean. By the brute?"

Stig nodded. Dachshund continued to speak.

"Your nemesis took them, put them in a truck and drove around with them. Then he stashed them, before going back to get them once more. Then he tried to sell them to us at that flea market, but we took them instead."

Stig nodded again.

"Has anyone come for them? Tried to find them?"

Stig shook his head.

Dachshund pressed his thumb into his chin, staring at the art pieces. He talked out loud to himself.

"Why? What do they know? What are these really? They're fakes, we know that. For sure. But why keep them? Why did Levi have them? For decoration? For his *der'movy* movies? For insurance?"

Stig stood silently. He knew better than to speak when the boss was monologuing.

"I say insurance. Fakes, copies to wave in front of adjusters. The movies are the cover. That's 'why' he has them, for filming. But that's the believable lie. The money is truly in the insurance, not in the paintings themselves. But they do have value. Critical value. Just not as much as the one we are owed." Dachshund, satisfied with his theory, nodded to himself.

"Get them out of here. I want these loaded in the SUV. Carefully. They need to travel with me for a while. I need some more answers before we make any final decisions."

Stig nodded and turned to head out the door just as Dachshund's cell phone buzzed. The trim man pulled the device from his jacket and read the display. He raised one eye and puts a hand in the air, halting Stig for the moment. He then moved a finger to his lips, cautioning Stig to remain quiet. Dachshund answered the call.

"Hello?"

Stig watched his boss carefully, looking for clues about the caller's identity.

"Well, I'm not very happy with you right now." Dachshund's face and demeanour did not betray anything. "Yes, I think we should. Yes. Do you know the Vulcan landfill in Sun Valley? Just off Sheldon? Yes, come there and we can talk. That's fine."

Dachshund replaced the cell phone into his pocket. A wry smile crossed his face. Stig looked at him, as if to say *"What? Who?"*

"Now, that is a most interesting turn of events. Don't load the paintings just yet. You and I, we are going to have a visitor."

64

DAVID PRESSED the accelerator hard, just making the yellow light. He had no intention of stopping anyway. Time could not be wasted. David had to move. He weaved in and out through the evening traffic on Pico Blvd.

Ben had been very helpful, which was usually what happened when you convince someone they are headed to jail if they didn't cooperate. Ben may have been "Zev's guy" when it came to making his little films and whatnot, but he knew screw-all about real life. And David Teck exploited that ignorance every single way he could. He smiled as he flew his car through another stale yellow.

Getting Ben to admit his role in the whole "secret" painting copy that he had facilitated for Levi was tough at first, but once he hit the right note, Ben folded like a cheap suit. He had stammered and whined and protested, claiming that he was nervous and suspicious about the whole thing all along. David knew he was lying, of course. Everybody lies when they're caught, but he had to say something. David had seen the look in the eyes of the liars and cheats and assorted scum. The look that always seems to absolutely glow as they detail whatever "big lie" is at the heart of their scam. These types could close their eyes to anything that might implicate them directly but getting them to flip on their partners required only the slightest of pressure, only so long as it was applied in the right direction.

Ben was a film "builder" guy. He put the physical movies together. Obviously, he knew little of whatever the hell Zevon was doing regarding the financing of his films. Which is likely why he gave no thought whatsoever to driving a blindfolded man, an hour each way, to and from a secret location just to do some painting. He was complicit but ignorant of the details, probably on purpose. He was smart enough for that. Ben didn't seem to know anything about what was being painted. In fact, he seemed totally clueless about those details. But that made sense. No reason for Levi to tell him what was being done. He only needed someone he could trust to deliver the guy back and forth.

David laughed to himself, thinking about Ben babbling away about picking up the guy and dropping him over and over at the same location and how he was innocent and didn't know what was going on, yada, yada. It had been a dry period for Zev's projects, which also made sense. That matched his need to get some funding together, which was why he was trying to use the "painting" in the first place. By the end he had almost begged David to let him draw a map of where he had taken Denny over and over for the joy of painting.

David leaned the car into the turn lane so he could make a curved left across four lanes without cutting his speed too much. He was not going to miss getting there in time.

Ben had explained that he had largely driven Denny around in circles, eventually delivering him each time to the production office on Sunset where Zev would switch out as driver and continue from there and that he had no idea where Denny ended up each time. David was pretty sure Ben was lying, but he didn't have any way to prove otherwise. He had to go back to Denny again.

David curved his car to the right now, skipping some construction and merging onto the 110 freeway. LA surface streets after 9pm were a dream but an open freeway was better than the Autobahn. High speeds and a ton of room to move.

Thinking back to Ben spilling his guts over the process, David's mind tried to recall something Denny had said before, in passing. Something about a smell. He tried to remember what it was. For whatever reason, it kept jumping out to him as he tried to figure out what to do next. What was it?

Bunny Levi was a trainwreck. That woman had jail-time written all over her and David needed to exit from her presence as fast as possible.

Originally, she had proposed an insurance scam, which was fine, that was David's stock-in-trade. And in most circumstances, it would have worked out fine. But she had managed to inadvertently cause the death of her husband and was refusing to deal with that reality. It was a minor miracle that the LAPD seemed to be uninterested in digging deep into what happened, though the narrative of home invasions was fairly ingrained by now and maybe they were ignoring it in hopes of improving their own PR. Never underestimate another's self-interest, no matter how objective or pure they claim to be. They probably weren't investigating because they didn't want to draw attention. Whatever the reason, Bunny was skating on thin ice and David had no desire to get stuck nearby.

Once he had realized that this was more than a simple insurance play, that it might involve an actual, long-missing masterpiece, things changed for David. That there might be an extremely famous, impossible-to-recover work of art up for grabs provided a prize worth chasing. A find like this had the ability to make David's career absolutely sing, and in more ways than one.

The spectacle at the funeral showed that there were more than a few folks chasing along behind, not to mention the dog lady from the mansion showing up. What was that? This piece was seriously "in play" and that meant it was up to David to get his hands on it before any of the others did. Which was also why he had split from the funeral as fast as he could, leaving a shrieking Bunny far behind as she wailed and carried on.

David exited into Pasadena, turning off and heading north. He pushed the throttle. *He better still be there,* thought David, as he scanned the road ahead.

David knew the game. Reproduction artists, legit ones, went to extreme lengths to make their copies. They mixed paint the same way it was done three hundred years ago, they used the same classic pigments produced in the same medieval ways. They even got brushes and utensils constructed exactly like they had been when the painting was first done. But because they were not crooks, they never copied the signature of the original artist and they never, ever made the painting the same size. That, in the reproduction world, was an absolute, unforgivable no-no.

But that was not what Denny did because how could he? The copies he made came from paintings that had been stolen, that had been cut out of their frames and not seen since. There existed no actual record of the current sizes of the missing pieces. So, he matched the size to what he had in front of him. Anyone seeing the copies was going to compare them to the official sizing from before they were stolen. It was a flawed way to determine their status. David had made that mistake when he had told Bunny they were worthless, when he had let Tranko take them at gunpoint. They could still be fakes though. The point was, David now wasn't sure.

So, the only person in the world with the actual, current measurements of *"The Concert"* was Denny. David hung a hard left, accelerated to a cross street, took a right and then slid down the alley, behind the condo he and Bunny had originally confronted Denny in. He could see light coming out back. He hoped he wasn't too late. Ben had said Denny was getting set to run. Which is why David had to work fast. Only Denny could answer the size question. He alone knew the true measurements, and David needed to be able to see his face when he got them from him. Throwing his car into park, David jumped out and made his way around to the open garage door of the studio where Denny was working.

But he wasn't painting.

Denny was packing. Furiously. He was pulling all manner of items off the walls and cramming them into large plywood crates. He was stacking art on cushioned pallets and wrapping things up with furniture blankets. He was bugging out. David spoke up.

"Hello Denny. Going somewhere?"

Denny turned, and audibly cursed. David smiled and walked towards him.

"Didn't think I'd be back, did you? I know what you're doing."

David lied. He didn't know what Denny was doing, but he figured a good bluff might make it seem like he did. And it might get him to admit things he would not otherwise say. Denny dropped his hands by his sides.

"Whatever, okay? I'm hooped. As soon as you showed up before, I knew my days were numbered. I have no choice but to get out of here. I got a truck coming for my stuff in a few hours. I'm relocating. I gotta go." Denny went back to packing up his warehouse.

David stepped in front of him.

"Look, I can get in your way over this, or you can tell me what I want to know. What I *need* to know. And then you can run as far and as fast as you want. I could not give less of a shit about where you're going. But if you lie to me, I'll know and I'm not going to stop coming after you. I swear, I will send every bad guy I know up your ass too. Wherever you end up."

Denny dropped the packing materials on the floor and looked David square in the eye. "So, what do you want to know?"

David outlined his ask, demanding the exact dimensions of the original painting *The Concert*, plus notes on the other two Denny had completed, along with details on how he could tell them apart. Satisfied that he had received the right answers, David stepped back.

"Well, get yourself packed. I'd say the last place you want to be is in LA, especially if what I think is going to happen, does."

Denny said nothing and went right back to loading his artistic life into crates and onto pallets. David started walking back to his car, staring down at the numbers he had noted. Pausing, he remembered about the smell. He turned back to Denny.

"You had said when they drove you to the painting each day that you remembered a smell or something? You commented on that before. What was it? I forget."

Not pausing in his efforts, Denny shouted back. "Chlorine. The smell of chlorine struck me. I figured the room they had me in had stored it once or had a bucket of it somewhere. It was a storage room, right? I never saw it or anything though. Some janitor stuff lying around made sense to me though."

David nodded his head and got back inside his car, fired it up and took off as fast as he had arrived.

65

"THIS IS A BAD IDEA," remarked Tranko Lutz, out loud.

Stewie looked at him but said nothing. Tranko spoke again.

"A really, really bad fucking idea." Stewie made a face. He couldn't not say anything. Finally, he looked right at Tranko and spat it out.

"Then why are you doing it, man?"

Tranko said nothing in response. He was sulking. Stewie tried again. "I said, why do it?"

"Because I don't know what else to do!"

Tranko sat in Stewie's truck. They had just exited the chaos of the Roosevelt Hotel but were now stopped by the side of the road. Tranko sat in the passenger seat, fuming. Out of nowhere he started yelling, pounding on the passenger door of the truck with his clenched fist. "Fuck, fuck, fuck!" He eventually caused the arm rest on the door to come loose. Stewie was horrified.

"Hey! C'mon man! This is my ride. I get you're pissed and all but…damn, hey."

Tranko looked sheepishly at Stewie and tried to "fix" the door. He couldn't. It was broken for sure. He mumbled under his breath, "Sorry, Stewie."

The duo sat in the idling truck, stopped in the red zone just down from the Chateau Marmont garage entrance. Tranko stared at his phone and eventually began talking to it.

"I'm not gonna wait. Fuck her. I don't even know why I answered it in the first place."

Stewie shook his head, as Tranko continued.

"She was the cause of all of this. It was a simple fucking job. Scare some rich dude by ripping off a few things, not a big deal. Then all of this. Bitch!" Tranko's face exploded in rage as he began pounding on the door again.

Stewie, annoyed about his truck being abused, couldn't hold it in any longer. "Dude! Will you cool it with beating on my truck? And it was sort of Howie's fault. I mean, he hit the guy, right? The chick had nothing to do with that."

Tranko turned and glared at Stewie. He knew he was right, of course. Tranko turned back. "Shut the fuck up, Stewie."

Stewie let out an exaggerated burst of air, as he raised both hands in surrender. "Whatever, man. I think you're letting things get way too complicated here. I'm speaking truth and my truck is paying the price. And that's not cool."

Tranko was in no mood for conversation. He went to get out of the truck by reaching for the inside door handle, but it wouldn't release. His pounding has caused it to dangle loose. Stewie noticed and let out a moan. "Oh, come on man! Damn it! See, now my door is fucked."

By this point, as embarrassed as he was angry, Tranko reached out of the truck window and opened his door by pulling the outside handle. He stepped onto the sidewalk and started pacing back and forth. He looked down at his phone again, thinking. *She's got two minutes, tops. Then I'm outta here.*

Just then, a black Mercedes limo pulled up behind the truck and stopped. The back door opened and a pair of legs in high heels got out. Bunny Levi, in full funeral attire, pulled herself awkwardly from the car but continued to face inside of it, pointing, yelling, and gesturing the entire time. Tranko walked toward her, but she ignored him, focusing instead on whoever remained inside the car.

"Well, I don't know what you expect me to do. You think I'm the one in charge? Neither one of you could give a shit for me. You never did. I'm your mother but you care more about the guy that signed freaking checks and gave you whatever you wanted. I gave you life!"

Someone in the car said something back to Bunny. She slammed the door in response and screamed into the open window.

"Fine! See if I care! Go back to the goddamn hotel then. You both made it very clear how little you need me. Well, I don't need you either! Or you!"

Bunny turned and stomped toward Tranko, passing him, and heading for the truck. As she did, the limo window slid back up and the long car pulled away from the curb and disappeared into the evening traffic of Sunset Blvd. Bunny screamed something unintelligible after the car.

"Don't ever have kids" she spat at Tranko. "Or a mother." Bunny strode aggressively to the truck passenger side, yanked the door open and crawled inside, planting in the center seat of the Ford truck. Tranko stared at her and then the open door. Stewie said nothing, looking left at the traffic rolling by. Bunny sat completely still, staring straight ahead. Tranko took a deep breath and walked over to the truck, got inside, and pulled the door closed. The three of them sat in silence for a few moments. Stewie, personally uncomfortable with the volume of rage permeating the pair, reached to turn on the radio, pressing the scan button as he did. Almost immediately he heard a song he liked, and his positive attitude sprang back to life.

"Hey, I love this one." He cranked the volume to *The Pina Colada song*.

Stewie hit the left signal light and slowly pulled the truck out into traffic.

Like Bunny, Tranko stared straight ahead. No one was talking, except for Stewie who was singing along to the radio.

Finally, Tranko gave in and turned to Bunny. "What do you want?"

Bunny glared at him. "What do I want? What do I want?" Well, I'm pretty sure what I didn't want was to see my dead husband's memorial turned into a fight club. And I didn't want my kids to hate me. And I didn't want my mother to tell me everything I'm doing is always wrong. And I sure as hell didn't want the asshole I hired to scare my ex-husband to kill him but HERE WE FUCKING ARE!"

Tranko wished he had never opened his mouth. He went back to looking forward, and pursed his lips. He knew it was a bad idea to re-engage with such an angry troll.

Bunny continued her tirade. "What do I want? What I want is to get some goddamn security for whatever is left of my life. That's what I want. You think this is gonna last forever?" She motioned to her body, as Stewie turned, mid-lyric, to appraise along with her, nodding approvingly.

Bunny's voice escalated, "Did you know I got nothing in the will? Nothing! Maybe it's not official-official but I saw the lawyer at the burial, and he made it clear I'm out. That's it for me. The kids are going to get everything, and they've decided the reason their father is dead is because of me. Me! Like they have any idea about anything."

Bunny went silent, grabbed lipstick from her purse and, after wrenching the rear-view mirror to suit her, began applying it. She kept talking.

"The insurance guy is a jerk. I thought I might get something there but that turned into a dead end. He's at least as dumb as you are, but he's dumped me off and sure as hell plans to cut me out of everything. That means you and I are all we got right now…and if either one of us hopes to get a damned thing out of this churning shit-show we better stick together."

Tranko just looked at her.

Finally, he asked, "Where are we going?"

She looked back at him. "I don't know where we're going. He's driving." Bunny aimed her thumb at Stewie, who ignored them both. He was busy singing to a new song on the radio.

Bunny aimed the question right back at Tranko. "So, where are we going?"

Tranko took a second. He was thinking hard. There had to be a way out of this. There had to be a solid play somewhere. He looked down at his phone again. He had an idea. Tranko punched keys on the phone and then held it to his ear. The call was ringing. Someone answered.

"Yeah. It's me. I know, I know. I think we should talk. Real talk. No bullshit this time. Uh huh. Yeah. Okay. That's about a half hour from us. Okay. Yeah."

Tranko pressed the button to hang up the phone. He furrowed his brow, unsure if he made the right decision or not.

"Who was that? Who did you call?"

Tranko breathed deep. "Stewie, turn us around. We gotta head out to the Vulcan landfill. Bunny, I think it's time you met Edward Dachshund."

66

MAGGIE NEEDED to protect Fatima. There was no other way around it. Aldo was dangerous. Far more dangerous than she realized. Maggie had known this, but she had pushed the thought from her mind, trying to respect her friend's heart. Getting between two people romantically involved was never a good idea, but she no longer had a choice. At the very least, Fati would have to find out the truth about Aldo, as in, who he was and what he represented. Maggie slowed her speed, steering the Honda down Stuart Ranch Road. She was headed for Malibu City Hall.

Fatima had said she was heading back to Vancouver today. Aldo was taking her in his jet, promising to drop her before he skipped off to who knows where. Fati had asked if Maggie wanted to join her, but she had declined. First using the whole "I've still got a little upset stomach thing", but then adding that with the crochet convention over she wanted to play tourist in LA for a few days. Fatima bought it and promised they would get together when they were both back in Vancouver. Maggie was happy to get Fatima out of LA. Things were getting dangerous and having Fati far away from the chaos was only for the best.

With her leverage over Aldo hidden in the motel room on Wilshire, Maggie felt personally protected. But Fati had nothing. And Maggie hated what it was going to take for her to be able to protect Fati.

She was going to have to tell Fatima the truth.

About her past. About everything. There could be no more secrets. Maggie winced at the thought.

Coming clean about everything sounded simple enough, but there was no way Fati could handle the knowledge. It would likely break their friendship apart for good, which Maggie hated. But it was a small price to pay if it meant she could get her away from Aldo. Maggie's own research, combined with Ivan finally coming clean, had revealed Aldo for the problem that he was. The trick was going to be getting Fatima to believe her.

And that was not going to be easy.

Maggie had successfully lied to her friend over and over. About her whereabouts, her actions, the truth of what she was doing in LA, everything. It felt awful. She couldn't keep doing it, even though it was for Fatima's own good. Maggie felt dirty, constantly having to keep her in the dark regarding her real life. She had genuinely believed it wouldn't be an issue back when they met. Maggie had been winding down. She had a normal job. She was trying to live like a regular person. She had really wanted to.

But she couldn't.

Yes, Maggie ended up needing more money, but the real draw was the excitement. Maggie hated that it pulled her back in, but she had to admit it to herself: she liked the life she led before. It was fun. It fed her in a way being a drone at the catalog counter could never achieve. But how would Fatima take it?

Steering into the parking lot of the Malibu City Hall, Maggie parked the bike, switched it off, and removed her helmet. The online world was a great one, and you could pick up the most amazing things when it came to collecting information in a fraction of the time, but some things just needed to be done in person. No matter how inconvenient. Maggie walked through the main doors and looked for signs indicating the planning department for Malibu. She needed access to Levi's secrets and what better place to dig in than a fresh branch of government.

Standing at the counter, Maggie waited as a young man noticed her and then stepped up.

"Hi, can I help you?"

"Hello. I'm trying to get some more detailed plan information on a home that was constructed along Birdview Ave in the last few years or so. I'm not sure of the exact date or time but I do have the plan numbers and some other details." She handed a piece of paper to the clerk.

"We do offer a lot of this online. You can even access it from one of terminals here in the building," he offered helpfully.

"Oh, yes, but my boss needed something that's just not showing up on the online file. It would take physically viewing the plans in question, you know how small that type can be in architecture plans. Is there any chance I'd be able to see the hard copies?"

The young man made a face. "Well, we usually require a little warning before allowing direct access to the hard copies. It takes a fair bit of time to get it them out of the archives. We don't make a habit of letting people in to go over them personally."

Maggie bowed her head. "Oh dear. I'm in so much trouble. I was supposed to do this two weeks ago and I got distracted by another job. Now my boss is on me to have it and if I delay any longer, I could be in serious trouble. Is there any way you can help? I know it's all my fault, not yours, but if there is anything you can do, I would totally appreciate it."

The guy breathed in and out, furrowing his brow. He looked around and then, leant in close to Maggie. "Look, it's not very busy today, at least not yet. I can't guarantee anything but let me have a look and see what I can do. Just have a seat over there. I'll talk to someone."

Maggie nodded and smiled appreciatively. Taking a seat just across from the planning desk, she prepped herself for a substantial wait.

Running things through her head, Maggie saw David Teck pop up. Now he really was a potential problem. Ivan had explained to her who he was, a wannabe thief who moved into insurance scams. She didn't know his exact role in things yet, but at least she knew who he was. Seemed like he was with the widow in some way. Might be in on things, might not be. He might even be playing it straight in his role as adjuster. Maggie would need more info on him to sort that out. Her brain spun farther afield. The Russians.

They were another problem. Maggie knew they were big trouble. Leverage on that crew wasn't going to be easy to come by, and they represented a threat at least as dangerous as Aldo. Aldo was lily white, in public, because he needed to be. That meant he was more squeamish when it came to dispatching people. And so long as someone was no threat to him personally, he'd probably leave them alone. The Russians on the other hand, they were straight organized crime. They were not shy about killing to send a message, and whether Maggie liked it or not she was now tangled up with them in a big way. The only way they were better was that they had no direct tie to Fatima.

Ivan had detailed the role of the Russians in the piece she was tasked with securing. They felt it was theirs, while Aldo wanted it for his own negotiations with them. Maggie was not privy to more details on that, and neither was Ivan. She only knew they had beef with each other, and that the Vermeer was the piece they were fighting over. Maggie was going to have to work that one out too. She hadn't met any of the Russians yet, but Ivan had pointed out a few of them at the memorial at the Roosevelt Hotel. The big one fighting in the center was the boss, apparently.

As Maggie let her gaze wander around the waiting room her mind finally drifted back to the immediate task at hand: she had been hired to get a picture for Aldo, and his right-hand Manheim was going to be up her butt about it until she did. She was certain he had even trailed her a few times, but she had worked hard to keep him off. Maggie was even confident he knew nothing of her visit to Aldo's yacht, but you could never know anything truly 100%. She just had to be careful, at least until she secured *The Concert*. Then at least she would have something to bargain with. And unlocking the location of Aldo's pride and joy gave even more credence to her belief that Levi's own "pride and joy" would have been hidden similarly close as well. The trick was finding it.

The clerk returned. He was smiling.

"Okay, I can let you into the physical records room. I'm not able to be with you but this binder has the codes to look up the actual drawings you need to see. Now, I can't authorize any copies, but you can write down whatever info you need to gather from the plans. Will that work for you?"

Maggie smiled broadly. "It will be perfect. Thank you so much for this. You have no idea how much this helps me."

* * *

The architectural plans for Levi's ego exercise on Birdview were detailed and voluminous, and most things you could imagine were noted, except the one item Maggie was looking for.

A secret room.

Obviously, the point of a secret room was that no one knew about it, but in the modern era building one was a little trickier than in days gone by. You couldn't just task your slaves with building something and then have them killed when you were done to protect the secret. Today there were zoning boards and inspectors and all sorts of checks and balances to review every stage of construction. Hiding the creation of a secret room took some doing. But if you knew what to look for, sometimes you could uncover it. Maggie set about paging through the plans again. Over and over, she studied them. Front to back. She even used a magnifying glass she had found on a side table. Nothing.

Maggie rubbed her eyes and looked at the clock. More than fifty minutes had passed. She had been through the plans a half-dozen times now. Her eyes were beginning to cross from staring at all the tiny text and the whisper thin lines that made up the drawings. Every time she thought she found something that contradicted another area of the house it checked out. She must be looking in the wrong place. There had to be something else.

Absently flipping the pages, Maggie decided to lean in on the areas she had not focused on already. What had she passed over without considering? She turned the pages slowly, eventually stopping on a landscape map. Landscaping? thought Maggie. Outdoors? Maybe he had put something into the backyard?

Obviously, Maggie had her own experience with secret rooms. She had been inside plenty of them, usually without the owner's knowledge. But she had also listened to her father explain how he had put his together. How much of the work he had done himself and the parts he had been able to let others do was simply because there was no way they could realize the true nature of what they were building. They didn't have the full picture.

And digging holes was a great way to hide things.

Maggie knew you could dig a hole bigger than it needed to be, appear to fill it in, but then expand it sometime later. So, what about Levi? Had he dug any holes?

Maggie stared at the page. A pool. According to the plans, Levi had excavated an existing pool on the property to re-do it, and, again according to the notes, enlarge it. Looking, Maggie saw the plans showing the pool significantly larger in the "after" rendering than the "before" outlines. Going back and forth between the two, Maggie could see a big difference between the old pool and the new one planned. Racking her brain, she tried to remember her time on site. She looked at the plans and tried to situate herself in her mind. And things were not adding up.

The plans showed a pool that was significantly larger than the one she remembered standing next to. But what if it was wishful thinking? Or her mind playing tricks on her? Still, the size of pool drawn out seemed too big compared to the one she had seen in person. Was that where the secret lay? Did Levi have a secret room outside, adjacent the pool? Maggie checked the clock again. She had enough time. Especially considering where her next stop needed to be.

67

THE GUY staring at them had the largest eyebrow Bunny had ever seen.

"Look at it," she said, almost mesmerized, "It's like someone put black body tape straight across his forehead. How can that be real?"

Tranko rolled his eyes. He wasn't going to engage with this.

"Look at it. It just completely dominates his face!" Bunny was transfixed.

"Maybe he shaves them," offered Stewie.

Bunny turned to Stewie, her face pinched. "No way, that's not real. That's an old wives' tale."

Stewie shook his head slowly, making clear he was not in agreement with Bunny's dissent. "Well now, I had a friend who was a swimmer guy back in the day and he shaved his legs all the time for racing, and he said the hair always grew back way thicker and coarser. He looked like he had pants on...even in shorts."

"That's leg hair. I doubt eyebrows are the same," answered Bunny.

"I don't know," said Stewie, "Makes sense to me."

"But why would he shave his eyebrows at all? I mean, who does that? And look at him. I'm not sure he even bathes, let alone grooms himself. That caterpillar on his face is real. He couldn't help it if he tried. He probably looks like a *Sasquatch* if he takes his shirt off."

Stewie craned his neck over the steering wheel, looking out the front window of the truck at the guard in question.

"You really think so? I can't imagine..."

Tranko had heard enough.

"Will you two idiots shut the fuck up? Enough, okay? Just sit still and shut up."

Bunny chided him, "How long do they expect us to just sit here and wait. I thought you said I was going to meet some big shot tough guy or something? Let's get on with it."

Tranko took a very deep breath, willing himself not to slam Bunny's head into the front dash of the pickup.

"They'll let us in when they're ready. Just stop, okay?"

Bunny crossed her arms angrily and slumped in the center seat.

"Ugghhh! So, we just sit here until the freak with eyebrows thinks it's okay to come in?"

"Not him. But yes."

Almost instantly, the large guard with the even larger eyebrows seemed to hear something in his ear, then he stepped to one side and waved at the trio to drive through. Stewie started the truck, put it in gear, and they rolled past the open gate, heading towards the series of old warehouses separate from the operating landfill. Tranko scanned behind them, in the mirror, seeing the secondary gate close. Immediately, he started searching for alternative exits, just in case.

As the truck approached the structures several dark SUVs become visible. Tranko looked ahead, straining to see.

He cautioned Stewie, "Slow down a little." Tranko spied five or six guys and made a quick decision.

"Stop here. We'll walk in. You stay with the truck." Stewie nodded and pulled the truck over. Bunny and Tranko got out. As Bunny started to walk towards the SUVs, Tranko hung back and leaned in the window, toward Stewie.

"Angle the truck that way, away from the road, towards the landfill access, where those big trucks are coming in." Stewie nodded and began moving the truck where he was instructed while Tranko caught up to Bunny.

Tranko leaned over to Bunny, speaking quietly. "Resist the urge to talk, ok? It's gonna be hard for you, I know, but you are not dealing with guys as "enlightened" as I am."

"What does that even mean?" asked Bunny.

"It means you might get belted. Or shot. So don't be a...uhh...." Tranko censored himself. He didn't want to antagonize her a few seconds before it mattered.

"Don't be a bitch, you mean?"

"That would be a good idea, yes." agreed Tranko.

"We'll see."

As Bunny and Tranko came to stop in front of the group, everyone assessed each other, looking up and down, left, and right. Stig (as Dachshund) stood in the center, flanked by his men while the real Dachshund hovered nearby in his "slim accountant" guise. Tranko spoke first.

"I think you already have what you want."

Stig looked at Tranko, saying nothing. Tranko had faced him and spoken directly to him, but he knew it was the real Dachshund nearby that was receiving the message.

Stig answered, "What you mean?" He motioned for his men to check them.

The group stood outside the Vulcan landfill, steps from the old warehouse where the paintings were now stored. Tranko and Bunny were patted down as she tapped her foot nervously, becoming more and more frustrated at what was happening.

"Ok, buddy, that's no gun and you know it. Hands off!"

Stig eyed Tranko with his chin jutted upwards, disdainfully. "I said, what you mean?"

Tranko spoke clearly. "Originally, you came at me wanting help, ordering me to help, really. And we went back and forth, with you guys getting all those paintings we had in the truck. What I'm saying is that you already have what you want…"

Before he could finish his sentence, Bunny unloaded on all assembled.

"You assholes ruined my husband's memorial! How dare you!" Stepping forward, she poked a finger directly at Stig.

"And you! You destroyed a food table and caused the scene. What the hell is wrong with you?" Stig raised his eyebrows and smirked a little, bemused at the mouthy woman coming at him like a small pet.

"Bunny!" said Tranko, trying to stay calm but barely holding on.

Bunny waved her arms in the air. "Why do I have to pussyfoot around these guys? The only one who got killed was my husband and that was your fault, right?"

Tranko wanted to punch Bunny in the face. Never, ever accept a job from a woman. How he had managed to break that rule still tormented him. Bunny wasn't finished. She took another step and shoved Stig in the shoulder. He didn't move, but he did lower his eyebrow and slowly turn his palm over, clearly prepping for a backhand slap. The "accountant", seeing this, stepped in and placed his hand on Stig's, looking him square in the eye while saying nothing. The tension in Stig levelled as the real Edward Dachshund stepped onto centre stage.

"Mrs. Levi. Your husband engaged in some…dealmaking…with my boss and, while the circumstances of his demise are indeed regrettable, they do not have any bearing on the promises that he made to us. His obligations remain, and they will be satisfied."

Bunny turned her focus from Stig to the more benign seeming accountant. Her wheels were turning, that much was clear.

"Satisfied? What does that even mean?"

Calmly, the trim, controlled man continued, "Your husband guaranteed something extremely important and valuable with a very special possession of his, and he was paid quite handsomely for this service. However, a problem arose when the item he was guaranteeing with failed to materialize. That meant that your husband had to forfeit his guarantee, as in, he had to hand over the item. He did not do this before he died. Now if this item can be produced, then we will go, and you will not hear from us in any way, shape, or form. However, if it is not produced then we will be forced to take alternate measures."

Bunny turned and looked at Tranko. "And back to the threats. Why is it always threats?"

The real Dachshund, smiling, took Bunny's hand gently and looked right at her. "Threats, my dear lady, are things people unwilling to back up their words resort to. Our words, however, are cast in iron and should represent a perfectly clear picture of the future. They are not threats. They are promises."

Bunny swallowed, even as she appeared likely to speak. She decided against it.

Tranko spoke instead. "Look, I don't think she knows anything. She's running around just as much as we are."

"Then why bring her here?"

"Because I think the weasel that she was dealing with does know something. And with her help, maybe we can get that guy onside with us."

The accountant looked right at Stig and the two of them walked a short distance away, talking. Stig was animated with large arm movements. The other, not. Eventually, the two men returned, and the real Dachshund spoke to Tranko, as if he was deferring to "his" boss.

"Mr. Dachshund would like some more details about the individual in question, and this time you will work in concert with us. No more freelancing."

"Whatever. I just want this settled, okay? So, what do you want to do?"

"Provide Mr. Dachshund with details of this person and make arrangements to get him in front of us."

"Do you want his name?"

"All that you can provide. I must go. I have a meeting I cannot miss. I'll touch base from the car later. You all talk."

And with that, the real Dachshund stepped quickly into a black SUV, slamming the door as it took off down the road. Tranko faced Stig and rolled his eyes slightly.

"Right. So, Bunny. We're gonna need the details on this guy you were dealing with." As he turned to look at Bunny, he was shocked to discover her making eyes at Stig.

"Bunny? C'mon, are you kidding me?"

She whispered to him, "I can't expect you to protect me. It's up to me, as usual." And with that Bunny tottered over to Stig on her platform heels, adjusting herself and primping all the way. Stig eyed her curiously as the odd group slowly went inside the warehouse to discuss the apparent apprehension of David Teck.

68

MAGGIE STARED at the swimming pool as the light shimmered in the afternoon sun.

The painting was here. It had to be. She could feel it.

Maggie had returned to Zev Levi's Malibu mansion. The staff were clearly gone as the gates were closed and secured. She had stored her bike inside the front gardens, behind a large palm, making it effectively invisible. Then she hopped herself over the fence. Maggie didn't see any grounds camera, so she wasn't worried about tripping anything exteriorly.

Besides, she didn't need to go inside the house. The answer was in the backyard. In the pool.

Maggie cast her gaze up and down the length of the pool, end to end, over and over again. She was good at eyeballing distances, always had been. No way did the physical pool match the approved dimensions on file at Malibu city hall. There was absolutely a difference in the size of the pool approved and the size of the pool built.

When Maggie's father had constructed his secret room, he had done it the old school way. He had done it himself. He had cut through the existing foundation wall of the house and simply dug it out, bucket by painful bucket, himself. It had taken forever, or at least it had seemed like forever. In truth, it was about six months. He had excavated the space, framed it, poured his own cement walls, ran his own wiring, and then built the false wall out of a broken piano he had bought at a yard sale for $50. He had reasoned that something that heavy would never be viewed as easily movable, causing most to skip their eyes right over it. And he had been right.

No tradesperson or individual who had ever entered the house for any reason suspected there was an entire secret room mere feet away.

But this wasn't her father's secret room.

Zevon Levi was a movie producer, not a builder. He'd have had to hire someone to do such things. And you couldn't exactly advertise to have a secret room built. Especially when things like building codes, tradesman, and snoopy inspectors ruled. You had to be creative. You had to do things like this in pieces, so that no one person could ever know the whole truth.

The first step was the space. Where could you hide it so that it seemed invisible? Maggie found the answer in the pool's plans. The excavation for the pool was massive, far larger than the pool she was standing in front of. So, why dig a bigger pool than the one you eventually install? An inspector could easily be convinced that the "size didn't match my vision" or that "the prices changed" or the "materials were not available." Whatever lie chosen, it must have been sufficient to explain the difference when the final pool was inspected.

But before that final inspection, before the pool was ever fully put into place, a foundation would have been laid to support the pool as currently presented with a concrete box directly adjacent. The trades people would have been told it was for shoring up the grounds, or maybe as a catch-basin overflow, or some other plausible lie. Someone paying attention might have suspected what was up, but those folks were few and far between.

And that is how Zevon Levi would have built a secret room that almost certainly lay adjacent to his backyard swimming pool.

At least, that's what Maggie had convinced herself was the case. The trick now was finding out how to get inside it. If it was accessible only from the house that would complicate things. The house was alarmed. Maggie could disable it, and she still might if she had to, but she couldn't shake the idea that the room was separate from the house for a reason. He didn't want anyone to find it, and in a modern designed home with large open spaces and few pieces of furniture, it might have been more difficult to hide the access to such a thing. Not a lot of grandfather clocks or heirloom bookshelves to pass through *Hardy Boy's* style.

Which brought Maggie right back to the pool. No obvious, nearby outbuildings. The shower/change area was minimalist in design too

– hard to see where a secret passage could be obscured. She looked around the pool equipment room. The door was unlocked but the space was small. Just large enough for a pump, heater and filter. Two five-gallon pails of chemicals stacked in one corner, few other tools, etc. Maggie slid her hands around the building's corners, and the equipment itself. She was looking for something that should be secure but wasn't. For something that might move.

Nothing.

The pool house was just too small. Maybe too obvious? If you have a secret pool room, maybe you don't access it through the pool? Thought Maggie. She walked over to the other side of the pool, between the edge and the view, looking over the cliff beyond. Could he access it from the cliff face? She just couldn't see that making sense. Too risky for being seen by some random guy on the beach looking up. Not right.

Maggie was getting frustrated. She was certain she had figured out where the secret room was. The issue now was getting inside it. Maybe she had to go inside the house after all.

Walking over to the sliding doors, Maggie eye-balled the edges while avoiding the exterior cameras. Sliding doors were great for gaining access to homes. They never had the security profile of a solid oak door and getting proper alarms on them was always a pain. Half the time the owners would disable the alarms on sliders just because they'd constantly go off every time someone slid a door too far or closed it wrong.

If she was going to break into the main house, she needed a small window. They were easier to break, plus they made less noise. Around the back of the house, she found one. Assuming she could get through it easily, it was unlikely she'd set off other alarms. Motion alarms inside the house were possible, but almost always set to allow for pet movements, etc. And having staff meant even more issues. Having their servants tripping alarms was always a pain for the rich. As a result, they turned most alarms off and just bought more insurance.

As Maggie examined the window she planned to break, she decided it might be better to use a rock or tool rather than risk a cut on her hand. Seeing a tiny gardener shack in the corner she opened the cedar door and spied a motley collection of lawnmowers, blowers, rakes, shovels and more. Looking for a small hammer or something similar, Maggie stepped inside and searched the tiny work bench, moving gardening gloves, buckets, and assorted tools.

Then she stopped.

The little shed was rickety. Decrepit seeming. The walls were thin. It matched exactly nothing on the site. Wood, yes, but not serious or secured in anyway. It was a piece of junk compared to everything on site.

But the floor sure wasn't.

The floor of the tiny shed was dirty, but it was solid in a way the rest of the structure was not. Maggie stomped on it to confirm her suspicion. No echo, no sound. Just solid. Thick.

Maggie dropped to her knees, feeling around the edges of the floor, looking for anything. A catch, a lock, an edge, something that might indicate a trap door.

Then she had a thought. Pulling herself all the way inside, Maggie closed the door behind her. Getting back down on the floor she looked for a catch. And there it was. It had been masquerading as the door stop, invisible when the door was open, obvious when it was closed. Because who would ever consider going inside a shed this tiny and closing the door? No one, except Zevon Levi.

Maggie pulled the "doorstop," nothing. Then, she twisted it to the left, and pulled. Instantly, she heard a lock release and a hatch in the floor open. Lifting it revealed a set of steel stairs heading down into the earth. It was lit with the tiniest of pin lights. Maggie's heart leapt. She had found it. Checking outside once more, Maggie descended into the passage, her heart pounding all the way.

The passage was concrete, with various pipes suspended along the ceiling. Understandable, as their purpose was to service the pool, meaning the construction could be justified, even though having a tunnel large enough to walk alongside would be an anomaly. Zevon was no dummy, clearly.

About 40ft in, Maggie came to a door. It was steel, with a solid handle and a keypad code. Maggie tried the door first. You just never knew when it might be left open. No luck. Locked. Maggie studied the keypad. Nothing fancy. Just a standard, hardware store coded lock. Probably ran on 4 AAs. But it required a code, nonetheless. Maggie stopped for a moment, considered her options, and looked around. If she tried too many codes and they were wrong, the keypad would lock up for a period before letting her try again. She didn't want that. There was always a key override, but where was the key? Remembering that people are people, and that the simplest solutions were usually the easiest, Maggie started hunting around the doorway for a backup key.

"There's no way he's leaving a key to this room inside the house," thought Maggie.

Nothing by the door. Turning around she looked at the pipes running along the roof. Studying them, Maggie spied a naturally occurring junction with the pipes that seemed blind, protected. Grimacing, she reached her hand up inside, expecting some manner of creepy crawly to touch her hand. She hated bugs. Searching around she felt something move. Success! Maggie withdrew a magnetic key locker.

Taking it down, she opened it and took the shiny key out. Sliding it into the lock, Maggie turned the key and opened the door.

The room was not what she expected.

Under construction would be the best description. Zevon Levi had had plans for it but clearly didn't get around to finishing the room before he died. It was a fair space, maybe 15 by 25 feet. The floor and walls were unfinished concrete. Some 2x4 strapping had been started at one end of the room but seemed to have been abandoned mid-job. There were tools lying around, plus some older furniture that appeared to have been chosen solely for its ability to fit down the hallway into the space.

It was a grown man's secret hideaway in progress, now doomed to remain unfinished forever due to Levi's death. Maggie searched around the room, looking behind plywood sheets leaning against the walls and under tarps holding unopened boxes of hardwood flooring.

Under one tarp was a pinball machine. A *Gilligan's Island* one. Plus, what seemed like pieces of a disassembled pool table. An old bar fridge stood nearby. Unplugged, empty. Next to it was a collection of framed movie posters, all resting against the wall, waiting to be hung. Maggie flipped through them. *The Godfather, Bladerunner,* something called *Stormchasers,* and then a piece of thick plexiglass...

Maggie's breath caught in her throat.

She slid the plexiglass out of the pile. It was two pieces screwed together at the four corners. The pieces were pressing what seemed to be an old canvas between them. Maggie slowly flipped it over.

The Concert, by Johannes Vermeer. The missing painting from the Gardner Museum robbery decades ago. The most expensive piece of art ever stolen.

It wasn't properly framed, probably because it couldn't be. When the painting had been stolen from the Gardner it had been cut out of the frame. That might have lopped off a good inch or more around the picture. Framing it correctly would shrink it further still. Maybe he decided to press it instead, like a flower in a book. Maggie studied the piece. It was real all right. The canvas had the age required. The sizing seemed right, and the painting, well, it was all legit. Maggie had found the Vermeer. Now she had to get it out of here.

Leaning the piece against one wall, Maggie took *Lola* out and tried to pry open one of the fasteners holding the plexiglass in place. It took a little bit of fiddling, but she finally jury-rigged a way to unscrew the parts and free the canvas from the plexiglass press. Once that was done, she could roll the canvas carefully and slip out easily. She went to work on the last screw plate.

Maggie didn't hear him enter behind her, at least until he spoke.

"Now you can't possibly tell me that poor little Roofie somehow wandered in here? That dog is amazing. Imagine that, trained to sniff out Vermeers? He's quite the dog, no?"

69

FATI TOOK a sip of her whiskey sour as she paged through a massive coffee-table book of vintage Los Angeles photos. Just behind her, to the left and through hidden pocket doors, was a continuation of the dark-hued bar, but in a lighter palette featuring more earth tones and wood. The Salon at LAX was easily the hippest place to await a flight she had ever experienced.

Fatima glanced up, seeing the sun stream through the windows by the attached garden, complete with water feature and outdoor lounge. It was all accessible from the full-service bar and restaurant. She watched Aldo playing cornhole in the outdoor area. Quite a departure from the stresses of a normal airline gate. Who would believe they were a runway separated from LAX itself? It was like another world.

The lounge was quiet, with only one other party visible. Three men, apparently on a golf holiday, threw back shots. Aside from their chatter, the room was blissfully peaceful. Fatima set her drink down and replaced the large book on a nearby end table. Getting to her feet, she went to join Aldo in the outdoor area, seeking natural sunshine and some fresh air of her own.

The Salon was set up as an elite gate providing exclusive access to the Los Angeles International Airport. For a fee, privileged travellers could use the private waiting area with its own TSA security check and chauffeured car service directly to the tarmac. Aldo had been praising the service for a few days now, as he readied plans for their trip overseas. Fatima sighed with satisfaction. It was wonderful being cradled in the bosom of luxury. Memories of her father swelled inside as she approached Aldo, who was cheering his success at the classic backyard game.

"*Mira vos!*" exclaimed Aldo, "Ha ha, see Fatima, no one beats the champ!"

"Lovely," replied Fatima, beaming as she went in for a hug. Aldo embraced her with one arm as he tossed a remaining game bag to the side.

"Are you ready for the trip home, my lovely?" asked Aldo as he swooped her into both arms.

"I am," replied Fatima, "but I still wish I could have seen Maggie before we left."

Aldo reached for an outdoor chair and guided it to Fatima, seating her. He pulled one over and sat down himself.

"Fatima, I've been meaning to discuss something with you. I...think maybe your friend does not have quite your best interests at heart."

Distressed, Fati looked at Aldo, confused. "I don't follow."

Aldo leaned back in his chair, smiling in his gregarious way, arms outstretched. "Look, I know Maggie, she does not...seem happy for you...for us. I mean, maybe it's jealousy or..."

"Jealousy? What are you saying?"

"I simply mean that she seems to not like me and you as a couple so much."

"Well, she was sick the other night, that's why she couldn't come."

"It's always something like that, and I didn't want to say before but...."

Suddenly, a firm voice to the side of them broke into their conversation.

"Pardon me, Mr. Neto?"

Aldo turned in his chair to face the man, rising to grasp his outstretched hand.

"I'm sorry, you are...?"

"My name is Edward Dachshund and I think it's time you and I met face to face."

Aldo's sunny disposition turned instantly stern. He looked to Fatima and gave curt instructions.

"Fatima, I need a moment with this gentleman. If you could..."

Fatima, immediately sensing the brush off, stood up and attempted to engage with the man herself.

"I'm sorry, we haven't met..."

Aldo cut her off brusquely.

"Fatima!" He turned to Dachshund. "Do you have someplace we can talk?"

Dachshund, all but ignoring Fatima, indicated he had a place and began to walk away. Aldo followed him, leaving Fatima fuming where she stood.

The two men walked down a hallway into suite #13, the only private berth with its own secluded outdoor space. They proceeded through the luxurious suite to the outside. Once there, Aldo pivoted smoothly and looked Dachshund right in the eye.

"Bold of you to show up without a detail, no?"

"I have nothing to fear, from you or anyone else," replied Dachshund.

Finding his calm, Aldo lifted his chin slightly, curling his lip as he spoke. "That's not what I've heard. You have made promises that are not being kept and it's putting you into some difficulties."

Dachshund smiled.

"Well, my 'difficulties', as you term them, seem to have a surprising relationship to certain strings that you pull. Why is that do you think?"

"I think you are imagining things, like a child looking to blame others for their own faults."

"Mr. Neto, I am very aware of the position you now hold, not to mention the ways in which you manipulated to make it possible. My indifference to such should not be seen as acceptance. What goes up, most certainly can also come down."

Aldo smiled, then turned, giving his back to Dachshund. He spoke while facing the opposite direction. "Down is the direction you are most certainly headed, especially when you have failed to meet your obligations."

Dachshund, determined to stake his own point, found a chair, and seated himself. He was facing the back of a standing Aldo.

"Do you like this space, Mr. Neto? I mean, it's very swish, but as luxuries go it doesn't come close to matching the sort of things available to individuals such as us, now does it?"

This caused Aldo to stop, turn, and face the now seated Dachshund. "What are you playing at?"

"Don't cheapen this. You know full well what I'm trying to collect is owed to me. Getting in the way of it, affecting it, tells me all I need to know."

"And that is?"

"That you are either working on behalf of my enemies to repay debts owed or for your own gain. Either is inadvisable. It's time for you to call off your dog."

* * *

Fatima sat at a table in the lounge, furious at being barked at by Aldo. Her own history with difficult men taught her enough about them to know the signs. She was not so naïve as to the affairs of powerful men, but she had hoped that Aldo was above such things.

Maybe he wasn't.

She was also not happy with the insinuations being tossed at Maggie. What was Aldo getting at? What was he accusing her of? Fatima took out her phone and searched up the hotel Maggie was staying at. She dialed the main desk.

"Hello? I'm trying to reach Maggie, Margaret Deacon? Yes, she's a guest there. Yes, I'll wait."

Fatima waited on hold while the clerk tried the room. She looked about for Aldo and his mysterious visitor. No sign of either. The clerk returned to the line.

"I'm sorry, we have Ms. Deacon checked out a day prior."

"That's impossible. She was just there yesterday. I spoke to her myself."

"I'm sorry. She is no longer a guest here."

Fatima clicked off her phone. Now what was going on? Where was Maggie? She had said she was going to stay around LA for a few days and check it out. Now she wasn't there? Was Aldo on to something? Was Maggie lying to her? Fatima began to tap her nails on the counter nearby.

Suddenly, Aldo strode back into the lounge. He had a hard look on his face. He was annoyed. Out the window, Fatima watched as a black SUV roared past the glass entrance. She guessed it was Aldo's tormentor leaving the scene.

"What was that all about?" asked Fatima.

"It's nothing. Get your things. We should board the plane now."

"I'm not boarding anything until I get some answers."

"Fatima, dearest, I love you with my heart, but now is not the time to make demands of me. My...business has thrown me some issues that must be dealt with and..."

"Your business? You were in the process of smearing my best friend before you jumped up and ran away with some stranger out of the blue. Am I supposed to not notice that? To not be concerned? What is going on?"

"My business is not your concern..."

"You want me to marry you, but your business is 'not my concern?' And what about Maggie haven't you told me? What do you think you know about her that I don't?"

Aldo, looking around nervously, disliked the escalating scene being created. "We should go now. We can talk on the plane."

Fatima was not going anywhere. She had had enough. "I'm not getting on any plane." She pulled herself away from Aldo and stepped up to the counter, waving for help. "Hello? Hello? I'd like my bags removed from the...his plane. Yes? Right now!" The clerk behind the counter froze, not prepared for confrontation. He looked at Fatima and then stared over to Aldo.

Aldo tried to placate her. "Fatima, you're overreacting. This isn't necessary."

"I want my bags NOW!"

Aldo turned to the clerk and nodded. Immediately, the clerk dialed a phone and began preparations to get Fatima's bags back to her.

Facing the clerk, Fatima spoke "I will be standing out front waiting for a car to take me out of here and it better have my bags inside it, or else!"

The clerk looked back to Aldo again, who nodded with resignation.

He continued to plead at her, "Fatima, I..."

Without giving him a second look, Fatima stormed out the door of the Salon and stood with her arms crossed in front of the main entrance. She took out her cell phone and started calling the number she had for Maggie's cell phone.

"C'mon Maggie, I need you to be there, right now. Please answer."

70

SLOWLY, Maggie turned. It was the guy from the party, and from here at the house. David Teck was his name, according to Ivan, and he was standing between her and the doorway. Only one of his hands was visible as he spoke.

"Nuh uh, slowly now. I know you aren't who you said you were, and I'm fairly sure you know that neither am I. Both of us are looking to take something that doesn't belong to us. Thing is, I've got an insurance card to play that gives me some legitimacy. I'm thinking you do not have something similar."

Maggie frowned. He was right about that. She had no excuse for being here, and whether he was lying or not didn't really matter. He had the drop on her. David spotted the Vermeer on the table. His eyes widened.

"It's real, isn't it? Damnit! I knew it! I knew it! Go ahead, finish what you were doing."

Maggie cocked her head at him. "Why? So, you can run out of here with it? You do it."

David smiled back at her.

"Now, now. No need to get salty. Sure, I'll do it, but you have got to hand me that fancy knife first. What do you say?"

Maggie sighed. No way was she giving up *Lola*, even if it might give her a momentary advantage. Time to play what the situation offered. She got busy removing the last of the screw catches on the plexiglass.

"Good, good," approved David.

As Maggie pulled the last screw out, she began to lift the large plexiglass sheet off the Vermeer canvas…then stopped.

"Ok, so what do want me to do here?"

David stalled. He still had not produced his other hand for viewing. Maggie was waiting to see what he had on offer.

"What were you going to do?" David thought he was being smart by turning the question back on her.

Maggie stared right at him. "I was going to expose the canvas, carefully, and then take my time rolling it up."

David nodded. "And you have a way to carry the rolled canvas?"

Maggie nodded. "I do."

David walked over to one side, slightly exposing the single doorway behind him. He leaned on a carpenter's sawhorse. "Here's the thing. I don't have a gun, never used the darn things. Makes your sentence too high when you get caught. In fact, I've never used violence at all really. Makes things too messy, you know?"

Maggie nodded. "It does."

David studied Maggie for a long moment. Really looked at her. Then he spoke.

"You're not who you present as, are you? You're far more trouble than even I realized. You might use that age thing you got to make people underestimate you, but I don't. Who brought you into this? You can tell me."

Maggie placed the top layer of plexiglass on the floor, leaning it against the table between her and David. She began to roll the canvas, very carefully.

"Why don't you tell me who brought you in first?"

At this, David laughed out loud. "Ha! I'm not shy about that. The widow, that horrible little creature. She was looking for an insurance payday. Figured she could use me to get a better settlement. I even think she had her old man offed in the first place. She keeps saying it was an accident and blames some other guy but she's as crooked as they come. She didn't even know what she had. In fact, I doubt she even recognizes it fully at this point."

"Where is she?"

"No, no, no. I told you something. Now it's your turn. Who brought you in?"

Maggie continued to roll up the canvas, smoothly and with care. She pulled a bag from her hip and flipped it out. It scared David.

"Whoa! What's that? Take it easy."

"Just a carry, I have to put it in something."

"Go ahead. You were saying?"

As Maggie slid the canvas into the bag she spoke matter-of-factly.

"I'm a cat burglar, and I've been doing things like this for a long time. Ivan Bosche brought me in, to do a job for a big shot. Then I found out there's another big shot who is also trying to get this impressive treasure and they have nothing to do with your widow, do they?"

David, interested, indicated he didn't really know.

Maggie continued, "So, here are you and I, a couple of little fish, swimming around between some very big ones who really couldn't care less what happens to anyone else in their little game of 'got your painting.' I'm not too fond of things like that. How about you?"

David nodded. "I'm going to have to agree with you on that. I've been a bit twisted up myself on how I was going to get out of this with my own head intact. I'm figuring that possession being nine-tenths of the law, as they say, will give me a leg up on making a deal with someone that should preserve my interests."

Maggie finished fitting the rolled canvas into the slim sack. She took the string along the side and went to slip it over her head and shoulder.

"Whoa. Hold it. Don't put that on yet."

Maggie froze, holding the rolled canvas in her back hand, away from David. He continued to lean on the sawhorse a good eight feet away.

David stayed genial, but his eyes were darkening. He didn't plan on leaving without the painting.

"Look, how much are you being paid? Why can't we make a deal that benefits both of us?"

Maggie said nothing. She just looked at him.

"It's not so crazy. Why do we have to fight? I'm sure you can handle yourself. Well, so can I. You might get away, might not. Why risk it? Let's throw in together and make something work."

Maggie didn't look away for an instant. She watched David like a hawk.

"I don't know you. And I don't do deals with people I don't know."

"Hey, I'm not playing a heavy here. It doesn't have to get rough."

"If you plan on getting this painting, it certainly does."

As soon as the words left Maggie's mouth, David lunged for her. Maggie had one eye fixed on his hidden hand. Now visible, she could see it contained a pipe or piece of wood, something he would strike with. Maggie waited a split second longer before kicking the plexiglass piece that had been leaning on the table towards the advancing David. The new element caused David to drop his eyes as he adjusted his rush to account for it. Maggie used this distraction to turn her body to the side and reach out with her fingers, aiming them right at David's eyes and face. As David fell forward over the plexiglass piece one of her fingers hit the goal. David screamed in pain. Maggie followed that with a sharp punch to the side of David's torso and a kick to his opposite leg's shin. The sequence sent him crashing into the table, grasping at his eyes and momentarily unable to stand.

Maggie had her opening. Spinning around the flailing David, she flipped the carrying case over her head and shoulder, strapping it across her back. She flipped *Lola* back into its handle and sprinted for the door. She didn't look back. She knew he would recover soon enough and needed to make space between them as fast as she could.

Maggie tore down the hallway as fast as she could, then up the ladder stairs and back into the garden shed. She didn't know if he had backup of any kind, but she trusted that speed and force would protect her if he did. She could hear scrambling behind her. She didn't have much of a head start. If David got his hands on her it could get ugly. She couldn't chance it.

Looking carefully, Maggie raised her head slowly. No one around. As she pulled her legs up, she could hear David approaching. She slammed the lid down and looked around for something to block it. The door! She closed the door halfway, just enough to cover part of the lid. If he tried to raise it, it should get stuck under the open door. As she sprinted into the garden Maggie heard the hatch hit the bottom of the open door. Success! Maggie kept moving.

Her bike was in the bushes out front. Running at the brick-block fence, Maggie took two steps up the wall, launching herself towards a branch about ten feet off the ground. Catching it, she flipped her body just enough to reach the top of the wall. Pausing only long enough to get her balance, Maggie scampered along the wall like a large cat and dropped down near the hidden motorcycle. She could hear yelling behind her. David had escaped the tunnel.

Jumping on the bike, Maggie went to kick it to life.

Nothing. *Now now!* She panicked. Kicked it again. Nothing. This was like the movies for God's sake. *The stupid bike fires every other time. Why not now?* Then Maggie looked. She hadn't turned the key. Flipping it, she kicked one more time and the bike burst to life. Jamming her helmet on her head, Maggie spun the rear wheel as she tore out of the underbrush, nearly hitting a passing car as she did.

Back on Birdview Road, Maggie headed away. She rolled the throttle on the bike as she commanded herself to calm down. "Easy, easy girl. Don't lose it all by going too fast. You're in the lead. Keep pushing."

As the bike headed down toward the beach, Maggie allowed herself a smile. She had found it! She had the Vermeer. Maggie turned and headed along the water, towards the highway back to Santa Monica. She could hear a car's engine behind her. She didn't know if it was David, but she had no plans on sticking around to find out. She needed traffic to lose herself in. Time to find some.

As Maggie raced down the PCH she passed a few cars on the right to create a buffer between her and whomever might be following. Once she felt a bit protected, Maggie slowed down and tried to ride easy, drawing less attention. It was at this point she felt her cell phone vibrating against her leg.

Traffic had slowed to a crawl near a flashing crossing, so Maggie grabbed at the phone to see who was calling. It was Fati. How? Her and Aldo were supposed to be in the air by now. What was going on? She did not have time for this now.

71

FATIMA STOOD outside the Stardust Motel on Wilshire. Nervously, she looked up and down the street, watching the traffic. She didn't know what she was looking for but somehow it made her feel better as she waited. Fatima walked back and forth, turning small circles every now and again. She studied the broken concrete of the parking lot.
Maggie had taken her call, even though she had sounded frantic. Maggie was rushed, that much was clear. She had been so abrupt on the phone. Fatima knew she could be long-winded, but she did want to talk about things. About Aldo, about what he said. About how she had gotten mad and was not flying home with him. Fatima tried to get out what was going on, but Maggie had shut her down the second she had explained that she'd left Aldo. She told her to get to the Stardust Motel and wait there. That she would be along as soon as she could.
So, Fatima had found the motel and waited. And waited. She watched as the traffic ebbed and flowed along the busy street.
The motel was not what she had expected. Maggie had stayed at simple airport hotels before, but this was far grimier and sort of…rough. It wasn't exactly Fatima's cup of tea, but she knew that Maggie was less afraid of things than she was. She could handle such a place. Fatima jumped when a nearby parked car fired to life, revving its seriously out of tune engine. She edged a little farther down the parking lot.
    Maggie hadn't said what room number she was. Not that it really mattered. Fatima doubted she would have been any more comfortable inside one of the rooms. Probably better to wait outside. Fatima turned her nose up as the dueling smells of burning marijuana and greasy fried chicken competed for space in her nostrils. This really

was a bad place. A motorcycle turned into the parking lot. Instinctively, Fatima tried to make even more space between herself and the quickly closing machine...until she realized it was Maggie.

"Fatima!" yelled Maggie.

Fatima's eyes went wide as saucers. "What are you doing on that?"

Maggie looked behind her and then all around, quickly. She turned back to Fatima. "No time to explain now, you've got to hop on. We have got to go, now!"

Fatima started to panic. "But, but I can't!"

Maggie yelled over the motor. "Why not?"

Fatima waved her arm towards a pile of matched luggage stacked beside a bush in the parking lot. "I have all my bags."

Maggie's eyes rolled so hard it looked as if they might stay pinned to the top of her head. Immediately, she killed the engine, jumped off the bike and grabbed two of the bags, running for a door in the motel. Picking up on what she was doing, Fatima did the same. Maggie fished a key out of her waist purse, opened the motel door, and tossed the bags inside. Fatima properly placed her bags in the room, almost getting clipped by Maggie who had run over, grabbed the rest and was already flinging them inside the room by the time Fatima was set to leave.

"Ok, now we have to go."

Fatima stopped again.

"What now?" pleaded Maggie. Fatima pointed to her head.

"I don't have a helmet."

Acknowledging her screwup, Maggie nodded and thought for a second. Then she ran into the motel office. Fatima took the time to stare at the motorcycle Maggie had ridden in on. It was very shiny, and...well, cool looking. Fatima liked motorcycles, even though she had never ridden one. Well, maybe some Vespas in Italy but not a real, actual, fast motorcycle. She looked back, remembering that she really had no idea what was going on.

Maggie burst out of the motel office, running towards Fatima and the motorcycle. She had something in her hand. She pushed it at Fatima.

"Here. Put it on."

Fatima looked at the helmet in her hands. It was a fluorescent orange helmet, with cartoon dragons or something on it. "What is this?" she asked.

"*Pokemon*, I think," replied Maggie, "It's a skateboard helmet. Not perfect but it's all he had. Let's go!"

Maggie had already fired the engine on the bike. Gingerly, Fatima stepped over the back of the bike, sitting down on the seat behind her. She wrapped her arms around Maggie's waist.

"Are you ready?" called Maggie. Fatima nodded, and then realized Maggie couldn't see or hear her.

She yelled back. "YES!" At that, Maggie rolled on the throttle and took off, steering out of the parking lot, onto Wilshire, across three lanes and gone.

* * *

Fatima was exhilarated. Riding on the back of a motorcycle was incredible. Sure, she was terrified at first, but once she got into the feel of things it was quite a fun way to travel. You could feel the wind whipping around you, see and feel everything. Even the smells of the road, they all came up to meet you. The two had been riding for almost a half hour. The one time they stopped long enough to be heard, Fatima asked where they were going. Maggie's answer didn't make much sense. All she could make out was two words: "The Strand."

The Strand, a paved bicycle path that hugged the Pacific Ocean shoreline in Los Angeles County, ran from Will Rogers State Beach in Pacific Palisades to Torrance County Beach. It was 22 miles long, with the midpoint falling somewhere near the southern end of the Playa del Rey residential area. Considered something of a boardwalk, the Strand was in fact paved end to end, with not a wood plank in sight. This was where Maggie was headed.

As Maggie cruised into the Manhattan Beach area, she slowed the bike down and Fatima caught the distinct smell of the ocean. Looking around Maggie's shoulder, Fatima saw a glimpse of blue, dead ahead.

Maggie slowed their ride even more, eventually coming to a halt at a junction point between some beach front houses and a walking path out towards the water. Finally, Maggie stopped the bike and turned it off. She reached up and pulled her helmet off.

"The Strand?" asked Fatima.

"The Strand." answered Maggie.

Both women, now off the bike and walking, set a curious picture. Fatima had to find her footing carefully. After nearly a half-hour on board the motorcycle, she was a little wobbly. Maggie was stretching her arms over her head. Fatima called to her.

"I thought we were going in the other direction, away from the water."

Maggie nodded. "We were. I had to rag around a little bit. Make sure we weren't being followed. When I was certain we were clean, I came straight here."

The women walked toward the beach. Fatima realized Maggie was wearing a long, slim purse or bag along her body. She also saw the helmet Maggie had been wearing.

"That's quite the look," she teased.

Maggie looked confused, but then realized what Fatima was noticing. She smiled at the helmet's design.

Fatima continued, "You know, I've got quite a few questions. Any chance I can ask them?"

Maggie stared out at the ocean. She took a deep breath of the fresh air. Then she took another. "Yeah, I think we both need to talk about some things. I just want to sit here for a moment first if I can. I need to catch my breath." Maggie spied a bench and walked across the pedestrian pathway to it and sat down. She was facing the houses that fronted the boardwalk. Fatima walked over and joined her.

Fatima looked out at the sea and spoke. "I think Aldo might not be who I think he is…or, I mean, who I thought he was. He just…I…." Fatima stopped. She wasn't sure what she was saying.

Maggie turned to her. "We are going to talk about him, and other things too, because they are important. Before we do that, I'm supposed to meet someone here. I can't see him yet, but he should be here shortly. Once I do that, we'll have all the time in the world to talk this through. Ok?"

Fatima nodded. She would wait, even though she didn't want to. Something was seriously wrong. Maggie was dressed like an insane biker chick, riding around like a lunatic on a motorcycle that she never mentioned having and staying in a dive motel, all while Fatima was trying to make sense of who Aldo really was. Things were not normal.

Suddenly, Maggie stood up, looking off to the distance. "I think I see him. Hold on. Just stay right here. I'll be right back, ok?"

Fatima nodded as Maggie walked quickly away, towards an approaching person. Then a group of people suddenly materialized, and Maggie froze. She did not take a step further. Immediately, she turned and started running back towards Fatima.

"Run!" screamed Maggie.

72

IVAN GOT the text from Maggie. She had it! His heart leapt. The end was in sight. Finally.

He quickly tapped out a reply, sending a location. They would meet, do the hand-over, and then Ivan could begin the process of extricating them both from the chaos. He sighed happily. It felt like he'd been holding his breath for days.

Soon, soon, it will be done.

He motioned to the waitress for his bill. She nodded from several tables over.

Foxy's wooden A-frame caught his eye, but it was the sign out front that made him want to come inside. Located in Glendale, not too far from the small hotel he was staying at, the heavy wooden planks, old 50's look, and massive windows set it apart on the street. But it was a sign promising "crystal chandeliers" that captured his imagination. Crystal chandeliers? In a retro A-frame diner? Well, Ivan simply had to know, so he'd scheduled today's breakfast with that specifically front of mind.

When he first went inside, Ivan was immediately drawn to the dimly lit, tightly packed interior. It was dark, but cozy, like a cabin. He looked for the crystal chandeliers but saw none. Only simple hanging lights coming off a dropped-V raftered ceiling with brass-colored fireplace hooks on either end of the main room. They were shaped like arrowheads. That was nice. Add in the menu, a gargantuan, multipage affair, with photos for almost everything they had on order, and he was sold. For Ivan, there was nothing better than being able to compare what you receive to the picture you'd fallen in love with.

But where were the chandeliers? After being seated, he looked outside at the main sign to confirm he hadn't imagined it. No, the sign was still there. "Foxy's Restaurant, breakfast, lunch, dinner, open 6am, crystal chandeliers. Was Ivan losing his mind?

He was about to ask the waitress when his eyes slipped across the parking lot to the business directly facing the restaurant. It was called Crystal Chandeliers. Ivan laughed at his own mistake, surprised to have been duped by something so simple. The two businesses were sharing the sign, one a restaurant and the other selling chandeliers. He was happy not to have made an obvious fool of himself by asking.

Taking a final sip of his coffee, the waitress breezed past, dropping off the bill.

"Thanks, honey. Just settle-up at the till over there."

Fed and happy, Ivan stepped into the sunshine. He considered calling Manheim and letting him know the job was near completion but decided against it. Never be counting the chickens until they all hatch. Wait until you had it in your hands. Always the best advice. Out of habit, Ivan looked around for a cab before remembering that taxis and big cities were a no-go these days. He turned to his phone, to the app Greta made him get. Uber. Just tap it and go, she'd said.

Ivan appreciated the ease with which such things worked, but he could not help worrying about the digital ropes it stretched across him. Always tracked, always watching. Big brother's face smiled. That's what North Americans never realized. They'd never lived under the old ways, under the boot of the state. Not like Ivan had. They surrendered their freedom because most had never really been without it. It was handed to them, as a birthright. They knew nothing else. How could they know the pains of life without it? They will, he thought.

Ivan felt the sun on his face. That much was clear. If you didn't have to fight for something you'll eventually lose it, because you don't truly see its value. He looked at the app. Ten minutes before the car would arrive. That was fine. He would make the meeting spot in plenty of time. He found a bus bench to sit on while he waited.

Ivan looked at the massive billboard of *Angelyne*. Still there, after all these years? He remembered seeing her decades ago. Surely, she didn't still look the same. Older of course, but still pushing the dream? Incredible. Kind of like himself, he guessed. Then Ivan looked again.

It wasn't one of the infamous billboards. It was a poster advertising for a new TV series with a young actress portraying *Angelyne*. He shook his head slowly. Everything original eventually got taken down, commercialized, bastardized, ended. Ivan bowed his head. He was tired. He wanted out of the game. It was time to leave this life. He had done so much wrong. So many mistakes. It needed to end.

This deal would bring a conclusion. He could provide Neto with his request, satisfy the gig, and separate. He would take less on the commission. More for Maggie. To make amends. He owed her that much. But he needed to stop. Maybe it was time to sell the place in Seattle. Downsize, simplify. Maybe travel someplace easy. Like Spain. Or Portugal. Lisbon! He'd always liked Lisbon. Maybe get a small flat by the sea. Spend his days watching the ships come in. It was a nice image, one that flooded his senses. The Uber arrived. Ivan went to the open window and ducked his head inside.

"For Ivan?" he asked.

The driver nodded. Ivan opened the door, sat down and buckled in.

"You're headed for Manhattan Beach?" inquired the driver.

"I am." Confirmed Ivan. "Near 3500 Ocean Drive. The neighborhood there."

"Nice neighborhood," replied the young driver.

"Anything by the water is usually nice, no?" Ivan winked at the young man.

The driver smiled back and nodded his head as the pair wheeled their way down the street. Neither took notice of the dark BMW pulling away from the curb on the opposite side of the road. It performed a swift U-turn across four lanes before settling in, comfortably disguised, behind them.

* * *

As the black SUV tore out of the airport, Dachshund's cell phone rang. He tapped the screen and put it to his ear. "Yes?"

"He's on the move. I've got him directly in front of me. What do you want?"

"Leave him, for now. But stay close. Don't let him see you. Find out where he's going and the second you figure it out, tell me. Immediately."

"Okay."

"Not after he stops. As soon as you figure out where he's headed tell me so I can send a team."

"Right."

"Do you know where the woman is yet?"

Silence from the other end of the line.

"Do you know?" pressed Dachshund.

"No, I uh…lost her after the first hotel she stayed in. I think she was on to me."

"You seem to have a habit of losing to this woman. Should I be concerned?"

More silence from the other end of the line, then a slight stammer. Dachshund stopped him.

"It's rhetorical. Don't bother trying to answer. Remember, the second you know the general area he's heading let me know. I'll send backup." At that, Dachshund pressed the off button and placed the phone on the seat beside him.

Dachshund had played carefully with Neto so far due to the potential of reciprocal blowbacks coming on other flanks, but that time was passing. He was now actively involved in attempting to steal something that did not belong to him. That could not go unanswered. He considered that it was reaching a point of having to become more personal.

Dachshund's phone flashed a text. They were headed for Manhattan Beach. Immediately he pressed a button to make a call, thinking to himself, *Perhaps Aldo Neto needs to have something a little closer to his heart put under threat.*

73

DAVID HEARD the motorcycle rev up and tear off down Birdview Ave., which allowed him to come to a stop. He didn't have to run anymore. He could focus on other important things, mainly reaching for his face and rubbing at the pain in his left eye where her finger had managed to connect.

"She better not have scratched the cornea. Damn, that hurts!" cursed David.

Walking back to the small garden shed, he looked at the open trapdoor just inside the door. Pausing, he went behind the shed and pulled a half-empty bottle of water and a sandwich wrapper off the ground, along with his coat. He had stood there for almost an hour, waiting for her to come. It had almost killed him standing so still and waiting. He wished it hadn't taken her as long as she did to find her way inside the bunker. But David couldn't make it easy for her. She might have become suspicious.

David had figured out the room was by the pool almost a day earlier. The comment by Denny on the smell of chlorine was what first tipped him off. Once back on-site, it had taken twenty minutes of poking around to find the entrance. Going inside, he found the missing Vermeer, but ultimately left it in place.

He needed someone else to find it. And he needed them to get away with it too.

As David gathered his things and headed out, he thought back to the memorial for Zevon Levi. The old man claiming to know him had caught him off guard. Then, when the guy had pulled "Babs" off to the side, only to disappear with her it became clear what was really going on. David had found himself in the middle of a professional heist. An underground painting "recovery."

He remembered the incident with his father very well, and the mysterious man who had intervened way back when. If this old guy was telling the truth, which it certainly seemed like he was, then David knew he needed to pay attention. The guy who saved his bacon all those years ago was connected to the stolen art world, which meant "Babs" was too.

David had leaned on a few contacts from his past. One came back with the old man's full name and a clear indication of who he was today: someone known for "getting things others could not". And knowing that suggested that the woman presenting as "Babs" was more than likely working for him in a collection capacity. Add in coming face to face with at least two versions of the long missing *Concert* by Vermeer, with the most recent seeming to be the actual one stolen from the Gardner in 1989, hammered things home further.

David needed to be very, very careful.

Visiting the forger again made him certain he had to come straight back to the Malibu house, and sure enough he found the painting. But he hadn't taken it. He'd left it there. Better to know where it was and use the information. Knowledge was almost always more valuable than the item in question. It was usually safer too.

The painting was a hot potato now, with at least two big players fighting over it. Bunny herself didn't seem to have the faintest idea it even existed, let alone who wanted it. She was still set on pulling an insurance scam. It had become something bigger now, a bargaining chip between two power players. That meant getting things right was crucial, at least if David wanted to keep his block from getting knocked off and maybe, hopefully profit a little.

He was still an outside party to all of this, separate from the goings on. His inclusion into things would not be seen positively, especially as he was not officially "employed" by either of the big dogs currently fighting. That needed to change.

The real question now was which side to sell his information to? Knowledge was a powerful commodity, but it could spoil like milk left in the sun if you held it too long.

His first realization was that he needed someone else to grab the painting. That made the most sense. Bunny was a waste of time. She'd only muck things up with her ignorance. But "Babs" was on one of the players' sides. Let her grab it and then sell her out to the other. It kept him out of the line of direct fire. Allowing for potential profit without doing something specifically illegal.

Smarter. Safer.

So, who was "Babs?"

After squeezing Ben on the night of the memorial party, David had left the Roosevelt Hotel and headed for Denny's. As he did, David had seen "Babs" leaving the hotel herself. He'd wanted to follow her but needed to get to Denny's ASAP. Not being able to split himself in two, he'd searched for the next best thing.

Looking around, David had spied a taxi sitting nearby, with a driver leaning on the hood and literally spitting at the numerous rideshare drivers who were picking up and dropping off their digitally sourced fares in front of the Roosevelt. David had appreciated his edge and walked right up to him.

"Hey bud! Wanna make $100?"

David offered the guy five twenties to follow "Babs" wherever she was going. He'd known it was a long shot. First, the guy might have kept the money and done nothing. That was more than possible, it was likely. Second, even if the guy had played along, "Babs" could have sensed the tail and lost him. Finally, maybe the guy did it for a bit and got bored, quit but lied about where she'd ended up, sending him on a wild goose chase. But a chance was a chance. The guy had agreed, so David had handed over the money along with his cell number. He'd pointed at the woman in question.

"Follow her. Find out where she goes."

So, the cabbie had taken off while David had headed away on his own journey. He'd expected very little to come of it but hoped for the best.

Which was exactly what David got.

Incredibly, four hours later the guy called him. It did seem like he'd been drinking, but David chose to believe it was from celebrating his cash score. The guy had sworn he'd followed her to a motel on Wilshire Blvd, which was how David had come to find himself spending six hours the very next day watching and waiting for "Babs" to emerge.

When she did, he'd followed her all the way to the Malibu City Hall. Once she was there, it hadn't taken long to see what she was up to. She'd gone to the planning dept. That meant she was re-focusing on the Levi house because, as David knew, that's where the painting was. She was smart, that much was clear.

But David was smarter.

So, he headed back to the mansion and hid himself on the grounds. And waited.

He'd waited for "Babs" to show up. He'd waited for her to find the secret room. And he'd waited for her to find *The Concert*. He also needed her to leave with it, but he had to ensure something else first.

He needed to know where she was going with it. And thanks to their little tussle, notwithstanding his red and now throbbing eye, he'd accomplished that easily.

As they had come together, he'd planted an RFID tag on her. Wherever she went, he'd know about it. David knew it was only a matter of time before she discovered the tag and tossed it away. But for now, she was panicked and on the run. And that gave him the best chance possible to follow behind, figure things out, and determine the best way to win.

Sitting in his car, David checked his cell phone and watched as the icon moved along the PCH. He placed the phone on the dash, started the car, and headed after her.

But David hadn't driven 50ft before the phone lit up with a call. The picture appearing on screen said it all, an image of a deranged Jessica Rabbit with the name "Bunny."

David shook his head slowly and chuckled to himself as he tapped the screen to accept the call.

74

ALDO WAS SULKING.

He did not like change that came from beyond his control.

First, he got ambushed by that wannabe oligarch Dachshund at the airport. Then he had to endure yet another tantrum from Fatima as she overreacted to the situation at hand. That, in turn, made the day's flight impossible causing him to cancel it, delay his own plans, and cool his heels in LA for yet another day.

Aldo was tired of LA. He was ready to move on. The chase seemed to be nearing its conclusion and he did not need to be nearby. In fact, it was usually better to be far away when such things come to a point. His own history was proof of that.

He made himself a drink behind the yacht's bar. The wait staff were gone and only a skeleton crew remained. He had released most of them due to shutting down the yacht's comfort services and prepping for its planned return to warmer waters. But Aldo would spend the night onboard. No point staying in a hotel for a single night. Better to sleep in a bed one owned.

Aldo dumped some ice in a glass, poured cachaça over it, two shots, and added sugar, lime juice and two pieces of pineapple. He stirred it and had a taste. Not a bad *Caipirinha*, if he did say so himself. Aldo walked into the lounge and took his personal seat.

Finding the remote control, he switched on some light music and sipped at his drink, before placing it on the small table nearby. He closed his eyes and began massaging his temples.

Aldo needed this fiasco to be over. He genuinely thought it would be easy to secure the painting ahead of Dachshund and get it back to the freeport. Thankfully, they were close now. The plan was to take possession and get it onboard the *Jimena* for a simple, uneventful trip overseas, while he flew separately to meet it in person. The yacht had plenty of impregnable stores that no customs crew had ever discovered. Neat and clean.

But the local fools Dachshund had tearing around Los Angeles had become more of an issue than he expected them to be. They were thugs, and Aldo did not think for a moment they'd have the finesse to secure something so hidden. All they seemed to do was draw attention and make a bunch of noise.

Besides, Aldo had hired professionals to retrieve the piece. It should have been no contest. A fine instrument vs. a blunt hammer. Perhaps the issue was the involvement of Americans? They did have a way of making things harder than they needed to be. The Levi widow had clearly made things worse, though, he had to admit, so had his unexpected romance with Fatima.

Maybe it was too perfect that one of the women he was dating happened to have a friend who was a professional art thief? It was just so…unexpected. Thrilling even. What a game! Fatima was wonderful, but to also have a friend who could do what Maggie did? And then her performance in Russia? How could he refuse Fatima? Aldo loved the drama, both romantically and professionally, laughing once more at the thought of lifting the Klee right from under the noses of some minor enemies. He loved that its disappearance had created a small firestorm within a specific crew of administrative sucklings inside the Kremlin, assisting in his ability to blackmail Dragic. Getting payback on a group that had worked to sabotage his rise at the UN was absolute perfection. He'd heard they were now engaged in a circle of finger-pointing, threats, and individual fear. One cannot underestimate the general instability that marked the day-to-day disbursement of their duties. Russians were sub-human in general, which to Aldo meant they deserved whatever abuse they got. They were ignorant of his involvement, at least for now. He would weigh when it might be worthwhile to change that.

But what to do with Fatima? And Maggie? Obviously, he was right to hire her. She had found the Vermeer, yet her presence was becoming a genuine thorn in his side. He enjoyed Fatima and hoped to continue with her, but he could not have this constant tension surrounding him.

Fatima was fun. He adored her helpless femininity, along with her sporadic outbursts. Why even have a woman if you didn't enjoy drama? But the connection between her and Maggie was proving troublesome. What if he couldn't split them apart? And what if he didn't want to? What if the sparkle came from the pairing? He sipped more of his drink. *Ahh, mulhares.*

Aldo raised his arms in the air and stretched, releasing his voice with a pronounced "Ohhhhahhh!" Maybe he was the one guilty of drama. Let it go. The chase was nearly complete. Manheim assured he would have the painting in hand which meant Dachshund would not and the rest would take care of itself. As it always did.

He laughed at himself, toasting the air with his drink. The chasing around of smears on paper. Such an endeavor. Such effort for beauty. Deliberately setting down his drink, Aldo stared hard at the "ironic" computer rendering of *Storm on the Sea of Galilee* and smiled. He had been so lucky to secure the original. The art world had written it off, gone forever, likely destroyed. But it wasn't. It had surfaced and found its way into one of his freeports. When he saw it, he didn't believe it was real. But it was. He had to have it. It took some…creative maneuvering to secure it as his own, but Rembrandt's most fascinating self-portrait had no better home than becoming the hidden centerpiece of the *Jimena*. It was his secret pride and joy.

He reached for the tiny button under the table and held it down, anticipating the reveal he enjoyed so much. But the false painting was sticking as the motor whirred. Aldo pushed the button on and off, hoping to make it work. Eventually the painting began to slide, but it was bending in the frame, catching on something. Concerned, Aldo stopped what he was doing and went to the wall, cursing the poor workmanship of the frame. He didn't want to damage the masterwork beneath.

As he pulled at the edges, trying to reset it within the track, Aldo caught sight of something that made his breath catch. The original was missing from underneath.

Rembrandt's *Storm on the Sea of Galilee* had been stolen. From him! From under his nose!

He could feel the rage inside him boiling towards explosion. He stomped around in a tight circle, tensing every muscle, squeezing his fists, longing to punch, to kick...to smash! Then he reached for his drink and heaved it as hard as he could at the back wall of the central lounge, breaking the mirror and sending ice and glass shards everywhere. He bellowed at the top of his lungs.

"MAGGIE!"

75

MAGGIE SPRINTED toward Fatima, motioning for her to follow. Fatima, looking confused, hesitated and didn't move. Not able to waste time, Maggie reached out and grabbed for her arm as she ran by, heading back to the motorcycle parked up beyond the walkway.

"Why? What?" was all Fatima could muster as Maggie reached for her.

"Not now. We have got to go. Those men, the ones coming. Just move now!"

But Fatima froze. She didn't move. Couldn't. Frustrated, Maggie gave up and ran for the motorbike alone, jumped on-board and fired it up. No helmet, she spun around and headed back to the boardwalk for Fati, pulling in tight beside her.

"GET ON!" Maggie screamed, revving the bike.

Finally, Fatima moved. Hesitantly she swung one leg over the bike and tried to get set. The running men were less than 6ft away. As she held onto Maggie with one hand, trying to get fully on, Maggie took off, tipping Fatima slightly to one side and unbalancing her. At the same time, a hand reached out and grabbed at her coat, pulling her backwards. Maggie didn't notice and continued to gun her engine, even as Fatima slid off the bike into the grasping hands of the two men.

Stunned at the fall, and still confused by all the yelling, Fatima found herself helped to her feet by the men, as a third jogged over.

"What is this?" she demanded. "What is going on?"

The third man stopped and stared at her. It was Manheim and he smiled, even as his eyes remained dark.

"Your friend is in some serious trouble. As it happens, so are you."

He indicated for one of the men to take Fatima away. Then Manheim stepped out into the center of the walkway, trying to see Maggie on the speeding motorcycle in the distance. Cursing that he had lost her again, he spied an unattended bicycle leaning against the beach washrooms. Running over, he grabbed it and got on, pedalling after Maggie. Once on board, Manheim realized it was an e-bike, so he pressed the throttle with his thumb and accelerated. He could still see Maggie up ahead but now he was starting to make up the distance, fast.

* * *

Maggie whipped her head to the side, catching a look behind her. She saw Fati fall off the bike and get grabbed. *Darn! That was my fault.* She also saw Manheim walking toward her, but the other faces she didn't recognize. Ivan was supposed to be there. He had said to meet her on this spot of the Strand, and he didn't say anything about Manheim. That spelled trouble in Maggie's mind. She couldn't take a chance. She had to run. But now Fatima was tied up with these guys. For the briefest of seconds, Maggie considered pulling up, turning around, and going back, just giving up. Then she shook it off. Whatever power she still had rested in the leather tube on her back, and that would only remain if she stayed ahead of them. Rolling on the throttle, Maggie pushed it, slowing just enough to dodge the various runners, walkers, and skaters, who screamed at her for riding a motorbike along the boardwalk.

* * *

Stumbling, Fatima was shoved/led towards an adjoining road as another man approached and directed her captors toward a dark SUV. He opened the back door as they pushed her inside the high vehicle. As she sat on the seat, Fatima came face to face with someone already inside. He was a small, older man and his hands were bound at the wrist with zip ties. He looked at her with warm eyes.

Fatima jumped as the door slammed behind her. She tried the handle, but it wouldn't open. Locked from the outside. She frowned and turned to the slight man. "What's going on? What is this?"

The old fellow bowed his head for a moment before returning her gaze. "You were with Maggie, yes? Her friend. You are Fatima? Was she able to get away?"

Surprised at hearing her name, Fatima answered, "Yes, but... uh...how do...look, who are you, exactly?"

"I'm Ivan. I think we should talk."

* * *

As Maggie continued her race down the Strand, Manheim was gaining ground. Between the people she had to slow to avoid hitting, plus the effort of regular shoulder checking, Maggie's motorcycle advantage over Manheim's stolen e-bike wasn't amounting to much. Looking back, she could see him in the distance, coming ever closer.

Looking forward, Maggie searched with her eyes, trying to see somewhere, anywhere, to pull off or hide. Unfortunately, the walkway was a long stretch, meaning any side street she cut up would be visible all the way back to her pursuer. She continued to press forward, even as she had to come to an almost full stop thanks to a group of pedestrians completely unaware of the bike approaching. She pushed the horn on the bike, but it didn't work. *Guess I never checked that before I bought it.* she thought.

As the Strand gave way to Hermosa Ave, running alongside, Maggie considered trying to get onto the main road and taking off that way, but the cars were almost bumper to bumper. It would be slower than she was already moving. Realizing that she had left the boardwalk and was on a parallel road she tried again to pull in to traffic. As she looked for an opening, a car backed across the paved boardwalk, exiting from one of the beach houses now to her right. Maggie squeezed hard on her brakes, almost flipping the bike over itself, and barely missed colliding with the car by inches. The woman inside the Porsche Panamera made sure to give her a serious frown, along with a determined finger wag.

Maggie had no time, revving the bike and peeling around the Porsche to the front before continuing forward. She needed to find an exit that would work. Looking to the right, Maggie spied an entry back to the boardwalk, figuring it might throw Manheim off a bit. Immediately, she fought the bike into a 90 degree turn and headed back to the beach. Success! Hitting the walkway, Maggie turned left and continued to drive on, trusting that something would present itself. She looked behind her, and, not seeing anyone in specific pursuit, allowed herself to breath once more.

Meanwhile, Manheim continued to run his e-bike down the boardwalk and, missing the same switchback Maggie had, found himself dodging the automobiles of people coming and going from their various beach abodes. He couldn't see her up ahead and, concerned that he might have lost her, pressed the electric throttle to its limit. He continued his pursuit, looking between the houses in case she might be hiding between them.

Manheim never saw the dump truck.

Backing out of a residential construction site, the huge machine completely blocked the pathway. By the time Manheim looked back to his direction of travel there was no time to stop, let alone change direction. He hit the truck going at least 35 mph, launching his entire body into the side of the steel rig, head-first.

Manheim was dead, instantly.

* * *

As Maggie emerged from the end of the boardwalk, she realized she was moving into a marina. The King Harbour Marina to be exact. Slowing down, she tried to figure out where might be a good place to either lie low or at least be able to stop for a bit and try to figure out her next move. Slowly, she made her way around the various parking lots and buildings, seeing a sign for the Portofino Inn. Following the arrows, Maggie figured a hotel might offer some chances to hide.

Cruising through the various parking lots toward the hotel, Maggie caught sight of a truck that seemed to be tracking her. It was certainly moving too slowly and deliberately to be a mistake. That was unless Maggie was being paranoid, which she knew she was. Everyone on the run was paranoid. Maggie looked to her left and saw some beach volleyball courts. Thinking that cutting through them would leave her potential pursuer in the dust, Maggie turned onto the sand. Unfortunately, because of her split focus and the sand being deeper than she expected, the bike dropped in on the front wheel and turned, flipping the whole unit over itself to a stop. Maggie flew over the handlebars and onto the thick sand. She landed with a comparatively soft, but still wind-removing thud. She struggled to get up.

Making her way, slowly, back to her bike, Maggie strained to stand it up. Without proper leverage she was in serious trouble. The sand was just too thick. Nothing would hold. And to make matters worse, out of the corner of her eye she saw that the pickup truck had circled around and was now stopped less than 5ft away from her. A voice called out from the truck.

"Are you Babs?"

This caused Maggie to stop trying to right the bike and peer into the truck cab. She didn't recognize the face, so she got a little closer. The big guy spoke again.

"I said, are you Babs?"

Maggie looked back at him, still unsure as to what she should do.

"Who are you?" she asked.

"If you're Babs, you need to get in."

Maggie let out a snort. "I'm not getting inside anything. Who the hell are you?"

The man in the truck looked around, then aimed a massive gun right at Maggie's face.

"I don't have a ton of time, ok? They might still be coming. Now get in."

Worried, but also curious, Maggie nodded and opened the passenger door, getting into the truck. Immediately, the guy hit the gas and they took off, headed away from the Portofino Inn and back into the maze of LA streets.

76

MANHEIM PRESSED a button, ending the call. He felt… conflicted.

Not at double-crossing Aldo. That part was easy. What bothered him was the chance that he might not get to catch Maggie personally. He wanted to wipe that arrogant smirk off her face himself. From the moment they had first come face to face on the train, and she'd bested him, Manheim had wanted to level the score. Badly.

This was the best way to make it happen.

Doing a deal with Edward Dachshund would also move him into a different sort of territory. He steered the BMW through the LA streets, following the private car carrying Ivan Bosche to his appointment with Maggie. Aldo was a taskmaster and Manheim had grown tired of being his man Friday. Maybe when he was younger such things could have continued, but not anymore. He had lived a life of servitude to such men, the most recent being Aldo Neto, and it was getting to him in ways he had not expected.

Manheim didn't recognize himself anymore. Rolling eyes, being frustrated when given an order. That was something you read about in books or saw in movies. It wasn't professional and it wasn't how Manheim acted. But the job was bringing it out in him which only meant one thing: It was time to change jobs.

The Uber carrying Ivan stopped at a light. Manheim drifted to a crawl two cars back and one lane over. Watching. Trying to get a sense of where he was heading. Where was Maggie going to meet him? The light changed and the car headed away. Manheim followed.

He had been in service to Aldo for almost eight years now. The position wasn't that bad. Aldo was an egotistical man, but most at his level of power and wealth were. Manheim just could not be kept anymore. The inability to make his own decisions regarding events was getting to him.

Dachshund wouldn't be any better, but Manheim wasn't selling himself as an employee. He was selling information, and he planned to collect handsomely. Enough to set himself up so that he could work one-off jobs versus responding to the too-often inane needs of one selfish man.

He had no wife. No children. No need of much at all. But he wanted his freedom. The ability to say and do whatever he pleased. As he aged, that became more and more important to him.

Manheim wasn't sure when that desire had struck at him so hard. It wasn't recently, that much was certain. He remembered back to a movie night several years earlier. Aldo had been entertaining a few women and decided they all had to watch the film *Pretty Woman*. Aldo loved reminding women what level they occupied in his existence. In one of the many trips in and out of the screening room fetching this or that, Manheim had found himself removing dirty plates as one scene played out on screen. In it the hotel manager, played by Hector Elizondo and established as a very powerful and influential man in his own right, was instantly brought low. He was exposed as a mere servant to the wealth of Richard Gere's disinterested Edward, as he was left limp, offering nothing more than a flaccid business card in hopes of proclaiming his status to a man who neither cared nor respected who he was or what position he held. The top hotel in all of Los Angeles, and yet there he was, a faceless functionary still. Manheim felt ill at the scene, and nearly dropped a plate. He forgot about it soon after, yet it would come back to haunt him many times over. The role player. The flunky. Yes, he was paid extremely well, but the price was just not enough.

The car turned left and headed south. It seemed to be a main road at this point. Would it continue? Manheim followed along.

Aldo was making his moves into the UN. That carried with it the promise of more administrative power. That had been attractive to Manheim at first. It presented a new challenge. Perhaps something more respectable than being a mere manservant.

And yet all it really meant was Aldo quickly became surrounded by even more accomplished sycophants, wiser in the ways of international politics than the comparatively sheltered Manheim. He couldn't win. But he endured.

Until that Maggie woman had come along.

That woman, as angry as she made Aldo, also excited him in ways no female ever had before. No matter what she did, or how much damage she caused, Aldo was intrigued. Engaged. Manheim wanted to thump her, and yet Aldo would never let him. He protected her, no matter what. He wanted to see "what was next."

Manheim knew what the fight was over. He knew of Dachshund, and his issues with Aldo. Manheim knew what Aldo was doing, trying to scoop the art first and replace it in the freeport. His attempt to embarrass Dachshund. Manheim didn't care, specifically, but as the fight intensified, and Maggie's role expanded, Manheim saw an opening. He could turn informer, but only if he waited for the right moment. For the exact moment which would provide the most opportunity to give one titan an advantage over the other.

That moment was now.

Manheim could tell Ivan was headed for the water. The signs pointed to Manhattan Beach. At the very least, it would be easier to send cars this way in preparation. He hit the redial button on his phone. It rang, and Dachshund answered.

"Manhattan Beach. They appear to be headed for the Manhattan Beach area.

"I'll get a team over there. Drop me a pin with your location when he comes to a stop. I'm advising the team to find you first and act on your directive. You're good with that?"

"I am."

"Good."

With that, Dachshund's voice disappeared.

Watching the car ahead of him move in and out of traffic, Manheim appreciated the symmetry of it all. He had found the needle in the haystack of Russia and now he would find her in the haystack of Los Angeles. The car ahead slowed and turned from Highland onto 11th Street. It was downhill, all the way to the ocean. Surely, they were reaching the drop off soon. Manheim texted with one hand as he drove, sending a final location.

After crossing several streets, Manheim could see the water. He slowed down and pulled to the side, watching the Uber car. Eventually, it came to a stop at the bottom of the hill, just off Ocean Drive. He watched Ivan get out of the car and walk towards the water. Immediately, Manheim swung the big car back onto the road and drove quickly, not wanting to lose sight of him for too long. As soon as he got close enough, he parked the BMW and headed out on foot.

As he reached the bottom of the street, and watched Ivan walk towards the public washrooms just down from the shoreline boardwalk. At the same time, he got a text. Dachshund's men had arrived. He told them to meet him one street over and headed that way immediately.

As the large SUV pulled up, Manheim strode up to it. The three men got out and gathered around him. Manheim laid things out.

"He's inside the public washroom. You two circle around and wait for him. I'll point him out when he emerges. Then we can walk him back here."

One of the men responded. "And the woman?"

"I haven't seen her yet. But when I do, I've got the lead, ok? No mistakes."

As the men waited for Ivan to come out of the washroom Manheim set his jaw. He would get Maggie on his terms this time around, or he would die trying.

77

"I THINK *Rockford* used to have his trailer somewhere around here."

Tranko, Bunny and David all turned to look at Stewie, who seemed surprised at the immediate, and clearly annoyed, attention.

"What? He did. Remember in the show? *The Rockford Files*? Jim Rockford lived in a big trailer parked near the beach, in a spot exactly like this. Or maybe it was closer to Malibu? So cool. Loved that show." Stewie swiveled his head around, admiring the scenery.

The group was gathered between their cars, just off the PCH near Pacific Pallisades. Bunny had called David and arranged to meet him at the closest spot they could all get to, which turned out to be a parking lot near the beach. And even though everyone assembled appeared to be on the same page, each person had an ulterior motive.

Bunny was trying to secure David for her new friend Stig (whom she believed to be Edward Dachshund, Russian oligarch). Tranko was supposedly helping her, but he was in fact trying to figure out an angle for himself to a) not get killed and b) maybe make back some of the money he was supposed to get on the original job Bunny Levi had hired him for. Finally, there was David, who was absolutely working on behalf of his own self-interest.

And Stewie, who was just happy to be there.

Choosing to formally ignore Stewie's pop cultural addition to the conversation, the rest re-focused on their discussion.

"I'm not sure what you're asking me, Bunny?" questioned David.

"Ugghhh!" fumed Bunny. "Hello! This is not complicated, okay? All we need to do is figure out who this woman person we saw at the house is and get her. Then we hand her over to the Russians."

Tranko said nothing. He didn't trust Bunny or the Russians. And he didn't trust Bunny's guy either. But the problem was he needed to trust somebody, or he wasn't likely to get out of this with his head intact. He'd been running around with this group of crazies for more than a week and he felt further away from any kind of success or payday at all. He'd grabbed a truckful of "art" but none of it was valuable. Or was it? He didn't know anymore. The real Dachshund had taken it all back. Now, the fact that he was still chasing after something suggested that what he had clearly wasn't what Dachshund wanted, but what did that mean? What did any of this mean? Tranko was more confused than ever.

"Hey. HEY!" Bunny shrieked at Tranko, breaking his semi-trance. "Dumbo! Do you have anything to add to this? Have you seen this woman they were going on about?"

Tranko shook his head. "No."

"Right. Well, David and I have seen her. Her name is…"

"Babs, she said," interjected David.

"Babs," concurred Bunny. "Right, and David here says he knows where she's headed." Bunny turned to David.

"Right, she said was going to meet someone and unload the painting right away, so there was nothing I could do about it," David responded to her pointed look.

"How did she get the drop on you?" asked Tranko.

David made a face. "I don't know, came up from behind and hit me with something. Caught me off guard."

"So, why'd she talk at all?" pushed Tranko.

"I don't know. Maybe so I wouldn't chase her? Ask her."

"Whatever," ruled Bunny. "The point is, David has some indication where she's headed. You said San Diego, right?"

David nodded. Bunny continued, "Now, I think the deal I've made with Mr. Dachshund will help things work out for everyone. You and Stewie take the truck and head for San Diego to find her. David and I will take his car and meet up with Mr. Dachshund."

Some deal. thought Tranko. Bunny had kissed up to Stig, offering who knows what to get in with him. Then she offered to double-cross her guy David, and bring him to Dachshund herself, probably hoping to align herself with a group even more powerful. And no matter what happened, Tranko knew it spelled the end of his deal with Bunny. He needed his own way forward, fast.

"How do I know this asshole isn't sending us on some stupid goose chase?"

Bunny rolled her eyes and stared hard at Tranko, trying to will him to hear her inner voice. *It doesn't matter, stupid 'cause all I'm trying to do is get him to the Russians.*

Tranko knew what she was up to, but he didn't care. He did not feel like playing along. He argued.

"What if this is all bullshit? Why should we go anywhere without you two? I don't trust either one of you."

"Oh, for fuck's sake…" cursed Bunny.

David interceded, "Bunny, just get in the car. It's all good. Let me talk to the men, okay?"

Bunny huffed away and plopped herself down in David's car, immediately grabbing for the visor mirror to check her makeup. David turned to Tranko and Stewie.

"Look, she's a lying bitch. I know it, so do you. She's trying to dump me with the Russians, right?

Tranko and Stewie said nothing but listened closely.

"It doesn't matter. I know what's going on. "Babs ain't going to San Diego. I got a trace on her, and I need someone to run her down. That's you two. Head along the coast, back towards the city and wait for me to text details, ok?"

Tranko paused for a moment. Then he spoke.

"How do you know we won't screw you over?"

"I don't," answered David, "but I also know you don't want to get that painting any more than I do. The big dogs chasing this thing will squash you or me to lay their hands on it. So, mess me over if you want, but right now I'm your best chance at making some bucks from all this. The cancer we need to cut out at this point will be riding with me. Let me handle that one."

Tranko thought for a moment. He still didn't trust David, but he liked the idea of getting rid of Bunny. He nodded acceptance of David's terms.

"Good. Here," said David, tapping his phone on Tranko's. "you've got my text now. Babs is on the move. When I get a static location on her, I'll send it. Go now."

And with that, David walked around the driver side of his car, got in, fired it up and took off in a plume of dust and spinning tires, leaving Tranko and Stewie standing alone.

"So do we trust him?" asked Stewie.

"No. But with nothing better to do right now we might as well do what he wants," replied Tranko. "At least until it's time not to."

Both men got into Stewie's truck and drove away.

* * *

Inside David's car, as they headed down the highway, Bunny asked a question.

"Do you think those guys will be able to get her?"

David shook his head. "Of course not. I sent them on a wild goose chase. You and I are going to go get her. Trust me." And with that David accelerated the car forward, pressing Bunny back in her seat. She smiled at finally being on the inside of the scam, secure in the knowledge that she was about to take David down and secure a big win for herself.

* * *

Ten minutes later, Tranko and Stewie were riding surface streets along the coast. They just passed Manhattan Beach when a text came in from David. Tranko read it out loud.

"She's heading towards the beach. Go towards Portofino Inn, near Redondo. She's on a motorcycle, on the boardwalk."

"*Cannonball Run*." said Stewie.

"What?" asked Tranko.

"The Portofino Inn. That's the finish line of the *Cannonball Run*. The real one. They even used it in the movie."

"Stewie you just...." Tranko swung his head around. "Stop the truck."

Stewie stopped the truck and Tranko ordered him out. Stewie complied and Tranko slid behind the wheel.

"Look, I still don't know if I trust this guy or not, but if we split up then whatever happens, only happens to me. If it's for real, I'll swing back and grab you once I've got her. If it's not a trap."

Stewie looked right at Tranko and cocked his head just a bit. He looked like he might shed a tear.

"Thanks, man. I really appreciate that."

Slightly exposed, Tranko looked away and nodded in response. Then he pressed the gas and took off, heading down towards the ocean in search of the mysterious "Babs."

78

"DOES IT HURT?"

Fatima looked at Ivan's wrists and grimaced at the way the plastic zip-tie was cutting into them. She reached over and tried to adjust them, making some room to relieve the pressure. Ivan pulled them back and spoke to her.

"You are not one for difficult conversations I take it?"

Fatima looked at him and smiled shyly. "No, not really. I'm also quite scared right now. I don't know what to do."

Ivan nodded his head. "That's fair, and you do find yourself in the middle of something...significant."

"What am I in the middle of, exactly?"

"Well, some gentlemen are having a disagreement over who gets to have something that doesn't belong to either of them."

"And you?"

"I work for one of the gentlemen."

Ivan saw Fatima look down at his zip-tied hands and then back up at him, making a face that said "bullshit." Ivan, feeling compelled to answer her look, responded.

"My work is for the *other* gentleman, not the one who did this to me."

"And what do you do for your 'gentleman?'"

"Arrange for the acquisition of the item in question..."

"...that doesn't actually belong to him." filled in Fatima.

"Correct."

Fatima took a deep breath. "And Maggie?" She asked the question but was personally terrified to hear the answer.

Ivan bowed his head slightly. "Maggie, my little vixen. She, I'm afraid, works for me."

Fatima exhaled and immediately started looking about, trying to see if the SUV door would open, or if she could crawl into the front seat. She was acting in a somewhat claustrophobic manner, speaking in bursts without looking directly at Ivan.

"So, I'm supposed to believe my best friend is a…..is a….?"

"Thief?" helped Ivan.

Fatima pursed her lips and furrowed her brow.

"That is the word you meant, yes?" asked Ivan.

Fatima nodded her head curtly.

"Maggie's story is not mine to tell, especially to someone close to her. But you should know that the person you thought you knew remains the same, except for a single reality of her life that, in many ways, she never truly had any control over. She is no different, no matter what you think."

"You have no idea what I think."

At that moment the driver door flung open and one of the men got in and fired up the vehicle. Then another entered the passenger side. The SUV was on the move before his door was fully closed.

The driver spoke, "Where is Bogdan?"

"He's going up the pathway, looking for the *osvedomitel*."

Ivan leaned into Fati's ear and whispered a translation, "Snitch."

The passenger instructed the driver, "Go along the water, as close as you can. We need to find him. I'll call the boss." He dialed a cell phone and began talking into it. Fatima was getting more nervous. Ivan put his clasped hands on one of hers.

"Don't worry. I am certain we are bargaining chips at this point. They will not hurt us, at least for now."

Fatima could not believe her ears. *For now?*

Then Fatima had a thought. Remembering her cell phone, she slid it from her jacket pocket, showing Ivan, who saw it but said nothing. Quickly, she began to tap out a message, hitting "send" before anyone in the front seat was the wiser.

*Let's see what he does with that…*thought Fatima, hiding her cell phone once more.

* * *

David pulled off the freeway and slid out the exit, turning hard onto a surface street directly beneath the on ramp. He followed along for a few hundred feet before coming to a stop. Bunny looked at him quizzically.

"What are we doing?"

"I'm meeting someone. He was supposed to be here already."

And then suddenly he was. Within 30sec, a yellow taxi pulled up behind David's car. He turned to Bunny.

"You stay here."

David got out of the car and walked to the back, meeting the cab driver. Bunny angled the mirror to watch what David was doing. He appeared to be looking at something in the back seat of the cab. She couldn't make it out directly, and she didn't want David to think she was particularly interested. She tried to listen to their words. No luck. Then she saw David hand the man something. Money. She couldn't see how much. The cabbie got back in his car, started it up and pulled away, taking off in the opposite direction. David walked back to the car and got inside.

"Who was that?" demanded Bunny.

"Interesting guy," answered David. I met him in the city the other night and he did a job for me. He liked it so much he asked if I had any other jobs he might do."

"So, what is he doing?"

David ignored the question and started the car, shoulder checked, then pulled it back onto the street. He steered toward a main road.

"Where are we going?"

"Santa Monica."

Bunny looked frustrated. "I promised that we would go meet my guy near the water. He's sending me an address."

"We have lots of time for that. I just have a stop to make first."

"You already made a stop."

"Yup, and now I have to make another."

Bunny didn't like what was going on. Had David realized she was setting him up? Had he caught wind of her agreement to hand him over to Mr. Dachshund? She didn't want to give anything away, but she also couldn't leave things to chance. Maybe she could change things up a little.

Bunny reached over and started stroking David's thigh. David looked at her and smiled.

"I thought you were mad at me?"

Bunny looked away but kept stroking his leg. "That's how I communicate. You know that. I thought you liked it." She gave his thigh a slight squeeze, causing David to flinch a little.

David turned and looked at her. "You really are something else," he said.

"What?" Bunny batted her eyes at him and smiled, crossing, and then re-crossing her legs beside him. She put two hands on his thigh now, moving one of them closer to the top. David shifted in his seat.

"Now Bunny, is that safe?"

"I'm not driving," she teased, "Besides, I've got nothing better to do and I'm bored."

As Bunny continued to rub David's leg, she simultaneously moved her hands closer to his crotch, bumping it with every third or fourth rub. Seeing David's expression, she felt confident enough to re-ask her question.

"What's Mr. Taxi man doing for you anyway?"

David's bemused expression formalized slightly. He reached over and cupped the left-side of Bunny's face with his right hand, holding her cheek. Then he let it go and put his hand back on the steering wheel.

"Funny thing about that. He was just at your Malibu place."

That caused Bunny to stop rubbing momentarily. Then she remembered what had got her this far and started up again.

"Ummhmmm," she answered, desperately trying to stay casual.

"Yes, I had him pick up some things for me. Remember all those junk pieces of art you and your idiot hitman picked up that I said were worthless?"

Bunny was getting more concerned but was determined not to show it. She kept stroking his leg, teasing him.

"Ummmhmmm."

"Well, it turns out they aren't worthless. They're quite valuable. And I plan to sell them to some people I know. I should clear mid-five figures."

This information was too much for Bunny. She pulled her hands from David's leg and sat bolt upright in the car. "What! That's my money! You said they were worthless."

David smiled, "I did say they were worthless. But that's because I lied."

Bunny's eyes blazed with fire. "I could kill you!"

David turned his face to her and put on a sad, puppy dog expression. "Now, Bunny. Don't be like that." He reached for her hands and pulled them back toward his leg. "You can keep doing whatever you were gonna do. It's all good."

David turned another corner and kept driving.

Bunny yanked her hands back from him and crossed her arms. "What's good about it?"

David, smiling calmly, spoke, "I haven't forgotten about you. There's something for you in all this too you know."

At that, Bunny immediately softened, leaning back in toward David. He reached for her nearby hand and led it back to his leg, encouraging her to continue what she had been doing. Bunny felt her mood shift enough to give in a bit. She started kneading at his thighs again.

"I knew I could count on you."

"You always can."

David came to a stop, signalled, and then turned another corner.

"Where are we?" asked Bunny.

"Almost there," answered David.

As Bunny went to unzip David's pants she had a flash of doubt, wondering if she should tell him about Mr. Dachshund and her agreement to deliver him up. Did she really want to double-cross David? Should she confess? He wasn't so bad after all. He had figured out how to get some money out of the art they found and had even told her about it. That was good. Still, she liked having an out. She might wait a bit. See if he was fair with the split. Maybe she could use the Russian to leverage him right out of his piece altogether. Bunny smirked as she counted her options.

Until she looked around. Something wasn't right. There were several police cars parked along the road.

"What is this?" asked Bunny.

"Santa Monica PD. They were helping investigate your husband's death, so I told them how you hired a guy to kill him. They were going to come for you, but I offered to turn you in myself. They're going to charge you with your husband's murder. It probably won't stick but it'll give me more than enough time to get away from you, not to mention those lunatic Russians you were dumb enough to try hooking up with…"

"YOU ASSHOLE!" screamed Bunny. She looked around at the police station and all the police cars and police officers moving around. She started to panic. She needed a way out. Her eyes bulged. She was spinning, trying to make sense. She needed a thread. Something to grab. Then she stared at David and accused him.

"It was you! You did it! You made me do this! And, and, and… you broke into my house! Yes! You stole my art! I'll tell them! You'll go to jail too! Not just me!"

David waved her off. "Hey now. I didn't break into anything. I certainly don't have any art in this car, do I? And it was your codes that opened the gate and doors, by the way. In fact, I bet the police are going to want you know where you stashed them, huh? That might be another big problem…for you." He pulled over and stopped the car.

At this, Bunny let loose a primal scream that started in the depths of her soul and escaped her mouth at maximum velocity and pitch. At the same time, she pushed through David's fly with both hands and grabbed onto his penis with an unbridled ferocity, squeezing and yanking as hard as she possibly could.

"OW! OUCH! HEY! AHHH AAAAHHH! DAMMIT! STOP!" Too late, David realized the awkward position he found himself in. He opened his car door and tried to get out, instead falling onto the sidewalk, still hollering in pain as Bunny attacked his crotch. She continued screaming curses at him, even as a handful of nearby police officers ran over to separate them.

79

MAGGIE SAT squished between Tranko and Stewie, wondering what came next. To say this job had gone off the rails was an understatement.

Tranko, who was driving, fiddled with his cell phone trying to call someone. No one answered and he slammed it down on the dash of the truck.

"He's not answering."

"Maybe he's busy."

"That's not the point. What the hell are we supposed to do now?"

Maggie interjects, "Either of you planning on telling me what's going on?"

No one said anything. Maggie pressed them again.

"Hello? Boys? Can we at least go back and get my bike?"

Tranko answered without taking his eyes off the road.

"No."

"Why not?"

Tranko continued to say nothing. He stared out at the road before angrily reaching for his phone to hit re-dial once more. When it went to voicemail, he again slammed it down on the dash of the truck. This triggered Stewie.

"C'mon man, that's still my truck, ok?" Tranko grunted in response. He was mad as hell at still being in the dark on things.

As the truck rolled to a stop at a red light, Maggie sprung into action. She struck Stewie in the throat, causing him to pitch forward as she slipped her legs up and pushed to go behind him and out the passenger door. She had the door open, and her torso headed outside, but not before Tranko reached over and grabbed her ankle, stopping her forward momentum and keeping her mostly inside the truck. By this point, Stewie had recovered and managed to pull her fully back in, but not before the huge commotion had become visible to anyone paying attention. Seeing this, Tranko slammed Maggie down in her seat between them and hit the gas, turning right on the red light, and getting the truck out of the area as fast as he could. Stewie was the first to say something.

"That really hurt!"

"It was supposed to," snapped Maggie.

"Do you want us to tie you up? Because we can, you know," said Stewie.

"What I want is to know who the hell you two are and why you are holding me against my will? And if I don't get some answers quick, I'm going to make even more trouble for the pair of you."

At this, Tranko slammed on the brakes and pulled the truck over to the side of the road. He reached aggressively for the cell phone and again hit redial. Nothing. Voicemail. Again.

"Fuck!" Tranko flung the phone on the dash and turned to look right at Maggie.

"Ok, 'Babs' here's the scoop. We know who you are and what you're carrying in that fancy little tube on your back...."

"And?" Maggie challenged.

"And...what? What else am I supposed to say?"

Maggie looked right back at Tranko. "And what are you going to do with it? You know who I am. So? What does that mean? You know what I've got on my back. So what? Are you going to take it? Then what? Who are you giving it to? Are you going to sell it? To whom? How much is it worth? What do you know about any of this? I'm getting the impression you don't have a single clue about what you've gotten yourself into, do you?"

Maggie's verbal attack sent Tranko's barely contained rage into a serious red zone. He gripped the steering wheel so hard that his fingers turned white before suddenly releasing and yanking the driver's door open, getting out and slamming it so hard the entire truck shook. Then he stomped around the front and started pounding both fists on the hood. Stewie put a hand on his head and dropped his eyes.

"C'mon man. You're killing me."

Maggie turned to Stewie. "What's his problem?"

"He's really frustrated. It's been a pretty tough week."

By this point, Tranko had stopped pounding the hood. He had turned his back to the truck and was leaning backwards against it, looking forward down the road. Maggie craned over and stuck her head out the driver window.

"Hey big fella. If you can calm yourself down enough to talk, maybe we can figure something out. I'll tell what I know, and you do the same. I'm not gonna pretend to trust you but I don't expect you to trust me either, so that kind of makes us even. At least we can try, ok?"

Tranko heard her. He said nothing but it was clear he was listening. He stood up fully and stretched his shoulders out before turning and coming back to the door of the truck. Leaning inside the open window he looked at both Maggie and Stewie.

"I'm hungry. Want to get some tacos?"

Maggie and Stewie looked at each other and then back to Tranko. Both nodded. Tranko nodded in return and got in, firing up the truck and heading off down the road in search of something to eat.

* * *

The taste was unbelievable. Maggie had eaten tacos before but never anything quite like this. Sitting at a wood picnic table with a tire shop to her left and the 110 freeway to her right was hardly the kind of location one expected for gourmet food, but the Tacos Los Guichos food truck dominated the scene, dishing out all manner of authentic Mexican fare to a steady lineup of hungry diners.

The most incredible sight was located directly to the side of the truck: a pair of prep tables holding two ridiculously large 3ft cones of twirling, marinated meat, flame-cooking constantly and being shaved repeatedly by two men wielding foot-long knives. The vertical spit, called a *trompo* according to Stewie, was how one spotted true *al pastor* aka shepherd-style tacos this side of Mexico City. Stewie likened it to *shawarma*, but Mexican. He was definitely on to something.

Maggie couldn't believe the flavor. She also hadn't realized how hungry she was, downing three tacos before taking a breath. She slowed down for the fourth, attempting to enjoy it even more. Taking a break, Maggie took a pull on a pineapple soda. Tranko and Stewie sat across from her, doing much the same. The sun was setting, and a light breeze was picking up. As the light faded a hazy orange and yellow glow filled the sky, causing their location to take on an almost surreal look, like a 3D, live-action velvet painting. Tranko spoke between mouthfuls of taco.

"Look, I've dealt with Russians before. You can't trust 'em. And I don't. But what the hell do I do? They're locked onto me and if I don't deliver, I'm dead."

Maggie nodded her head. Tranko continued, "I think we're all screwed, to tell you the truth. That bitch, sorry Bunny, I mean. She started all this trying to scare her old man. At this point, I just want out."

"Well, what do we have?" asked Maggie.

"You say you got the big deal painting they want. I had some ones they said were fakes but they got those now too. The Russian promised me money if I brought *The Concert* painting to him, but he never said how much, and I doubt he'd pay anyway. He's probably gonna shoot me. What about your guy?"

Maggie explained, "My deal is a little more clear. I get paid if I deliver to my contact, but I think your Russian has already grabbed him up. And I'm pretty sure he's got my friend too."

"So, we do a trade? Give him the painting for your contact and your friend? And if I deliver maybe I get my ass out of it too?"

"It's a possibility, but I've still got my big shot on the other side. I do have some insurance I can leverage against him, so I'm not too worried about blowback on that one. He's still dangerous though. But either way, we both lose out on a payday. I hate giving in on that to these jerks."

Tranko slapped the table with his hand. "At this point, I don't even care. I just want out."

"I'd still like some money," commented Stewie.

"What about the slickster? Bunny's 'friend?' Is he a problem?" asked Maggie.

"He could be. I still can't reach him. He was the one said to pick you up. He put a tracker on you, by the way."

"Yeah, I found it when I visited the porta-potty over there. It'll be staying onsite. I dare him to go looking for it now."

"I don't trust him, but if he gets rid of that broad I ain't gonna cry. She is trouble and she won't hesitate to take me down with her."

Maggie sat for a moment and sipped at her drink. She looked up into the darkening sky, searching for answers. Then she spoke.

"We're going to have to meet with them. All of them. A big meet. Where we get everyone together with an interest in this."

"What will that do?" asked Tranko.

Maggie sighed. "I don't know, yet. We need to create a situation where we can get the big guys fighting each other instead of wasting their time on us. I just don't know exactly how to do it."

Stewie perked up. "If you want a place for a big meet-up I got the perfect spot. And I know all sorts of secret ways in and out. It'd be impossible for 'em to cover the whole thing."

Tranko turned and looked at Stewie. "Where?"

"The Hollywood Bowl."

# 80

ALDO STOOD in the foyer of the Highland Park Bowl, a painstakingly refurbished, one-time 1920's speakeasy, now transformed into one of LA's hippest hangouts. It was a throwback, standing in such a place. An anachronism to modern Los Angeles, designed to make the visitor feel like a time-traveller. Unfortunately, Aldo felt something else: impotence. He was suddenly unsure of himself in ways he had not experienced in decades.

Not since the tennis match.

As a young man, Aldo loved sport. Especially tennis. So athletic and powerful, yet so graceful and disarmingly internal. You could turn the worst game around with a mere thought or lose the surest of things via little more than a slip of the mind. Tennis was brutal. His first coach likened it to boxing, only worse.

"A boxer has a corner man to tell him what to do and remind him that things will be okay every few minutes. In tennis you compete alone, trapped alongside whatever chaos grows within your own mind. Tennis, as a sport, is far crueler than boxing could ever be."

And yet Aldo was very good at it. He was a natural who practiced relentlessly and competed obsessively. Which meant he rose quickly. At one point he had harboured the idea of becoming a top player, maybe even challenging for the Davis Cup.

Back then, Aldo had few doubts about anything. The son of wealth, he had led a privileged and connected life. Young Aldo wintered in San Moritz and spent summers chasing around the US, Cuba, Mexico, or whatever other trendy hot spot beckoned, kissing the girls, and closing most of the bars each night. He was young and strong then, wandering the world with his skill and charm, determined to prove to his father what a grand sportsman he was. It was an incredible time, but for the one match that changed it all.

It was in some small Euro backwater whose borders have almost certainly shifted several times over. He'd agreed to play on a dare, certain of a win mainly due to the apparent lack of skill offered by the locals in attendance. Aldo was a snob, but he didn't care. He knew his pedigree and his talent. Victory was assured.

And sure enough, his match went off as expected. The other player was tough but not of Aldo's calibre. He beat him soundly, his only regret being the lack of an audience or even linesmen to applaud his success. Matches then were played on the honor system, with each man calling his own lines. Officials were only present during the semi-finals and beyond. This being merely a first round meant such formalities were unnecessary. Or so he thought.

Cooling down after the match, and seated together at their shared bench, the other player beckoned for Aldo's attention. Once captured, he opened his bag and encouraged Aldo to look inside. In doing, Aldo saw a gun, an automatic weapon, lying provocatively within reach. The other player then suggested that perhaps Aldo had in fact lost the match he had just won, and that he would be better served reporting the final score as the reverse of what had occurred.

Aldo, smug about his talent and position, laughed at the attempted intimidation and went on to report the other player to the tournament, ensuring that he would be credited with the match win and that the offending player would be sanctioned. He would not be bullied. Not someone as successful as he.

Unfortunately, the other player and his friends had waited for Aldo that night. As he stumbled home after celebrating his victory they surrounded him, beating him mercilessly. Afterward, he was so injured he had to withdraw from the event, unable to play. Never before had Aldo experienced that level of humiliation. It had taken years to build himself back up from being laid that low.

Until today. When he looked around and found himself being forced to stare once more at a metaphorical weapon inside a bag.

Dachshund had taken Fatima. Manheim was missing and Maggie had stolen his pride and joy. Between the three, Aldo's confidence was shaken, his success in question. Fatima had texted him, begging for help. What could he do? He was a man of angles, not violence. In America, he was without the "enforcement" he might otherwise count on. At least not easily found.

Aldo texted her back, but Fatima never answered. He assumed her phone had been compromised or grabbed by her captors. Either way, she was now a prisoner, and it was his fault.

And Maggie's too.

Trying to reach Manheim had become a lost cause. For whatever reason, he had dropped off the face of the earth. And knowing that coincidences were rare, it only multiplied the fear that was rising inside him. Aldo preferred to be the one in control. He counted on being the one with a "gun in the bag."

Which is exactly what he hoped to acquire in the bowling alley tonight.

Aldo didn't have anyone in LA, outside his yacht crew which, by definition, were not muscle. Manheim was his fixer, and with him unreachable Aldo was at a distinct disadvantage. He needed to find leverage. He needed help.

Aldo knew the Boolis were behind the incomplete deal with Dachshund. And he had found out that Sauf, the older brother, was being held until the deal was complete. So, he called Rael, who by this point was apoplectic about his brother still being held by the Russians. Rael was panicked in his own right and did not want to do anything to risk harm coming to him, let alone stand obviously against Dachshund. But Aldo pressed him, demanding help. Finally, Rael gave in, telling him to wait for details. Eventually, Aldo got word to visit this place, this specific bowling alley and to wait. Rael had said that someone would come.

As he paced the area, watching the pin machines in the distance set and reset, a voice behind him called out.

"You are Mr. Aldo?"

Aldo turned and came face to face with one of the largest human beings he had ever seen. The man's shoulders seemed to be three feet across, with a huge head between them. The man's beard looked like it was a solid mass, topped by eyes as dark and cold as smooth black stones. He was at least 6'7", maybe more, and had similar jet-black hair on the backs of both hands. Aldo turned fully to face him.

"I am. You are?"

"I am Malik. My cousin Rael told me to meet with you. Shall we?"

Aldo followed massive Malik to the center bar area facing the restored lanes. He watched as the huge man sat on a stool and still seemed taller than he. Not wanting to be shrunk further, Aldo chose to lean against the table.

"Drink?" asked Malik.

"No. I need help, not a drink. I've got a situation that has spiralled out of control."

"I am aware. Rael has clued me in, but mostly in how my other cousin Sauf is at risk. You cannot act rashly regarding the person with whom you are dealing."

"Well, I am aware," snapped Aldo, "but what are you suggesting we do?"

"At Rael's urging, I am to assist in providing a path forward. Specifically, you are to let Dachshund take his painting. Do not fight him."

Aldo was stunned.

"How is that a plan? Give him what he wants? How does that protect my interests in any way?"

"It doesn't protect you. It protects Sauf, who is under his direct control. As a side benefit it might also protect your lady, at least for a time. That is where I can help."

"You just said we are doing nothing."

"I said do nothing to antagonize Dachshund. I did not say do nothing. Big difference."

Aldo nodded. "Okay, what did you have in mind?"

"I am going to need a few things."

"As you know, I have no specific people here in Los Angeles. None that can be called upon that I trust...for issues like this."

Malik answered, "That is no problem. I have people. But I need other items." At this, Malik pulled a list from his waistband and handed it to Aldo, who scanned the paper quickly.

"Do you really need that much?"

Malik focused his dark eyes on Aldo. "Lives are at stake."

Chastened, Aldo conceded, "Alright, I think I can arrange this. But I'm not sure how it's going to help get us into a better position."

"It will help fine, Mr. Aldo. Now, If I may ask, has Dachshund made any attempt to meet with you at all since?"

Aldo shook his head. "No, not yet."

"Are you able to reach out to him?"

"I can."

"Do this. But not too soon. I need several hours."

Aldo looked at the large human, marvelling once more at his size. "What exactly do you do? What is your job?"

"Day to day?" asked Malik. "I sell custom coasters. Branded bar ware and similar."

"Really?" exclaimed Aldo in disbelief.

Malik caught the look. "I do other things as well."

Aldo rubbed the back of his neck, taking things in. "And you really think this can work?" he asked.

"It must. This is for family, for Sauf first. Then, your lady. After that, it is whatever it is."

To Aldo's left, a nearby bowler let out a loud cheer and pumped his fist as a ball smashed a strike. Aldo turned and watched the pins reset themselves, ready to absorb another monstrous hit. He nodded his head slowly and looked away from Malik.

"It is whatever it is." agreed Aldo.

81

"REAL OR NOT?" Edward Dachshund stood in the warehouse, just off to the side of the three paintings leaned against the wall. Ivan knelt in front of the set, studying them carefully.

"It does not seem so, to me," replied Ivan.

Fatima stood to one side with her hands zip-tied together in front of her. She watched quietly.

"But the one your woman has, *The Concert,* that one is real, you know this?"

Ivan nodded. "I do."

Dachshund pressed, "And how? How do you know this?"

Awkwardly, Ivan used his tied hands on his knee to struggle back to his feet. He turned and faced Dachshund. No one else, save Fatima, remained in the large warehouse. He spoke simply but with authority.

"Provenance. I know how Levi got the painting in the first place. And I know where it came from before that. Zevon Levi had *The Concert*. Maggie took it from his home, which means what she has is real. I cannot vouch any stronger than that."

Dachshund nodded his head. He looked again at the paintings against the wall.

"And these?"

Ivan waved towards them. "Not originals, of course, but they are not without value. They would fool some. Maybe not art experts but some insurance firms, those less skilled."

"So don't destroy them then?"

"That would be foolish. They exhibit significant skill."

"Worth keeping?"

"I would," replied Ivan.

Dachshund paced a small area. The entire goal of the Los Angeles excursion was to seize the original piece that the Boolis had guaranteed their product with, and he had been thwarted in that goal since day one. Even now, all he had to show for his efforts were three supposedly well-done fakes plus two local captives and one missing snitch. He was in a pissing match with Aldo Neto and whatever local police trouble the damnable widow of Zev Levi brought down on him and the apparent murder of her husband.

This had to stop.

He already held Sauf Booli back home. That should have been enough to close things out, but for the involvement of Aldo and the mess made by the wife. There was no reason any of this nonsense needed to continue. Dachshund needed to get out of America and get back to his own world. The longer he was here the worse things got. Rather than clean things up, each turn had merely made things messier and messier.

His cell phone rang. Dachshund pulled it out and answered.

"Hello? ....Are you certain? And there are police on scene? He had nothing that can tie him to us, right? Okay. Leave it then. Come back here." He pressed the call off.

"Our turncoat is dead," said Dachshund to no one in particular. Ivan turned to him, looking unsure. Seeing his confusion, Dachshund clarified.

"Neto's right hand, Manheim. You dealt with him, I'm sure."

Ivan's face betrayed the shock he felt. His eyes must have struck Dachshund, who immediately protested.

"It had nothing to do with me. He was chasing your woman when it happened."

This caused Fatima to speak up.

"Is Maggie okay?"

"She must be if Manheim isn't. Anyway, that's a question for you. Where is she?"

Ivan looked directly at Dachshund. "She was coming to meet me. Your people intervened and she took off. What did you expect?"

Dachshund looked at the two of them individually, then focused on the pair.

"Each of you needs to contact someone who can help me right now. Get my painting! I am not going to be patient any longer. I've wasted too much time on this already."

Fatima looked perplexed. She had no idea what to say and began looking left and right. Ivan answered for them both. "She's not going to answer if we call. She knows you have us."

Dachshund looked hard at them both. "This is the point in our relationship where I pull out a gun, level it at you and order you to do what I say or else. I would do this so that you know I'm serious. Well, I don't need a gun to make it clear. I mean what I say. I've got plenty of leverage and if you have no value to her then you have no value to me. One of you better get her or Aldo on a phone to me in the next few minutes or I have no reason to keep you around. Am I being clear enough for you?"

Ivan nodded and held up his hands, indicating that he'd like his bonds cut. Dachshund pulled out a knife and severed them. Ivan then indicated the same for Fatima.

"They took our phones," offered Ivan.

"I'll get them." Dachshund walked out of the building and slammed the warehouse door shut behind him.

Fatima looked at Ivan, who was rubbing his wrists.

"What do we do?"

"I think you would agree our options are limited, yes? We will have to reach out to those that care about us. Where it goes from there, I have no idea. But it is not looking very good right now."

"He'll kill Maggie."

"He will very likely kill all of us, dear lady. If it is at all possible, we need to find a way to stop him from doing that."

"Well, what can Maggie do against an animal like this?"

"Don't underestimate the Vixen. She is far wiser in the ways of things than even I realized. In fact, I would suggest our fate rests in her capable hands right now."

The warehouse door whipped open, and Dachshund walked back in carrying two cell phones. He handed them to Ivan. "Each of you make a call. You get Maggie and you get hold of that frivolous, man-child Neto and make it clear that if they don't take some immediate steps to get my painting to me that your lives will be forfeit. I want this carnival of insanity wrapped up."

Ivan paused in dialing, turning toward Dachshund.

"With all due respect, it is unlikely either will immediately come if they think you are lying in wait. Could I propose an alternative idea to satisfy your demand?"

"I'm listening."

All of a sudden, the warehouse door opened. Stig barged in.

"...I...uh...there is something you should know. About the widow...and the insurance guy."

Dachshund held a finger up to stop Ivan from speaking as he turned to hear what Stig had brought by way of information.

"The broad is with the police and..."

Before Stig could get the rest of his sentence out the room filled with the voice of Gloria Gaynor singing *"I Will Survive."* The music was coming from Fatima's cell phone. Everyone turned to look at her. Fatima looked down at her phone and then up at Dachshund.

"It's Aldo."

Dachshund, frustrated at all the interruptions, barked back at her.

"Answer it then."

Fatima pressed the accept call button and put the phone to her ear.

"Hello?"

Dachshund, Ivan, and Stig all stared at Fatima, waiting for something. She made a face and looked at the phone, then up at Dachshund. She lifted the phone toward him, "He wants to talk to you."

82

ALDO WALKED the gangplank back onboard the *Jimena*, replaying the events of the evening. A hastily arranged sit-down with a bearded giant, set up by an angry, and objectively cornered, brother who had screwed over a Russian mobster. And now here he was, somehow having to put his faith in the unknown abilities of a bar salesman who wasn't even really on his side anyway. This was not good. Not good at all.

He felt the paper he'd been given crinkle inside his jacket pocket, reminding him that he'd been handed a to-do list as if he was someone's junior lackey. This was not his role, at least not for a very long time. How had it come to this? Running around getting "supplies" for an unknown enforcer without any guarantees that he'd even come out the other side unscathed? This was insanity. The temptation to pull up anchor and simply sail away from everything was almost overpowering. That the only obstacle to making such a decision was his attachment to Fatima gave him pause. How did he allow himself to fall for this woman? That reality alone was too much to handle, and personally troubling.

Now on deck, he looked across the water. It was quiet, or at least as quiet as the populated shore could be. Music could be heard playing from a far-off pub while small boats traversed the marina, arriving to tie up and shut down for the night. Aldo opened a hidden cooler and fished out a bottle of water, twisting the lid off and immediately took a deep drink. He breathed in the evening air while mentally weighing the possibilities still available to him. Suddenly, a voice from the shadows broke his solitary spell.

"Are you going to run?"

Turning in the direction of the voice, Aldo strained his eyes to see. He shook his head from side to side as Maggie stepped out from the darkened side of a large bulkhead.

"Ms. Deacon. Of course, it's you."

Maggie walked over to Aldo, sitting down on the edge of an outdoor lounger just removed from him. She re-asked her question.

"Well, are you?"

Aldo looked at her, then took another drink from his bottle. Slowly he re-screwed the cap. "It has certainly crossed my mind."

His admission caused Maggie to smirk, even as she rolled her eyes with disdain over his answer. She looked away, towards the quickly blackening horizon.

"Even you must admit it's the smartest play, at least in this circumstance, yes?" he offered.

Maggie heard him, but chose to ignore his provocation, keeping her eyes glued elsewhere. She spoke without facing him.

"I knew you were weak when she told me about your 'harem.' Having women compete for you? At least you're consistent," deadpanned Maggie.

Aldo, taking exception to the insult, raised his head and set his jaw. "I care deeply about Fatima."

"You're not showing it."

"What would you have me do?"

Maggie turned her eyes toward him. "Save her."

"I'm not the one holding what that Slavic *pessoa má* wants. That would be you."

This caused Maggie to turn around fully, and then rise to her feet, squaring off directly against him.

"Believe it or not, I have a few things certain people would like back. And I'm prepared to use every one of them to get Fatima out of this, but I need some clarity on what your end is. You hired me to grab *The Concert* in the first place. Why?"

Aldo paused for a long minute, considering how he might answer such a question. Then he became expressive, flitting his hands into the air as he paced away from her.

"Quick answers, easy explanations. Make it all go away, yes?"

Maggie stepped after him. "There's nothing easy in life, Aldo. You and I both are old enough to understand that. I just want to know what I don't already know. I have two people that are very special to me at risk. Yes, I accept my share of the blame for that, but not all of it. I'm here first because you hired me. Why? Why this painting and this man? You knew he was chasing it. What's it to you?"

Aldo tapped his foot on the deck. "Would it anger you if I said, 'it's just business?'"

"Probably."

"Fair. I had a commercial relationship with some people that guaranteed certain things to Mr. Dachshund, but I was not a party to these guarantees. Still, I became involved tangentially. As the situation unfolded, an opportunity presented itself to…cause some embarrassment to Mr. Dachshund, so I took it. Or, should I say, tried to take it."

"You have a history with him?"

"We navigate similar waters and have traded…indirect blows in the past, but nothing this specific, at least until now."

Maggie nodded her head. "I love when it comes down to guys cocking around about who's got the bigger bat in the fence."

"Ms. Deacon, power isn't static. It ebbs, flows, and requires constant maintenance. If you don't use it, you lose it. Still, wherever this started, I am fully committed to rescuing Fatima. Her safety is paramount."

"Well, we're going to need more than that. The man you hired me through, Ivan. He is also at risk now. I'm going to need your help to save them both."

Aldo nods. "What do you propose?"

"I have a list…"

"That seems to be a theme tonight."

"I don't follow." Maggie looked at him, confused.

Aldo seated himself on a railing near the stern. "You, dear lady, are not the only one reminding me of my obligations tonight."

Momentarily stopped, Maggie stepped back and surveyed Aldo, for once really looking at him. He was an attractive man. More so right now, as a certain amount of vulnerability appeared to be showing. For once, the smooth operator wasn't in complete control. Maybe this is what Fatima had caught glimpses of? A stripped down, emotionally bare Aldo Neto? Maggie wondered, then spoke, "I'm going to need you to level with me about what you have going on."

Aldo dropped his hands into his pockets. "Honestly, I can't even be sure myself at this point. I have been given a new partner."

"Do you know where Manheim is?"

"That is another problem. I'm at the conclusion that he has either abandoned or double-crossed me. Or perhaps left on a sudden vacation? Or died? Or something. Either way, I have no idea where he is."

"Well, he was chasing after me not that long ago, but I personally haven't seen or heard from him since. I will need to know if he's an issue or not."

Aldo nodded his head in agreement. Maggie continued, "You will also need to get some money. A lot. In cash."

"Yes, that was on the list."

"Can I see this other list?" asked Maggie.

Aldo handed her the small paper. Maggie opened it and read aloud.

"A flame-thrower? Really?"

"Apparently," answered Aldo.

Maggie continued, "Two vans - identical, three commercial rolls of plastic cling wrap, duct tape – three rolls, binoculars, $1 million in US cash, a kids' plastic pool, four 60-lb kettlebells, two wood pallets, two extra-large lifejackets, fishing line, case of frozen water bottles, satellite phone with service. This is insane. Who the heck are you in bed with now?"

"Family. Related to one of the detained."

"Not Fatima or Ivan? There are more?"

"One more. Overseas."

"I don't see you going to get all this stuff. Would you even know where to start?"

"I was going to have my steward get most items."

"A flame-thrower?"

"That one might be trickier."

"And the money?"

"I can arrange that."

"Not so fast. I'll need you to get a little more."

"Of course, you do."

"I'm not coming to this party empty-handed. You know what I have of yours. I'll give it back. But only if I can trust you. And I swear to God, if any harm comes to Fatima, *Storm* will disappear forever."

Aldo looked right at Maggie. "I'm sure it will." He paused before speaking again. "I guess I never should have made fun of you that night in my apartment, hmm? I'm paying for that now, yes?"

Maggie ignored the jibe. "Aldo, my opinion of you is open to adjustment, but only when Fati is home safe. Until then, you remain as much an enemy to me as you ever were."

"Understood."

"OK, let's go over what needs to happen if we are going to get things back the way they should be. And do not spare any details on "Mr. Flamethrower" either. I think he and I will need to meet before this is over as well."

"That can happen."

"Great. But first, you need to make a phone call."

"To whom?"

"Let's just say I'm fairly certain you have her number saved in your phone."

83

TRANKO SAT in the cab of Stewie's truck with his arms crossed and eyes closed. He was trying to catch what little shut eye he might find before things start up again. It had been a long day and he was tired. The sounds of sea gulls beyond the marina provided a somewhat annoying background, even as the sun finished setting. He shifted in his seat, trying to find some comfort. Stewie, sitting in the driver's seat and staring out the front window, spoke up.

"How long do you think she'll be?"

Tranko grunted, "I don't know." He shifted again in his seat, trying to find a position that would work. Maggie had convinced the guys to drive her back to the marina so she could speak to Aldo. Having them park out of sight, a few hundred yards away, Maggie then slipped back on board to wait for him. Tranko, against it at first, eventually agreed with her idea, but he was very reluctant. His experiences thus far with the players involved did not suggest adding more of them would make things any better for him. He felt certain he was somehow being pushed back into a no-win corner. Again.

"You think she'll come back? I think she'll come back." nodded Stewie, answering his own question.

"Well, why wouldn't she? You clap like a seal at every word she says. You even got suckered into getting her bike back for her."

"We couldn't leave it out there, man. It's a CB750. Do you know how rare those things are? And especially one in great shape like that one. Look at it. It's amazing" At this, Stewie turned and craned his neck trying to see the motorcycle in the back of the truck, secured under a tarp.

"You're a sap," remarked Tranko as he stretched his neck side to side.

"She did ask nicely."

"Whatever."

A few beats passed and the silence built up once more between the two men. Tranko looked like he might have finally found a comfortable static position and felt himself drifting off. Stewie split the silence once more, "You think she's gonna be long over there?"

This time Tranko didn't even open his eyes as he spoke. "She said she was gonna try to get this big shot on side against the other big shot, the Russian asshole that I've been dealing with. I don't know how long that's going to take so I'd like to get a little sleep in the meantime, ok?"

Stewie nodded. "I guess."

"So, can you friggen can it for a bit?"

"Sure, sure. Sorry, man."

Stewie settled in, getting himself cozy and the truck went quiet once more. But the peace only lasted for a few moments before a cell phone suddenly went off. Immediately, Stewie checked himself.

"It's not mine."

"No, it's mine." Tranko sighed loudly and reached into his bag pulling out the phone. He looked at the display before answering and his eyes got big when he saw who it is. "Fuck! It's Bunny. I thought that guy was getting her locked up. What the hell?"

Stewie looked at Tranko. "You gonna answer it?"

"No, let it go to voicemail." Tranko put the phone on the dash of the truck and pulled his hand away. Then they waited, watching the phone. Eventually, a light began to flash, indicating that a voicemail message was waiting to be played. Tranko grabbed the phone, clicked in, and hit play. He put the message on speaker.

"Hi, it's me. Bunny. Levi. That asshole David tried to have me arrested but the cops had nothing on me, so they let me go. I need to see you, like NOW! David is trying to scam some art out of me that could mean some serious money…for both of us. By the way, I didn't say anything about you when the cops asked all their questions, but I could still turn you in if you don't call back. We have got to meet right away. Call me back or things go nuclear!"

Stewie, hearing her threat looked over at Tranko. "You believe her? What do we do?"

As Tranko started to speak, his cell phone lit up once more, announcing another incoming call.

"She's calling again?" asked Stewie.

Tranko looked down at the display. "No, now it's that David guy."

Once more, the pair did the exact same routine, watching the phone until the ringing stopped, placing it on the dash of the truck and waiting for the flashing light to reappear. When it did, Tranko again entered the code to play the new message.

"Hey, okay. Bunny is caught up with the police now, but I need to find out what's going on with the larger situation. You hooked up with "Babs" like I told you, right? I think she's an important key in all this that we need to figure out. Don't trust her, whatever you do. I'm finishing a deal that could mean some cash heading your way, but I can't be sure until I know all the angles. I need to hear from you before anything else happens. We need to meet up. Just call me back, ok? Thanks."

Stewie looked over at Tranko, who was just staring straight ahead. Finally, Stewie spoke, "Do you believe him? Or her?"

Tranko rolled the muscles in his neck and flexed his shoulders in and out. He cracked his neck to the left and right before speaking, "Stewie, what I believe is that you and me, we are about to get royally fucked over by this entire group of crazies unless we do something about it first."

Concerned, Stewie pressed Tranko, "What did you have in mind?" Tranko thought for a second and then raised his eyes. He had an idea.

"You still have that .50 CAL? The M82?"

"Yeah."

"Good. We're gonna need it, plus a few other things. How about that buddy you said worked on *The Fall Guy* TV series?"

"Geez, Trank. He's pretty old now."

"Not too old, I hope."

"I can call him. I think he's still around."

"Ok, but you cannot say anything about any of this to anyone. Especially not to the broad when she comes back. We need to keep this totally between us."

"Sure. OK."

"No. I mean it Stew. This is for all the marbles. This gets out and you and I are done. Dead. No do overs." He stared right at Stewie without flinching to make his point. Stewie looked right back at him, his eyes fixed and jaw set.

"I'm locked down, Trank. For real. You can count on me."

* * *

As Bunny pressed her phone to 'off' she turned to the officer seated across from her and flashed a sassy smile.

"He's totally going to call me back. He's an absolute meathead but if he thinks there's money coming his way, not to mention me saying that I might turn him in, he'll totally come running. I guarantee it."

"He better," the officer responded, before looking down to start writing notes on the pad of paper on the table in front of him. The pair were inside a small interrogation room at the Santa Monica police department. Bunny tried to make eye contact but got frustrated as the officer continued to write.

"I'm not going down for something I had absolutely nothing to do with. It was all him."

"Ummhmmm," grunted the still writing officer.

"It was! He had this grand plan to scare my ex with a phony home invasion and stuff and then he kills him. I tried to talk him out of it, but he wouldn't listen. All he wanted was my ex's art collection. He said he was going to sell it for cash…to the underworld. He deserves to get the electric chair for this."

"California halted use of the death penalty in 2019."

"Why?" asked Bunny.

"I don't know, politics?" answered the officer.

"Well, then he better get locked up for life. He's so guilty it's ridiculous!"

"We'll see about that," said the officer.

Bunny, annoyed at not seeing some direct action, rattled her handcuffs. When the cop looked up, she smiled at him and looked down at her bound hands. He shook his head.

"I'm not taking them off."

Immediately, Bunny frowned. "You said if I told you about the other people involved that you'd let me go."

The officer shook his head again. "No. I said any information you provide will help your chances at being let go. We aren't there yet Mrs. Levi. Not by a long shot."

"Well, I'm innocent," responded Bunny, "totally innocent."

* * *

"Good?" asked David.

"For now," answered the detective. David replaced his cell phone in his jacket pocket and leaned on the side of his car. He and the cop were standing outside the Santa Monica police station. The officer, a standard issue suit-jacket-and-tie police detective, looked frustrated.

"I'm not too hot on this, Dave. The girl is sketchy as hell, but I don't think we really have all that much to hold her. Her alibi on the day of the murder is pretty solid."

"Look, Roy, I told you I'd bring you something. Bunny Levi is a great catch. This guy I called just now, 50-50, ok? I mean, she hired him, and he was in it with her, but I can't guarantee him for anything."

The cop answered, "I'm not looking for guarantees but letting you skate away on any involvement here means I'm going to need a little more than you dropping a voicemail on some cell phone. Help me out. I know you got an angle. Give me one. A real one."

Playfully, David grabbed the detective by the shoulders, rubbing at his neck. "Chill Roy. He'll call me back. Don't worry."

The detective pulled away from David. "C'mon, man. Don't, ok? I can't officially let you go until I hear something I can use. Maybe we should go inside."

David tensed. He had no intention of going inside the police station. No matter what, he knew enough that once inside it became that much harder to get out again. He projected as much calm as he could muster.

"No sweat, Roy. Seriously. You won't be sorry on this one. I promise." As David started to follow the detective inside, he furiously scanned his brain for a follow-up move. Just outside the first entrance, David finally figured out what to do, and offered it up.

"Say, Roy? Would you be interested in closing off a super-famous, heavy-duty stolen art case from the late eighties? They even did a documentary about it on *Netflix*."

Suddenly, with a hand outstretched to open the door, detective Roy stopped dead in his tracks.

"Oh yeah? Tell me more."

84

THE LOCATION of the Hollywood Bowl was a natural amphitheater. A well-shaded grove and popular picnic spot in Bolton Canyon. It had natural acoustics and was close to downtown Hollywood, making it the perfect place to construct a live show venue. The Bowl officially opened on July 11, 1922, and never really closed since. Being formally listed as a public park meant practically anyone could wander inside and have a look around. Other than dress rehearsals, the park remained accessible most hours of the day. Which was exactly why Stewie suggested it for the big meet.

"So, this is it?" asked Maggie.

"Yeah," replied Tranko, "quite the place."

Maggie looked around. "Where's your shadow?"

"He'll be here."

"He'd better."

The two walked up to the highest levels of the Bowl before stopping and looking back down towards the stage. A paved, single lane ring road encircled the seats, allowing for workers and other vehicles to service the facility and its landscaping. At that very moment, two teams were working away, mowing, pruning, and clearing brush as Mexican music played from a boom box atop one of their vehicles.

"Where's your big shot?" asked Tranko.

"He's in the parking lot. He's ready when we need him."

As they neared the top of the venue, Maggie looked at Tranko and stopped, unshouldering her backpack, and letting it drop near her feet. She studied the massive flak vest he was wearing under his open jacket.

"How in heck do you breathe in that thing? It looks like it weighs fifty pounds."

"It's gotten me through some tough times. It's good luck."

Accepting his explanation, she turned back to the commanding view of the bowl. "He's late."

"He ain't late," assured Tranko. "He's just casing the place."

Almost on cue, two black SUVs appeared in the lower area, stopping at the bottom. One of the two reversed and turned around, stopping again but this time facing out. The other crawled slowly up the side of the bowl until it came to a halt about halfway up. Several men exited the vehicle, Stig and Dachshund first among them. The crew stayed close to the SUV while the two men walked along the rows, headed towards Maggie and Tranko.

"Where the hell is Stewie?" asked Maggie again.

"Don't worry," replied Tranko.

Now, with Stig and Dachshund a mere fifteen feet away, Maggie called out.

"Hold it! I think that's close enough."

The two men stopped. Stig looked annoyed. Dachshund raised his hands slowly.

"This better not be more game playing."

"The only game I'm playing is to stay alive," answered Maggie, "and keeping you two there is a good first step."

"Do you have my painting?"

Maggie nodded. "I do."

Dachshund made an exaggerated show of looking left and right. "Well, I'm not seeing it."

"It's here. I give my word. Where are my friends?"

At this, Dachshund nodded and turned to Stig, indicating for him to do something. Stig then turned and waved at the men outside the nearest SUV. One of the men opened the rear door and gestured for someone inside to come out. At this point both Ivan and Fatima appeared, hands tied in front of them.

Dachshund faced back to Maggie. "They're not coming a step closer until I see my painting."

Maggie nodded. She pulled out a cell phone and typed a text message. The presence of the phone unnerved Dachshund.

"What's that for?"

"Just getting your property delivered."

Maggie turned and looked down, toward the opposite side of the bowl, near the bottom. Eventually, Aldo entered, on foot, and began the long hike up the opposite side of the bowl, towards Maggie and Tranko. He was carrying a long leather satchel.

Dachshund started to laugh. "You got him here? To deliver it in person? I'm honored."

Maggie said nothing, continuing to wait for Aldo to get closer. As he made his way up the concourse, Aldo passed the group of landscapers busy with pruning. Suddenly, one of the men turned around and reached out, grabbing Aldo. He pinned his back against him with an arm around his neck, then screamed at the top of his lungs, "FREE SAUF!"

Maggie wheeled back to Dachshund.

"What the hell is this? Is this you? This wasn't part of the deal. What's going on?"

Dachshund immediately protested. "I have nothing to do with this. This is you and your theatrics."

The man yelled louder. "FREE SAUF!" Two other men stepped out from the side of the work truck. One of them was Malik. He stepped forward and yanked the slim leather satchel from Aldo. He held it above his head and shouted.

"I have your bounty Russian. Free my blood!"

Both of Dachshund's crews aimed their automatic weapons on the yelling man, but no one fired.

Dachshund looked at Maggie. "This is going to go worse for you."

Maggie jeered him right back. "I made a deal to get my friends back. What in the hell is he even talking about? What's a Sauf?"

Malik called to someone behind him, who emerged from behind the work van. He was holding a lit flamethrower. Malik removed the painting from the satchel and unrolled it with another man. They were holding *The Concert*.

"FREE SAUF OR SEE IT BURN!" he screamed, as flamethrower-man released just enough to confirm the gun worked.

Dachshund told Stig something, who then turned and put his hands in the air, commanding his crew to hold fast. Dachshund spoke to Maggie.

"Did you know of this?"

"I knew about Aldo. He's got the painting I stole which I was giving to you in exchange for my friends."

"How do I even know it's the real one?"

"Make him let you see it."

Dachshund pondered this and then directed Stig to order something. Stig waved his hands and yelled to his crew something in Russian. One of them pushed Ivan forward.

Dachshund yelled to Malik, "Let the man examine it. I need to know if it's real or not."

He turned and spoke quieter, to Maggie, "If it's a fake, I will kill you all."

Tranko tensed. He didn't like how this was going.

As Ivan was led toward the painting the atmosphere in the Bowl was heavy. The place was so big that random workers and hikers moved about without realizing they were in the middle of a public standoff, no doubt confused by the fake "workmen" and semi-official look to the goings on. They might have even thought it was a movie being filmed. It was LA, after all.

As Ivan finally got near the painting, Maggie watched him like a hawk. He studied the canvas, nodding in a smooth and consistent manner, officially authenticating the very piece Maggie had stolen and tried to deliver to him mere days earlier.

And then he stopped.

It was almost imperceptible. Maggie could see, but could anyone else? She wasn't sure. But it was so clear to her. She moved her head and looked around slowly to see if anyone else noticed, but they hadn't. Only her. During his examination, Ivan had locked up for an instant. He had frozen. Something was wrong. She felt his energy change, even from a distance. Then, during confirmation. She saw it. Unmistakable. He reached down and scratched the outside of his knee with his little finger, while at the same time turning and giving a thumbs up to everyone assembled.

"It's real," Ivan called out.

Maggie's heart sank.

"Bring him up here." Said Stig.

As the Russian goon pushed Ivan up the hill, Malik and his team of fake gardeners stood fast in their positions, the small flame continuing to flicker in the barrel of the flamethrower.

As they waited for Ivan, Dachshund shouted to Tranko. "You have chosen yet another side?"

"I've always been on my side. Anyway, you're getting what you told me you wanted."

"Who rewards you now, hmm?"

"I delivered like I said I would. Nothing more."

"You know of this?" Dachshund indicated the massive east Asian man holding the painting hostage down below.

"I don't know him at all," answered Tranko

With Ivan shoved back behind him, Dachshund spoke, "So, who do I believe? You say you brought my painting, but now it's not in your hands? How did that happen?"

Maggie was furious. "Oh for...." Then she unloaded on Dachshund.

"Can it, ok? I'm a hired gun. So is he. That clown down there hired me to get the painting. I did and I gave it to him, like I was supposed to. I didn't know about you or have anything to do with you. You kidnapped my friends and told me to give it to you or else. Fine. I get it here to trade for the lives of my friends, like I said I would. Then I find out I'm in the middle of some other deal you have going? You tell me what to do now, because personally I haven't got a flipping clue!"

Dachshund considered this. He whispered something to Stig, who nodded and immediately walked back to the van. As he did, Dachshund called out to Malik, "If I release Sauf how will you know?"

Malik held up a satellite phone.

Dachshund stared at him for a few moments, then looked toward Stig, who was returning to the group with Fatima. She was absolutely terrified by what was going on, shaking, and barely holding it together. Aldo saw her, and even though he was restrained, tried to pull away from his captor, calling out.

"Fatima!"

"Aldo!" responded Fatima.

Dachshund rolled his eyes at the sentiment. He took out a cell phone and made a call. Once connected, he spoke in hushed tones, all Russian. Then he waited. After almost thirty seconds he spoke again, then hung up.

"Watch this," he said to Maggie and Tranko, before turning once more to face Malik down below.

Time ticked very slowly, but within two minutes the satellite phone held aloft rang. Malik answered it and listened. Then he yelled.

"SAUF IS FREE!" Immediately, he indicated to release Aldo, handing back the unrolled canvas and encouraging him to take it to Dachshund.

Aldo moved quickly up the hill, stopping just between Maggie, Tranko, Dachshund and Stig.

"Careful with it," cautioned Dachshund. He instructed Stig to take the painting from Aldo and return it to the SUV. As Aldo handed off the painting he rushed to Fatima, embracing her, only to be roughly separated and held apart by a Russian crewman.

"You got your painting. Let her go!"

Dachshund looked at him and then at Maggie, shaking his head.

"The deal was two people for one painting. Having just released one, the account no longer balances." He looked right at Stig, who had returned from handing off the painting, and levelled an order. "Kill him."

Without hesitating, Stig took out a massive handgun, aimed it at Ivan and pulled the trigger, blasting a round directly into his chest. Ivan slumped to the ground. Fatima screamed as Maggie yelled, "NO!!!!!"

Suddenly, all hell broke loose. Tranko ran at Stig, crashing into his body with a full force. The two men struck the nearby seats and tumbled to the ground, punching, and kicking at each other. The Russian crew started firing rounds at Malik and his crew. Simultaneously, some of Malik's men appeared behind Dachshund's group, dropping their masquerade as landscapers. One Russian got pulled backward while another was smashed in the back with a swinging kettlebell. Once on the ground, their legs were cocooned in cling wrap as Malik's men worked to incapacitate whoever they could get close to. The fight up high continued as Tranko smashed Stig in the face, even as he countered that with a knee into Tranko's thigh, knocking him backwards. At the core of the chaos, Maggie rushed to Ivan's side and knelt beside him.

"No, no, no. This wasn't supposed to happen. I'm so sorry. Ivan, I'm sorry," she cried.

Ivan struggled to speak. "Stop Maggie, little vixen. No more tears. It's done now. This….is all my fault. Circles close….uhhhh….."

"Ivan! Hold on. I'll get help," Maggie pleaded.

Ivan touched her face. "There is no help. It's okay. I will see my son now, maybe. I love you little vixen. I'm so sorry I did this to you. I'm sorry." And Ivan breathed his last. Tears streamed down Maggie's face as she continued to try and stop the bleeding, refusing to accept that Ivan was gone.

"Come on Ivan. Come on!" she pleaded.

In the meantime, Aldo was running with Fatima, trying to find cover away from the insanity. But Fatima was resisting, looking backwards. "What about Maggie? We can't leave her!"

Aldo didn't care. "I don't know who's getting shot next. We have got to get out of here!" he shouted.

Eventually, Fatima shoved him away, rushing back towards Maggie, who herself was struggling to get Ivan moved, even as she slowly accepted that he was dead. Maggie sat on the ground, gutted, while Tranko and Stig, still fighting, were finally running out of juice. Tranko stumbled backwards and landed on his back, momentarily stunned. He looked up to see Stig aiming his gun right at him.

"Bye-bye, baby."

Just as he went to pull the trigger, Stig's chest exploded out the front of him. He was hit from a long-distance round, a high shot that went right through him. Stig fell forward, dead at Tranko's feet.

As a new explosion of gunfire by the crew near the SUVs started, Malik's men began moving in, starting to surround the Russians. At the same time, a hidden sniper seemed to be taking out random players, causing everyone on all sides to panic.

Two more of Malik's men came from behind the lower SUV, smashing a rear window open with another of the massive kettlebells.

One got inside and took control of the van, attempting to use it to block access to the Bowl. On the other side, two Russian goons ran at some of Malik's men, only to see a kiddie pool burst out of a landscape van. Two men pushing from behind it, landing on the Russians and wrapping the pool around them while they kicked and punched at the confused men.

Through it all, Dachshund had run for cover, carrying the painting. Now inside the first SUV, he fired it up and accelerated backwards at top speed, ramming into the lower SUV that was trying to block the way. The powerful vehicle continued to spin its wheels, eventually pushing the angled SUV out of the way. Dachshund ran into the edge of a large wall and seemed jammed as he tried to get the SUV turned around.

With bullets continuing to fly everywhere, Tranko waved his arms and yelled at Maggie, Fatima, and Aldo.

"Get your asses down! There's shit flying everywhere. Seriously, get out of here! Just go!"

Maggie, finally releasing Ivan, spied the backpack she was carrying near Tranko. She yelled at him. "The backpack, grab the backpack! It's yours!"

As Tranko stopped and looked down, he saw the backpack, reached down, and grabbed it. He held it up and looked at Maggie, as if to say, "What is this?"

Maggie yelled, "I made him pay extra...for you!" She indicated Aldo.

"Thanks, but...." And before Tranko could utter another word his chest exploded out the front of him, another victim of the sniper, his face frozen mid-yell. Tranko touched the gore of his chest and said dumbly, "Ah, Stewie...man...." before falling forward and landing face-down.

Maggie screamed, "NO!" instinctively trying to run back to him. Aldo stopped her, pulling her back with Fatima as he directed them along the ground. "We've got to get out of here. We're next!"

Maggie struggled against Aldo's grip, trying to get him to let her go. "He's dead Maggie. That's a sniper round. He's gone. We have got to get out of here!"

As the firefight wound down, Malik and his crew continued to advance on the Russians, even as Dachshund managed to get his SUV out of the Bowl and into the parking lot. Two Russians jumped in with him as he finally roared away, with Malik and company spraying bullets as they went. Maggie, Fatima, and Aldo escaped out an emergency exit to a hidden area where Aldo had a car waiting.

"This place is going to be overrun with police. I can't be here."

Aldo headed for the car, waving at the driver. Maggie was in disbelief.

"THAT'S what you came in? A Fiat?"

Aldo said nothing, waving for the women to get in the car. As they finally made their escape, sirens began to sound in the distance.

* * *

Back inside the Bowl, silence reigned. Other than the trills of far-off emergency vehicles, nothing moved or spoke. Everyone previously involved was either dead or long gone. The smell of spent ammunition hung heavy in the air. Nothing made a sound.

Except for a light staccato that seemed to be getting closer.

A punctuating sound of metal bumping metal, but also brushing against fabric. Over and over, *tsink-tsink, tsink-tsink*. It got closer and closer until eventually a mass of leaves appeared to roll over the rear-wall of the Hollywood Bowl. It was someone in a *Ghillie* suit, carrying a high-powered rifle. The leafy mass stopped, dropped the weapon, stripped off the suit and stepped from the shadows of the trees.

It was Stewie, dressed head to toe in fatigues. He reached down and picked up the massive sniper rifle, then looking left and right, slipped through the seats until he got to where Tranko was laid out flat. He dropped down beside him and softly patted his back.

"You good big man?"

Slowly, Tranko shifted his weight and rolled over. He took a deep breath.

"Fuck, Stewie. What'd you hit me with? That felt like a full round."

"No way man. I dropped a plastic dud on ya. It was big though. Couldn't take the chance it wouldn't go the distance. Buddy's rig worked great, huh? Your chest looks like Jesse Ventura's from *Predator*."

"Is everyone gone? Did they see?"

"You're a ghost buddy. They all saw you get dead. Now, let's get outta here. Cops are coming."

As Tranko strained to get up he paused, reaching for the backpack Maggie had thrown at him.

"What's that?" asked Stewie.

"Compensation, finally," replied Tranko, "I think you and me need to head for calmer shores, like Guatemala."

"I like bananas."

Tranko, about to roll his eyes and tell Stewie to shut up, stopped. He smiled instead.

"Y'know Stew, I like bananas too. Let's go."

As they returned to the wall and began climbing back over, Stewie asked a question.

"What about that Bunny chick and her guy…David?"

Tranko heaved Stewie over the wall, and then jumped up and grabbed on himself, as Stew helped pull him over.

"Don't worry about them. I took care of it."

And with that, the two men disappeared into the surrounding forest.

85

"TEST, TEST." David looked down and spoke into his chest.

"I've got you. Don't worry. It works."

"I am worried. I don't like doing this 'wear a wire' shit. It's a good way to get shot."

"You're the one waving 'famous art crimes' in the face of my bosses. What did you think would happen?"

"I thought you'd do your jobs and catch them yourself. I'm a civilian."

The detective snorted at David's complaints.

"What if he's a no show? What if he lied?"

"You're the one that said they were coming here. We're trusting you."

"I know that. He said the Russian would be stopping here after their big meet, and he swore he'd have the painting with him."

"Okay, so what's the deal then? I had to pull a lot of strings to get this team in place."

"I know, I just…it's these damn Russians, ok? They play for keeps. You gotta make sure they don't kill me."

"You do what we said to do, and it all goes fine. We'll be watching. Don't worry."

David stepped out from the hidden van. He walked away from the grove of trees and onto the dirt road toward the warehouse in the Vulcan landfill. Nervously he looked around as he got closer, paranoid that someone had eyes on him. He spoke into his chest.

"Testing? You still have me?"

"Yeah, we got you. Now shut up, okay? Don't blow this."

David approached the warehouse and stepped inside. He looked around. It seemed abandoned, but Tranko swore they were coming back after their big meeting. He said the Russian had left the copies there to be picked up.

As he poked around some more, David found a tarp covering some items. As he peeked underneath the covering, he saw them: *Storm, Concert and Flowers*, all the fakes Tranko had taken from him and Bunny at the house. *Maybe he wasn't lying after all*, thought David. He tensed as he heard a car approach.

David waited as the vehicle came to a stop. He counted forty agonizing seconds between hearing a car door open and finally close again. Then he counted the footsteps as they approached the warehouse door.

One, two, three, four, five, six...and then the door pulled open.

It was Bunny Levi.

David stepped out from the back area. "What are you doing here?"

"Me? What the hell are you doing here? That lugnut Tranko said the Russians would be here with their paintings. I want my cut."

That asshole, thought David, *he's messing with us. There are no Russians coming. He's screwing us over by aiming us at each other. Well, two can play at that game.*

"How far away are they?" asked David.

"I don't know. He just said to be here if I wanted to see them."

"How'd you get out of jail?"

"I never went in the jail, and thanks for that, by the way, you jerk. Nice trick trying to frame my ass with this. I'm innocent, and once those stupid cops realized they couldn't hold me on anything they had to let me go. And where's my money from that other art? That's mine and you know it. I never gave you permission to take it or sell it. That's a crime you know. You're guilty as hell."

David wasn't hearing it, but he wanted to make sure the detective did. "No way, Bunny. You tried to trick me from the very beginning, and you know it. All your talk about crooked insurance deals and then seducing me. It was all you."

Bunny raged. "In on it? It was your idea to kill my husband and take his art. You said that he was an idiot and..."

"Hold on now. That's BS. I never did...and what is that?"

"What's what?" Bunny looked around.

"That! In your hair? Is it a filament or something? Are you fucking wired-up you crazy bitch? Seriously?"

Immediately Bunny started yelling "Octave! Octave!"

"Octave?"

Suddenly, the warehouse door burst open as a group of police officers rushed in, guns drawn. They were followed shortly by David's group of undercover detectives, also with their guns drawn. Both sides were screaming "police!" at each other. In the meantime, the ones first through the door had thrown David to the ground and pulled his arms behind him. They were reading him his rights. He turned his head and looked up at Bunny.

"Octave, huh? That's the safe word they thought up? Mine was 'insane bitch.' I got to pick it."

Bunny just sneered at him as the two groups of undercover police finally stopped shouting and aiming guns at each other. David's detective appeared and spoke to the officers holding him down.

"He's with us. Where are the paintings?"

David, still hogtied, was about to answer. He paused, thinking for a moment and then spoke. "They're right over there."

"What?" said Bunny. "He told me before that they're fakes but I don't know what they are."

"You two are both in a lot of trouble. And I'm not seeing any Russians, David. This does not look good." said the detective.

* * *

From a significant distance, Dachshund watched through a pair of massive binoculars. He saw the undercover vehicles pulling in and surrounding his warehouse. He turned to the two men still with him.

"I think we're officially done in LA. Call the port. We need an exit. Now."

The men got back inside the battered SUV and tore off, headed for Long Beach.

* * *

Maggie and Fatima were squished in the back of a tiny car racing through the streets of LA. Aldo was in the passenger seat while the driver was a clean-cut young man in a polo shirt. Maggie looked at him and then at Aldo.

"Haven't I seen this guy somewhere before?"

Aldo answered, "That's Bryan. He's crew. On board the *Jimena*."

Maggie nodded her head. "That's right. You made me a pina colada. It was good."

"The secret is to use heavy cream. No one does," said Bryan.

"Just drive, ok?" barked a frustrated Aldo, "Look, I don't exactly have a bunch of roughnecks. I mean, this isn't even my car."

Bryan spoke up again, "It's my girlfriend's. She lives in LA."

Embarrassed, Aldo tried to change the subject. He spoke to no one in particular, "Where are we going?"

Maggie talked first. "To the Stardust, on Wilshire. I've got something for you."

* * *

As Dachshund's black SUV ripped through the port of Long Beach, he was waved through three separate security checks, eventually coming to a stop near the edge of the main loading terminal. The SUV was motionless only momentarily, just long enough for the doors of a massive shipping container to be opened. Then it drove right inside as the doors were pushed closed and latched tight by three massive longshoremen.

Less than three beats passed as the container was hoisted into the air, directly on-board a huge container ship parked nearby. Inside the steel box, all three men, and Dachshund's precious cargo, were fully on board.

Squeezing out of the passenger side inside the darkened container, Dachshund pulled three glow sticks from his jacket and cracked them, tossing them onto the floor of the container, lighting it up with a green glow. He walked to the back of the SUV and opened the rear hatch, pausing only to gaze at the canvas now lying flat. He sighed, smiling.

"I'm done with North America. Get me home to Mother Russia."

A loud bang on the side of the container alerted them to the steel doors opening, as more members of Dachshund's crew entered with flashlights to get the men out of the box and onto the ship proper for the long voyage home.

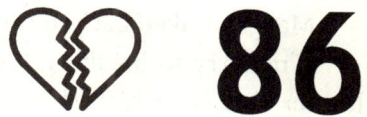

86

STOPPED AT the Stardust Motel, the group exited the tiny Fiat. Instantly, Maggie spied something that caused her to smile from ear to ear. She almost ran to reach it.

There, parked just in front of her motel room, was the Honda CB70 she had been forced to ditch near the Portofino Hotel. Walking up to it, Maggie slid her hand along the seat. Spying a piece of paper taped to the handlebars, Maggie pulled it off and read aloud.

"Enjoy!" with *a friend* scrawled underneath. Maggie grinned as she appreciated Stewie's efforts on her behalf. She fished a key out of her waist bag and went into her room.

Aldo and Fatima got out of the car as well, but they were less calm.

"Fatima, please. Don't do this. You know how much I care for you."

"I....just can't. Why won't you see that? How can you pretend what has happened over the last few days is normal?"

"I'm not pretending anything. It's only that..."

"This can't be swept away, Aldo. I liked you so much, but I don't like any of this. You need to leave me be."

"I don't want to leave you be. I risked a tremendous amount for you. You matter to me."

But Fatima couldn't be dissuaded. "Maybe I do, but I don't see a place for myself in your world, whatever it is. I'll admit I had stars in my eyes for awhile, but I can't be a part of..." she waved her hands around, indicating the space surrounding Aldo. "This."

Aldo bowed his head. "I could never force you. You've broken my heart."

Fatima cracked a wry smile. "I highly doubt that Mr. Aldo Neto. I'm thinking you're quite resilient when it comes to affairs of the heart."

Maggie walked back to the pair.

"I'm sorry to break in, but this is for you." She handed Aldo a leather slipcase, which she opened just enough to reveal the aging canvas inside. "It's in good shape. I was careful with it. After I cut it." She smirked a little as she spun *Lola* in her fingers.

Fatima stepped back, almost recoiling.

"And this only highlights how out of all this I am. What the heck is that?"

Maggie smiled awkwardly. "A long story?"

"Honestly, at this stage, I don't even want to know. I need space." Fatima walked purposefully away from the pair, staring off into the distance.

Maggie started after her. "Fati, wait. Please, I'm sorry. There's just so much we really need to talk about."

"You think?" answered Fatima with a sarcastic edge.

"Ok, I deserved that. I never meant to hurt you."

Fatima was about to say something but thought twice, holding it in. Then, she furrowed her brow and decided to speak after all.

"Maggie, look, I love you, ok? I really do. You are my very best friend and I think you always will be. But right now, I just can't really talk to you about all of this. I will, but I can't do it now. I need some time to let this all roll around inside me for a bit. What I want right now is to go home."

"Well, we can…" Fatima cut her off, shaking her head firmly.

"No. First of all, I'm going home by myself. Not in his jet. Or on his yacht. Or on the back of your motorbike. Or with anyone. I'm going alone. You and I will talk when you get back to Vancouver. But for now, I need space and I'm going to have it."

Maggie bowed her head. "I understand."

Aldo stepped forward to Fatima. "How will you go? You have no…"

Fatima stopped him mid-sentence. "I've got my own money, thank you very much. I'll buy a ticket and fly home."

"Can I offer a ride to the airport at least?" begged Aldo.

"Taxi." replied Fatima.

Maggie walked to the motel office and requested a taxi be called. The trio stood around, awkwardly but calmly, waiting for its arrival.

Once the car finally came, Fatima opened the rear door and got inside. Aldo pushed the last of her luggage into the rear of the car and walked around. She rolled the window down and addressed Aldo.

"You," she said "were as troublesome as you were fun. I don't know what to think about it right now."

"Fatima, please."

"Goodbye Aldo," said Fatima firmly.

"Goodbye, Fatima."

Fatima then looked to Maggie and reached her hand out the window, indicating for her to grab it. Maggie did.

"And you? Come see me when you get back, ok? We'll get through…whatever this is. I can't imagine the story you have to tell but hopefully by then I should be ready to listen, ok? I love you, crazy lady. Friends forever."

Maggie, with tears misting in her eyes, answered back. "Friends forever."

And at that, Fatima released Maggie's hand and instructed the cab driver to go. The bright blue car turned into traffic and disappeared down Wilshire.

Maggie breathed in, rubbed her eyes quickly, and composed herself. She turned back to Aldo.

"Are you and I good?"

"She's quite something, isn't she? You must know why I'm so taken with her," said Aldo, still staring after Fatima.

"I think you kind of blew it with her."

"Likely, yes. Perhaps not for always though. I don't give up easily. If she ever has room for me, I will find a way to return."

"I bet you will."

Aldo turned and faced Maggie, "You are quite formidable in your own right Ms. Deacon. I incurred your wrath and, dare I say it, suffered as a result. Thank you for returning this." He indicated the canvas she had handed him. "You didn't have to return it, but you did. You have my gratitude."

"You did what I asked you to do."

Aldo nodded and stepped back slightly. "Well, it was my duty. I will go now. Do you need anything else? Can I get you back to your home?"

"No, I think I can handle it."

Aldo started to walk away but stopped and turned back to face Maggie. "No fun when the bad guy wins, is it?"

Maggie stood for a moment, considering Aldo's words. Then she cocked an eye skyward. "Well, a whole bunch of stuff happened and somehow, I'm still here. I can't really complain about that."

"I guess not."

"And I'm keeping the *Klee*, by the way."

This news caused Aldo to laugh. "With my compliments."

"Where are you going?" asked Maggie.

"Back to the *Jimena*. I'm going to stay on board as they reposition. I need to be at sea for a while. Hide out for a bit, yes?" He returned, took Maggie's hand, leant down, and kissed it gently before turning and walking over to the embarrassingly small Fiat. As he prepared to step inside, Aldo stopped and took a full look at Maggie. Then he offered a genteel salute before settling down inside. The small car zipped away, leaving Maggie by herself in the parking lot.

Turning, Maggie looked at the motorcycle, realizing it was now her only mode of personal transportation. She considered the insanity of driving all the way home on an aging Honda motorbike and shook her head.

Still, thought Maggie, *maybe a good ride is just what the doctor ordered.* Besides, she still had to make a very important stop. Some time to prepare might be just the ticket.

87

SEVEN HOURS of riding is a lot for anyone, no matter how fit and strong you might be. And when you're in your 60's, that pain will eventually come calling in a big way. Maggie could feel her muscles cramping. She had stopped for a rest after the first full day of riding, but even a good bed and a hot meal didn't make the remaining hours any easier. She was done being on a bike.

Vale, Oregon sat about twelve miles west of the Idaho border, at the intersection of U.S. Routes 20 and 26, along the Malheur River near where it joined up with Bully Creek. Once upon a time it was the first stop on the Oregon Trail. As Maggie rode through town, she found herself on the main drag, remembering instantly how quiet a truly small town can be. Spying an older man waiting at the corner, she pulled her bike over to ask for directions.

"Hi. Do you know where the Treasure Valley mobile home park is?"

"Sure, good lookin'," said the spry fellow, "just follow along that way until you get to West St. Then hang a left and go along until you cross the train tracks. You'll come to road called Hope. Go left again and follow that on back. Treasure Valley will be on your right."

"Thank you."

"Anytime Ms. Pretty."

Maggie couldn't believe the old coot's sass, but still blushed slightly at his exaggerated flirting. She rolled on the throttle and glided away.

* * *

Cruising past the mobile homes, Maggie swiveled her head left and right, looking for space number 33. Finally seeing it, she turned in and came to a stop, parking the bike and removing her helmet. She stepped off and did a huge stretch, cracking her own back as best she could. She placed the helmet on the seat.

Still a little creaky, Maggie made her way toward the front door when she heard movement down the side of the trailer. Abandoning her first idea, Maggie turned and went walking in that direction instead, quickly ending up behind the home and seeing a young man busy moving things around in a large, old shed. He didn't see her, so she called out.

"Denny Cooper?"

Involuntarily, the young man turned, immediately tensing. "Who's asking?"

Maggie continued to walk towards him.

"Ivan's dead."

Denny made a face like he didn't know what she was talking about, but Maggie held her gaze on his until he finally gave in, visibly acknowledging that the name meant something by dropping his head.

"What happened?" he asked.

"He got shot. Protecting me. And you too, apparently."

"What are you talking about?"

"I know who you are, Denny. Ivan told me. I know what you do. It took a bit to find you here, but it wasn't that hard."

Denny looked at her but said nothing.

"How did you first meet him? What was the connection that brought you to him?"

"I think you're making a mistake."

Maggie stopped walking. She spied an aging lawn chair to her right. Looking at Denny, she indicated the chair, "May I?"

He nodded and she sat down, putting her hands on her hips and stretching her back and shoulders upwards, releasing a slight groan of effort. Sitting normally felt wonderful.

"That's better. Ok, Denny. Now, I know you don't know me. But that doesn't matter. I know about your skills and the work you did for Zev Levi. I know about *The Concert*."

Denny let out a sigh and seemed to release the idea of running away or arguing. In what could only be read as resignation, he leaned heavily against the wall as Maggie continued to talk.

"You ever hear of Bob Ross, Denny? You know that TV painter? The 'happy little trees" guy? Of course, you do. Everybody knows him. He'd do an entire painting in one little half hour TV show. They weren't extraordinary but they were kind of special, at least in their own right. Lots of folks learned to paint from him."

Denny acknowledged this with a nod.

"Anyway, what most folks don't know is that he didn't paint just the one picture each show. He would do three of them. Three! Can you believe that?"

Denny didn't say anything. He just looked down.

"He'd decide the image or view he was going to paint and then he'd do a version prior to filming, just to work the kinks out, right? Then, he'd do another one for the camera. That's the one people watching would see him do. Finally, he'd do a third, after filming was done. That was for him, to clarify whatever he thought he'd missed or not done well enough during the broadcast. Sort of obsessive sounding to me, but I'm not really a creative like that. You are though, aren't you Denny?"

Denny continued to say nothing, but shifted uncomfortably in his spot, looking away.

"We all thought it was pretty cut and dried. Well, I certainly did. You did a copy of *The Concert*, from the original, because Levi wanted to keep a version even though he had to sell it. But when he saw how good you were he thought he might be able to fool the very people he had to surrender it to, thinking maybe they couldn't tell? Then he could keep the real one. Because your forgery was so darn good. And it was good. No one could tell for a second which the real one was. Except someone who knew you. Someone like Ivan."

Maggie remembered back to the Hollywood Bowl and Ivan's barely hidden shock when he came face to face with the painting. He knew something was off and he had signaled such to Maggie the only way he could. The tap on his knee with his little finger. It was from long ago, a thing between Maggie and her father. A way to know that whatever was being said, the opposite was true. When Ivan gave his full-throated guarantee that the painting was real, he signalled to Maggie that it absolutely was not. It had been a fake too.

Maggie continued to speak, "So, now I've seen two fakes floating around LA and I've got to wonder, where did the real one end up? The Russian mobster thinks he has it, and that's good for all of us that he does. He can disappear and leave the rest of us alone. Didn't help Ivan though. He's dead. Zev too. A lot of folks died for a painting they never actually got to really see. But you got to see it, didn't you Denny? You saw it a lot."

Denny crossed his arms and looked down at his feet.

"It's here, isn't it? The real one?" Maggie let the question hang in the air.

Eventually, Denny gave in, nodding. He looked up at her through his shaggy hair.

"Can I see it?" asked Maggie.

Denny lifted himself away from the wall and walked into the shed. He dug somewhere in the back. All around were the hurriedly packed art supplies, canvases, and pallets of materials and paintings he had boxed up and shipped when he fled Los Angeles. Here, clearly in the middle of unpacking and setting up a new home for himself, away from the chaos of the big city, was his attempt to escape the problems that had been created.

Denny pulled a section of canvasses back and slid out a fully framed canvas, wrapped in multiple drop rags. He pulled the fabric clear and angled the painting towards Maggie.

There it was, *The Concert* by Joannes Vermeer, painted in 1664, lost to eternity in the 1990 robbery of the Isabella Stewart Gardner Museum in Boston, leaning like so much junk against the wall of an old shed in some Oregon trailer park. The most valuable missing painting in the world.

"I didn't plan on keeping it. I switched it once, just to do some study on it back at my place when I was working on it for Levi. But he never noticed. Not when I took it, or when I got it back. Eventually, I had done two copies that were near perfect, and I wondered if anyone would know? So, I switched it, and they never noticed. And then it was too late to switch it back and things kinda went crazy when Zevon died. I didn't know what to do."

Maggie stared at the painting. After everything that had happened, no one had ended up with it after all. It was just as lost as it had been after the original Gardner robbery. Denny pushed it toward Maggie.

"I don't want it. You take it. Seriously, that thing has caused me trouble since I first saw it. I just want it gone. You give it back or something."

Maggie shook her head.

"I don't want it."

"That painting is incredible. I was lucky to have even spent the time with it that I did. I thought I was so smart when I kept it but who cares, right? And nothing good has happened. I mean…Ivan."

"How'd you know him?" asked Maggie.

"Sometimes I'd buy drugs off his kid. We were close in age. I liked him. He was messed up but a good guy. When Ivan found out I could paint, he'd toss me jobs every now and again. But I want to be done with all that. I just want out of this. Take it. Please."

"I can't," insisted Maggie, "I'm on a bike."

"I'll trade you my car, straight across. What do you think?"

* * *

As Maggie cruised into the small town of Oroville, WA, she slid her hand across the massive bench seat beside her. Agreeing to trade her mighty Honda CB70 for a rusted out 2006 Grand Marquis might have seemed crazy at first, but watching the miles spin by from the comfort of what amounted to a living room on wheels was a hell of a lot easier on her back and hips than the bike was. And there did come a time in every life when comfort replaced the shallow need to look cool.

Maggie saw a sign indicating the US/Canada border only a few miles away. Looking around, she spotted the place she planned to stop. Pulling over the car, she parked and turned off the engine.

Getting out and heading around to the massive trunk, Maggie pressed the button and popped the latch, lifting it to survey the cargo inside. *The Concert* stared up at her, looking way less impressive thanks to its humble location. She hefted the fully framed masterpiece from the trunk and onto the street. Looking up, she faced the small goodwill thrift shop. The OPEN sign beckoned. With effort, Maggie struggled the large painting inside the shop.

As the door opened, a woman similar in age to Maggie saw her straining to move the painting inside.

"Goodness! That's quite the masterpiece you've got there. Just lean it against the bookcase." Maggie did as she was directed and walked over to the counter.

"How can I help you?"

"Well, I'd like to donate this painting to goodwill. Found it in my uncle's attic when he passed. I have no need for something so big. Thought it might be something someone else would like."

"It's very nice. Old-timey looking, as they say."

"Yes, I guess it is." The two women turned back toward the painting, as the counter lady studied it intently.

"I can get an appraisal done if you like but it may take a few days. That way we can give you the fair value for a proper tax receipt."

Maggie smiled. "That's okay, it's not very expensive. Just an old print or something. I don't need anything for it. It's all yours." With the woman continuing to study the piece, Maggie started to walk away. Suddenly, the woman stopped her.

"Hold on there. I can't let you leave."

Maggie froze in place. Had her ruse been discovered?

"We have this thing. It's called the *Antiques Roadshow* rule. So many people would give something away to thrift shops and similar that eventually turned out to be very valuable and then they'd come back and sue, claiming they were cheated. We learned the only way to protect against that was to make sure something official traded hands. With a receipt."

Maggie smiled in relief. "OK, how about a dollar? Would that work?"

"That would work just fine," the woman nodded.

* * *

As Maggie drove into the receding sunlight, she held up the dollar bill she had received for the most famous missing painting in the world. Shaking her head at the irony, Maggie turned on the radio and fiddled with the buttons until a song she liked started playing. The chords of *Free Fallin'* filled the car as Tom Petty's voice dropped into the chorus. Maggie joined in.

With a relaxed smile and a very easy feeling, Maggie aimed the massive car at the horizon, heading for home in the yellowy-orange light of a cool summer evening.

While writing has been a constant for more than three decades, Jarrod Thalheimer has also seen service as a hotelier, actor, security guard, union leader, hot receptionist, truck driver, scrap metal chucker, movie producer and more. Vixen is his first fiction novel.